## Secular States, Religiou

This is a pioneering comparative study of the two major attempts to build secular states – where the constitutional identity and fundamental character of the state are not based on or derived from any religious faith – in the non-Western world. A few decades ago, the secular nature of the republics of India and Turkey was considered axiomatic. Not so any more. Alternative, anti-secular visions of nationhood have risen decisively from the political margins to centre-stage and won state power in both countries. The secular definition of nationhood has effectively been replaced by a Sunni-Islamist majoritarian definition in Turkey, where the secular state is dead in all but name. In India, majoritarian Hindu nationalism has emerged as by far the country's single largest political force, and the future of India's secular state is in the balance.

The book explains the political transformations of India and Turkey with deep insight and exceptional clarity. It shows the similarity of the two non-Western secular states in not being based on a Western-style principle of separation of church and state, but rather on an operational doctrine of state intervention in and regulation of the religious sphere. At the same time, the work highlights the very different motives behind the establishment of secular states in the two cases, and demonstrates that while state-secularism took a culturally deracinated and deeply authoritarian form in Turkey, it assumed a culturally rooted and democratic form in India. The author critiques the flaws of what he calls India's 'really existing' secular state, but argues that unlike the fatally flawed Turkish model, secularism retains relevance in the Indian context and is indispensable to its future as a democracy.

In a lucid, accessible style, *Secular States, Religious Politics* combines encyclopaedic knowledge of the cases with a sophisticated comparative framework. Its subject, and argument, are extremely topical to the times we live in.

**Sumantra Bose** is Professor of International and Comparative Politics at the London School of Economics and Political Science (LSE). His many books include *Transforming India: Challenges to the World's Largest Democracy* (2013), *Contested Lands: Israel-Palestine, Kashmir, Bosnia, Cyprus, and Sri Lanka* (2007), *Kashmir: Roots of Conflict, Paths to Peace* (2003), *and Bosnia after Dayton: Nationalist Partition and International Intervention* (2002). Born and raised in Kolkata, India, Bose graduated from Amherst College in Massachusetts in 1992 and received his PhD in political science from Columbia University in New York in 1998. He lives between London and India.

# Secular States, Religious Politics
## India, Turkey, and the Future of Secularism

Sumantra Bose

 CAMBRIDGE
UNIVERSITY PRESS

# CAMBRIDGE
UNIVERSITY PRESS

University Printing House, Cambridge CB2 8BS, United Kingdom

One Liberty Plaza, 20th Floor, New York, NY 10006, USA

477 Williamstown Road, Port Melbourne, vic 3207, Australia

314 to 321, 3rd Floor, Plot No.3, Splendor Forum, Jasola District Centre, New Delhi 110025, India

79 Anson Road, #06–04/06, Singapore 079906

Cambridge University Press is part of the University of Cambridge.

It furthers the University's mission by disseminating knowledge in the pursuit of education, learning and research at the highest international levels of excellence.

www.cambridge.org
Information on this title: www.cambridge.org/9781108472036

© Sumantra Bose 2018

First published 2018

Printed in India by Rajkamal Electric Press, Kundli, Haryana.

*A catalogue record for this publication is available from the British Library*

*Library of Congress Cataloging-in-Publication Data*

Names: Bose, Sumantra, 1968- author.
Title: Secular states, religious politics : India, Turkey, and the future of
    secularism / Sumantra Bose.
Description: Cambridge, United Kingdom; New York, NY : Cambridge University
    Press, 2018. | Includes bibliographical references and index.
Identifiers: LCCN 2017061664| ISBN 9781108472036 (hardback) | ISBN
    9781108454865 (paperback)
Subjects: LCSH: Secularism--Political aspects--India. | Secularism--Political
    aspects--Turkey. | Religion and politics--India. | Religion and
    politics--Turkey. | Hinduism and state--India. | Islam and state--India. |
    Islam and state--Turkey. | India--Politics and government--1977- |
    Turkey--Politics and government--1980-
Classification: LCC BL2765.I5 B67 2018 | DDC 322/.10954--dc23 LC record available at https://lccn.
loc.gov/2017061664

ISBN 978-1-108-47203-6 Hardback
ISBN 978-1-108-45486-5 Paperback

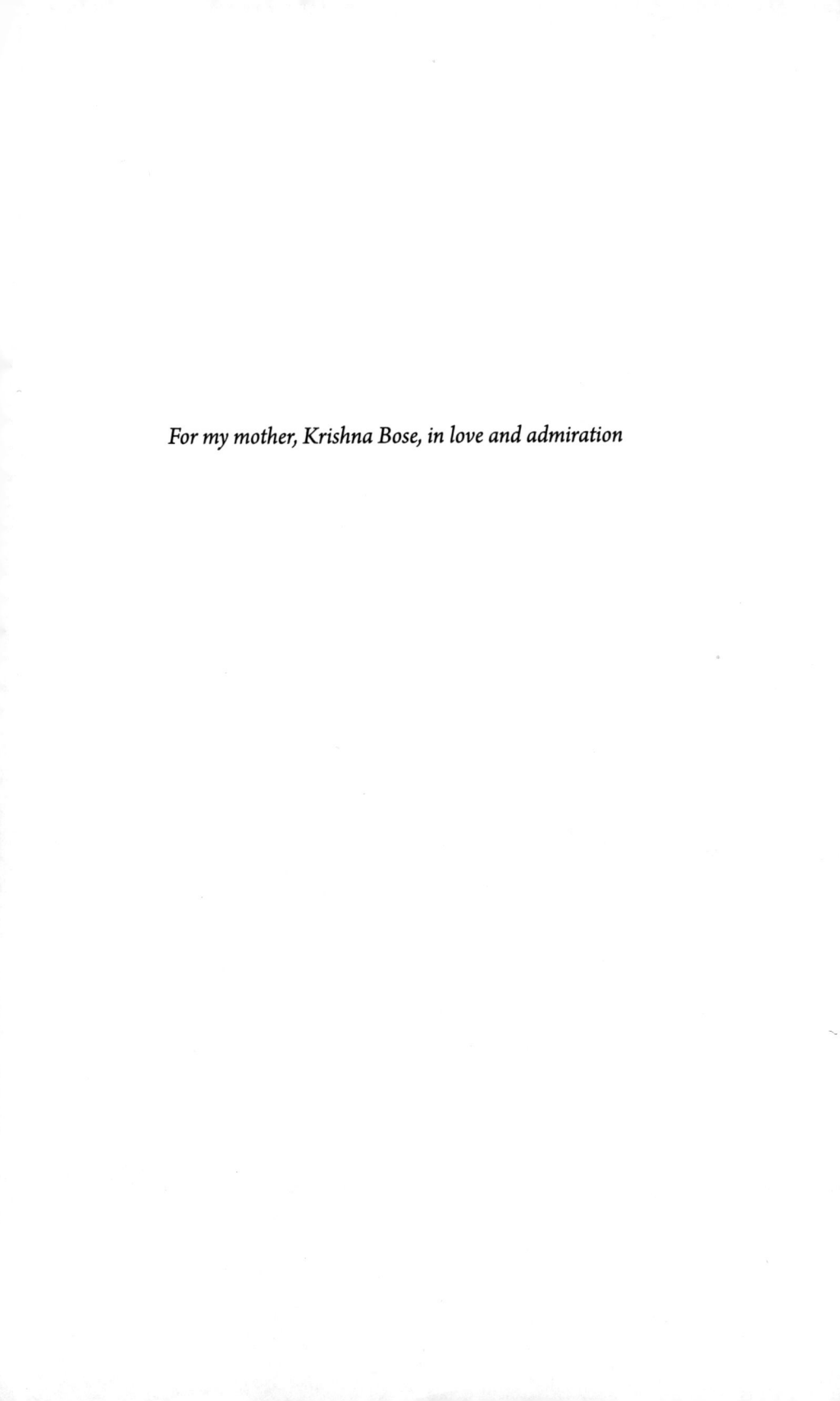

*For my mother, Krishna Bose, in love and admiration*

# CONTENTS

# PREFACE

Although I wrote this book in 2017, it has been in gestation for nearly twenty years, since the end of the 1990s.

Growing up in India during the increasingly turbulent decade of the 1980s, coupled with my immediate family's keen interest in and engagement with the political life of the country, spurred my interest in Indian politics. I left my hometown, Calcutta, in 1988 for undergraduate studies in the United States, but stayed closely interested, visiting often and spending considerable time in the country. The challenge to Indian secularism escalated dramatically during those years. When the Babri Masjid in Ayodhya, the symbolic focal point of the challenge, was razed in December 1992, I was finishing my first semester as a PhD student in political science at Columbia University in New York. I returned for the winter vacation to an India in crisis, engulfed in 'communal' (religious) violence.

My family background and upbringing had instilled in me a deeply felt sense of love of country which applied to all its people, without any question of distinction or discrimination. This mainly stemmed from my paternal family, in which my granduncle, grandfather – and, in the 1940s, my father, as a very young man – had been extremely active in India's struggle for freedom from colonial rule. My maternal family was not as political, but they came from an enlightened tradition of the (East) Bengal intelligentsia which lent itself to the same kind of view. The parental influence shaped, as is natural, my own conceptions and convictions. Nevertheless, I realised from the political events that unfolded in India from the early 1990s onward that the form of national identity which had been dominant since before our independence (from the 1920s) faced a very serious challenge, and equally that our 'secular state' established after independence could no longer be taken for granted.

I did write an extended academic essay on those developments in 1993, which was eventually published as a long chapter in an anthology on contemporary India in 1997. My perspective drew attention, but I was too immersed in pursuing various other research and writing interests to work further on the topic. At the same time, I stayed engaged with the evolution of Indian politics as a participant-observer of

PREFACE

the mass electoral politics that is the lifeblood of our democracy, and the India-related parts of my scholarly work, such as on the Kashmir conflict, also fostered that engagement.

My interest in Turkey dates to the first half of the 1990s. It initially derived from one of my main areas of interest and work as a student of comparative politics – conflict between states and aggrieved ethno-national groups therein. During that time, an armed conflict between the Turkish state and Kurdish ethno-nationalists reached its peak and regularly made headlines. I followed the conflict, though I did not work on it directly. Gradually, that led me to the broader context of the conflict: the nature and political history of the Turkish state established in the 1920s. In the process, I became explicitly aware of something I had known more vaguely earlier – that this was the other major example of a non-Western state, aside from my own, which had loudly proclaimed secularism to be a central aspect of its identity since its formation.

I spent two months in Turkey in the summer of 1999, teaching in the summer school of a well-known university in Istanbul. That first visit was simultaneously a learning and an unlearning experience. I had been harbouring the impression that Turkey was an (almost) European country, as proclaimed by its elite for over seven decades. I lived on the university's scenic campus in a posh suburb on the 'European' side of Istanbul, overlooking the Bosphorus Strait, and even there Turkey struck me as a thoroughly Middle Eastern and – to use an outdated term – 'Third World' country. It was distinctly 'Oriental' in many different ways, and nothing like even the nearby, formerly Ottoman territories of the Balkans in the former Yugoslavia, where I spent a lot of time during the 1990s (and since). Cities like Sarajevo and Mostar in Bosnia-Herzegovina, which retained many signs of four centuries (until 1878) of Ottoman Turkish rule, are distinctly (East) European in a way Istanbul is definitely not. Istanbul is much more like an Indian metropolis than any European city. I did not have the opportunity to travel in Turkey on that occasion, but from my perch in an affluent, 'secular' part of Istanbul I wondered what the rest of the country was like culturally, especially its heartlands in central and eastern Anatolia.

That first sojourn in Istanbul in 1999 also gave me a powerful sense, in ways tangible and less so, of the profoundly authoritarian nature of Turkey as a state, despite its democratic trappings. I had thought that this was a more or less democratic country, not too dissimilar to India. I realised that it was in fact a country where a state-sponsored ideology of national(ist) homogeneity and conformity had been strictly enforced, often through draconian means, over more than seven decades. An atmosphere of repression pervaded. At that time, the Kurdish insurgency in eastern and south-eastern Turkey was on its last legs after fifteen years of increasingly brutal warfare, Turkey's first Islamist-dominated government had been forced out of office by a 'soft' military coup just two years earlier, and Recep Tayyip Erdogan, the Islamist movement's stormy petrel, was serving a short prison term after being convicted on charges of anti-secular politics and banned from politics. It was a disquieting experience, because I had spent all my life in flawed democracies – in India, and since the late 1980s also in the United States.

# PREFACE

I decided that I wanted to do a comparative study of the secular state and its travails in India and Turkey, and wrote up a book proposal to that effect in 2000, shortly after I joined the London School of Economics and Political Science (LSE) as a faculty member. But then I never got around to it as many other non-academic and academic preoccupations, including several book projects, intervened in the subsequent years.

Fifteen years later, in mid-2015, it occurred to me that the original project I had neglected to pursue was even more relevant to the times than it had been back then. I retrieved the old proposal, dusted it off, and began afresh with a revised version.

I am grateful to the Syndicate of Cambridge University Press for approving the proposal, to the three anonymous reviewers who commented on the proposal for the Press, and to Qudsiya Ahmed, the Press's Delhi-based publishing manager for the humanities and social sciences. The Suntory-Toyota International Centre for Economics and Related Disciplines (STICERD) at LSE kindly gave me a grant in 2016 for the final stages of field research.

This book is for my mother, Professor Krishna Bose, who has been in somewhat frail health physically since 2016 but remains more lucid than ever mentally and indomitable in her spirit. Moreover, my late father, Dr Sisir Kumar Bose, has featured either on his own or jointly in the dedications of three of my four books published since his death in the autumn of 2000, whilst my Mamma has had only one dedication – jointly with him – in my very first book published aeons ago in 1994. It's time she gets her due.

# 1

# THE DISCONTENTS OF SECULARISM

*In 1945, the Turkish lexicon prepared by the Turkish Language Association provided the following in its entry for religion: 'An idea or ideal to which one fervently adheres. Kemalism is the religion of the Turk'.[1]*

*In 1961 I asked an Indian professor why he supported the principle of the secular state. The reply was: 'Because I have always been a nationalist'.[2]*

For decades after the formation of the Republic of Turkey in 1923 and the Republic of India in 1950 as sovereign nation-states, the principle of 'secularism' (*laiklik* or laicism in Turkey) was held to be a cornerstone of both state and nation in the two countries. It was seemingly impossible to think of national identity without reference to the 'secular' principle, or to conceive of the state without reference to its 'secular' character. In Turkey, as the first epigraph above conveys, the official ideology of nation-statehood had supplanted Islam – the religion of the vast majority of the population – with a new creed of 'Kemalism' named after the Turkish Republic's founding leader Mustafa Kemal, known after 1934 as Ataturk (Father of the Turks). Under Kemal's leadership, a series of radical reform measures were enacted starting in 1924 to make Turkey a secular state. In 1928, Article 2 of the Republic's Constitution, which had

---

1   M. Sukru Hanioglu, 'The Historical Roots of Kemalism', in *Democracy, Islam and Secularism in Turkey*, ed. Ahmet T. Kuru and Alfred Stepan (New York: Columbia University Press, 2012), 44–45.

2   Donald E. Smith, *India as a Secular State* (Princeton: Princeton University Press, 1963), 139.

stated that 'the religion of the Turkish state is Islam' was summarily deleted. The secularizing drive culminated in 1937, a year before Kemal's death, when Turkey was constitutionally declared a 'laicist' state.

The word 'secular' did not feature in India's Constitution until 1976, when it was inserted via an amendment made during a relatively brief, 18-month period of authoritarian rule known as the 'Emergency'. Nonetheless, that multi-religious India was a 'secular state' became a central tenet of the official discourse during the 1950s and the state-sanctioned version of Indian nationalism incorporated secularism as a core principle of independent India's identity. In March 1950, two months after the proclamation of the Republic of India's Constitution, Prime Minister Jawaharlal Nehru wrote to Vallabhbhai Patel, his Home (interior) Minister and Deputy Prime Minister, 'We talk of a secular state. That of course simply means any normal state today, leaving aside the abnormality of Pakistan's Islamic state.' Patel replied two days later:

> As regards the differences in our approach, as far as I know there has been none as regards the secular ideals to which we all subscribe and for which we all stand ... At the same time, I have not ignored ... what is happening in Pakistan and the bitterness that engenders in this country (this was a reference to severe violence ongoing at that time against the Hindu minority in Pakistan's eastern wing, which has been sovereign Bangladesh since 1971).[3]

In 1952, Sheikh Mohammad Abdullah, the main political leader in India's part of the disputed territory of Jammu and Kashmir (claimed also by Pakistan), asserted following talks in New Delhi with Nehru's government, 'The supreme guarantee of our relationship with India is the identity of democratic and secular aspirations, which have guided the people of India as well as those of Kashmir in their struggle for emancipation.'[4] And in 1958, Nehru told the French writer Andre Malraux about his two priorities, 'Creating a [socially] just state by just means ... [and] creating a secular state in a religious country.'[5]

---

3   Madhav Godbole, *Secularism: India at a Crossroads* (New Delhi: Rupa Publications, 2016), 276–277.

4   Sumantra Bose, *Kashmir: Roots of Conflict, Paths to Peace* (Cambridge, MA and London: Harvard University Press, 2003), 45.

5   Swapan Dasgupta, 'The Toppling of the Nehruvian Political Order', *Hindustan Times*, 1 December 2016.

Five years later, in 1963, the American scholar Donald Smith published a substantial monograph titled *India as a Secular State*, the pioneering study of its topic, from which the second epigraph above is sourced.

♦

India and Turkey are the two leading examples of avowedly secular states in the non-Western world. What makes them secular? The state is constitutionally secular in both countries in that there is no official or state religion – the state's identity is not based on nor derived from (any) religion and is independent of any particular faith. Article 15 (1) of India's Constitution defines the basis of citizenship thus, 'The state shall not discriminate against any citizen on grounds of religion, race, caste, sex or place of birth.' Donald Smith noted that India's 'striving to be a secular state is remarkable ... in contrast with neighbouring countries.' Thus, Pakistan 'proclaimed itself an Islamic Republic ... its 1956 constitution required that the head of state be a Muslim and forbade enactment of laws "repugnant to the Holy Koran".' In Burma, which was a province of British India until 1937, the state, 'after independence embarked on a course of extensive promotion of Buddhism through legislation and state patronage' and 'the constitution was amended in 1961 to make Buddhism the state religion'.[6] A very similar course of events unfolded in Sri Lanka (then Ceylon) from 1956 and culminated in a new constitution in 1972 which formalized the Sinhala–Buddhist basis of the state's identity and policies.

Turkey has had three constitutions in the course of its existence as a republic: the first constitution adopted in 1924 was replaced by a new constitution in 1961 following a military coup, which in turn was replaced by the third constitution of 1982 enacted after yet another military takeover of the state. All the constitutions have enshrined *laiklik* (laicism, based on the French term *laicite*) as a core principle of the state, and the Turkish Republic's notion of the shared national identity of its citizens has drawn on a hybrid of ideas of blood descent (not infrequently by invoking dubious theories of racial origin), language (modern Turkish, written in the Roman script since the end-1920s, when it replaced the Arabic script as part of state policy), and geography (the

---

6 Smith, *India as a Secular State*, vii.

territory of Anatolia). The common – indeed monolithic – conception of 'Turkishness' promoted by the regimes of the post-1923 republic chose to emphasize these binding factors rather than Islam, which is, with considerable diversity of practice across denominations and sects, the faith of some 99 per cent of the population. In his magnum opus, *The Development of Secularism in Turkey*, published in 1964, the Turkish scholar (of Cypriot origin) Niyazi Berkes pointed out that 'the central issue around which the Turkish transformation took place', as a Turkish national state emerged in what had for hundreds of years been the political centre of the vast, sprawling Ottoman Empire, was 'the adoption of complete secularism'.[7]

The Western versions of state-secularism are based – albeit in differing specific forms and to varying degrees – on the doctrinal principle of separation of church and state. The Indian and Turkish models of state-secularism are, in sharp contrast to this broad Western prototype, not premised on any 'wall-of-separation' doctrine. Instead, the state has acted as a nearly omnipresent and often intrusive regulating authority in matters to do with religion and over religious institutions, resulting in entanglement of the state and the religious domain, rather than separation. In both cases, the state is legally and constitutionally empowered to do so, and this is the salient common feature of the Indian and Turkish secular states. Writing in the mid-1950s on Turkey, the American scholar Howard Reed noted,

> the state maintains a close, formal control of Islam by means of three central government agencies. The first two, established on 3 March 1924, are the Directorate-General of Religious Affairs and the Directorate of Pious Foundations. The heads of these offices are appointed by the President of the Republic on the recommendation of the Prime Minister, to whom they are directly responsible and on whose Prime Ministry budget they depend. The third is the [state's] Ministry of Education, which has been ultimately responsible for all formal instruction, including religious education, since 1924.[8]

---

7 Niyazi Berkes, *The Development of Secularism in Turkey* (London: Hurst and Company, 1998), 431. The book was first published in 1964 by McGill University Press in Canada, where Berkes was then living as a political exile.

8 Howard Reed, 'The Religious Life of Modern Turkish Muslims', in *Islam and the West*, ed. Richard Frye (The Hague: Mouton and Co., 1957), 109–110.

Indeed, the new-born Turkish Republic's sensational abolition of the Caliphate in March 1924 was accompanied by the immediate establishment of the *Diyanet Isleri Baskanligi*, or the Directorate-General of Religious Affairs, as a key organ of the new state. The sweeping mandate of this institution included administrative oversight over all mosques in the country (as well as dervish monasteries or *tekkes*, until these were summarily banned in 1925 along with the deeply-entrenched and widespread religious brotherhoods or *tarikat*s), and supervision of the appointment and dismissal procedures of all *imam*s (head clerics and prayer leaders of mosques) and *hatip*s (ordained preachers) across Turkey. The mandate of the Directorate of Pious Foundations (*Evkaf*) included the administration of religious endowments, maintenance of mosques, and from the early 1930s, the remuneration of clerics. The elimination of the autonomous system of religious schools was accompanied by the promulgation of a Unity of Education Law, which brought all institutions imparting religious education (*medreses* and *mekteps*) under the authority of the central state's Ministry of Education. This structure and set-up of the secular state has been described as a 'control model', in which the state seeks not to stand apart from and distance itself from the domain of religiosity and religious practice but systematically intervenes in that domain to control religious affairs and co-opt and subordinate religious bodies and institutions.

In an early study of India's secular state published in 1964, the Indian scholar Ved Prakash Luthera observed that the Indian Constitution 'does not embody the spirit of the concept [of the secular state] which consists of ensuring the freedom of the church ... from regulation and control by the state'. 'On the contrary', Luthera noted, 'the constitution vests immense powers in the state over the affairs of the church (religious bodies)' and sets up 'a jurisdictionalist state' which 'is intertwined with all the churches [religious faiths] and controls and regulates the affairs of all [of them]'.[9]

Indeed, Article 25 (1) of the Indian Constitution states that 'all persons are equally entitled to freedom of conscience and the right freely to profess, practice and propagate religion' but 'subject to public order, morality and health' – as implicitly, but quite obviously, defined by the state authorities –

---

9   Ved Prakash Luthera, *The Concept of the Secular State and India* (Calcutta: Oxford University Press, 1964), 146, 150.

'and the other provisions of this Part [of the constitution]'. Article 25 (2) lays out those other provisions,

> Nothing in this article shall affect the operation of any existing law or prevent the state from making any law a) regulating or restricting any economic, financial, political or other secular activity which may be associated with religious practice b) providing for social welfare and reform or the throwing open of Hindu religious institutions of a public character to all classes and sections of Hindus.

Article 26 states that it is 'the right of every religious denomination or any section thereof … to manage its own affairs in matters of religion', provided it is 'subject to public order, morality and health' – as interpreted by the state. The Indian secular state put these open-ended, self-arrogated powers of intervention in religious matters to extensive use as early as the mid-1950s, when the national parliament enacted a set of legislation that codified Hindu personal and family laws on marriage, divorce, inheritance and adoption with the explicit objective of progressive reform, especially regarding the rights of women. The state also intervened on a large scale to combat and curb the most egregious manifestations of the caste-based social order, such as opening up access to Hindu temples and shrines to so-called untouchables – referred to in contemporary India as *Dalit*s, or the oppressed, they comprise one-sixths of India's population – as well as to supervise and regulate the administration and endowments of Hindu religious bodies.

Luthera argued that 'the [Indian] constitution does not establish a secular state' because, far from separating and distancing the state from religious matters it actively promotes the opposite – the irretrievable entanglement of the state with the domain of religion. He noted that Donald Smith, whose book had appeared the previous year (1963), had read his manuscript and disagreed with its conclusion that India could not claim to be a secular state, principally on the grounds that Luthera had used 'too narrow a definition of the secular state' which 'equates "secular state" with separation of state and religion'.[10] Smith, for his part, acknowledged in his book that the Indian secular state was replicating 'the tendency of traditional religions to regulate virtually every aspect of life', so the perspectives of the two authors did significantly

---

10 Ibid., 146 and viii.

overlap. Smith differed with Luthera in that, he felt that the Indian example of the secular state had 'no clear parallel in Western experience' and therefore, it was inappropriate to apply the typical criterion of the Western secular-state paradigm as the benchmark for the Indian case.[11] Luthera did apply an overly restrictive and West-centric definition in his judgment of the Indian state's secular credentials, and Smith had the more nuanced and context-sensitive position in this debate. Luthera's own observation that 'the constitution of India does not establish any religion'[12] places India in a completely different category from Pakistan, Burma or Ceylon, and fulfils my own definition of a secular state (as elaborated above) – a trait the Republic of India shares with another non-Western country, the Republic of Turkey.

If Western-style separation, or put in less ideal-typical terms, distance of the state from matters of mosque, temple and church does not define the secular state in India and Turkey, then what does? As twentieth-century republics, both states are founded on the doctrine of national self-determination and its twin precept, popular sovereignty. In 1921, as nationalist Turks clustered around Mustafa Kemal, he struggled to salvage a Turkish national state in Anatolia in the face of a Greek invasion, and French and (particularly) British machinations. Meanwhile, the National Assembly formed in Ankara in 1920 adopted a constitution for the state in the making. Article 1 stated, 'Sovereignty belongs unconditionally to the [Turkish] nation ... based on the principle of the people's direct rule over their own destiny'.[13] The doctrine of popular sovereignty, born of the French Revolution of 1789, implies the equality of all citizens who comprise the nation. In an avowedly secular republic, where the identity of the state is not based on or tied to (any) religious faith, it additionally means that all confessional communities are equal in the eyes of the state, and none should receive either preferential or discriminatory treatment. As Luthera put it, 'all religions are placed on a basis of equality' by 'the constitution of India', which seeks to establish 'a religiously impartial ... state'.[14] This constitutional framework provides the basis of the Indian

---

11  Smith, *India as a Secular State*, viii.

12  Luthera, *The Concept of the Secular State and India*, 149.

13  Berkes, *The Development of Secularism in Turkey*, 446.

14  Luthera, *The Concept of the Secular State and India*, 149–150, 155.

secularist concepts of *dharma-nirapekhshata* (neutrality or impartiality, usually meaning state neutrality and impartiality, towards the nation's diversity of religions) and *sarva-dharma-sambhava* (equal status of all religions).

But in the cases of India and Turkey, staying aloof from the religious domain is not an option for the state. This is because entanglement rather than separation, and proximity rather than measured distance, defines the relationship of the state with religion. So, the activist secular state in India has been saddled with the complex challenge, and delicate balancing act of treating all of India's faiths – Hinduism, Islam, Sikhism, Christianity, Jainism, and Buddhism – with absolute impartiality, *sans* any kind of favour or prejudice. In Turkey, the challenge of impartiality has also been significant for the state. Just as the common description of India as a predominantly Hindu country – 79.8 per cent of Indians were classified as Hindu in the national census of 2011, Muslims being the largest religious minority at 14.2 per cent – obscures the enormous diversity among the nearly one billion people classified as Hindus, the common description of Turkey as '99 per cent Muslim' is simplistic and indeed misleading. In fact, Turkey is rife with ethnic, sect, denominational and ideological diversity. As the Turkish scholar Ergun Ozbudun has argued, the Turkish Republic's chronic problem has been that the plural nature of its society is at odds with the nature of its state, which has been fixated on imposing an untenable homogeneity on all citizens and groups of citizens.[15] Turkey's society is defined by multiple, criss-crossing fault-lines based on ethnic identity (majority Turks and a substantial minority of Kurds), outlook and lifestyle (a pious Muslim majority and a substantial Westernized minority) and ideological divides between conservatives and relative liberals. And while Turkey is majority Sunni (among both Turks and Kurds), there is a large confessional minority whose position in society and politics is analogous to that of India's Muslim minority. These are the Alevis, usually estimated at around 20 per cent of Turkey's population of 80 million, whose faith is a particularly heterodox form of Shi'ism mixed with crypto-Christian practices (such as the drinking of wine during devotional ceremonies) and paganistic elements. Alevis, who are a sizeable minority among both Turks and Kurds, do not have mosques but congregate in *cemevi* (prayer halls which also serve

---

15 Ergun Ozbudun, 'Turkey: Plural Society and Monolithic State', in *Democracy, Islam and Secularism in Turkey*, ed. Kuru and Stepan, 61–94.

as community centres) where men and women sit together, and collective dances are performed. Many Sunnis, especially Sunni Turks, of a pious and traditional mentality do not regard Alevis as fellow-Muslims, but as heretics.[16]

In both India and Turkey, the secular state has floundered in living up to the very demanding criterion of impartiality towards religions, sects and denominations. In the process, it has attracted criticism and hostility from the advocates and agitators of all sides. Since the 1950s, India's (then marginal) Hindu nationalists have attacked the secular state for (allegedly) denying what they regard as the essence and cornerstone of Indian nationhood – the Hindu faith of the majority – and as 'pseudo-secular' for practicing 'appeasement' of the Muslim minority. Indian Muslims, for their part, have grievances towards the state as well, including well-founded notions that a strong strain of Hindu communalism – the word used in India to denote religious bias and prejudice – has existed within the secular state throughout its history and that, especially since the 1980s, ostensibly secular leaders and governments have encouraged and colluded with Hindu majoritarian politics. In Turkey, the stunning political rise of anti-secularists in the twenty-first century is rooted in the longstanding feeling among numerous Sunni Turks that the superficially Westernized elite which dominated the secular state since its inception ignored, and even demeaned, the real essence of Turkish nationhood – Islam, in the Hanefi-Sunni tradition of the majority (the Hanefi tradition, one of the four schools of Sunni jurisprudence, is dominant among Sunni Turks, although Sunni Kurds mostly belong to the Shafi tradition).

Many Alevis, on the other hand, believe that the secular state has actually embodied, and practiced, a deeply ingrained and insidious partiality towards the Sunni majority. Indeed, in the 1980s Turkey's then nearly all-powerful military brass – the self-appointed guardians of Kemalist secularism – started to promote a so-called 'Turkish–Islamic Synthesis' as the official ideology of the state. This provided a fertile context for the rapid growth of Islamist politics in the 1990s (and beyond), just as the permissiveness of Indian secular leaders

---

16 On the Alevis, see David Shankland, *The Alevis in Turkey: The Emergence of a Secular Islamic Tradition* (New York: Routledge, 2003); Tord Olsson, Elisabeth Ozdalga and Catharina Raudvere, eds., *Alevi Identity* (Istanbul: Swedish Research Institute, 1998); and Nur Yalman, 'Islamic Reform and the Mystic Tradition in Eastern Turkey', *Archives Europeennes de Sociologie* 10, no.1 (1969): 41–60.

towards Hindu majoritarian politics in the 1980s resulted in the meteoric rise of Hindu nationalism from the margins to the centre-stage of India's politics in the 1990s, and into the twenty-first century. Ultimately, the Alevis prefer the imperfectly secular state to the Sunni Islamist conception of nation and state, just as India's Muslims prefer the flawed Indian secular state to the Hindu nationalist alternative. But it is the anomalies and contradictions of the secular state that have, in the longer term, enabled the once unthinkable – the rise of avowed anti-secularists to the helm of the secular states of India and Turkey.

◆

In June 1996, the Turkish Republic had an openly Islamist Prime Minister for the first time since its birth on October 1923. That Prime Minister was Necmettin Erbakan (1926–2011), Turkey's best-known Islamist politician since the end-1960s, when he founded a movement called *Milli Gorus* (National Outlook) and was elected to the Turkish parliament from Konya – a city in west-central Anatolia famous as the hometown of the thirteenth-century Sufi saint Rumi, who is known as 'Mevlana' in Turkey and beyond. The main figure behind the political emergence of Erbakan (an engineering professor with a doctorate from Germany) was Mehmet Zahid Kotku (1897–1980), a leader of the Naqshbandi *tarikat* (religious order) and the *imam* of the Iskenderpasha mosque in Istanbul's devout Fatih district. The Naqshbandi order was banned along with all other religious brotherhoods by the secular state in the mid-1920s but continued to maintain a clandestine existence and to command widespread social influence in Turkey. In the words of Lutfi Dogan, the head of the state's Directorate-General of Religious Affairs (the *Diyanet*) from 1968 to 1971, Kotku believed,

> the core identity (*kimlik*) and character (*kisilik*) of this wounded [Turkish] nation is Islam. Your main heritage is Islam and ... you can heal the wound by listening to what our Turkish Muslim people want. What they want is an Islamic sense of justice, and the restoration of their Ottoman-Islamic identity.[17]

As the Turkish scholar M. Hakan Yavuz writes, Erbakan and his supporters

---

17 M. Hakan Yavuz, *Islamic Political Identity in Turkey* (New York: Oxford University Press, 2003), 207.

used the word *milli* to denote the religiously rooted essence of the Turkish nation and its integral place in the community of Muslim nations, in sharp opposition to the secular and Europe-oriented definition of Turkish national identity represented by the Kemalist republic.[18]

Erbakan had previously served as Turkey's Deputy Prime Minister in unstable coalition governments during the 1970s. He was not the first politician of Islamist leanings to head Turkey's civilian government – Turgut Ozal (1927–93), who was Prime Minister from 1983 to 1989 and then the President until his death in 1993, came from what might be called a 'soft Islamist' background, and had even stood unsuccessfully as a parliamentary candidate in 1977 for the National Salvation Party (*Milli Selamet Partisi*, MSP) led by Erbakan. But in comparison to Ozal, a pragmatic politician whose Islamist sympathies and connections Turkey's military hierarchy found tolerable and even useful as they carefully supervised the gradual restoration of civilian government following their violent seizure of power in 1980, Erbakan represented an ideological brand of Islamist politics that the military's leadership could not live with.

In parliamentary elections in December 1995, Erbakan's Welfare Party (*Refah Partisi*, RP) won the single largest number of seats – 158 of 550 – in a fractured Turkish Grand National Assembly or TGNA (a 'hung' parliament in Indian political parlance). In June 1996, the RP concluded a post-poll coalition agreement with the second largest party in parliament, a nominally secularist right-wing party, and Erbakan became Turkey's Prime Minister.

The RP's rise to leadership of Turkey's government, with a veteran Islamist politician occupying the office of the Prime Minister, was too much to bear for the high echelons of the Turkish military's officer corps, the guardians of the Kemalist republic's secular foundations and character. They were already alarmed by the RP's steady advance in Turkey's politics – in nation-wide local elections held in March 1994, which saw a turnout of 94 per cent of the registered electorate, the Islamist party had won in some 300 cities and towns across the country, including the largest city Istanbul and the national capital and (then) bastion of the secular elite, Ankara. The RP's most charismatic young leader, Recep Tayyip Erdogan (b. 1954) had taken charge as Istanbul's mayor following those elections. In February 1997, the military brass initiated

---

18 Ibid., 223.

what is widely regarded as Turkey's fourth military coup in four decades – following direct seizures of power in 1960 and 1980 and a somewhat less direct but still decisive intervention in 1971 – in the form of an eighteen-point 'directive' to Erbakan's government. The first point stated, 'The principle of secularism should be strictly enforced'. A tense stand-off ensued and in June 1997 Erbakan threw in the towel and resigned. The Turkish Islamists' taste of national power had lasted just a year. That was not all. In January 1998, Turkey's constitutional court, another watchdog institution of the secular state and effectively the military command's partner-in-arms, closed down the RP, the nation's largest political party, for violating 'the principles of the secular Republic' and banned ex-premier Erbakan from politics for five years. The secularist onslaught continued thereafter. In late 1998, the banned RP's youthful icon Tayyip Erdogan was compelled to step down as mayor of Istanbul and in 1999 convicted and sent to prison for several months; he was also banned from politics, a ban not overturned until early 2003, when he returned in triumph to take over as Turkey's Prime Minister. He was sentenced and banned for the alleged anti-secularist heresy of reciting a poem by Ziya Gokalp (1876 –1924) – a leading Turkish nationalist ideologue of the early twentieth century whose ideas were partially and selectively incorporated into the post-1923 Kemalist republic's ideological framework – during a visit to predominantly Kurdish south-eastern Turkey, then torn by over a decade of armed conflict between the military and police forces of the Turkish state and the Kurdish nationalist Workers' Party of Kurdistan (PKK). The offending verses from Gokalp he had recited were, 'Turkey's mosques will be our barracks, the minarets our bayonets, the domes our helmets, and the faithful our soldiers'. The constitutional court's chief justice from 1998 to 2000, an arch-secularist, went on to serve as Turkey's President for a seven-year term from 2000, in which capacity he feuded continuously with the first government (November 2002–07) of the *Adalet ve Kalkinma Partisi* (AKP, Justice and Development Party) – the successor to the banned RP. That first AKP government was headed initially by Abdullah Gul (b. 1949), who would later serve as Turkey's President from 2007 to 2014, and from March 2003 by the triumphantly rehabilitated Erdogan.

In an uncanny coincidence, anti-secularists also assumed the helm of the ship of state for the first time in India at nearly the same moment, in mid-

1996. In independent India's eleventh general election in May 1996, the Hindu nationalist party, the Bharatiya Janata Party (Indian People's Party, BJP), for the first time emerged as the single-largest party in the parliament, winning 161 of the 543 seats in the Lok Sabha (House of the People), its directly-elected chamber. The BJP's rise had been nothing short of meteoric – in the eighth Lok Sabha (1984–89) the party had held just two of the 543 seats. The 1996 result was a fractured one. The Congress party, the hegemon of India's democracy until the late 1980s, did very poorly, winning just 140 of the 543 seats – its worst ever showing at the time, surpassed in a mid-term national election in autumn 1999 when it won only 114 of the 543 seats, and then again in the current Lok Sabha elected in mid-2014 when it won just 44 of the 543 seats. The other 240 or so seats were taken in 1996 by a diverse and disparate spectrum of so-called 'regional parties': parties with a mass base usually in only one of the then 25 (now 29) States of widely varying population sizes that comprise the Indian Union.

India's Hindu nationalist party was formed in 1951, just before independent India's first general election. From then until 1980, when its name was slightly amended, it was known as the Bharatiya Jan Sangh (Indian People's Organization, BJS). From its inception until today, the BJS/BJP has been one member of a 'Sangh Parivar' (family of organizations) which constitutes India's Hindu nationalist movement. The core organization of this 'family' is the Rashtriya Swayamsevak Sangh (National Volunteers' Organization, RSS), founded in 1925. The RSS, which is headquartered in the city of Nagpur in India's western Maharashtra State, has several million members organized in tens of thousands of local branches (*shakhas*) across India and is known for both ideological commitment and organizational discipline. In March 2017, the RSS's annual all-India conference heard that 57,233 *shakhas* operate across the country. The RSS leadership has tended to disavow political aims but the purpose of its existence has been to ultimately realize the goal of making India a Hindu Rashtra ('Hindu State'), reflecting its belief that Indian nationhood is defined by the common Hindu identity of the large majority of Indians. In this view, India being a secular state is not just inappropriate, it is an abomination. The initiative for the formation of the BJS in the early 1950s came largely from the RSS's leaders of the time, who felt that a political party was needed to represent the movement and its anti-secular struggle in the arena of competitive politics. Since then, almost all top BJS/BJP leaders have been indoctrinated and politically socialized in the RSS, including India's two BJP Prime Ministers: Atal Behari Vajpayee (b. 1924), who was Prime Minister very briefly in 1996 and then for over six years from 1998 to 2004, and Narendra Modi (b. 1950), who has been Prime Minister since mid-2014. Indeed, prior to becoming the Chief Minister of the State of Gujarat in western India at the age of 51 in late 2001, Modi spent almost his entire adult life as a cadre of the RSS, which seconded him to the BJP in the late 1980s.[19]

In 1996, India's President, the titular head of state, acted in accordance with constitutional and democratic norms despite his background as a lifelong Congress politician. He gave the BJP, as the single largest party in the newly-elected parliament, the first chance to form a government. The BJP accepted the invitation with alacrity and the veteran Hindu nationalist Atal Behari Vajpayee was sworn in as Prime Minister along with a BJP-dominated cabinet of ministers. Vajpayee had spent his early political life in the RSS before being seconded by the RSS leadership to the newly formed BJS in the early 1950s, and he had earned a reputation as an excellent orator of the Hindu nationalist viewpoint over nearly four decades as a member of parliament ever since his election to the second Lok Sabha in 1957.[20]

The Hindu nationalists' first sojourn in the corridors of power in New Delhi lasted thirteen days. Just before the government completed its second week, Vajpayee resigned without seeking the required vote of confidence on the floor of parliament when it became clear that the BJP had no chance of mustering or even approaching the majority threshold (272) in the 543-member Lok Sabha. With its 161 MPs, BJP was 111 short of the threshold and along with three regional party allies it could count on 185 MPs in total. The deficit of 87 MPs proved to be a mountain too high to climb.

---

19  On the RSS, see Walter Andersen and Shridhar Damle, *The Brotherhood in Saffron: The Rashtriya Swayamsevak Sangh and Hindu Revivalism* (New Delhi: Sage Publications, 1987). On the BJS/BJP, see K. R. Malkani, *Principles for a New Political Party* (Delhi: Vijay Pustak Bhandar, 1951); Craig Baxter, *The Jana Sangh: A Biography of an Indian Political Party* (Philadelphia: University of Pennsylvania Press, 1969); and Bruce Graham, *Hindu Nationalism and Indian Politics: The Origins and Development of the Bharatiya Jan Sangh* (Cambridge: Cambridge University Press, 1990).

20  An account of Vajpayee's complex political life can be found in Ullekh N. P., *The Untold Vajpayee: Politician and Paradox* (Delhi: Penguin Random House India, 2017).

These dramatic episodes twenty years ago in India and Turkey were not aberrations, but early signs of fundamental shifts in the politics of the two leading non-Western secular states. The thirteen-day Hindu nationalist government was replaced in mid-1996 by a shaky coalition government cobbled together from some of the regional parties represented in parliament, propped up by 'outside support' given by the defeated Congress party. The government fell when the Congress withdrew support in end-1997 and a mid-term general election took place in the early spring of 1998. In this election, the BJP once again emerged as the single largest party in parliament, winning 182 of the 543 seats in the Lok Sabha, one-third of the total. This time the BJP was able to stitch together a majority government with the support of a number of regional parties. Vajpayee again became Prime Minister, on this second coming for slightly over a year. In April 1999, the BJP-led coalition government lost a vote of confidence on the floor of the Lok Sabha by just one vote after a temperamental regional party leader withdrew from the government. But in a fresh mid-term general election in autumn 1999, the BJP yet again emerged as the single largest party, winning 182 of the 543 Lok Sabha seats, exactly the same number as in early 1998. The BJP entered the 1999 election at the head of a pre-poll alliance styled as the National Democratic Alliance (NDA), which included a dozen regional parties – most of a secular orientation – from across the length and breadth of the country. These regional parties won 88 parliamentary seats between them and a BJP-led coalition government was formed without difficulty. Vajpayee, a virtually unique specimen of a lifelong Hindu nationalist respected by many secularists for his personal civility and probity, became Prime Minister for the third time in three years. In return for the support of the (mostly secularist) NDA regional parties, the BJP agreed to put in abeyance the three main points of its anti-secularist programme. These were:

(a) The campaign by the Sangh Parivar to build a grand temple dedicated to the Hindu deity Ram at the site of a sixteenth-century mosque in the town of Ayodhya in Uttar Pradesh (Northern Province), India's most populous State which is a gigantic sprawl across northern India's Indo-Gangetic plain. The site, claimed by the Hindu nationalists to be Ram's birthplace, was the focus of a strident agitation by the Sangh Parivar between 1990 and 1992 which climaxed with the razing of the mosque by a mob of

Hindu nationalist activists in December 1992, and the very polarising and inflammatory campaign played an important role in the growth of support for the BJP in northern India and to a lesser extent elsewhere in the country.

(b) The demand for a Uniform Civil Code (UCC) for all Indian citizens regardless of religion. A 'directive principle of state policy', incorporated as Article 44 of India's 1950 Constitution, reads: 'The state shall endeavour to secure for the citizens a uniform civil code throughout the territory of India'. Religious codes can be invoked by both Muslims and Christians in India in personal and familial matters, but Hindu nationalists focus on the right of Muslims to have recourse to Sharia law in such matters, and cite the secular state's complete inaction over decades on enacting a UCC as prime evidence of its hypocritical 'pseudo-secularism' and 'appeasement' of Muslims – especially given that Hindu personal and family laws were codified on reformist lines by the same state as early as the mid-1950s, particularly with a view to improving the rights of women in matters of marriage, divorce, inheritance and adoption.

(c) Lastly, the demand for the abolition of special autonomy provisions for Jammu and Kashmir, India's only Muslim-majority State, as specified in Article 370 of India's Constitution.

The NDA government completed its full term of five years, but unexpectedly fell significantly short of gaining a parliamentary majority in the general election of mid-2004. Following this failure, an alternative 'secular' coalition government was stitched together by the Congress with a range of regional parties, and the Congress-led alliance won a second five-year term in the general election of mid-2009. However, the BJP was not relegated back to the margins of Indian politics, its status until the end-1980s. It continued to be the main opposition party, and in India's sixteenth general election in April–May 2014 it regained power, winning an absolute majority of the Lok Sabha – 282 of the 543 seats. This was the first time in three decades, since the eighth general election of December 1984, that one party won an outright majority in the Lok Sabha (on that occasion, the Congress had benefited from a nationwide wave of sympathy following the assassination of Prime Minister Indira Gandhi). The charismatic and controversial Narendra Modi, who headed the stunningly successful campaign as the BJP's declared candidate for Prime Minister, became India's second Hindu nationalist Prime Minister, and the first person born in independent India to assume the post. Unlike Vajpayee, this next-generation icon of Hindu nationalist politics came to the job with a hard-core right-wing image, which he tried to temper by emphasizing a message of socioeconomic development – *sab ka saath, sab ka vikaas* (with all, for the development of all).

If India's politics has undergone a sea-change since the late 1990s and into the new century, Turkey's politics has witnessed a transformation of seismic proportions. Following the forced closure of the RP in 1998, the banning of Erbakan from politics and the banning of Erdogan from politics along with his conviction and imprisonment – all for alleged violations of the Turkish Republic's secular ethos – the Islamists seemed condemned to a bleak political wilderness. The military's leadership and its allies in the handpicked high judiciary of the state appeared to have delivered a knock-out blow to their anti-secularist challengers. But the restoration of the secularist *status quo ante* proved both unsustainable and an optical illusion.

In early 2001, the Turkish economy, always unstable, and barely sputtering along by the late 1990s, the currency (Turkish lira) nearly worthless in international terms, suffered a meltdown. The collapse, a British journalist then based in Turkey recalled, 'triggered an upward lurch in inflation, a brutal recession and an almost unbearable dose of economic misery for ordinary citizens', and the crisis

> forced thousands of businesses into bankruptcy and threw hundreds of thousands of people out of their jobs ... the speed with which the crisis spread was extraordinary. It was as if a house of cards had collapsed. Turkey suddenly became a cash-only economy. There was no credit available, even between longstanding business contacts, because no one knew who might be unable to pay. It wasn't just the poor who were suffering. Countless small businesses went bust as people stopped buying all but the bare necessities, and companies relying on imports couldn't afford them any longer. Many middle-class people, who had taken out mortgages denominated in foreign currencies, lost their homes after the repayments became unaffordable overnight.

As the currency crashed further, the social consequences were devastating,

> In big cities like Istanbul and Ankara, a crime wave followed as some

people began to steal to survive. Others set up makeshift pavement stalls to sell valuable possessions, and the number of prostitutes working the streets suddenly increased. Shopkeepers who hadn't made a single sale in days were joined by taxi drivers who could no longer afford the price of imported fuel. A quarter of the 14,000 journalists and technicians working in Turkish media were fired as big media barons trimmed their margins, and 200,000 workers in the shoe industry alone lost their jobs. Many people only managed to get through because extended families and religious communities rallied around.

As for the political implications,

> Popular disgust at the way politicians reacted to the crisis intensified as people began to realise how long-established corruption had contributed ... State-run banks controlled by political parties in power had run up losses of twenty billion dollars by handing out bad loans ... The cosy alliance of politicians, bureaucrats and businessmen who had carved up the spoils for decades could never rest easily again.[21]

As this carnage unfolded, the secularist establishment doggedly pursued its persecution of the perceived anti-secularist menace. In June 2001, the *Fazilet Partisi* (Virtue Party, FP), the renamed RP which had been banned in 1998, was closed down upon an order by Turkey's constitutional court. The disbanded FP then split into two factions. In July, some members of the party's old-guard loyal to the aged and played-out Erbakan reformed as the *Saadet Partisi* (Felicity Party, SP). But most of the erstwhile RP chose to follow the younger generation of leaders – Abdullah Gul (b. 1949), Tayyip Erdogan (b. 1954) and Bulent Arinc (b. 1948) – in the launch of the Justice and Development Party (AKP) in August 2001. Apart from the bulk of RP adherents, the AKP gained a small number of disillusioned leaders of nominally secular right-wing parties, including several who had been close to Turgut Ozal, the 'soft Islamist' who was Prime Minister from 1983 to 1989 and President from 1989 to 1993.

---

21 Chris Morris, *The New Turkey: The Quiet Revolution on the Edge of Europe* (London: Granta Books, 2005), 158–161. There already was widespread discontent with the military-backed coalition government which had been in office since a parliamentary election in April 1999 over its inept response to a major earthquake that had hit northwestern Turkey in August 1999.

There was an attempt to close down the AKP just prior to early national elections held in November 2002, once opinion polls showed it leading the field. The state's chief public prosecutor asked the constitutional court to ban the party on the usual charge of anti-secular ideology and intent. However, the ban did not materialize in time, and the AKP surpassed all expectations, its own included, by winning a two-thirds majority in parliament, the Grand National Assembly – 363 of the 541 seats.

The AKP achieved this two-thirds majority on the basis of just over one-third, 34.3 per cent, of the nationwide popular vote. The reason for the apparent anomaly was the unusually high threshold of 10 per cent of the nationwide votes that any candidate list in Turkey must poll in order to secure representation in parliament (in countries that do have such a requirement the threshold is typically much lower and rarely exceeds 5 per cent, which is the required level in Germany for instance). The high threshold was made a requirement for parliamentary seats after the 1980 military coup and was intended to simplify Turkish politics and curb its increasing fractiousness by preventing smaller parties from getting into parliament. That the threshold has been maintained at such a high level since multiparty politics was reinstated in 1987 is usually ascribed to its use in keeping any Kurdish nationalist party from gaining parliamentary representation – until 2015, when the major Kurdish nationalist party finally broke through the threshold and entered parliament. Due to popular disgust with the political class, only one of the established political parties breached the 10 per cent threshold in 2002. This was the Kemalist Republican People's Party (CHP), whose share of 19.4 per cent was far behind the AKP's. Thus only two parties, the AKP and the CHP, were represented in the 2002–07 parliament, with 363 and 178 seats, respectively. The nearly one-half (46.3 per cent) of the electorate who had voted for a range of other parties had no representatives in parliament.

Nonetheless, the AKP's national vote share of 34.3 per cent in November 2002 was a huge increase on the 21.4 per cent Erbakan's RP had polled in December 1995, and an even bigger increase on the 15.4 per cent the banned RP's initial successor (the FP), had polled in yet another early parliamentary election in spring 1999. Apart from gaining the vast bulk of the FP's 1999 support, a devoutly religious vote base, the AKP benefited from a consolidation of right-wing (conservative nationalist) voters behind it. Between 1999 and

2002, the vote shares of two established and nominally secular right-wing parties declined sharply, as did the vote share of a far-right nationalist party, and these defections by voters of established conservative nationalist parties benefited the AKP. With its relatively fresh image, the AKP gained from the collapse in the credibility of these established parties in the wake of the 2001 economic meltdown, and became the beneficiary of a backlash to the secularist establishment's relentless hounding since 1997 of the religiously-minded political alternative. The popular backlash to that extraordinarily anti-democratic and vindictive campaign, a blatant case of punitive overkill, combined with the effects of the economic crisis and the partial disintegration of the established party system, all caused to propel the new generation of Turkish Islamists to power at the beginning of the twenty-first century.

It was far from evident then, however, that a new political era had arrived in Turkey. The AKP had, after all, won only slightly over one-third of the national vote and owed its huge parliamentary majority to the electoral rules, as explained above. Moreover, the military brass, the ultimate arbiters of Turkish politics, lurked as menacingly as ever in the wings, ready to cut Prime Minister Erdogan's government to size and even bring it down in the name of saving secularism. The military commanders had crucial allies in other institutions of the state: the high judiciary, with the apex constitutional court acting as the military's fellow-guardian of the secular state, and the presidency, occupied from 2000 to 2007 by an arch-secularist who had been the head of the constitutional court when it banned the RP in 1998.

The AKP's somewhat fortuitous win in November 2002 turned out to be the first of five consecutive AKP victories in national parliamentary elections. In 2007, Erdogan's party was re-elected to government with a resounding parliamentary majority, with a vastly expanded national vote share of nearly 47 per cent. In 2011, even this impressive performance was surpassed as the AKP won its third parliamentary majority with nearly 50 per cent of the national vote. In the next election, held in June 2015, the AKP's relentless ascendancy stumbled somewhat – its vote share fell to 41 per cent and the party fell slightly short of an outright parliamentary majority, winning 258 of the 550 seats in the Grand National Assembly. But in fresh elections in November 2015 the AKP bounced back, regaining an absolute majority (316 of 550 seats) with a revitalized vote share of nearly 49 per cent, close to the all-time high of 2011. Voter turnouts are consistently high in Turkish national elections; it was 84 per cent in June 2015 and 86 per cent in November 2015.

Turkey's political landscape has been transformed since 2002. The most important change has been the decisive assertion of civilian supremacy over the military. During the AKP's second term (2007–11), Erdogan's simmering confrontation with the secularist military hierarchy escalated. But the outcome was in stark contrast to previous confrontations between civilian politicians and the military's command, which had invariably ended in abject defeat for the civilian leaders. This conflict went in Erdogan's favour and the result was a thoroughly tamed and defanged military leadership, a truly incredible development by the Turkish Republic's standards, where the military hierarchy had been the ultimate authority for a half-century, since the first coup of 1960.

The second change is the rise and entrenchment of a hegemonic political party for the first time since the advent of multiparty politics in Turkey after World War II (for its first quarter-century the Turkish Republic was a one-party state ruled by the Republican People's Party, *Cumhuriyet Halk Partisi* or CHP in Turkish). To some extent the Democrat Party (*Demokrat Partisi*, DP), which emerged as an opposition force after World War II and then defeated the CHP in the first genuinely multiparty election in 1950, did emerge as a dominant party in the 1950s. But during its decade in government (1950–60) it faced increasingly strong competition from the CHP – in the 1957 national election, for example, the DP and CHP vote shares were 48 per cent and 41 per cent, respectively. By contrast the AKP was ahead of its closest competitor, the Kemalist-secularist CHP, by sixteen points (41 per cent to 25 per cent) even in the election of June 2015, when the AKP stumbled and failed to win an outright parliamentary majority. The political map of this inconclusive election shows the AKP dominant, often by wide margins, across most of Turkey except for a band of provinces on the western edge of the country, where the CHP led, and a swathe of provinces in predominantly Kurdish-populated eastern and south-eastern Turkey where the Kurdish nationalist party, the *Halklarin Demokratik Partisi* (People's Democratic Party, HDP) was the frontrunner. Indeed, in June 2015 the AKP failed to win an outright parliamentary majority because the HDP, which seeks to advance Kurdish rights and autonomy in Turkey, broke through the 10 per cent threshold required for representation in parliament and won 80 parliamentary seats with an impressive 13 per cent share of the national vote. The HDP was able to achieve this by broadening its Kurdish rights platform and positioning itself as a progressive force for democratization in Turkey, a strategy which won it a sizeable vote from young, urban, educated and pro-secular ethnic Turks in addition to its core Kurdish base. In the snap November 2015 election that followed, the AKP won nearly twice as many votes (49 per cent) as its closest competitor, the CHP, which remained stagnant at 25 per cent. Most of the AKP's vote gain between June and November 2015 came from voters who had supported the far-right Nationalist Movement Party (*Milliyetci Hareket Partisi*, MHP) in June but opted for the AKP in November, as Erdogan hardened his stance on Kurdish rights, a non-negotiable issue for Turkish ultra-nationalists, and launched a police and military crackdown in the Kurdish nationalist regions in the second half of 2015. The MHP's national vote share slumped from 18 per cent in June 2015 to 12 per cent in November; the HDP declined from 13 per cent to 11 per cent but managed to hold on to a somewhat diminished presence in parliament.

The third change is the dominance of political life by a commanding mass leader – possibly for the first time since the death of Ataturk in 1938, and certainly since the demise of Adnan Menderes, the charismatic DP Prime Minister from 1950 to 1960, when he was deposed by the military and executed by hanging a year later. Recep Tayyip Erdogan is a famously divisive figure in Turkey; he is adored by his supporters and loathed by his critics, who are overwhelmingly of a secularist political orientation. He holds the upper hand over his rivals, though. In August 2014, Erdogan contested the first-ever direct election to the presidency of Turkey, after relinquishing his prime ministership of eleven years to a handpicked acolyte (who was replaced in May 2016 by another handpicked acolyte). By 2014, Erdogan was already buffeted by growing criticism for his authoritarian behaviour, and for growing corruption in his government and party. The second and third largest parties in the country, the Kemalist-secularist CHP and the far-right, ultranationalist MHP, put up a joint candidate in hopes of defeating him. A defeat would have dealt Erdogan a political body-blow. The opposition's gambit did not work. Erdogan prevailed with 52 per cent of the popular vote; the joint CHP–MHP nominee got 38 per cent while the youthful leader of the Kurdish HDP, who stood separately, polled 10 per cent. Since Erdogan got an outright majority (>50 per cent) of the nationwide vote, a second round France-style 'run-off' between the two frontrunners, to be held in case no candidate crossed the 50 per cent mark in the first round, became moot. The opposition had failed to even push Erdogan into a second-round decider. Although Turkey's President had limited powers under the constitution and executive authority was, supposedly, principally vested in the Prime Minister and his cabinet, President Erdogan has been the ultimate authority and decision-maker in Turkey since that election. He has further enhanced his overbearing domination of the state in the wake of the failed military putsch of 15 July 2016 against him and the AKP government, which was apparently orchestrated by a secretive Islamist sect led by the United States-based septuagenarian preacher Fethullah Gulen, who was a key AKP ally during Erdogan's first decade in office but split bitterly from him and the AKP in 2013.[22] Turkey today has what political scientists call a 'neo-sultanistic regime', a leader-centred polity defined by the leader's personal authority. A century after the demise of the Ottoman Empire, a peculiar twenty-first century version of its integrated sultan-caliph form of authority has partially reappeared in the Republic of Turkey. All other AKP government officials and party leaders are followers; the state revolves around Erdogan.

The fourth change is that Turkey's state and society do not revolve any

---

22 Hakan Yavuz noted in 2003 that 'the [Gulen] movement functions like a beehive ... [based on] loyalty and discipline ... [and] is conditioned by nationalism and statism', specifically a blend of 'the state-centric Ottoman culture and Turkish-Islamic nationalism'. He also noted its rigidly hierarchical organizational set-up and that 'members of the movement are socially conservative, and not very open to critical thinking'. Yavuz, *Islamic Political Identity in Turkey*, 179, 181, 195, 201. Indeed, the Gulen movement, which built widespread networks in Turkey's state and society since the 1980s, as well as a global presence, and enjoyed the post-2002 AKP governments' indulgence and patronage until 2013, has clear attributes of a religious cult. It is partly descended from the ideas of the Islamic thinker Bediuzzaman Said Nursi (1876–1960), who was from eastern Turkey and of Kurdish origins. Nursi was closely monitored and persecuted by the authorities of the Kemalist state but his philosophy, especially as contained in his *kirmizi kitaplar* (red books), continued to have a significant following in the secular Republic, especially among petty-bourgeois social groups. Adherents of the *Nur* (Light) movement inspired by him are known as '*nurcus*'. See Serif Mardin, *Religion and Social Change in Modern Turkey: The Case of Bediuzzaman Said Nursi* (Albany, SUNY Press, 1989).

more around a (substantial) minority – the urban, mainly metropolitan elite of Istanbul and Ankara of Westernized habits and Europhile outlook schooled in 'Kemalist' values, above all secularism. The non-elite Hanefi-Sunni Turkish masses of Anatolia's rural areas and provincial towns – millions of whom live in Istanbul, Ankara and other big cities due to several decades of internal migration – believe that the AKP's rise has given them voice, equality and opportunity in twenty-first century Turkey. The AKP's remarkable electoral performances during its first decade in power owed much to economic recovery and healthy growth under its governments, coupled with nationwide anti-poverty and infrastructure initiatives, in the wake of the mess left by secular governments at the beginning of the century. But the de-secularization of the conceptual basis of Turkish national identity has also been a powerful rallying point. The AKP era has given millions of Sunni Turks whose Turkish national identity is inseparable from their religious faith a sense of validation and empowerment. They see Erdogan, a self-proclaimed 'Black Turk' of religious, working-class background, as personifying a certain levelling of Turkish society, where the 'White Turk' elite of the Kemalist epoch no longer rules and is not able to impose its values such as the former ban on headscarf-wearing women in state institutions and premises, including public schools and universities (approximately two-thirds of women in Turkey use some form of covering in public for their head and hair).

After a long and bitter struggle with the secularists of the CHP and the constitutional court, the AKP government was able to more or less end this restriction in 2013, except in the courts, military and police. Since August 2016, female police are also permitted to wear a simple headscarf the same colour as their uniform under caps or berets. Prime Minister Erdogan told the Turkish parliament in October 2013 that 'those who wear the headscarf are as much owners of the Republic as those who do not'.[23] Then, in February 2017, women officers and cadets in the Turkish military were extended the right to wear a headscarf if they so choose under their caps or berets, subject to the same rules regarding simplicity and colour as their counterparts in the police. The ultimate bastion of Kemalist secularism, the military, had fallen to the anti-secularist war of attrition on the headscarf front. Writing in 1973, the

---

23  Guney Yildiz, 'Turkey Lifts Headscarf Ban in State Institutions', BBC News Online, 9 October 2013.

Turkish scholar Nur Yalman called the Kemalist elite's imposition of a secular state on a Muslim and religious society nothing less than a 'cultural revolution', and he was quite right.[24] One can say without too much exaggeration that to committed AKP supporters, Erdogan and the AKP are engineers of a second revolution – overdue, welcome and democratic. To Turkey's beleaguered and outnumbered secularists, and to communities such as the heterodox Alevis, this is a creeping, foul counter-revolution reeking of majoritarian tyranny.

India's BJP can only aspire and strive, as yet, to the kind of hegemony the AKP has achieved in Turkey. The BJP's single-party parliamentary majority in 2014 was based on a relatively modest plurality – 31.3 per cent of the nationwide votes polled. The explanation lies in the electoral system. India's British-style plurality electoral system in single-member constituencies tends to disproportionately reward the political party, or the pre-poll coalition, that receives the plurality or single largest share of the vote. In the first general election of 1952, the Congress party won a nearly three-fourths majority in the Lok Sabha (364 of the then 489 seats) though it polled just 45 per cent of the nationwide votes. The Congress party in fact never won a simple majority (>50 per cent) of the nationwide vote in any election during its four decades of hegemony in Indian politics. It came closest, with 48 per cent, in 1984; that gave it 77 per cent of the seats (415 of 543) in the Lok Sabha. In 2014, the BJP's national vote share of under one of every three votes cast likewise gave it 52 per cent of the Lok Sabha's seats. The BJP contested 427 of the 543 constituencies, leaving the rest to a clutch of allied regional parties, whose candidates won another 54 constituencies between them, making a total of 336 MPs for the BJP-led alliance with 37 per cent of the nationwide votes.

Moreover, support for the BJP is very uneven across India. Generally speaking, the party is stronger in northern and western India and weak in most of eastern and southern India. The BJP's single-party parliamentary majority in 2014 was powered by Modi landslides in most of the States of northern and western India. For example, in the giant northern State of Uttar Pradesh, India's most populous State which elects 80 of the 543 Lok Sabha members, the BJP took 71 of the 80 constituencies (89 per cent) in a near-total sweep, albeit with only a good plurality (42.5 per cent) of the vote. However, even

---

24 Nur Yalman, 'Some Observations on Secularism in Islam: The Cultural Revolution in Turkey', *Daedalus* 102, no.1 (Winter 1973), 139–168.

in northern India, the BJP faces strong challengers, especially in States where powerful regional parties are present. In the populous northern State of Bihar, where the BJP won most of the 40 parliamentary constituencies in 2014 riding on the pro-Modi wave, the Hindu nationalists lost badly in an important election to constitute the State's legislature and government in late 2015 – to an alliance of two regional (Bihar-based) parties. So even in northern and western India, where the BJP is on a strong footing, it cannot take its prospects and dominance as assured in most of the States. And in most of the States of eastern and southern India, which largely bucked the Modi wave in 2014, its presence and base remain weak compared to entrenched regional (State-specific) parties. Even as Modi won nationally in 2014 with his purposeful image and promise of strong leadership, regional parties swept the eastern States of Bengal and Odisha and the southern State of Tamil Nadu, three States that together account for 102 of the 543 seats in parliament.

The extraordinary complexity of India's social and political landscape means that the Hindu nationalists' ambition of emerging as the nation's hegemonic party is fraught with uncertainty. But the prospects of this ambition should not be underestimated. The BJP is the only party in India today which can remotely claim to be a nationwide party, in spite of its very uneven footprint across the country. The Congress party, the grand old party of India, has withered away across most of the country both in popular base and organizational capacity, and is on the brink of extinction. The proliferation and growing clout of regional parties has been the defining feature of the evolution of India's democracy since the 1990s, following the end of the era of Congress hegemony.[25] But the regional parties are limited to their respective States, and the potential of an alliance of regional parties that can challenge the BJP is severely limited by their disparate nature, conflicts of ego and ambition between the chieftains of regional parties, and the fact that regional parties are in competition with each other in a number of States. Thus the BJP, its own limitations notwithstanding, has an advantage over its assortment of rivals. That advantage is amplified by the fact that the BJP has a leader, in Narendra Modi, who stands head and shoulders above any other politician in contemporary India in popular appeal and credibility. Like

---

25 See Sumantra Bose, *Transforming India: Challenges to the World's Largest Democracy* (Cambridge, MA and London: Harvard University Press, 2013), especially Chapter 2.

Erdogan, Modi remains a controversial and divisive political personality. His high-voltage 2014 campaign successfully exploited the weakness of his adversaries. The Congress-led government was severely unpopular and crashed to a humiliating defeat – the Congress itself won just 44 of the 543 Lok Sabha seats – and there was no alliance of regional parties that could act as the focal point for a national alternative. But since his ascension to the prime ministership in 2014, he has pursued a crafty strategy of positioning himself as the only politician with a national vision for India's progress and development. Like Erdogan, he presents himself, and possibly regards himself, as India's 'man of destiny' in the early twenty-first century. And he projects a distinctly presidential aura and style in India's parliamentary democracy, the first politician to plausibly do so since Indira Gandhi, Nehru's daughter and Prime Minister from 1966 to 1977, and 1980 until 1984 – a charismatic populist who is chiefly remembered today for her autocratic politics.

♦

The rise of anti-secular parties and leaders to the helm of the secular state in India and Turkey defines their politics in the early twenty-first century. In a most intriguing paradox, the state remains constitutionally secular but has leaders and parties whose ideology is fundamentally anti-secularist at the helm.

The deeper significance of the Indian and Turkish experiments in secular statehood can hardly be over-stated. Turkey has long been regarded as a test-case of whether a secular state is possible in a Muslim society. Nearly a century after the secular Republic's founding (the centenary is in 2023), the answer to that general question is far from obvious. What is clear, however, is that secularism has ceased to be the ideology of the Turkish Republic of the early twenty-first century. The same is becoming true of India as it approaches the 75th anniversaries of its independence (August 2022) and of the proclamation of the Republic of India (January 2025). For nearly a half-century after independence, secularism was considered essential to holding a vast, multi-religious country together. That is not axiomatic any longer in the early twenty-first century.

Secularism was a core element, perhaps *the* core element of the Kemalist and Nehruvian conceptions of national identity and of modernity. In those frameworks, it was impossible to conceive of the Indian and Turkish nations without the secular principle, and impossible for those nations to be 'modern' without simultaneously being secular. The secular state simply reflected this conception of modern nationhood. For four to five decades in the Republic of India and seven to eight decades in the Republic of Turkey this conception of nation, state and modernity was hegemonic, the anti-secularist alternative largely confined to the margins as a deviant phenomenon. With political transformation and the loss of secularist ideological hegemony, the anti-secularist argument that their alternative conception of nationhood is legitimate – indeed more culturally authentic than the secularist construct, and that it is quite possible to be modern *without* being secular – has moved from the margins to the centre-stage. The result is that the societies and polities of India and Turkey are deeply split on a secularist/anti-secularist fault-line. It is difficult to over-state just how fundamental this conflict is. The divide is over which form of nationalism is legitimate, and what the true or real basis and nature of society – its soul or essence – is. What is ultimately at stake in this conflict is the nature of the state. If the secularists are right, the secular state is essential; if the anti-secularists are right, it is not.

It should be noted that the anti-secular parties and leaders at the helm of state power in India and Turkey often don't overtly emphasize or foreground their opposition to the secular state, although that is the bedrock of their ideology and politics. As mentioned earlier, the BJP agreed to put in abeyance the three major demands of its anti-secularist manifesto in the late 1990s in exchange for the support of (mostly secularist) regional parties, whose support enabled it to lead coalition governments in New Delhi from 1998 to 2004. Since assuming the reins of the national government with an outright parliamentary majority in mid-2014, Narendra Modi, a politician of ideologically hard-line background and credentials, has not personally emphasized or even explicitly spoken about the Hindu nationalists' opposition to the secular nature of the state. Instead, his speeches and pronouncements have focused on (socioeconomic) development, about meeting the needs of the poor and improving their lives and opportunities, and about fulfilling the aspirations of India's youth (two-thirds of Indians are under 35) to jobs and economic security. All of his government's major policy initiatives stress these priorities, and he speaks in ambitious, even grandiose terms about a new India that will eliminate poverty, foster inclusion and equality – the slogan is *sab ka saath, sab ka vikaas* – and take its rightful position as an important country on the global stage. Explicit invocations of Hindutva ideology, which claims that Indianness is essentially based on the Hindu identity of the large majority of Indians and the character of the state should reflect that fact, have been conspicuously absent from his rhetoric. This is in stark contrast to the highly ideological and agitational mode of politics, with its full-frontal attack on the secular state, which the Hindu nationalist movement pursued during the first half of the 1990s. Secularists believe that as at the turn of the last century, Modi's change of discourse is a deceptive feint and the Hindu nationalists remain committed to realizing their ultimate objective of Hindu Rashtra, which they are continuing to promote in various insidious ways for the time being, until such time as they achieve the pan-Indian political hegemony necessary to dismantle the secular state.

During the AKP government's first term in Turkey (2002–07), some of its ideologues developed an ideological framework for the party that defined its political creed as 'conservative democracy', seemingly shifting away from the Turkish Islamist political identity of its forcibly dissolved parent party, the RP, and the RP's predecessor parties of the 1970s. An influential exponent of this reformulation was Yalcin Akdogan, a young (b. 1969) AKP politician close to Erdogan who served as one of the several Deputy Prime Ministers from 2014 to 2016. In an essay published in 2006, Akdogan wrote that 'according to conservative democrats, politics should be firmly grounded in a culture of reconciliation' and defined the party's agenda as 'gradual change and moderate reform that will accept the spectrum of Muslim beliefs and expression in public life' derived from the 'moral and family values' of Turkish society. Akdogan frankly acknowledged that the 'conservative democratic' self-label had been devised due to 'the acute sensitivities regarding secularism and the Islamization of the state in Turkey' and that avoiding a polarizing rhetoric of religious versus secular citizens was a better way of furthering the agenda of 'gradual change and moderate reform' because while the AKP 'could not afford to ignore the demands of the periphery', meaning its following in the non-elite and religious sector of society, it also could not 'afford to antagonize the centre'

29

(the Kemalist/secularist civilian and military elites).[26] To a typical Turkish secularist, this would have sounded suspiciously like the old anti-secular potion with the bottle's label changed to avoid another military intervention and/or proscription of the AKP by the constitutional court, and as a strategy designed to incrementally change the character of the state until the time was ripe for a full takeover of the 'centre'. Indeed, the battle between diehard secularists in the military's leadership and the AKP's civilian government escalated from 2007, and the AKP came perilously close to being banned by the constitutional court in 2008. After that, the tables turned as Erdogan neutralized the military brass's power and prevailed in a series of policy battles with the secularist establishment, including on the headscarf issue.

Erdogan himself has been careful not to totally disavow the Turkish secular state. In September 2004, the state's Directorate-General of Religious Affairs, the *Diyanet*, organized a high-level symposium in Ankara. The attendees included Prime Minister Erdogan and Bulent Arinc, the speaker of parliament and a top AKP founding member of 2001, alongside Ahmet Necdet Sezer, Turkey's President, who as head of the constitutional court had presided over the closure of the RP in 1998. The arch-secularist President, who sparred continuously with the first AKP government until the end of his term in 2007, told the audience: 'Secularism is a way of life, which should be adopted by the individual. A secular individual should confine religion to the sacred place of his conscience and not allow his belief to affect this [temporal] world'. In their speeches, both Erdogan and Arinc countered Sezer, arguing that they were willing to abide by secularism as a constitutional principle of the state but did not agree that it was a 'way of life' to be adopted by all individuals.[27] In September 2011, Erdogan visited Egypt after the fall of the Mubarak regime, fresh from his resounding third successive election victory in Turkey. He was given a rapturous welcome in Cairo by the Muslim Brotherhood, Egypt's largest and oldest Islamist political party-cum-social movement founded in the late 1920s. To their dismay, Erdogan seemingly defended the Turkish secular

---

26  Yalcin Akdogan, 'The Meaning of Conservative Democratic Political Identity', in *The Emergence of a New Turkey: Democracy and the AK Parti*, ed. M. Hakan Yavuz (Salt Lake City: University of Utah Press, 2006), 49–65.

27  Ahmet T. Kuru, 'The Reinterpretation of Secularism in Turkey: The Case of the Justice and Development Party', in *The Emergence of a New Turkey*, ed. Yavuz, 136.

state. An annoyed Brotherhood leader sulkily responded that 'Turkey violates sharia law. In Turkey, when a man finds his woman in bed with another man, he can't punish her by law'. A few days later, Erdogan repeated his point in Tunisia, where the so-called 'Arab Spring' had begun with an uprising against the longstanding secular authoritarian dictatorship in December 2010. He received a more sympathetic hearing in Tunis from supporters of the moderate Islamist *Ennahda* (Renaissance) party and movement – which won the single largest share of Tunisians' votes in democratic elections just a month later – when he highlighted himself as an example that 'a Muslim can govern a secular state in a successful way'.[28] Just after midnight on 1 January 2017, a lone gunman massacred 39 people, two-thirds of them foreigners, at a trendy but sleazy nightclub popular with a *nouveau-riche* secular Turkish clientele and some tourists in a fashionable Istanbul district located on the Bosphorus strait. This was one of a spate of terrorist incidents with high casualties in Turkey, perpetrated by Islamist radicals (as in this case) or Kurdish militants. A few days later, President Erdogan said in Ankara that there was 'no point in trying to blame the attack on lifestyle differences'. He added, 'No lifestyle is under threat in Turkey. We will never allow that'.[29] The reassurance notwithstanding, the AKP government's *Diyanet* had issued a statement in December to advise the people that celebrating the New Year was not consistent with 'Muslim values'.

Fifteen years after the AKP was first elected to govern Turkey, Turkish society is as divided and polarized as it was back then – between secularists and anti-secularists, nationalist Turks and disgruntled Kurds, orthodox Sunnis and heterodox Alevis. But there has been one decisive change. The control of the state has changed hands, reducing the old Kemalist elite and their social constituency to an embattled minority much like the Kurds and the Alevis. The erstwhile 'periphery' has become the 'centre', and the erstwhile centre the periphery. An analogous situation could, many Indian secularists fear, take root in India unless the Hindu nationalist ascendancy is politically checked, and sooner rather than later.

---

28  Jenny White, *Muslim Nationalism and the New Turks* (Princeton and Oxford: Princeton University Press, 2013), 189–190.

29  'Lifestyle Not under Threat, Says Erdogan', Reuters, Istanbul, 4 January 2017.

◆

Despite the enormous significance of the cases of India and Turkey as experiments in non-Western secular statehood that now face perilous futures, there has been no comparative study of the two countries. The two countries and their experiences of state-secularism are the subjects of two entirely separate bodies of scholarly literature. Since the 1950s American, European and Turkish scholars have written extensively on various aspects and problems of secularism and the secular state in Turkey. In the 1990s, sharply critical perspectives on the hitherto sacralized but now faltering secular state began to be published by Turkish scholars.[30] But all of this very extensive literature over the last six decades seems blind to the existence of India, the other major non-Western secular state, with the sole exception of a review article by the Turkish scholar Nur Yalman published in an Indian academic journal in the early 1990s.[31]

The scholarship on India's secular state and the problems of Indian secularism has been equally case-centred. The pioneering works by Smith and Luthera appeared in the first half of the 1960s. After a long hiatus, the topic received a very pronounced revival of attention as the 1990s progressed, in response to the dramatic rise of Hindu nationalism in Indian politics. Such liberal luminaries as the development economist Amartya Sen and the historian of ancient India Romila Thapar weighed in with uncritical defences of what I would call India's 'really existing secular state' (*a la* the 'really existing socialism' of the former Soviet Union). The political theorist Partha Chatterjee reflected on the crisis of Indian secularism with his brand of eclectically Marxist (or post-Marxist) analysis, and the flamboyant social psychologist Ashis Nandy engaged in an imaginative attempt to rescue India's tradition of religious tolerance from the clutches of the secular state. These eminent scholars stayed focused on just the Indian experience, however. In

---

30  See for example Sibel Bozdogan and Resat Kasaba, eds., *Rethinking Modernity and National Identity in Turkey* (Seattle: University of Washington Press, 1997); Nilufer Gole, 'Authoritarian Secularism and Islamist Politics: The Case of Turkey', in *Civil Society in the Middle East, Vol. II*, ed. Augustus Richard Norton (Leiden, New York and Koln: EJ Brill, 1996), 17-43.

31  Nur Yalman, 'On Secularism and its Critics: Notes on Turkey, India and Iran', *Contributions to Indian Sociology* 25, no.2 (1991):233–66.

1998, a useful anthology titled *Secularism and its Critics* was published from Delhi. It combined theoretical pieces on the idea of secularism and essays on the Western variants of secularism with contributions to the debate about secularism in India, the latter mostly from the 1990s. Its editor, the Indian political theorist Rajeev Bhargava, noted in his introduction that the volume could not aspire to be 'a comprehensive anthology of secularism … nor provide an adequate comparative perspective on secularism' partly because none of its fifteen chapters dealt with 'the experience of secularism in Turkey', among other cases.[32] In his work *India as a Secular State* (1963), Donald Smith did note that,

> a discussion of the problems of applying the idea of secularism in Asia would be very incomplete without at least a brief treatment of the first conscious endeavour of a free Asian country to become a secular state. For, a full twenty-five years before the secular Indian Constitution was adopted, the Turkish Republic made such an attempt, and largely succeeded.[33]

Smith's discussion of the Turkish case however consisted of two pages in a book of over 500 pages.

♦

The comparison of India and Turkey is extremely illuminating of the problems and future of the secular state in the non-Western world because the two cases combine the striking similarities and parallels already discussed with significant differences in their historical and political contexts. In the method of 'structured, focused comparison' in social and political inquiry, a comparison across cases makes sense and is potentially fruitful in illuminating the issue or problem being studied if the cases are substantially similar on the main axis or focal point of the comparison – i.e. the secular character of the state and its decline over time – but also different in contextual specificities.

---

32 Rajeev Bhargava, ed., *Secularism and its Critics* (New Delhi: Oxford University Press, 1998), 4. In this volume, see Ashis Nandy, 'The Politics of Secularism and the Recovery of Religious Toleration', 321-344; Partha Chatterjee, 'Secularism and Tolerance', 345-379; and Amartya Sen, 'Secularism and its Discontents', 454-485. See also Romila Thapar, 'Communalism and the Historical Legacy: Some Facets', in *Communalism in India: History, Politics and Culture*, ed. K. N. Panikkar (Delhi: Manohar Books, 1991).

33 Smith, *India as a Secular State*, 52.

That is because comparing 'apples and oranges' (cases which are utterly different) or cases which are totally identical are both meaningless.[34]

The genealogy of the secular state in India and Turkey has two salient differences. The first is the reason the two republics adopted secularism as a core principle in the first place. The statements of the two leaders at the helm as the secular states came into being, Jawaharlal Nehru and Mustafa Kemal, are revealing of the very different motivations and objectives at work in the two cases.

The formative period of India's secular state was 1947–49, as independent India's constituent assembly debated and formulated the Constitution of the Republic of India, which came into effect on 26 January 1950. On 3 February 1948, the daily newspaper *Hindustan Times* reported that Nehru said, 'We are planning to create a secular state, where one community or group ... will not be permitted to usurp the rights of another'. On 4 June 1948, the *Hindustan Times* reported, Nehru defined the 'secular state' as 'not [being] tied to any religion'. On 18 April 1949, the same paper reported Nehru's elaboration of the rationale of the secular state in the making,

> I am convinced that the measure of India's progress will be the measure of our giving full effect to what has been called a secular state. That, of course, does not mean a people lacking in morals or religion. It means that while religion is completely free, the state, including in its wide fold various religions and cultures, gives protection and opportunities to all and thus brings about an atmosphere of tolerance and cooperation.[35]

In short, Nehru believed that a state whose identity was not based on or tied to any religion, and which was impartial towards the nation's multiple religious faiths and traditions, was essential due to India's multi-religious composition. A secular state was both natural, and indispensable, given India's historical heritage of the coexistence of a multiplicity of religions.

Mustafa Kemal's argument for a secular state in Turkey during its formative period invoked a very different rationale. In 1923 he declared, 'The war [to establish the Turkish nation-state in Anatolia] is over with ourselves

---

34  On the use of the case-study method in comparative inquiry, see Alexander George and Andrew Bennett, *Case Studies and Theory Development in the Social Sciences* (Cambridge, MA and London: MIT Press, 2004).

35  Luthera, *The Concept of the Secular State and India*, 159.

victorious, but our real struggle for independence begins only now—this is the struggle to achieve Western civilization'. On 1 March 1924, two days before the Republic proclaimed on 29 October 1923 abolished the Caliphate as an autonomous source of religious authority, he told the National Assembly in Ankara,

> The important point is to free our legal attitudes, our codes, and our legal organizations immediately from principles dominating our life that are incompatible with the necessities of the age ... The direction to be followed in civil law and family law should be nothing but that of Western civilization.

As the secularizing project of the Turkish Republic moved rapidly into high gear, he elaborated further in October 1925,

> The Turkish Revolution ... means replacing an age-old political unity based on religion with one based on another tie, that of nationality. This [Turkish] nation has now accepted that the only means of survival ... lies in the acceptance of the contemporary Western civilization. This nation has also accepted that all of its laws should be based on secular grounds only, on a secular mentality that accepts ... change and development.

This explicit advocacy of the secular path fleshed out what he had said a year earlier, in late August of 1924, in a speech on the second anniversary of the Turkish military victory in the war of independence:

> Surviving in the world of modern civilization depends on changing ourselves. This is the sole law of progress ... Changing the rules of life in accordance with the times is an absolute necessity. In an age where inventions and the wonders of science are bringing change after change in the conditions of life, nations cannot maintain their existence by age-old rotten mentalities and tradition-worshipping ... superstitions and nonsense have to be thrown out of our heads.

Even earlier, in 1922, he had said, 'Social life dominated by irrational, useless and harmful beliefs is doomed to paralysis ... progress is too difficult or even impossible for nations that insist on preserving their traditions and beliefs lacking in rational bases'.[36]

---

36  Berkes, *The Development of Secularism in Turkey*, 463–470.

The obsession with joining 'Western civilization', in effect a vague and idealized notion of Europe, had its roots in the failure of the Ottoman Empire to stem its long decline that began in the seventeenth century. As the nineteenth century progressed, the decline escalated sharply and efforts to modernize the Ottoman imperial state (such as the *tanzimat* reform programme of the mid-nineteenth century) failed to turn the tide; it resulted in the Ottoman Turks' losing contest with its European rivals: the Habsburg, Russian and British Empires. The once vast and mighty Ottoman Empire shrank progressively and between the late 1870s and 1913 the Empire lost practically all its European and Mediterranean territories. World War I (1914–18) resulted in the loss of its remaining Middle Eastern, mostly Arab-populated territories and being on the losing side of the Great War meant the demise of the Empire. After the end of World War I, Istanbul (Constantinople until its conquest by the Ottoman Turks in 1453), the centre of the sprawling empire for several centuries, came under the occupation of French and British forces and Anatolia was invaded by Greece, which had been an Ottoman colony until 1829. The war of resistance (1919–22), led by Mustafa Kemal, managed to eject the occupiers and invaders and salvage a Turkish nation-state, but even in this victory the traumatic experience of having failed to compete with European powers had convinced Kemal and his core group of followers about the superiority of 'Western civilization'. From the beginning of the twentieth century, a 'Westernist' current had gained ascendancy in the Committee for Union and Progress (CUP), the so-called 'Young Turks'. Active under slightly different names since the late 1880s, initially as a movement of dissident intellectuals based in continental Europe, the CUP, joined later by bureaucrats and army officers, essentially ran the unravelling Ottoman Empire during its last decade. One of its most influential ideologues, Abdullah Cevdet (1869–1932) famously proclaimed, 'There is no second civilization; civilization means European civilization, and it must be imported with both its roses and thorns'.[37]

This was the mentality that underpinned the determination of Kemal and his core group of followers to make the Republic of Turkey a secular state. The general model was their nebulous conception of Europe's separation

---

37 Metin Heper and Nur Bilge Criss, *Historical Dictionary of Turkey* (Lanham, MD: The Scarecrow Press, 2009), 57.

of church and state, and especially France, where laicists had prevailed over religious conservatives in 1905 after over a century of ding-dong struggle since the French Revolution of 1789. In the words of Nur Yalman, the Kemalists' secularizing programme of the 1920s and 1930s aimed 'to set up a new culture ... uncontaminated by ... a past ... regarded as backward, corrupt, rotten, weak, and shameful. And since Islam was at the heart of the *ancien regime*, it was Islam that received the heaviest blow'.[38] Ottoman-style piecemeal modernization would not suffice; root-and-branch change had to be implemented.

So, the Kemalist state's new legal system copied existing European models. The Republic introduced a new civil code in 1926, at one stroke replacing both the late nineteenth-century Ottoman code, the *Mecelle*, and the *Seriat* courts dealing with personal and familial matters. The new code imitated Switzerland's civil code, in operation since 1912. A new Turkish penal code introduced in the same year imitated Italy's, and the new commercial code imitated Germany's. In 1925, a so-called Hat Law banned the traditional *fez* worn as headgear by men and made European-style top hats compulsory. Failure to wear a top hat in public was punishable by one year in prison.

The longed-for tryst with Europe signally failed to materialize for Turkey. The embrace of Western civilization proved to be a sad case of unrequited attraction. Turkey and its people remained outsiders to Europe. Today, nearly a century after Turkey became a secular state in order to shed inferiority and join the West as an equal, Turkish people are not regarded as fellow-Europeans in any part of Europe, and Turkey's prospects of joining the European Union as a full member-state remain extremely remote, practically non-existent. Meanwhile, history has come nearly full circle in Turkey itself. After decades of being marginalized and demeaned, the nation's Islamic identity rooted in a millennium of history, particularly the Ottoman centuries, began a political resurgence from the 1980s. The AKP's early twenty-first century doctrine of 'conservative democracy' is just another label for the political ideology of 'Turkish–Islamic Synthesis' that emerged during the 1980s as an alternative to Kemalist secularism. Kemalist Turkey failed to secure the external acknowledgment its architects and successive generations of leaders craved. The West-oriented, Europhile and secular vision of the

---

38 Yalman, 'Some Observations on Secularism in Islam', 154.

small coterie of Kemalist pioneers failed, over decades and generations, to win the acceptance of more than a substantial minority of Turkey's population. Today that minority, approximately one-quarter of the population, are truly stranded – alien as ever to the West and beleaguered at home.

By contrast, the secularism adopted by the Indian state was not inspired by an outwardly focused motivation and had nothing to do with any desire to imitate the West, contrary to the claims made by its Hindu nationalist critics from the 1950s to the present time. In contrast to the early Turkish secularists who emphasized rupture with tradition, the architects of the Indian secular state actually emphasized *continuity with* and *preservation of* an Indian tradition: mutual tolerance and coexistence of different religious faiths. As Nehru stated in 1950, 'The government of a country like India, with many religions that have secured great and devoted followings for generations, can never function satisfactorily in the modern age except on a secular basis'.[39] And Indian secularists drew their inspiration *not* from a Turkish-style puerile, inferiority complex-laden fascination with Europe or the Western world, but from the commitments made by the Indian National Congress during the long struggle it spearheaded to liberate India from colonial subjection that all religions would enjoy equality and parity of esteem in independent India. In 1931, during a nationwide civil disobedience agitation against British rule waged by the Congress under Mahatma Gandhi's leadership, the party's annual conference, held that year in Karachi, adopted a resolution on the fundamental principles of the future constitution of free India. The resolution included this sentence, 'The state shall observe neutrality in regard to all religions'.[40] Even earlier, in 1928, a high-level committee had been appointed by the Congress 'to determine the principles of the Constitution of India'. The committee of eight members was chaired by Jawaharlal Nehru's father Motilal Nehru and included Subhas Chandra Bose, a rising young leader from Bengal who was to become a legendary figure of India's freedom struggle. The committee's report asserted:

> There shall be no state religion for the Commonwealth of India ... nor shall the State either directly or indirectly endow any religion or give

---

39 Smith, *India as a Secular State*, 139.
40 Ibid., 92–93.

> any preference or impose any disability on account of religious belief or religious status ... No person shall by reason of his religion, caste or creed be prejudiced in any way in regard to public employment, office of power or honour and the exercise of any trade or calling.[41]

In comparison to its Turkish counterpart, Indian secularism has far deeper indigenous roots, and continues to have a much more compelling rationale today in the twenty-first century.

The second salient difference between the contexts of the secular state in India and Turkey is equally crucial. Turkish secularism was, from the outset, an ideology and policy promoted by a deeply authoritarian state. The programme of radical secularization – the core of the Kemalist 'revolution from above' – was imposed by a ruling clique on the country. The Turkish scholar Resat Kasaba has written that 'during the early decades of the twentieth century, the tired and defeated people of Anatolia were in no position to debate or resist Ataturk's radical message'.[42] This is only partly correct. There *was* dissent and opposition in the 1920s and 1930s, all of which was ruthlessly crushed by the Kemalists, sometimes with brutal violence. The long period of single-party rule by Kemal's CHP came to an end in 1950, but its legacy of an all-powerful, domineering state[43] (*devlet*) proved enduring, and is the central pillar of Turkey's politics to this day. Despite extended periods of multiparty politics, punctuated of course by recurrent military coups, the authoritarian 'state tradition', as the Turkish scholar Metin Heper called it in the mid-1980s, dominates Turkey. The country's political culture is based strongly on the nationalist–collectivist ethos originally implanted by the early- Kemalist Republic, and competing ideas of pluralism and accommodation are very weak in comparison. In the twenty-first century, that authoritarian state has been taken over by anti-secular forces headed by Erdogan (who has developed his own Ataturk-style personality cult), and this regime uses the same harsh rhetoric and punitive techniques against dissent that the Kemalist secularists deployed through the twentieth century against their opponents. In short, anti-secular authoritarianism has replaced secular authoritarianism in contemporary Turkey.

---

41 Godbole, *Secularism*, 71–72.

42 Resat Kasaba, 'Kemalist Certainties and Modern Ambiguities', in *Rethinking Modernity and National Identity in Turkey*, ed. Bozdogan and Kasaba, 16.

43 See Metin Heper, *The State Tradition in Turkey* (Beverley: Eothen Press, 1985).

India's secular state was, too, no doubt an elite-driven project, but it emerged through a process of democratic deliberation in comparison to Turkey and was not imposed through coercion and violence. More important, the Indian state's secularism became an integral part, from the early 1950s onwards, of a flawed but functioning democracy. As Donald Smith noted in 1963, 'the secular state ... stands or falls as a basic and inseparable component ... [and as] a fundamental aspect of ... India's total democratic experiment'.[44] The Indian secular state has of course not been free of the virus of authoritarianism. The self-appellation 'secular' was formally inserted in India's Constitution, as noted at the beginning of this chapter, by Indira Gandhi's thuggish 'Emergency' regime in 1976, which was eager to appropriate and exploit all progressive-sounding principles in a cynical bid to justify its authoritarianism. The Indian state has also been extremely repressive since the 1950s, and has deployed brutal force from the 1990s onwards, towards the people of the Kashmir Valley – a policy very dubiously justified in the name of secularism. But given that democracy, with all its flaws and warts, is at the heart of India's political system and its political culture, its integral component, secularism, can only be eliminated if the political ideology of Hindu majoritarianism – which is a fanciful construct at variance with India's diverse social and political landscapes – can provide an alternative democratic formula for a state with popular legitimacy. That is most unlikely, this book argues.

These differences in the origins and trajectories of the secular state in India and Turkey suggest that the principle of secularism, contested in both, may have very different futures in the two key test-cases of secular versus anti-secular politics in the non-Western world.

---

44  Smith, *India as a Secular State*, viii, 500.

2

# PATHS TO THE SECULAR STATE

*The religious conceptions in this country are so vast that they cover every aspect of life from birth to death. There is nothing which is not religion … We ought [therefore] to strive hereafter to limit the definition of religion in such a manner that we shall not extend it beyond beliefs and such rituals as may be connected with ceremonials which are essentially religious.*

—Bhimrao Ramji (B. R.) Ambedkar,
addressing India's Constituent Assembly (1947–49) as Chairman of its
Constitution-Drafting Committee and Minister of Law and Justice[1]

*The fundamental point … is the separation, in an absolute sense, of religion and the state. Religion is to be revered as long as it remains a matter of conscience from the point of view of the state … In separating religion from the world, the state of the present century … allocates religion to the conscience as the real and eternal throne for it.*

—Mahmut Esat, Minister of Justice,
in his speech to the Turkish Grand National Assembly in February 1926
tabling the Republic's secular Civil Code based on the Swiss model[2]

In the late 1980s, the Turkish scholar Serif Mardin observed 'the idea of a secular state' to be the 'foundation myth' of the Turkish Republic.[3] Indeed,

1  Smith, *India as a Secular State*, 105.
2  Andrew Davison, *Secularism and Revivalism in Turkey: A Hermeneutic Reconsideration* (New Haven: Yale University Press, 1998), 167–173.
3  Mardin, *Religion and Social Change in Modern Turkey*, 1.

41

the nearly transcendental status accorded to secularism (*laiklik*, based on the French *laicite*) in the ideological framework of the Republic after its formation, obscures the fact that the establishment of a secular state was not a declared goal of the Turkish struggle for national statehood of 1919–23 and hardly features in its discourse. To the contrary, during the Turkish war of independence (1919–22) Mustafa Kemal often deployed the rhetoric of Islamic solidarity, including the idiom of the 'holy war' against infidel enemies (Greeks, British, French, Armenians) to mobilize the masses. Whilst touring Anatolia, he would go into mosques, especially during the Friday prayer, take the *minbar* (pulpit) and deliver rousing *khutba*s (sermons) to the faithful gathered for the congregation. He frequently stressed the shared religious faith of the Turks and the Kurds, the two Muslim peoples inhabiting Anatolia, particularly in eastern Anatolia, where the large population of Kurds made them a critical factor in the struggle. The objective of the war waged under his leadership was to liberate the part of the disintegrated Ottoman Empire predominantly populated by non-Arab Muslims (i.e., mainly the territory of Anatolia) from the occupation or control of foreign powers and forces.

Between 1920 and 1923, a diverse range of views on the character of the national state in the making and the place and role of Islam in that state were expressed in sessions and debates of the National Assembly, formed in Ankara in April 1920 as the legislative body of the nascent state (Istanbul, the Ottoman capital, was under French and British occupation). It would be no exaggeration to say that perspectives based on and inspired by faith (Islam) dominated the discussions. Indeed, 'the Assembly appeared to some as the herald of the felicitous age of the Prophet', and 'the spirit of Seriatism made itself felt frequently'. The Assembly passed legislation banning not just the drinking of alcohol and gambling, but also the playing of cards and the game of backgammon (the latter a pastime popular across the Middle East) as un-Islamic practices. All bills presented to the Assembly by its members had to be referred to its Seriat committee for approval in addition to the committee responsible for the bill's subject. In 1921, the Assembly decided a national anthem was needed for the state in the making. It adopted an anthem penned by Mehmet Akif (1873–1936), a highly regarded poet and himself a member of the Assembly. Most of the members 'were carried away by its intense religious tenor' and 'the poem … was adopted with great enthusiasm as the national anthem of Turkey' (which it continues to be to this day). Also in 1921, two clerics who were members of the Assembly took the initiative to form a powerful parliamentary caucus called the Group for the Preservation of the Sacred Traditions, to oppose the more vaguely named Group for the Defence of Rights of the emerging Kemalist faction. The conservatives stated:

> Our aim is to preserve the rights of the Caliph-Padisah [the Ottoman emperor's dual role] and to work for the absolute avoidance of the republican form of government which will do enormous harm to the country and the world of Islam ... It can be sensed that the Group for the Defence of Rights, which has been formed by Mustafa Kemal in the National Assembly, aims to replace the Sultanate-Caliphate with a Republican form of government.[4]

Their sense was correct, but at the time the sweeping 'cultural revolution' (in Nur Yalman's 1970s phrase) that would envelop the Republic of Turkey from 1924 onward, starting within a few months after the Republic's proclamation in October 1923, would have appeared an improbable if not impossible prospect. That program of radical change, 'one of the most astounding ... transformation projects of the twentieth century ... aimed at the elimination of everything that made Turkey look non-Western'[5] and of course, non-secular.

The Turkish struggle for national survival and self-determination against an assortment of Christian enemies caused waves in faraway India, ruled by the British Raj. A movement in solidarity with the embattled Turkish people, and in particular their perceived defence of the Sultanate–Caliphate as a key focal point for the community of believers across the world, emerged among Indian Muslims in 1919. Known then and ever since as the Khilafat Movement, it peaked in 1920–21 and attracted the support of Mohandas Karamchand Gandhi, the new leader of the emerging Indian mass-based struggle against colonial subjugation, who was keen to forge an alliance of the subcontinent's Hindus and Muslims against the Raj. In December 1922, with the opportunist Greek invasion of Anatolia decisively defeated by the forces operating under Mustafa Kemal's leadership and the military aspect of the conflict clearly decided in favour of the Turkish resistance, the

---

4   Berkes, *The Development of Secularism in Turkey*, 447–449.
5   M. Sukru Hanioglu, 'The Historical Roots of Kemalism', 47.

leaders of India's Khilafat Movement conferred a grand title on Kemal: *Saif al-Islam* (Sword of Islam). They were somewhat disturbed by the Turkish National Assembly's decision to abolish the Sultanate just a month earlier, in November 1922 – after the last, entirely nominal and powerless Ottoman monarch in Istanbul thoroughly discredited and disgraced the institution by his complicity with British imperialist designs. But they were optimistic that while the Sultanate had been abolished, the Caliphate – which had been separated from the Sultanate and retained as an institution – was set to remain as a prime source of spiritual authority for Muslims worldwide.

Indeed, 'in a long speech' to the National Assembly, Kemal had explained

> the evolution of the Caliphate and Sultanate and claimed that the two
> could be separated as they had [once] been separated in history, and the
> second could be abolished while the first was retained. The Sultanate was
> nothing but temporal sovereignty, and that sovereignty has been taken
> over by the [Turkish] people [as per the interim constitution adopted by
> the National Assembly in 1921].[6]

Article 1 of that Constitution had asserted, 'Sovereignty belongs unconditionally to the nation. The government is based on the principle of the people's direct rule over their own destiny'. The wording was similar to Article 3 of the French Revolution's *Declaration of the Rights of Man and the Citizen* in August 1789, 'The sources of all sovereignty resides essentially in the nation. No body, no individual may exercise authority that does not proceed from it'. When, in early March 1924, the Turkish Republic (proclaimed just four months earlier in late October 1923) abolished the Caliphate as well, the Indian Khilafatists were left aghast. The cause they had championed had been rendered defunct. The Indian movement's two top leaders, who were (biological) brothers, bitterly denounced Mustafa Kemal in June 1924 as a 'traitor to Islam'. An alternative viewpoint within the movement, represented by Maulana Abul Kalam Azad – who was to become the top Muslim figure in the Indian National Congress, the secularist party spearheading the Indian struggle for independence – argued that the Turks were entitled to make their own decisions and the former Caliphate could now be regarded as vested in the sovereign government of Turkey and the person of its president. His erstwhile compatriots refused to accept this argument as that person was none

---

6   Berkes, *The Development of Secularism in Turkey*, 450.

other than the traitor-cum-apostate, Mustafa Kemal. Of the two brothers who pioneered India's Khilafatist agitation, one died in 1931 and was buried in Jerusalem in accordance with his wishes. The other, who lived until 1939, re-emerged in the second half of the 1930s as a collaborator of Muhammad Ali Jinnah, the leader of India's Muslim League and the eventual founder of Pakistan. In October 1927, Mustafa Kemal elaborated on the decision to abolish the Caliphate in the course of a six-day speech (known as the *Nutuk*) to the Turkish nation. He said,

> The Caliph and the office of the Caliphate which we maintained and safeguarded have, in reality, no *raison d'etre*, in either a political or a religious sense. The Caliphate may have a significance for us only as a historical recollection. For the sake of the utopia of establishing a worldwide Islamic state, the Turkish state and its handful of people cannot be subjugated to the service of a Caliph. We must put an end to the delusion of imagining ourselves the masters of the world. Enough of the calamities to which we have dragged the nation by our ignorance of the conditions of the world and our real position in it, by following the fools![7]

The abolition of the Caliphate by the infant Turkish Republic was, it turned out, just the beginning of the purposeful construction of a secular state. It was followed by the outlawing of all religious orders or brotherhoods (*tarikats*) in 1925; the introduction of a new Civil Code borrowed from the Swiss version in 1926; the deletion in 1928 of Article 2 of the Republic's Constitution (1924) which had stated that 'the religion of the Turkish state is Islam'; the replacement of the Arabic script by the Roman script between the late 1920s and early 1930s; and the inclusion of secularism (*laiklik*) in the early 1930s as one of the six 'arrows' or guiding principles of the CHP, the single party of the Kemalist regime. In 1937, a year before Kemal's death, Turkey was formally declared a secular (laicist) state.

◆

In *India as a Secular State* (1963), Donald Smith noted a seemingly paradoxical fact, considering the centrality given to secularism in the self-definition of the

---

7   Ibid., 457–460. The authoritative study of India's Khilafatist agitation is Gail Minault, *The Khilafat Movement: Religious Symbolism and Political Mobilization in India* (New York: Columbia University Press, 1982).

Indian state after independence – before 1947, the term 'secularism' was rarely used in the discourse of the Indian independence movement led by the Indian National Congress. He was quite right. References to secularism are rare in the voluminous pre-independence writings of Jawaharlal Nehru, the leader of the post-independence secular state as Prime Minister for nearly 17 years, from August 1947 until his death in May 1964. A gifted writer, Nehru wrote prolifically despite his hectic public life, and was particularly productive when imprisoned. The first explicit, if passing, mention of secularism in Nehru's writings dates to 1933, and refers to the far-reaching secularizing reforms enacted and under implementation in the Turkish Republic. The reference can be found in his book *Glimpses of World History*, first published in 1934. Secularism begins to feature in the writings and speeches of Mahatma Gandhi only in the final years of colonial rule, from 1944 onward, in response to the growing urgency of the 'communal' (Hindu–Muslim) question and the rising appeal of the Pakistan movement among the subcontinent's Muslims. Prior to that, Gandhi had largely neglected the difficult issue of how the relationship between India's confessional majority (Hindus) and its largest confessional minority (Muslims) should be structured in an independent Indian state. A deeply religious Hindu, Gandhi nonetheless regarded all religions to be equally true. His profoundly held humanist–universalist view of all religious faiths and traditions as equally true was admirable, but left him grasping for a response once the Hindu–Muslim question emerged as the major fault-line of Indian politics in the 1940s; moreover with a theory of Muslim nationhood based on a shared religion providing the charge to Jinnah and the All-India Muslim League's campaign for political sovereignty (or at least a status approximating sovereignty) for Muslim-majority areas of north-western and eastern India. In Gandhi's world-view, religious difference should not have become a matter of political contention at all, let alone such a divisive matter. For, he believed that all religions were essentially the same,

> I believe with my whole soul that the God of the Koran is also the God of the [Bhagavad] Gita [a sacred Hindu text] and that we are all, no matter by what name designated, children of the same God. My whole soul rebels against the idea that Hinduism and Islam represent two antagonistic cultures ... To assent to such a doctrine is for me denial of God.[8]

8  M. K. Gandhi, *To the Hindus and Muslims*, ed. Anand T. Hingorani (Allahabad: Law Journal Press, 1942), 415–416, 428.

When Jinnah's movement asserted that not only were the two faiths not the same, but also that the subcontinent's Hindus and Muslims comprised two separate 'nations' – each entitled to self-determination in its own sovereign state – Gandhi was at once horrified and lost for an answer. In his presidential address to the Lahore session of the Muslim League which passed the 'Pakistan Resolution' in March 1940, Jinnah said that,

> the Hindus and Muslims [of India] ... belong to two different civilizations which are based mainly on conflicting ideas and conceptions ... To yoke together two such nations under a single State, one as a numerical minority and the other as majority, must lead to growing discontent and final destruction of any fabric that may be so built up for the government of such a State.

Gandhi's response was simply that this claim was both 'baffling' and an 'untruth'. He wrote in his paper *Harijan*,

> I feel deeply hurt over what is now going on in the name of the Muslim League. I should be failing in my duty if I did not warn the Muslims of India against the untruth that is being propagated amongst them. This warning is a duty because ... Hindu–Muslim unity has been and is my life's mission.[9]

Subhas Chandra Bose, a top leader of the Indian independence movement alongside Gandhi and Nehru, was the President of the Indian National Congress when Mustafa Kemal – by then known as Ataturk (Father of the Turks) – died in November 1938. It fell to Bose to compose the official tribute of the Indian independence movement to the founder of the Turkish nation-state,

> Of the romantic figures thrown up by the Great War, Kemal Pasha was undoubtedly one of the most striking. His meteoric rise to fame and popularity is indeed rare in history. Kemal Pasha was, however, much more than a romantic figure or a conquering hero. He was at the same time a shrewd strategist and an acute diplomat, and his unprecedented

---

9   Mushirul Hasan, ed., *India's Partition: Process, Strategy and Mobilization* (Delhi: Oxford University Press, 1993), 69–71. This anthology provides a range of useful perspectives on the complex constellation of factors and dynamics which led to India's partition in 1947.

success in life would hardly have been possible without a unique combination of manifold qualities of head and heart. Kemal Pasha was revolutionary not merely on the battlefields of Anatolia, but also in the field of national reconstruction. He was a magnificent example of the dictum that those who strive for liberty and win it should also put into effect the programme of post-war reconstruction. Great as a general, great as a diplomat, great as a social reformer, great as a statesman, great as a fighter and great as a builder—Kemal Pasha, or Kemal Ataturk, is undoubtedly one of the greatest men of this century. To him goes the credit of saving his country from the jaws of the European Powers and of building up a rejuvenated Turkey on the ashes of the erstwhile Ottoman Empire. Should the European Powers try once again to overrun Asia, Kemal's Turkey will guard the western flank of our continent. The death of such a unique personality cannot but move the whole world and particularly all oppressed and exploited nations like ours. It is our bounden duty to pay our respectful homage to this great lover of freedom and of humanity. I, therefore, suggest that we observe 'Kemal Day' on the 19th November next and utilise the occasion for holding meetings at which resolutions should be passed paying our respectful homage to the memory of Kemal Ataturk and conveying our friendly greetings to the emancipated people of his beloved Turkey and our heartfelt sympathy in their national bereavement.[10]

This eloquent and substantive tribute shows deep understanding of Ataturk's personality, role and contributions. But it conspicuously lacks any reference to the creed of secularism Ataturk had placed at the heart of the Turkish state's identity. That Bose's detailed eulogy would refer in general terms to the Turkish leader's credentials as a 'social reformer', but with no mention of his secularizing legacy, is puzzling because of the top leaders of the Indian nationalist movement, Bose was closest to Ataturk's uncompromising views on the necessity for a secular state. In the words of Abid Hasan, one of Bose's close associates during the climactic phase of the latter's life in Europe and Southeast Asia between 1941 and 1945,

---

10 Subhas Chandra Bose, 'On Kemal Ataturk: Tribute to the Leader of Turkey on his Death, November 1938', in *Netaji Collected Works, Volume 9: Congress President— Speeches, Articles and Letters, January 1938–May 1939*, ed. Sisir K. Bose and Sugata Bose (Calcutta: Netaji Research Bureau and Delhi: Oxford University Press, 1995).

*Netaji* ['The Leader', as Bose is popularly referred to in India] divorced religion completely from [Indian] nationalism. Although a deeply religious man himself, he would not permit public display of any religious practice. Religious devotion thus became the individual concern of each person or, if practiced in a group, restricted to the congregational centres set apart for this purpose.

Hasan recounts an anecdote from 1942, when Bose visited a training camp in Germany where Indian prisoners of war captured by the Germans during fighting with British forces in North Africa had been organized into a pro-Indian independence military formation. In contrast to the British practice, separate kitchens for soldiers from different castes and faiths had been abolished and 'even the smallest units were mixed, not one being composed of men from the same region or religion'. Before Bose's visit, the men decided to compose a common prayer 'using only the word "*Malik*" [Master] for God' to recite in his presence. Hasan writes that 'composed by men from remote villages [of India], this prayer had Kabirian simplicity and charm' (Kabir was a fifteenth-century Indian mystic, poet and saint). When Bose arrived, 'we all, Hindus, Muslims, Sikhs and Christians, proudly recited it in front of him in one voice'. Bose did not react but later, he called Hasan aside and chided him for 'this stunt'. According to Hasan, Bose said, 'If you use religion to unite yourself today, you leave the door open for someone to attempt later to divide you using the same sentiments'.[11] Bose's view is the polar opposite of Jinnah's, whose politics fused religion, nation and state. But it is also very different from Gandhi's, who jumped on the Khilafatist bandwagon in order to promote Hindu–Muslim unity. Bose believed that the path to Indian unity lay in transcending rather than indulging religious affiliations and sentiments. He was emphatic that Indian nationalism should not, indeed must not, be grounded either in inter-faith solidarity or in a narrative of religious syncretism. This was reflected in the slogan-cum-greeting of the Indian National Army (INA) and the broader independence movement under his leadership in Southeast Asia from 1943 to 1945. It was simply *Jai Hind!* (Victory to India), devoid not just of any religious tone but any attempt to combine the slogans

---

11 Abid Hasan, 'Netaji and the Indian Communal Question', *The Oracle: A Quarterly Review of History, Current Affairs and International Relations* 1, no.1 (January 1979): 42–46.

and greetings particular to Indian religions. After independence, 'Jai Hind' became India's national slogan. Since the mid-1990s, it is also the form of greeting used between Indian Army personnel. *Kadam kadam badhaae jaa* (march forward), the INA's marching song with a catchy tune, is the marching song of the Indian armed forces.

Bose's failure to cite Ataturk's secular convictions and secularizing legacy is probably just another example of the relative paucity of explicit invocations of secularism in the discourse of the Indian freedom movement. Of course, the Congress-led movement's broad secularist commitment was unambiguous. As noted in Chapter 1, the 1931 Karachi convention of the Indian National Congress had declared that 'the [future, independent] state shall observe neutrality in regard to all religions'. As also noted in that chapter, the high-level committee appointed by the Congress in 1928 'to determine the principles of the Constitution of India' – this committee included the youthful Subhas Bose – had bluntly asserted that 'there shall be no state religion'. Still, the relative lack of emphasis on secularism *per se* in the discourse of the independence movement contrasts strikingly with the explicit centrality given to the principle in the Indian state after independence. Bose did not live to see independence; he died in a plane crash in Taiwan in August 1945. Gandhi did, and spent his final months in deep disquiet and mourning over partition and the savage violence it had unleashed. By early 1948 he too was dead, shot by a Hindu militant for continuing to advocate tolerance and amity between Hindus and Muslims. In the Republic of India that came into being under Nehru's leadership two years after Gandhi's death, secularism became a core tenet, almost an article of faith.

◆

The paths to the formation of the secular state in India and Turkey are marked by significant parallels as well as, of course, contextual differences. Yet the contextually distinct evolutions of the two secular states over time share certain paradoxes, anomalies and contradictions.

Nehru and Mustafa Kemal broadly shared a sceptical view of religion. As noted in Chapter 1, Kemal's public pronouncements between 1922 and 1924 are replete with derisive references to 'irrational, useless and harmful beliefs', 'age-old rotten mentalities and tradition-worshipping', 'superstitions and nonsense', and 'principles dominating our life that are incompatible with the necessities of the age'. His tone became progressively sharper between 1922 and 1924, and in 1925 he explicitly asserted that 'all ... laws should be based on secular grounds only, on a secular mentality that accepts ... change and development'. His opinion of men of religion and their role in society was as harsh. He commented on his regime's 1925 decision to ban all *tarikat*s (religious brotherhoods of the Naqshbandi, Kadiri and Bektashi orders) in these terms, 'Primitive individuals seeking moral and material prosperity through the guidance of such and such a sheikh [traditional religious leader] despite the enlightenment of science, technology and civilization ... should not exist in Turkish society'.[12]

Nehru did not express his views in this blunt and authoritarian style of an army officer turned national leader, but the difference is one of tone rather than substance. In 1933 he wrote to his leader Gandhi, the deeply religious seeker of 'truth', that religion was nothing but 'a begetter of confusion and sentimentality'.[13] In 1937, he wrote in exasperation about 'the communal feelings on either side' (Hindu and Muslim) in an essay published in *The Modern Review*, an influential nationalist journal of the time, 'When will people behave like grown-ups? How childish all this is and religion, as of old, warps the mind and confuses the issue'.[14] Nehru retained this attitude till the end of his life. In 1958, eleven years into his nearly seventeen years as India's Prime Minister, he told a gathering of students that he liked cows and horses equally. This was a snide reference to demands since the late 1940s for a total, nationwide ban on cow slaughter – the cow is considered holy in Hindu orthodoxy – which had triggered a failed 'Indian Cattle Preservation Bill' in parliament in 1955. That proposed legislation had been backed by several MPs of the Congress party in addition to Hindu nationalists. Nehru's apparent irreverence for the holy cow did not amuse dogged proponents of the

---

12  Hanioglu, 'The Historical Roots of Kemalism', 43.

13  Eleanor Newbigin, *The Hindu Family and the Emergence of Modern India: Law, Citizenship and Community* (Cambridge: Cambridge University Press, 2013), 165.

14  Anikendra Sen, Devangshu Datta and Nilanjana S. Roy, eds., *Patriots, Poets and Prisoners: Selections from Ramananda Chatterjee's The Modern Review, 1907–1947* (Delhi: Harper Collins India, 2016), 187.

movement against cow slaughter. One such figure accused him of 'deliberate and malicious intention of outraging the religious feelings of the Hindus'. Nehru's stance on the sanctity of the cow contrasts, at one level, with that of Gandhi, a devout Hindu. Writing in *Harijan* in 1940, Gandhi declared himself 'a worshipper of the cow, whom I regard with the same veneration as I regard my mother'.[15] However, amidst the bloodbath of the partition of India in 1947, Gandhi clarified the limits of his personal beliefs,

> The Hindu religion prohibits cow slaughter for the Hindus, not for the world. The religious prohibition comes from within. Any imposition from without means compulsion. Such compulsion is repugnant to religion. India is the land not only of the Hindus but also of the Mussalmans, the Sikhs, the Parsees, the Christians and the Jews ... In India no law can be made to ban cow slaughter ... I have long pledged to serve the cow, but how can my religion also be the religion of the rest of the Indians? It will mean coercion against those Indians who are not Hindus.[16]

Nehru and Mustafa Kemal also broadly shared a strong modernizing vision for their societies, with the sovereign state as the essential agent of modernization in all its interrelated forms – political, social, economic and cultural. The common denominator was their belief in the potential of science and technology to transform traditional societies. Chapter 1 has noted Kemal speaking breathlessly in 1924 about 'an age [of] inventions and the wonders of science'. Nehru, too, in contrast to Gandhi, subscribed to this belief in scientific progress. And like Kemal, he saw religion as an obstacle. He wrote in prison in 1944, 'Religion, though it has undoubtedly brought comfort to innumerable human beings and stabilized society by its values, has checked the tendency to change and progress inherent in human society'.[17]

Nehru's world-view was not at all unusual but widely found among leaders of non-Western societies struggling to emerge as sovereign states, India prominently included. In November 1938, coincidentally at the same time that he penned the effusive tribute to Ataturk, Subhas Chandra Bose took the

---

15  Smith, *India as a Secular State*, 484, 489.

16  Godbole, *Secularism*, 203–204.

17  See Jawaharlal Nehru, *The Discovery of India* (New York: John Day Company, 1946), 180–183, 511.

initiative as the President of the Indian National Congress to form a 'National Planning Committee' to prepare guidelines for India's post-independence economic reconstruction. Bose appointed Nehru as the committee's chairman. A photograph exists of Bose addressing the first meeting of the committee, which included prominent Indian scientists, as Nehru listens in rapt attention. The committee formed by Bose in late 1938 was the predecessor of India's Planning Commission established in March 1950, a few weeks after the proclamation of the Republic of India, to direct India's strategy of state-led economic development. It discharged this role for the next six decades. The Prime Minister of India held the chair of the commission with a deputy chairperson, usually a senior technocrat, functioning as its chief executive, so Nehru served as the commission's chairman until his death in 1964. It is not surprising that both India and Turkey adopted an emphatically state-led paradigm of economic development, with very extensive state control and regulation of the economy. In India, this was referred to as the state occupying the 'commanding heights' of the economy, with state ownership of a range of industries classified as 'basic' or 'strategic' or 'heavy', a limited role for private entrepreneurship in the manufacturing sector, and strict controls on the entry of foreign capital. This centrally directed, state-dominant paradigm began to be dismantled in favour of a de-regulated system much more open to private entrepreneurship as well as foreign investment in India only from the early 1990s, and in Turkey from the late 1980s. The parallel state monopoly of radio and television broadcasting also ended in the two countries at about the same time, during the first half of the 1990s.

The longevity of the statist approach reflects the similar beliefs of the founding elites of the two republics that the state must exercise control and supervision in all domains if their nations were to make the transition from poverty to prosperity, from medievalism to modernity, from obscurantism to enlightenment, from superstition to reason, and from stagnation to progress. In 1954, Nehru famously called dams the temples of modern India. Although he back-tracked somewhat in 1958 and lamented 'the creeping disease of giganticism', a reference to the emphasis on large-scale, state-owned projects of socioeconomic development, and called for this to be balanced by 'small irrigation projects, small industries and small plants of electric power', he remained resolute in his basic perspective. While India's second

Hindu nationalist Prime Minister, Narendra Modi, re-named and sharply downgraded the Planning Commission, a long overdue step, after assuming office in mid-2014, he echoed the secularist Nehru in a way by asserting that the national priority should be to build not temples but toilets; this being a reference to the lack of access to toilet facilities for nearly half the Indian population, and the majority in rural India. The origins of the activist, interventionist state that regulates and even directly controls (in the case of Turkey) the practice of religion – the salient common feature of the secular states of India and Turkey noted in Chapter 1 – lies in the shared emphasis of the shapers of the two republics on rationality and a scientific temper in all matters, with the state as the embodiment of reason and the engine of progress. Just as the state needed to be dominant and pro-active in driving the agenda of economic development, the state had of necessity to operate as a regulating and even controlling authority vis-à-vis the practice of religion if society were to be purged of various dogmas and atavisms, and become 'modern'.

The Indian and Turkish frameworks of state-secularism however also diverge in crucial ways. Kemal saw a secular state as absolutely central to his regime's quest 'to achieve Western civilization' (as noted in Chapter 1). This could simply not be an argument, let alone *the* argument as it was in Turkey, for the adoption of secularism in the Indian republic, the product of a mass struggle against two centuries of bondage to Western imperialism. In the early 1930s, Gandhi was asked his opinion of Western civilization by a pompous and probably racist British journalist. In what became one of his most famous quotes, the Indian leader replied, 'I think it would be a good idea'. One of the most haunting songs of India's national poet, the Bengali Rabindranath Tagore (1861–1941) begins like this: *Sarthako janam amar, jonmechhi ei deshe, Sarthako janam ma-go, tomai bhalobeshe* (My life is fulfilled by being born in this country, My life is fulfilled by loving you, my mother[land]). The most famous composition of the Urdu poet Muhammad Iqbal (1877–1938), published in 1904, begins: *Sare jahan se acchha, Hindustan hamara, Hum bulbulain hai iski, yeh gulistan hamara* (Our India, the best country in the world; we are like nightingales in a rose garden). While Iqbal veered towards the politics of Muhammad Ali Jinnah in later life, the song remained one of the leading hymns of the Indian independence movement and is one of India's most popular patriotic songs to this day. Colonial rule in India was underpinned by an ideology (if one can seriously call it that) of the racial and cultural inferiority of Indians. India's freedom movement rejected this and asserted pride in Indian history, heritage and culture. Jawaharlal Nehru, a man of somewhat westernized, European-style habits in his personal lifestyle, was steeped in this proud Indian nationalism. 'Ancient India', he wrote, 'was a world in itself, a culture and a civilization which gave shape to all things'.[18]

One of the first actions of Kemal's republic was to impose sartorial reforms on the population. A particular target was the *fez*, the brimless cap worn by Turkish men since its adoption in the 1820s by the then Ottoman sultan as a compromise between the traditional turban and Western-style hats. A Hat Law enacted in 1925 banned the *fez* and made it compulsory for Turkish men to wear brimmed top-hats in public. Kemal stated,

> It was necessary to abolish the fez, which sat on our heads as a sign of ignorance, fanaticism and hatred of progress and civilization, and to adopt in its place the hat, the customary [head]dress of the civilized world, thus showing that no difference existed in the manner of thought of the Turkish nation and civilized mankind.[19]

This was part of his drive, as he put it in a rambling forty-hour speech (*Nutuk*) to the nation delivered over six days in 1927, to join 'the really civilized and cultured peoples of the world'.[20] A deputy in the National Assembly, who was formerly a commander in the 1919–22 war of independence, pointed out that while certain dress regulations might be reasonably required of state officials, no other country, whether in Europe or Asia, imposed such rules on citizens at large. His objection was ignored. Some citizens, confused, struggled to cope with the new dress code. Kemal observed during a public meeting,

> I see a man in the crowd in front of me. He has a fez on his head, a green turban on the fez, a smock on his back, and on top of that a jacket like the one I am wearing. I can't see the other half. Now what kind of outfit is

---

18  Nehru, *The Discovery of India*, 62.

19  Bernard Lewis, *The Emergence of Modern Turkey* (London: Oxford University Press, 1961), 268.

20  Davison, *Secularism and Revivalism in Turkey*, 148.

that? Would a civilized man put on this preposterous garb and go out to hold himself up to universal ridicule?[21]

Protests against the authoritarian imposition of Western dress broke out across Turkey; one problem was that the mandatory brimmed hats impeded the Muslim prayer ritual, which requires the touching of the forehead to the ground. The protests were ruthlessly suppressed. Special tribunals tried arrested protesters and executions took place in towns in both central Anatolia and the Black Sea coast to the north. Veils as well as headscarves for women were not similarly prohibited, except for those employed in state institutions, but discouraged in more informal and insidious ways as out of step with the times and the secular republic's notion of 'civilization'. The ideal lifestyle of the citizen of the Kemalist republic

> included wearing neckties, shaving beards and moustaches, going to the theatre, eating with a fork, husband and wife walking hand in hand in the street, dancing at balls, shaking hands, wearing hats [in public], writing from left to right [unlike Arabic], and listening to classical western music.[22]

The contrast with the Indian freedom movement's sartorial, and more broadly, cultural and civilizational ethos, which endured in the dress code of independent India's ruling political elite for three to four decades after 1947, could not be greater. When Gandhi assumed the reins of the Indian National Congress after the end of World War I and turned it into a vehicle for a mass movement for emancipation from colonialism, he popularized the wearing of traditional-style Indian clothing made of *khadi* – a rather coarse homespun cotton-based cloth made by spinning a wheel-shaped contraption known as the *charkha*, another classic Gandhian symbol. This was part of his *swadeshi* (indigenous/self-reliance) campaign, which involved a boycott of all British-made goods and products. As my father Sisir Kumar Bose (1920–2000), who grew up with the freedom struggle in an ardently nationalist family and himself became an active participant from the beginning of the 1940s, writes in his memoir, 'Wearing khadi was a statement of patriotism and one's commitment

---

21 Lewis, *The Emergence of Modern Turkey*, 269.

22 Nilufer Gole, 'Authoritarian Secularism and Islamist Politics: The Case of Turkey', in *Civil Society in the Middle East, Vol. II*, ed. Augustus Richard Norton (Leiden, New York and Koln: EJ Brill, 1996), 23.

to the freedom struggle ... In nationalist families, buying British goods or wearing clothes made in England was considered disgraceful and Indians who did so were looked down upon'.[23] Alongside *khadi* attire, Gandhi introduced what became known as the Gandhi or Congress *topi* (cap), a longish cap pointed at the front and rear ends. This too was made of *khadi*, of course. Wearing traditional Indian clothing made of *khadi* – typically a waist-knotted *dhoti* for the lower body and legs with a long, full-sleeve shirt (*kurta*), along with the emblematic cap, was *de rigueur* for millions of Congress members and supporters. Top leaders such as Nehru and Subhas Bose almost always appeared in public dressed in this fashion, a picture of understated elegance. Bose spent most of the time between early 1933 and early 1936 in Europe. According to his nephew Sisir, 'Uncle had very definite views on how he would dress in Europe. He had decided to dress in Indian attire for public meetings and receptions and when he met important people'. Because of the very different climatic conditions of Europe, 'he chose an achkan-style coat [a distinctly subcontinental knee-length coat buttoned down the front], worn with European-style trousers, a Kashmiri cap and laced shoes ... He did of course make exceptions and would occasionally appear in public in well-cut Western suits'.[24] As Prime Minister after independence, Nehru too would routinely wear an *achkan*-style coat, paired with white *churidars*, a tight-fitting Indian leg garment. The nationalist cap almost always sat on his head.

Gandhi, the supreme leader, differentiated himself from his colleagues by dressing in a (longish) *khadi* loin-cloth; his upper body was either completely bare or partially covered by a simple white khadi *chadar* (piece of cloth). He had decisively moved on from his earlier life as a suit-wearing lawyer in South Africa. After the early 1920s, he also left his bald head bare, abjuring the cap worn by his colleagues and followers. His appearance horrified and repulsed Winston Churchill. Churchill had a very low opinion of Indians, whom he regarded as sub-human. That opinion was reinforced by the fact that a 'half-naked, seditious *fakir*', as he described Gandhi, was the leader of the Indian resistance to the British Empire. One wonders what Mustafa Kemal thought

---

23  Sisir Kumar Bose, *Subhas and Sarat: An Intimate Memoir of the Bose Brothers*, edited and with an introduction by Sumantra Bose (New Delhi: Aleph Book Company, 2016), 15–16.

24  Ibid., 48.

of the deliberately half-naked Gandhi, or of the assertively Oriental sartorial style of the Congress-led movement. He may have been puzzled, or perhaps he was simply too immersed in his insular preoccupation with remaking Turkey to care.

The nationalist dress code scrupulously followed by Nehru, Bose and other leaders, as well as millions of grassroots Congress activists, endured among India's political elite for several decades after independence. Nehru's successor as India's Prime Minister, Lal Bahadur Shastri (1904–66), schooled and socialized in the traditions of the freedom movement, strictly adhered to the same dress code. So did Morarji Desai (1896–1995), India's first non-Congress Prime Minister from 1977 to 1979. Desai, an ethnic Gujarati like Gandhi as well as India's current Prime Minister, Narendra Modi, was a social and ideological conservative who spent his entire political life until the late 1960s in the Congress, when he lost an internal power-struggle for control of the nation's historic party to Nehru's daughter Indira.

In August 1942 Gandhi launched the 'Quit India' movement, his last mass agitation against the Raj. My mother Krishna Bose (*nee* Chaudhuri), then aged eleven, had just started reading newspapers. She writes in her memoir of her early life,

> One morning [in Calcutta] I was reading the papers when I saw my father putting on a tie as he got ready to go to work. I said to him: '*Baba*, the newspaper says that crowds in the streets are forcing those wearing ties to take them off and burning them in bonfires'. Father replied: 'No problem, my tie is made of pure khadi!' He went off and returned sheepishly a short while later, *sans* tie.[25]

The Kemalist obsession with 'Western civilization', sometimes also referred to in Turkish secularist discourse as 'European civilization', was an early example of what the leftist Iranian writer Jalal al-e Ahmad called *gharbzadegi* (variously translated as 'Westoxication' or 'Occidentosis', among other terms) in a book published in the 1960s. Ahmad decried a tendency among Iran's social elite to regard the West (particularly Europe) as superior and worthy of imitation, and argued for an alternative that reposed confidence in Iran's own

---

25  Krishna Bose, *Lost Addresses: A Memoir of India, 1934–1955*, translated from Bengali by Sumantra Bose (New Delhi: Niyogi Books, 2015), 62.

values and strengths. Kemal's Turkey was an earlier and more extreme version of the syndrome Ahmad attacked in his own national context, Pahlavi Iran.

The desire of Kemal's regime to copy Europe and indeed, make Turkey a part of Europe, a European country and a member of the European comity of nations, was the overriding stated motivation for its espousal and promotion of a secular state. In this view, Turkey could never hope to join 'the really civilized and cultured peoples of the world' (Kemal's own words in 1927) if its polity remained based on and its society defined by Islam. This ardent Europhile perspective requires some explanation. It probably had something to do with Kemal's own origins and socialization – he was born and grew up in Salonica (now the city of Thessaloniki in Greece) and gained most of his training as a military officer, his chosen career, in the Balkans.[26] The Ottoman Empire progressively lost its vast Balkan territories through the nineteenth century and was almost totally evicted from the region by the 1912–13 Balkan Wars. This lost Ottoman-ruled Europe, referred to as Rumelia, continued to occupy a special place in the memory and nostalgia of the early (and even later) Turkish nationalists of the twentieth century.

The Turkish Republic's form of *gharbzadegi* however has its fundamental roots in the failure of a series of nineteenth-century modernizing efforts in the Ottoman Empire to enable effective competition with the Empire's European rivals (Russia, Austria–Hungary, Britain) or to stem the terminal Ottoman decline. Following the final disintegration of the Empire precipitated by defeat in the Balkan Wars of 1912–13 and then World War I (1914–18), Kemal, a practical and pragmatic man, decided to adopt a policy perhaps best described by the colloquial phrase 'if you can't beat them, join them'.

The ideological package that was to become known as 'Kemalism' originated in the Westernist stream of the Committee of Union and Progress (CUP). The CUP, often referred as the 'Young Turks' in popular parlance, emerged in the 1890s as a secret society of students and intellectuals united by opposition to the autocratic rule of the Ottoman sultan, Abdulhamit II, who had prorogued

---

26 On Kemal's life and personality, see M. Sukru Hanioglu, *Ataturk: An Intellectual Biography* (Princeton: Princeton University Press, 2011); and Ali Kazancigil and Ergun Ozbudun, eds., *Ataturk: Founder of a Modern State* (London: Hurst and Company, 1997).

the first Ottoman parliament in 1878, a year after its formation. Important CUP members were based in exile in continental Europe, in cities such as Paris and Geneva. From the beginning of the twentieth century the CUP started to acquire members among Ottoman officialdom, especially military officers. Some members of the CUP – the movement was diverse and chronically factionalized – essentially ran the Empire during its final, tumultuous decade, after the deposition of Abdulhamit II in 1909. The Westernist tendency represented one stream within the CUP fold but gradually gained currency as it became clear during the Empire's terminal crisis during that decade that neither 'Ottomanism' (a multinational and religiously plural concept) nor Islamic solidarity (primarily between Turks and the restive Arab populations of the Empire) were viable, and pan-Turkism – an ideology of ethnic unity of Anatolian Turks and the 'Turkic' populations of Central Asia and the Caucasus – was equally utopian in practical terms.

The Westernist current of the CUP movement gleaned an extremely simplistic notion of 'progress' from the works of Auguste Comte (1798–1857), the French mathematician and philosopher who is regarded as the progenitor of positivism and believed that human history had evolved in a linear fashion from fetishism to religion and thence, ineluctably, to scientific reason. The Comteist motto, *Ordre et Progres*, influenced the name of the CUP. Darwinist notions of evolution or extinction were also influential; as noted in Chapter 1, Mustafa Kemal declared in 1924 that 'surviving in the world of modern civilization depends on changing ourselves. This is the sole law of progress'. Another influence was the mid-nineteenth century German philosophy of *Vulgarmaterialismus* (vulgar materialism), which took a negative view of religion. This cocktail of 'European' ideas formed the basis of the strand of thinking that evolved into the creed of 'Kemalism' after the birth of the Turkish Republic.

Many elements of what became the Kemalist program for a new Turkey can be found in the writings of Ziya Gokalp (1876–1924), a commentator and polemicist who also wrote poetry. Gokalp was born and grew up in south-eastern Anatolia's Diyarbakir province, part of the predominantly Kurdish region of the later Turkish Republic, and was influenced by the work of the French sociologist Emile Durkheim (1858–1917). Gokalp became a member of the central committee of the CUP in 1909. His ideas were collected in a book titled *Turkculugun esaslari* (The Principles of Turkism), published in Ankara in 1923.

Gokalp expressed visceral hostility towards the Ottoman Empire and indeed the entire Ottoman era. His view had three major elements. First, he regarded the Empire as the embodiment of a shallow, unsustainable cosmopolitanism that was doomed to collapse. He wrote that it was

> no longer possible for artificial communities composed of many different nations to survive; henceforth every nation would be a separate state with its own homogenous, genuine and natural social life. This social evolutionary movement, which started five centuries ago in Western Europe, would inevitably start in the East also.

He dismissed the Ottoman Empire as a 'temporary community' – a rather odd label since it lasted over half a millennium. Second, and even more remarkably, he saw the Turks as the greatest victims of the Ottoman Empire. He wrote,

> The Ottoman elite disdained the Anatolian peasant as a 'stupid Turk', and the Anatolian townsman was labelled as *tashrali*, provincial ... When the Ottoman Empire was founded the Turks became *rayah* [serfs] within the feudalism this community brought into being. They had no time to progress educationally and economically as they spent their lives serving the community as soldiers and gendarmes. Other ethnic groups in Ottoman society became educated, civilized and rich, but the wretched Turks received only a broken sword and an old plough.

Third, nineteenth-century Ottoman modernizing reforms had simply resulted in dualism and confusion. That was because the reforms 'attempted to reconcile Ottoman with Western civilization ... A nation is either Eastern or Western, a nation cannot have two civilizations'. Gokalp was particularly incensed by the mid-nineteenth century *tanzimat* reform's introduction of 'an educational amalgam of Eastern and Western civilization', which permitted both secular and religious schools. He derided and decried 'the two kinds of courts, of schools, of laws' which the Ottoman system had brought into being during its final decades. He wrote,

> How can the Muslim World resist Europe under these circumstances? How can we defend the independence of our religion and our fatherland? There is only one way to escape, and that is to emulate the progress of

the Europeans in science, industry, and military and legal organization, in other words, to equal them in civilization. And the only way to do that is to enter European civilization completely. The tanzimatists also recognised this necessity and endeavoured to borrow from European civilization, but they borrowed only partially, not completely.

The imprint of this thinking is strongly evident in the discourse and the policies of 'Kemalism'. In his 1927 speech to the nation, Mustafa Kemal asserted that the Ottoman Empire had 'passed into the dustbin of history ... in perpetuity'.[27] Until the 1980s, the Ottoman centuries were indeed consigned to the dustbin of the official narrative of the secular Turkish Republic, either overlooked completely or disparaged as a dark era of backwardness. The headlong rush to Western/European civilization involved the wholesale borrowing of a civil code from Switzerland, a criminal code from Italy, and a commercial code from Germany. Ottoman hybridity was a particular target – the civil code enacted in 1926, apart from eliminating Seriat courts in personal and family matters, superseded the 1870s *Mecelle* code which had combined Islamic and European legal principles. Gokalp had argued that 'the indispensable condition of Turkey's entrance into the ranks of modern nations is the elimination of vestiges of theocracy and clericalism from all branches of national law'. The Unity of Education Law targeted the dualism in the education system that had so infuriated Gokalp, and strongly emphasized secular education.

There were several other aspects in which Gokalp's thinking was put into practice. Gokalp exalted ancient Turkey; he claimed that 'democracy and feminism were the two bases of ancient Turkish life' and that 'ancient Turkish women were all amazons'. During the first half of the 1930s, Kemal's regime propagated two theories of the Turkish past. One, the 'sun-language theory', asserted that Turkish was the first language of humanity and all other languages were derived from it. The other, the 'Turkish history thesis', asserted that the roots of all the world's peoples could be located in the migratory travels of the ancient Turkish 'race'. Gokalp also wrote that 'in order to create a national language, we must discard Ottoman [Turkish] as if it never existed and accept the Turkish language ... We must write this language as the people and

---

27  Davison, *Secularism and Revivalism in Turkey*, 148.

especially the women of Istanbul speak it'. The banning of the Arabic script in 1928, as only the Roman script was to be used, sent the literary heritage of Ottoman Turkish into the dustbin and a flood of 'pure-Turkish' neologisms were introduced to expunge Arabic and Persian words from the vocabulary as much as possible. Gokalp further advocated that 'all religious books, sermons and prayers shall be in Turkish'. In 1933, the state directed that even the *ezan* (call to prayer) should be in Turkish and not Arabic, and attempted to replace the invocation of Allah with a reference to *'tanri'*, a god of ancient Turkish mythology.

Finally, Gokalp was an early exponent of the unique greatness of Mustafa Kemal, foreshadowing the construction of the personality cult of the 'Eternal Chief' – as he was regularly referred to in Turkey through the twentieth century, particularly by committed secularists. Gokalp, who was a deputy in the National Assembly and a member of the state's committee supervising the overhaul of the education system at the time of his death (in October 1924, a year after the proclamation of the Republic), described Kemal as 'a great genius' and 'our great saviour'. In the early 2000s, *The Economist* magazine aptly described the cult of Ataturk as the world's most grotesque state-sponsored cult of personality outside North Korea. Kemalettin Kamu (1901–1948), a poet and National Assembly deputy from Izmir in western Turkey – representing the CHP, the single party of the first quarter-century of the Kemalist Republic – penned the following ode to the founder, 'Cankaya [the Ankara neighbourhood of the president's residence] ... Here Moses reached spiritual perfection, here Jesus ascended ... Let the Arab possess the Kaaba, Cankaya is sufficient for us'.[28]

The Kemalist state however also *departed* from Gokalp's vision in crucial respects. Gokalp made a distinction between 'national culture' and 'international civilization', and he expressly wanted the Turks to retain and indeed cultivate their national culture whilst becoming part of Western/European civilization (it does not seem to have occurred to him that his frame of analysis reproduced the kind of dualities he so despised in the Ottoman scheme). He was particularly taken with the example of Japan and its modernization. According to him, 'the Japanese became Western [sic] without abandoning their religion and nationality and, as a result, have caught

---

28  Hanioglu, 'The Historical Roots of Kemalism', 45.

up with the Europeans in every respect'. He asked rhetorically, 'Cannot we, too, fully enter Western civilization while retaining our identity as Turks and Muslims?' As for the content of the 'national culture', he believed it resided in the popular and folk traditions of Anatolia's people, traditions he claimed had been ignored or demeaned for centuries by Ottoman high culture. He wrote that the emerging elite of the Turkish Republic

> must go among the people, live with them, note the words and phrases they use, listen to their proverbs and maxims, grasp their way of thinking and feeling, listen to their poetry and music, watch their dances and plays, share their religious life and moral feelings, learn to appreciate the beauty of the simplicity of their clothing, architecture and furniture. They must learn the people's folk-tales, anecdotes and epics ... They must read the books of the people ... discover the hymns of the mystics [and] the people's humour ... They must seek out the old coffeehouses of the people ... They must enliven the nights of Ramadan, the Friday communal feasts and the exuberant religious holidays children await so impatiently every year. They must collect works of popular art and create national museums.

Gokalp argued that the elite had a two-fold duty, 'to receive a cultural education from them [the people] and to carry civilization to them'.

Gokalp's hostility to the Ottoman Empire did not lead him to reject Islam, especially as manifested in Anatolian popular and folk culture. To the contrary, he wrote approvingly that 'the Turkish hymns and incantations recited during a dervish [Sufi] *dhikr* are a great source of rapture'. He simply wanted religious services, ceremonies and rituals to be conducted in Turkish, in keeping with the established traditions of the common people; he noted that 'during Ramadan it is principally the Turkish-language poems and music which bring the prayers alive'. In 1925, Kemal's regime closed down all dervish lodges and banned all Sufi orders. Gokalp had written, 'The first dogma of our social catechism must be: I am a member of the Turkish nation, the Islamic community, and Western civilization'. He claimed that 'the elements of Eastern civilization that we will abandon are all things we obtained originally from Byzantium'. And while he believed that Turkish 'women have sunk into slavery or at least an inferior status', he blamed this 'on the influence of Persian and Greek civilizations'.

Ziya Gokalp's hopes of a harmonious confluence of national culture and

Western (European) civilization, achieved through an equal, reciprocal partnership of the elite and the masses, were not realized in Kemalist Turkey. Gokalp had written,

> The fatherland is a museum, an exhibition of religious, moral and aesthetic beauties … We cannot regard any nation as our cultural superior. For us, Turkish culture is the most beautiful culture that exists or shall ever exist, so we cannot possibly be imitators or vassals of French *culture* or German *Kultur*.[29]

Mustafa Kemal did adopt one aspect of Gokalp's prescription – that the embrace of Western/European civilization should be total and not partial and selective as under the Ottomans. But crucially,

> he rejected the separation of culture and civilization … Kemal considered civilization as a concept that included all cultures but was shaped by the most advanced European ones … [So] those aspects of a non-Western local culture that clashed with the universal civilization should be eliminated … [In the process] Kemal rejected the [very] concept of a non-Western modernity, despite having lived in one of the major examples of such an environment, the late Ottoman Empire.[30]

Thus, the abolition of the Caliphate and the office of the *seyh-ul-Islam* (the head of the *ulema*, the clerical hierarchy) in 1924, a decision compatible with Gokalp's aversion to theocracy and clericalism, was followed a year later by an all-out attack on the popular and folk versions of Anatolian Islam (which, unlike the official and institutionalized Islam, survived and continued in clandestine forms).

Instead of a reciprocal dialogue between the elite and the people, a top-down approach sought to inculcate the new values in the villagers and townspeople of Anatolia. As part of state policy, so-called 'People's Houses' (*halk evleri*) were set up in the larger towns in 1932, and 'People's Rooms' (*halk odalari*) in 1940 in smaller towns and villages, and functioned as re-education centres for adults. The chasm between a distant, bureaucratic

---

29 This and all of the above quotations from Gokalp are taken from Ziya Gokalp, *The Principles of Turkism*, translated from the Turkish and annotated by Robert Devereux (Leiden: E. J. Brill, 1968).

30 Hanioglu, 'The Historical Roots of Kemalism', 46.

'centre' and a vast 'periphery' comprising the bulk of society, apparent in the Ottoman Empire, continued and perhaps even deepened in the Republic, as Serif Mardin argued in a well-known article published in 1973.[31] In the mid-1950s, three decades after the emergence of the new Turkey, the American scholar Dankwart Rustow observed that 'Kemal's revolution has carried along the educated upper class but has had little effect on the peasant masses' (at this time, Turkey was 80 per cent rural).[32] The capital changed from Istanbul to Ankara but the elitist character of the Ottoman state carried over in a reconfigured form in the Kemalist republic, despite its ideological rupture with centuries of history and tradition. The Turkish anthropologist Nur Yalman's experience of conducting fieldwork among villagers in eastern Turkey in the late 1960s, at a time Turkey was still a largely rural country, convinced him that the state–secularist 'intellectuals of Istanbul and Ankara had completely misunderstood what Islam or religion was all about' and that they were 'cut off … from the common people'.[33]

The new order's Europhile ideology was obnoxious and even repugnant to numerous Turks. One such person was Mehmet Akif, composer of the poem whose first two stanzas were adopted as the Turkish national anthem by the first National Assembly in 1921. The poem continued thus, 'Though the West girds itself with a wall of steel, my bosom filled with faith is my fortress. Fear not; how can this faith of a people be smothered by that monster called "Civilization" which has but one tooth left in its jaw?' Thoroughly disillusioned by Kemal's regime, Akif emigrated in 1925 to Cairo and taught classical Turkish there at al-Azhar, the hallowed institution of Sunni theology. In his exile, he wrote, 'People of a nation … whose world is imitation, whose customs are imitation, whose dress is imitation, whose greetings and language are imitation, in short, whose everything is imitation, are clearly themselves mere imitation human beings'.[34] There were dissenting voices in later generations born and socialized in the Kemalist Republic of

---

31 Serif Mardin, 'Center-Periphery Relations: A Key to Turkish Politics?''', *Daedalus* 102, no.1 (Winter 1973), 169–190.

32 Dankwart A. Rustow, 'Politics and Islam in Turkey, 1920-1955', in *Islam and the West*, ed. Frye, 107.

33 Yalman, 'Islamic Reform and the Mystic Tradition in Eastern Turkey', 47.

34 Yalman, 'Some Observations on Secularism in Islam', 158.

rigid dogma and strictly enforced conformity. One such free-thinker, the leftist and secularist public intellectual Attila Ilhan (1925–2005), lamented in 1976,

> We read Sophocles in the lycee. We learned to curse classical Turkish music, to look down on *Divan* [Ottoman] literature. We learned to admire the terrible translations of Western classics published by the State Printing House. You would think that [Mimar] Sinan [the royal architect of Suleiman the Magnificent, the *kanuni* or law-giving 16th-century Ottoman sultan] was less important than Leonardo, that Mevlana [Rumi] was inferior to Dante, that Itri [a late 17th-century composer of mystical music] could not be compared to Bach. We put the noose of cultural imperialism around our necks with our own hands. The sickness … has gripped us. We are unable to search for our own synthesis.[35]

Other notable critics of Kemalism were even more forthright, and withering. The celebrated novelist Yasar Kemal (1923–2015), a leftist and a Kurd, told the *Milliyet* (Nation) daily in 1971,

> For 200 years the Turkish intellectual has aped the West, imitated the West. An Ape is not creative. It may look human, but it is not creative. Since Turkish intellectuals have aped the West for 200 years, they have not made any contribution to humanity for 200 years.[36]

Yasar Kemal clearly traced the 'Westoxication' that became the state's ideology in the post-1923 republic to its beginnings in the late Ottoman era, perhaps unfairly. But his point about 'aping' is well-taken. The Museum of Modern Art (MOMA) in downtown Istanbul, popular with secular Turks and some Western tourists, is packed with mediocre (and worse) imitations by twentieth-century Turkish artists of French artistic forms. It is a far cry from the repositories of Anatolian popular and folk art Gokalp had recommended the republic foster, and an utter contrast to the culturally distinctive and innovative forms of modern art, inspired by indigenous traditions, which emerged in India during the first half of the twentieth century. Another important contrarian voice, the academician Nurettin Topcu (1909–75) looked to the spiritual legacy of the thirteenth-century Anatolian Sufi mystics

---

35 Yalman, 'On Secularism and its Critics', 245.
36 Yalman, 'Some Observations on Secularism in Islam', 158.

Rumi and Yunus Emre as the source of an authentic national culture. Topcu, who was strongly hostile to orthodox, bookish Islam, wrote in 1972,

> The powers of ... Europe ... are not the powers which have given life to our people. The people of Anatolia, with a thousand years of history behind them, are products of the religion of Islam ... Just as our ancestry is Asian, our ethics ... are the honest works of Asia. The movement of our reform, renaissance and a return to our own identity will be different from ailing Europe ... This awakening will move towards Asia ... The moment has come for our idea of a nation to make its last and final separation from the idea of Europe.[37]

Topcu's political philosophy has some similarities to that of Ali Shariati (1933–77), the revolutionary Iranian intellectual who published a famous essay, 'Return to the Self', in 1971. Topcu and Shariati both earned doctorates at the Sorbonne in Paris but a generation apart, in the 1930s and 1960s, respectively.

Kemalist secularism was motivated by a craving to emulate the West, the one and only civilization of the times according to Kemal, and be accepted as a European (and therefore 'civilized') nation. The Kemalists were particularly excited by the example of the French Third Republic (1870–1940), where between 1875 and 1905 republicans committed to secularism (*laicite*) decisively prevailed over monarchists and other conservatives supporting a Catholic state and the supremacy of the Catholic Church. A series of secularizing measures culminated in the 'Law of 1905' which sealed the victory of the secularist vision of the state over the alternative religiously grounded model. If France, an overwhelmingly Catholic society, could become a secular state, so could Turkey with its overwhelmingly Muslim population, the pioneers of Turkish secularism felt. And if religious reaction and clericalism could be tamed in France, where Catholicism had been the state religion for most of the nineteenth century, why couldn't the same be achieved with regard to Islam in Turkey?

In fact, as the Turkish scholar Ahmet T. Kuru among others has shown, the contexts of France and Turkey were markedly different. In France, the victory of the secularists at the beginning of the twentieth century came

---

37 Yalman, 'On Secularism and its Critics', 244–245.

after a long 'war of the two Frances' – republican/laicist versus monarchist/clerical – which had lasted over a century. After the militant anti-clericalism of the years immediately following the 1789 French Revolution, Catholicism was reinstated as the religion of the French state from the beginning of the nineteenth century and the Church and its allied conservative forces dominated until the Third Republic. The tables gradually turned during the first half of the Third Republic because the republican/secularist side consistently demonstrated greater popular support than their conservative rivals. The latter lost eleven successive elections to the former during the first four decades of the Third Republic, up until the outbreak of World War I in 1914, and their vote progressively declined over that time. The main reason was that the French peasantry, the major component of society, increasingly supported the republican/secularist forces over their conservative/clericalist foes. The Law of 1905 was democratically passed by decisive majorities in both chambers of the French parliament: by 341 to 233 votes in the Assembly and 179 to 103 in the Senate. The republican/secularist parties then won the 1906 elections resoundingly and further increased their dominance in parliament, reinforcing the popular legitimacy of the secularization of the French state. Even so, the Law of 1905 contained some elements of compromise with the Church. The French Constitution of 1946 enshrined secularism as a fundamental principle; by that time, religious conservatism had been weakened further and the Catholic Church discredited by its support of the collaborationist Vichy state set up by Nazi Germany during its 1940–44 occupation of France.[38]

The Turkish secular state signally lacked these attributes of evolution over time and popular and democratic legitimacy. To the contrary, as the Turkish scholar Kemal Karpat pointed out in 1959,

> secularism in Turkey ... was not voluntarily accepted at the end of a natural and peaceful evolution but was imposed upon society by Mustafa Kemal's modernist-secularist group [by] taking advantage of special historical circumstances between 1919 and 1923 which had discredited the Sultan-Caliph.[39]

38 See Ahmet T. Kuru, *Secularism and State Policies Toward Religion: The United States, France, and Turkey* (New York: Cambridge University Press, 2009), 136–157.

39 Kemal H. Karpat, *Turkey's Politics: The Transition to a Multi-Party System* (Princeton:

That the Kemalist group was able to push this through was substantially due to their leader's sky-high prestige as the victorious commander in the 1919–22 military conflict which established the Turkish state. But, as Rustow notes, in the 1920s 'Kemal and a handful of intimate associates were the only determined secularists' in Turkey.[40] Their vision and agenda had to be implemented, and it was, through the enforcement of a draconian approach that routinized harsh repression and included episodes of brutal violence in the 1920s and 1930s. Thus from its beginnings, Turkish secularism became identified with authoritarianism, vividly reflected in Mustafa Kemal's grim visage and stentorian words.

Nonetheless, Kemalist secularism developed a significant following of ardent and even fanatical devotees over the next few decades. Writing in the mid-1950s, Rustow observed that 'today the secularists include a large majority of the urban educated class ... of the Turkish Republic'.[41] Five decades later, the Turkish scholar Sukru Hanioglu wrote that,

> a large section of the elite internalized the new modernism and considered it the only form of modernity ... the importance of the emergence of elite and urban upper and middle classes enthusiastically embracing the new ideology should not be underestimated. This class and its ideology have ruled modern Turkey since the inception of the republic.[42]

This was indeed the case until the beginning of the twenty-first century, when the tables finally turned and the two major weaknesses of Turkish state-secularism – the original deficiency of cultural and national authenticity and the limited base among an elite (albeit large) minority of society – caught up with the secular state. The copycat attempt to replicate French *laicite* in Turkey was not successful. In late 2007 a survey conducted by the (secularist) daily *Milliyet* reported that 78 per cent of the Turkish public were opposed to the then ban, enforced since the 1980s, on women wearing headscarves in all universities, whether state-run or private (the other 22 per cent were in favour). Around the same time, 72 per cent of the French public supported

---

Princeton University Press, 1959), 288.

40  Rustow, 'Politics and Islam in Turkey, 1920–1955', 106–107.

41  Ibid, 107.

42  Hanioglu, 'The Historical Roots of Kemalism', 49.

the prohibition applied in state-run institutions of learning in France on headscarves and other symbols of religiosity.[43]

♦

The Indian secular state has very different origins and premises, and does not have the birth defects that have plagued its Turkish counterpart since inception. India's secular state was *not* formed to copy the Occident in the hope of being accepted as 'civilized' and 'modern' equals. It instead grew from an emphatically Indian vision of modernity, incubated in the three decades of popular mobilization for freedom from British colonialism led by the Indian National Congress. This vision was rooted in an aspect of Indian tradition – mutual tolerance and coexistence of the subcontinent's various religious communities down the centuries – and sought to continue that aspect of tradition in a free Indian state, in stark contrast to the rupture with the past promoted by the Kemalists (Hindu–Muslim violence was very rare in India until the 1920s, when it emerged in some urban centres). That necessarily meant the equality of all of India's faiths in the eyes of the state. As Nehru said weeks after the enactment of India's Constitution in 1950, 'the government of a country like India, with many religions that have secured great and devoted followings for generations, can never function satisfactorily in the modern age except on a secular basis' (see note 39, Chapter 1). This was consistent with the Congress's declaration in 1928 (see Chapter 1) that 'there shall be no state religion' in independent India, 'nor shall the State either directly or indirectly endow any religion or give any preference or impose any disability [on citizens] on account of religious belief or religious status'. Even Vallabhbhai Patel, Nehru's Deputy Prime Minister and Home (interior) Minister, and the person closest to a Hindu-centric viewpoint among the top Congress leaders, said in January 1948 that 'if we cannot act as trustees for the entire population irrespective of religion, caste or creed, we do not deserve to be where we are'.[44] As the Indian Republic's Constitution took shape, Nehru the scientific rationalist clarified in April 1949 that the secular

---

43  Kuru, *Secularism and State Policies Toward Religion*, 192–193.

44  Reported in *Hindustan Times* on 17 January 1948. Cited in Luthera, *The Concept of the Secular State and India*, 161.

state was not about promoting atheism: 'The measure of India's progress will be the measure of our giving full effect to … a secular state. That … does not mean a people lacking in morals or religion … [the profession and practice of] religion [will be] completely free' (see Chapter 1). Here there is a similarity to Mustafa Kemal's 1927 statement that 'it is indispensable, in order to purify and elevate the Islamic faith, to disengage it from its condition of being a political instrument which it has been for centuries'.[45]

The differences in the paths to the secular state in India and Turkey are however much greater than the similarities. The Republic of India's 1950 Constitution, which established a secular state in all but name, emerged through a process of democratic debate and deliberation in the 1947–49 Constituent Assembly. This was no doubt an elite-led exercise, but its process of deliberative democracy still stands in contrast to the shotgun imposition of secularism on Turkey by the Kemalist clique from 1924 onwards. One member of the Constituent Assembly tried twice to formally include the term 'secular state' in the Constitution. He proposed that an article of the Constitution should assert that 'the state in India being secular shall have no concern with any religion, creed or profession of faith'. This suggestion, with its implication of distancing the state from religion altogether, did not pass. As Donald Smith observed in his 1963 book, 'the inclusion of such an article in the Constitution, however laudable the intention behind it, would certainly have produced a conflict with Article 25, which permits extensive state intervention in matters of religion in the interest of social reform'.[46] This activist, controlling, regulating and interventionist model of the secular state is of course the salient common feature of the secular state in India and Turkey, as described in Chapter 1. The consequences of this model are discussed in Chapter 3. As noted in Chapter 1, the term 'secular' was formally inserted in the identity of the Republic of India via a constitutional amendment in 1976, passed in parliament during Nehru's daughter Indira Gandhi's dictatorial 'Emergency' regime of June 1975–January 1977. My point here is that the Constituent Assembly which produced the *de facto* secular state that came into being on 26 January 1950, India's Republic Day, was a truly deliberative body in which a range of views were expressed and discussed. The foundations of

---

45  Davison, *Secularism and Revivalism in Turkey*, 151.

46  Smith, *India as a Secular State*, 101.

state-secularism in India are not just indigenously rooted but democratically crafted, both quite in contrast to the Turkish case.

The differences were reflected in foreign policy as well, where Nehru's regime followed a doctrine of 'non-alignment' – meaning equidistance from the post-World War II superpowers, the United States and the Soviet Union, and their respective blocs. The Indian emphasis was on building friendship and solidarity among Asian, Middle Eastern and African states emerging from the grip of European colonialisms. During the 1950s, Nehru also pursued a vision of Asiatic cooperation with the People's Republic of China, which he viewed as a state with a great civilizational heritage similar to India's and which too had shaken off Western domination after much struggle (this vision collapsed by the early 1960s as Sino–Indian relations deteriorated). Turkey, by contrast, joined the North Atlantic Treaty Organization (NATO) in the early 1950s after nearly three decades of self-imposed isolation from regional and global geopolitics and became a member of the US-led Western bloc in the Cold War. This choice was consistent with the Western and European orientation of its elite.

Contrary to what many Indians reflexively think based on their own experience, there is no intrinsic connection between secularism and democracy, as the case of Turkey amply demonstrates. During the first two decades of independent India, most American and European commentary was sceptical if not dismissive about its prospects of sustaining democracy. In the words of one Indian author,

> in the 1950s and 1960s [Western] reporting on India was full of metaphors of the region-of-uncertainty and area-of-darkness kind. There was a great deal of superior moaning about how awful, poor, divisive and filthy India was … Of course democracy simply had no chance in this illiterate and hungry land; at best it would be a farce and at worst a chaotic Babel that would encourage all the latent fissiparous forces, ensuring the destruction of the country.[47]

However, as democracy took root in India, albeit with many flaws and warts, so did the idea of secularism promoted by the state – notwithstanding the many paradoxes, anomalies and contradictions of Indian state-secularism

---

47 M. J. Akbar, *India, the Siege Within: Challenges to a Nation's Unity* (New Delhi: Roli Books, 2003), 95.

explored in Chapter 3 and throughout this book. As Donald Smith noted in 1963, secularism became 'a fundamental aspect of ... India's total democratic experiment' (see Chapter 1).

In Turkey, by contrast, secularism was paired from the outset with a harsh, snarling authoritarianism. Mustafa Kemal toyed with the possibility of allowing token opposition parties early on in his dictatorship but two such decorative parties, set up in 1924 and 1930 with regime approval, were rapidly dissolved by the regime, which feared they would become a rallying point for anti-secular forces. As Rustow notes, such decisions as the abolition of the Caliphate (1924) and the outlawing of all religious brotherhoods or *tarikat*s (1925) were above all motivated by the regime's goal of eliminating all potential sources of opposition as it consolidated its authoritarian rule: 'political considerations were decisive in determining the place of Islam in the Turkish Republic'.[48] So an armed rebellion against the new regime led by a Kurdish sheikh of the Naqshbandi brotherhood in the Diyarbakir area of south-eastern Turkey in 1925 triggered the closure of the first opposition party, which had been formed 'by a number of Kemal's most prominent military and political associates' in the 1919–22 war of independence, and the second, founded by another 'loyal associate of Kemal's', was precipitately shut down after a much more minor rebellion in 1930 led by Naqshbandi sheikhs near the coastal city of Izmir in western Turkey.[49]

From the time of Turkey's first military coup in 1960, the commanders of the Turkish military emerged as the self-appointed guardians of Kemalist secularism. This military hierarchy cultivated ties from then on with Pakistan – a state founded on a religion-based concept of nationhood, which would presumably have been anathema to Mustafa Kemal – but rather similar from the late 1950s onwards to Turkey in its record of recurrent military coups, military dominance of the state, and of course, shared membership of the US-led bloc in global geopolitics. The Turkey–Pakistan connection persists today, in the very different era of the ascendancy of anti-secularist forces in Turkey. In May 2016, President Erdogan harshly criticized the government of Bangladesh after it hanged a religious fundamentalist who had led a pro-

---

48 Rustow, 'Politics and Islam in Turkey, 1920–1955', 79.
49 Ibid., 87–88.

Pakistan militia during the 1971 conflict in East Pakistan which ended with the emergence of sovereign Bangladesh after India's military intervention in the conflict. In late 2016, Erdogan, a suspect character in most European democratic capitals after his regime's descent into vicious authoritarianism following the failed putsch by a small section of the military in July 2016, made an official visit to Pakistan and was warmly received there.

In sum, Turkish state-secularism was motivated by a desire to embrace and emulate a historical 'Other' – Europe. In 1926 Mahmut Esat (1892–1943), an ardent young follower of Mustafa Kemal and the Minister of Justice, tabled the republic's new civil code, an imitation of the Swiss Code of 1912, in the Grand National Assembly in Ankara in a long speech. He was dismissive of the late Ottoman (1870s) code, the Mecelle, which combined Islamic and modern European principles of jurisprudence. He averred that all but 300 of the Mecelle's 1,851 articles were 'primitive', a jumble of 'slapdash … religious principles', and 'doubtlessly irreconcilable with contemporary civilization'. By contrast, he said, 'the Ministry of Justice deems the Swiss Civil Code, which is the most recent and most perfect of its kind, as a civilized work' (Esat had earned a doctorate in law in Switzerland). He then pointed out that 'Switzerland, Germany and France have strengthened and fortified their political and national unities' by enacting uniform and secular civil codes and urged the parliamentarians to support his bill for the sake of realizing 'at any cost the political, social, economic and national unity' of Turkey. The otherwise droning speech ended on a rousing note: 'The day the Turkish Civil Code … is put into force our nation will have been saved from the faulty and confusing beliefs of thirteen centuries … and closing the doors of the old civilization, will have entered the contemporary civilization that grants life and light'.[50]

B. R. Ambedkar (1891–1956), the champion of Dalit rights and empowerment who served as the Chairman of the Constitution-Drafting Committee of India's Constituent Assembly and as independent India's first Minister of Law and Justice, was an exact contemporary of Esat's and was also Western-educated, having earned a master's degree at Columbia University in New York, and then a doctorate at the London School of Economics and Political Science (the LSE). He had not been part of the anti-colonial

---

50 The full text of the speech is reproduced in English translation in Davison, *Secularism and Revivalism in Turkey*, 197–203.

movement led by the Congress – preoccupied with the caste question and the oppression of the 'untouchable' communities at the bottom of Hinduism's social hierarchy, he had had a difficult and even adversarial relationship with the Congress leadership, particularly with Gandhi (who also pursued the eradication of untouchability as a top priority). Ambedkar's co-optation into independent India's ruling elite lasted just a few years, since he left the government in 1951. But his politics left an imprint on the Constitution, as in Article 17, which prohibited untouchability and made its practice a punishable offence. He also led the early debates (1948–51) on the reform and codification of Hindu personal and family law, which eventually happened in the mid-1950s (on this subject, there is much more in Chapter 3). Ambedkar broadly shared the secular-modernist mindset of leaders such as Nehru and Bose and was like them influenced by exposure to the West. In his 1936 work *Annihilation of Caste*, he described his ideal Indian society as one founded on 'Liberty, Equality, Fraternity', the slogan of the French Revolution. But his outlook, as those of Gandhi, Nehru and Bose, contained nothing of the grovelling adulation of the West/Europe as the sole source of civilization and modernity apparent in Mahmut Esat and other members of the Kemalist vanguard.

Although the Indian secular state was emphatically not inspired by or based on a Western 'Other' turned model, as Turkey's was, its architects did have an 'Other' they desired to differentiate and distance their state from. This was the other country born in the subcontinent in August 1947, Pakistan. Throughout his tenure as Prime Minister, and particularly in the early years after independence, Nehru was gravely concerned about India turning into a Hindu version of Pakistan in the aftermath of the traumatic partition of 1947, which had badly damaged the secular concept of Indian nationalism. His concern was motivated not so much by the activities of Hindu nationalist groups as by the sympathy and even support for their views he discerned within the Congress, including among senior leaders. He wrote to one such leader, his deputy Sardar Vallabhbhai Patel, in March 1950, 'A secular state … simply means any normal state today, leaving aside the abnormality of Pakistan's Islamic state'. Nehru believed that a secular state was essential to (re)building national unity in a multi-religious country in the wake of the partition – and not national unity 'at any cost', as the authoritarian

Kemalists would have it, but in a framework of political pluralism. Later that year, Nehru strongly opposed the candidacy for Congress's national President of Purushottam Das (P. D.) Tandon, a party veteran from north India's Uttar Pradesh State. In an August 1950 letter to Patel, Tandon's main backer, Nehru complained that Tandon was 'being widely supported by Hindu Mahasabha and RSS elements' (the Rashtriya Swayamsevak Sangh or National Volunteer Organization, founded in 1925, is the core of India's Hindu nationalist movement). Tandon was elected Congress President, defeating the candidate preferred by Nehru, the socialist Acharya Kripalani. But Nehru re-asserted his control of the party after Patel's death in December 1950, becoming Congress President himself in 1951 and 1952. On the eve of India's first parliamentary election, Nehru told a party rally in Delhi in September 1951: 'The moment you talk of a Hindu Rashtra [State] you speak in a language no other country except one can comprehend and that is Pakistan, which is familiar with the concept'.[51]

The desire to distinguish India from Pakistan explains the absolute centrality given to secularism and the secular state in official Indian discourse after independence, in contrast to the rare use of these terms in the discourse of the movement for independence. Deendayal Upadhyaya (1916–68), a Brahmin from Uttar Pradesh and a leading RSS activist who served from 1953 to 1967 as general secretary of the Hindu nationalist political party, the Bharatiya Jan Sangh (Indian People's Organization, re-named Bharatiya Janata Party or BJP in 1980), commented acidly in 1965, 'Nowadays the word "secular state" is being used ... the adoption of this word is mere imitation of western thought pattern. We had no need to import it. We called it a secular state to contrast it with Pakistan'.[52] Upadhyaya's allegation of imitation of the West is unfounded, but the point about Pakistan is well-taken. A few months before his assassination on 30 January 1948 by a Hindu militant, Gandhi had said while strongly opposing the clamour for a ban on cow slaughter in India,

> If they can prohibit cow slaughter in India on religious grounds, why cannot the Pakistan government prohibit, say, idol worship in Pakistan on similar grounds? I am not a temple-goer, but if I were prohibited from

51 Godbole, *Secularism*, 6, 277–278.

52 See Christophe Jaffrelot, *Hindu Nationalism: A Reader* (Princeton and Oxford: Princeton University Press, 2007), 154.

going to a temple in Pakistan, I would make it a point to go there even at the risk of losing my head. Just as sharia cannot be imposed on non-Muslims, the Hindu law [sic] cannot be imposed on non-Hindus.[53]

The paths to the secular state in India and Turkey are thus very different – indigenously rooted and democratic in India, and West/Europe-inspired and authoritarian in Turkey. Nonetheless, the paradoxes, contradictions and anomalies in the nature and functioning of the two secular states are remarkably similar. This is explored in the next chapter.

---

53  Godbole, *Secularism*, 203–204.

# 3

# PARADOXES OF THE SECULAR STATE

*Congress shall make no law respecting an establishment of religion, or prohibiting the free exercise thereof.*
 — The First Amendment to the Constitution of the
United States of America, 1791

The classic conception of the Western secular state is expressed in the first amendment to the United States' Constitution, proposed by James Madison in 1791. The amendment strengthened the secular basis of the US Constitution ratified in 1789 – the same year as the French Revolution shook Europe with its rejection of monarchy, aristocracy and clericalism – which had made no reference to God and specified that 'no religious test shall ever be required as a qualification to any office or public trust under the United States'. In 1802 President Thomas Jefferson famously wrote, in a letter to a local association of adherents of the Baptist denomination in a town in the State of Connecticut, 'I contemplate with sovereign reverence that act of the American people which declared that their legislature should make no law respecting an establishment of religion or prohibiting the free exercise thereof—thus building a wall of separation between the church and the state'. Of course, that doctrine of separation has not been absolute in practice; Donald Smith listed such practices as 'the appointment of Protestant, Catholic and Jewish chaplains in the armed services, the tax exemption granted to churches and synagogues, [and] the opening of State and national legislative sessions with prayer'. We might add to that list the habit of US Presidents to end important speeches to the nation with 'God bless the United States of America'. But, as he argued, 'the basic [twin] principles of religious freedom and church–state separation have been adhered to throughout ... American history'. In a landmark ruling in 1948, the US Supreme Court declared religious instruction in the public school system of the State of Illinois as unconstitutional in unequivocal terms, 'Separation is a requirement to abstain from fusing the functions of government and religious sects, not merely to treat them all equally ... Separation means separation, not something less'.[1]

The founding fathers of America would certainly have found it paradoxical that far from following the wall-of-separation doctrine, the twentieth-century secular states of India and Turkey adopted a model of secularism that irretrievably entangles the state with the religious domain, as a constantly monitoring, controlling and regulating authority (self) invested with extensive, even vast powers of intervention in matters of religion. The Indian and Turkish states are secular in that they don't establish any official religion, and so their constitutional identities are not based on or tied to any faith. Moreover, as the two epigraphs with which Chapter 2 began show, pioneers of the secular state such as B. R. Ambedkar in India and Mahmut Esat in Turkey did try to assert a conceptual distinction between the state and the domain of religious belief and practice. The common theme in their pronouncements is an attempt to demarcate a separate, private sphere for the matters of 'conscience', 'beliefs', 'rituals' and 'ceremonials' connected with religion and religiosity, away from the state and the public sphere. However, the 'jurisdictionalist' character of the Indian secular state (in Luthera's term) and the structurally similar 'control model' (as it has been described by scholars of Turkey from the 1950s on) of the Turkish secular state had the effect of blurring, indeed dissolving, the public/private and state/society distinctions. So, *contra* the wall-of-separation doctrine of American provenance, these two non-Western secular states have been defined not by the distancing of the state from mosque and temple, but rather by the state's role of oversight and supervision of religious affairs and institutions. This is a striking similarity of the democratic Indian and authoritarian Turkish variants of state-secularism. It is true that India has never had a Ministry of Religious Affairs in the manner of the Turkish Republic's *Diyanet* (the Directorate-General of Religious Affairs), which was established

1   Smith, *India as a Secular State*, 17, 499.

to subordinate the practice of religion to an encompassing state control, but the Indian state has not been significantly less activist in watching over religion and exercising its constitutional powers of intervention and regulation in matters pertaining to religion. Thus, the society/state and private/public distinctions asserted by Ambedkar and Esat remained conceptual rather than empirical and nominal rather than actual. The reasons for the appearance and institutionalization of this model of the secular state in India and Turkey have been discussed in Chapters 1 and 2. The common denominator seems to have been the judgment of the founding elites that in their societies, religion could not be left to its own devices.

India and Turkey are both Republics, polities founded on the twin precepts of popular sovereignty and the equality of all citizens regardless of group, class or community. The avowedly secular character of the two Republics additionally mandates that in its outlook, policies and behaviour, the state must maintain and uphold equality of status and treatment of all confessional communities, without preference or discrimination. This is what the Indian constitution enshrines, and is the essence of the Indian secularist concepts of *dharma-nirapekhshata* (impartiality, usually meaning state impartiality, towards the nation's multiplicity of religious faiths) and *sarva-dharma-sambhava* (equal esteem of all religions). Chapter 1 has noted that while Turkey is not an obviously multi-religious country in the manner India is, with its Hindu, Muslim, Sikh, Christian, Jain, Buddhist and Zoroastrian traditions and citizens, Turkey's overwhelmingly Muslim population contains layers of diversity: between majority Sunnis and minority Alevis, different schools of Sunnism (the Hanefi tradition dominant among Sunni Turks and the Shafi tradition prevalent among Sunni Kurds), and popular *tarikats* or sects (for example, the formalist Naqshbandi order found among Sunnis and the mystical Bektashi order among Alevis, both officially illegal since 1925). Turkey's ideological (secularist/anti-secularist) and ethnic (Turkish/Kurdish) fault-lines intersect in complex ways with these cleavages. The logical implication is that Turkey, as a secular state based ostensibly on the equality of all its citizens – a principle incorporated as Article 88 in the Turkish Republic's first Constitution in 1924 and re-stated in the subsequent Constitutions of 1961 and 1982 – ought to practice impartial treatment of the multiple denominational and confessional traditions, identities and allegiances which exist in its society.

◆

The secular state has failed to live up to this very demanding standard of impartiality in both countries. In the process, it has drawn criticism from the spokesmen, advocates and agitators of both majority and minority standpoints.

The virtually open-ended powers of regulation and reform of the practice of religion conferred on the Indian state by Articles 25 and 26 of the 1950 Constitution were soon put to use. The project was the codification of Hindu personal and family laws, a vast and ambitious undertaking no less revolutionary in its intent and implications than the Turkish civil code of 1926. In 1955–56, India's parliament enacted four pieces of legislation: the Hindu Marriage Act, the Hindu Succession Act, the Hindu Minority and Guardianship Act, and the Hindu Adoptions and Maintenance Act (there was also a Special Marriage Act, passed in 1954, which liberalized provisions for inter-faith marriage of a colonial-era law). Prior to this, there had been no uniform Hindu code for personal and familial matters; 'Hindu' laws governing such matters existed and were applied in diverse and often conflicting forms in different parts of India. The 1955–56 reforms had a two-fold purpose: to end this fragmentation in the newly-established Republic and to promote and secure the rights of the female gender, who were denied recognition, or equality, or both, in most of the prevalent versions of Hindu law. Cumulatively, the body of laws enacted in 1955–56 aimed to secure equality for Hindu women and girls in matters of marriage, divorce, inheritance and adoption. The mid-1950s reform had been preceded by high-level discussions of the subject during the first half of the 1940s, when the colonial power still ruled India, and then again in the years immediately after independence (1948–51). The matter was shelved in autumn 1951 amid mounting acrimony between proponents and opponents of the reform agenda. In his presidential address to the annual convention of the Congress in October 1951, delivered on the eve of the elections to constitute independent India's first parliament (the inaugural Lok Sabha) and democratically-mandated government, Nehru observed that 'the Hindu Code Bill, which has given rise to so much argument', had become 'a symbol of the conflict between progress and reaction in the social domain'. Sounding almost like Mustafa Kemal of the 1920s, he lauded 'the spirit underlying the Bill ... a spirit of liberation and of freeing our people and especially, our womenfolk, from outworn customs and shackles'.[2] The reform agenda was revived as several distinct but closely related and mutually reinforcing bills during the tenure of the first parliament, and despite strenuous opposition and criticism both inside and outside the legislature, eventually passed with large majorities. Six decades later, it remains the single most important instance of regulation and reform of religious practice implemented by the Indian state since independence.

In the debate on the legislation inside and outside parliament, proponents and opponents both based their arguments on (differing) interpretations of the essence and teachings of Hinduism as written in its holy texts. Donald Smith noted the paradoxical situation in which H.V. Pataskar, who as Law Minister tabled the bills to parliament, found himself,

> an official of the secular state, he became an interpreter of Hindu religion, quoting and expounding the ancient Sanskrit scriptures in defence of the bills. In a speech on the Hindu Marriage Bill, Pataskar explained the Hindu concept of *dharma* and contrasted it with the ... dogma in Christianity and Islam.

The Hindu Marriage Bill contained three especially contentious points: provisions for inter-caste marriage, divorce and prohibition of polygamy. In the government's interpretation and argument, Hinduism was an inherently progressive faith whose sacred texts permitted and even sanctioned these reforms. The opponents argued against the reforms on precisely the same grounds – the essential nature and precepts of Hinduism. The most articulate voice of the traditionalist opposition (or 'reaction', in Nehru's term) to the reforms both inside and outside parliament – the latter for example at an 'all-India convention' organized in Delhi in April 1955 to oppose the government's agenda – was N. C. Chatterjee, a Hindu nationalist MP who had been elected to the Lok Sabha from the State of West Bengal in eastern India. A highly educated Bengali Brahmin, he was a London-qualified barrister who pursued a career as a lawyer and became a judge of the Calcutta High Court. In the Lok Sabha, he represented the Hindu Mahasabha, an organization founded during colonial rule, and not the Bharatiya Jan Sangh (forerunner of the BJP), the RSS-backed political party formed in late 1951 under the leadership of Syama

---

2   Ibid., 280–281.

Prasad Mookerjee, another patrician Bengali Brahmin and London-qualified barrister who was also elected from West Bengal to the first Lok Sabha but died in mid-1953 while agitating against the autonomous status granted to Jammu and Kashmir State in the Indian Constitution. Both Mookerjee and Chatterjee were staunchly loyal to Britain during India's struggle for independence.[3]

In an impassioned speech in the Lok Sabha, Chatterjee pointed out that the ancient Vedas had described Hindu marriage as a sacrament (*sanskara*) – 'an inviolable union, an indissoluble union, an interminable union, an eternal fellowship' – and appealed to parliament to not 'tamper with Hindu sacramental marriage and introduce divorce into it'. On the subject of legalizing adoption of girl children as proposed by the government's legislation, Chatterjee and other opponents cited the ancient Hindu saying *putrarthay kriyatay bharja, putra pinda prayojaka* – a man acquires a wife because a son is required to perform the rituals upon his death. In the absence of a biological son, the man is allowed to adopt a male child who can fulfil this essential requirement, but never a female, because a girl child cannot by scriptural tradition perform this task. On the legislation giving daughters equal inheritance rights with male heirs, the opponents contended that this amounted to an attempt to impose Sharia principles on Hindus. This objection was on the grounds that while daughters in Hindu families did not customarily receive a share of a deceased father's property, because they already were or in due course would be a member of another family through marriage, Muslim law did grant inheritance rights to daughters. On the prohibition of polygamy for Hindu men, N. C. Chatterjee claimed that this would act as an incentive for them to convert to Islam, because Muslim men in India could continue having up to four wives as sanctioned by Islamic religious law. He told the all-India convention in Delhi that 'imbued with western ideas, some people in power are seeking to change Hindu dharma by making laws which are repugnant to the basic principles of Hinduism. What is this secularism [but] the negation and destruction of religion?'[4]

In addition to the defence of Hindu traditions as laid down in ancient scriptures, the Hindu nationalist criticism of the government's agenda had

---

3   N. C. Chatterjee's son Somnath Chatterjee was from the early 1970s onward elected to the Lok Sabha multiple times from West Bengal as a candidate of the Communist Party of India (Marxist), and served as the Lok Sabha's speaker from 2004 to 2009.

4   Smith, *India as a Secular* State, 281–288.

another, quite distinct and very contemporary argument, that the agenda was discriminatory because it violated the state's constitutional obligation to treat all religions equally. Chatterjee asked at the all-India convention, 'Why is this attempt to change the personal laws confined to Hindu society alone? Is this not communal legislation repugnant to the clear directive principle of the constitution that there should be a uniform civil code for all the citizens of India?' This aspect of the Hindu nationalist stance was echoed by other critics of a very different political persuasion. One such figure was Acharya J. B. Kripalani, the senior pre-independence Congress leader who had contested in 1950 to become Congress President with Nehru's tacit support and lost to a right-wing candidate sympathetic to Hindu nationalism. Kripalani had subsequently left the Congress and eventually joined the Praja Socialist Party (PSP), an opposition party formed by ex-Congress members with leftist leanings. Speaking in the Lok Sabha as a PSP parliamentarian, Kripalani said,

> I submit that we must not make laws for one community alone. Today the Hindu community is not as much prepared for divorce as the Muslim community is for monogamy ... Will our government introduce a bill for monogamy for the Muslim community? [Or] will my dear law minister apply the part about monogamy to every community in India? I tell you this is the [only] democratic way.

Kripalani reiterated the point to *The Hindu* newspaper,

> If they single out the Hindu community for their reforming zeal, they cannot escape the charge of being communalists in the sense that they favour the Hindu community and are indifferent to the good of the Muslim community or the Catholic community ... Do we want one community to be in advance of other communities in India, simply because it happens to be in the majority?

From two radically opposed sides of the Indian political spectrum, the Hindu nationalist and socialist critiques agreed on one point – that the authorities in charge of the secular state were violating its bedrock principle of impartiality.

The progressive critics also detected that in attempting to justify its position by claiming that the 'true' spirit and teachings of Hinduism were compatible with the proposed reforms, the government had introduced a substantively dubious and politically undesirable, potentially dangerous element into the debate, by implying and even asserting the innate superiority of Hinduism to allegedly more rigid and dogmatic faiths (primarily Islam, the second largest religion of India). Kripalani noted in the Lok Sabha, 'We call our state a secular state. A secular state goes by neither scripture nor custom. It must work on [ideological] grounds'. Another opposition MP elected from the far south of India (the present-day State of Tamil Nadu) criticized the Law Minister for inviting 'trouble' by 'bring[ing] in quotations from the Vedas', for which 'there was no necessity'. This lawmaker pointed out that while selective passages of the *Bhagavad Gita* might support the reformist argument, the very first chapter of this religious text advocates against inter-caste marriage.[5]

Nehru's government was pressed in parliament on why it was concentrating on Hindus instead of seeking to realize the 'directive principle of state policy' clearly stated in Article 44 of the Constitution, 'The state shall endeavour to secure for the citizens a uniform civil code throughout the territory of India'. Law Minister Pataskar replied that because the new Hindu code would apply to nearly 85 per cent of citizens, it represented a big step towards uniformity. During a parliamentary debate in 1954, Prime Minister Nehru responded thus to a member concerned about the government's approach,

> Well, I should like a civil code that applies to everybody, but … wisdom hinders … The honourable member is perfectly entitled to his view. If he or anybody else brings forward a Civil Code Bill, it will have my extreme sympathy. But I confess I do not think that at the present moment the time is ripe in India for me to try to push it through. I want to prepare the ground for it and this kind of thing [the new Hindu code in the making] is one method of preparing the ground.[6]

Nehru was Prime Minister for another full decade after he made this statement. Subsequent to his death in office in mid-1964, the Congress ruled India as its dominant party for another quarter-century, until the end of 1989 (except March 1977–December 1979). For 21 of those 25 years his daughter Indira and then her elder son Rajiv held the prime ministership, for sixteen and five years respectively. No initiative was taken by Congress governments over this period of more than three decades to realize a uniform civil code

---

5   Ibid., 286–288.
6   Ibid., 290.

for all Indians which, the nation's supreme court noted in 2015, 'remains an unaddressed constitutional expectation'. Prior to that, the Supreme Court had observed in 1995 that 'when 80 per cent of citizens have been brought under codified personal law [since the mid-1950s], there is no justification whatever for keeping in abeyance any more the introduction of an Uniform Civil Code for all citizens of India', a view it repeated in 2003.[7]

Meanwhile, ever since the 1950s, the violation of the impartiality principle became a prime plank of the Hindu nationalist attack on the Congress-run dispensation as 'pseudo-secular', guilty in particular of 'appeasement' of India's largest religious minority; these terms are a staple of Hindu nationalist discourse. Once the Hindu nationalists began their dramatic rise in Indian politics in the 1990s, the demand for a Uniform Civil Code or UCC featured as one of the three core points of their manifesto. Today the issue simmers dangerously as a movement against the habit of some Muslim men in India of divorcing wives through 'triple *talaq*', by simply uttering the word *talaq* thrice, a practice outlawed in numerous predominantly Muslim countries, emerged in the twenty-first century among some Indian Muslim women activists, with their cause receiving opportunist backing from the BJP. In late 2016, India's Law Commission, a central government body, initiated a public consultation exercise on the matter of the UCC and at the same time, the BJP-run government informed the Supreme Court that it opposed the legal right of Muslim men to polygamy and triple-*talaq* divorce because those rights violate the constitutional principle of gender equality. As the feminist scholars Brenda Cossman and Ratna Kapur wrote in 1996,

> there has been surprisingly little attention to the meaning of equality in the dominant vision of [Indian] secularism. The continuing silence ... has become a dangerous silence that the Hindu Right has been only too willing to exploit to claim the terrain of secularism as its own ... [by] bringing a very particular understanding of equality to the debate.[8]

---

7 'SC Bats for Single Moms, Uniform Civil Code, Says Keep Religion away from Law', *Times of India*, 7 July 2015.

8 Brenda Cossman and Ratna Kapur, 'Secularism Benchmarked by Hindu Right', in *Economic and Political Weekly* 38, no.21 (September 1996), 2622. See also Cossman and Kapur, *Secularism's Last Sigh? Hindutva and the Mis(Rule) of Law* (Delhi: Oxford University Press, 1999).

The Turkish civil code of 1926 had very similar provisions, and consequences, for women's status and rights as the Indian reforms three decades later. It prohibited polygamy, made the legality of marriage subject to a civil contract between the parties executed by a state official authorized to do so, made divorce obtainable only through a (secular) court of law with clear reasons given for the divorce plea and the participation of both parties in the proceedings, gave equal rights to women in inheritance and succession, and recognized a mother's equal rights in guardianship of children.[9] Unlike its Indian counterpart, the Turkish code escaped the partiality conundrum because it applied to the population at large and not to a confessionally defined sector of society.

The other major focus of the Indian secular state's regulatory-cum-reformist activism in the 1950s and 1960s was the administration of (privately-run) Hindu temples and shrines. The state's extensive interventions in this sphere included a particular emphasis on ensuring access for Dalits (or Harijans, 'people of God', the Gandhian term for 'untouchable' communities widely used until the 1990s) to such sites. This was consistent in general terms with Article 25 (2a) of the constitution, which empowered the state to regulate or restrict any activity associated with religious practice, and specifically with Article 25 (2b) which empowered the state to act in the interests of social welfare and reform and especially for 'the throwing open of Hindu religious institutions ... to all classes and sections of Hindus', as well as with Article 26, which made the right of any religious denomination or section thereof to manage its own affairs 'subject to public order, morality and health'. Further, the 1950 Constitution's Article 17 'abolished' untouchability and forbade 'its practice in any form'. This was followed in 1955 by the enactment of a nationwide Untouchability (Offences) Act by Parliament, which stipulated a prison sentence of up to six months and/or a fine for infractions of the constitutional prohibition. The legislation's 'punishment for enforcing religious disabilities' applied to 'whoever on grounds of "untouchability" prevents any person from catering [sic] to any place of public worship open to other persons professing the religion' and 'from worshipping or offering prayers or performing any religious service in any place of public worship ... in the same manner and to the same extent permissible to other persons professing the same religious denomination'. Geographically, the problem was most widespread in western and southern India, where the

9   Berkes, *The Development of Secularism in Turkey*, 472–473.

authorities of numerous Hindu temples and shrines barred 'untouchables' and social movements challenging the exclusion existed or were emerging.

The combating of curbs on entry into temples had been an integral part of the politics of unity and equality promoted by leaders of the Indian independence movement. In mid-1943 Subhas Chandra Bose, a top nationalist leader and two-time Congress President in the end-1930s whose vision and practice of secularism is discussed in Chapter 2, arrived in Southeast Asia after a three-month voyage by submarine from Europe and assumed the leadership of the anti-colonial Indian National Army (INA), formed with Japanese support principally from Indian soldiers and officers of the British army who had surrendered *en masse* on the Japanese capture of Singapore in early 1942. Bose's arrival in Southeast Asia touched off a wave of patriotic fervour among the large population of Indian origin across the Japanese-occupied territories of Southeast Asia. People flocked to the charismatic leader's rallies and the INA's numbers swelled from an influx of eager civilian volunteers. On the occasion of the autumnal Hindu festival of *Dussehra* which celebrates the triumph of good over evil and commemorates the deity Ram in north Indian society and the goddess Durga in Bengal (Bose's home region, where the day is known as *Vijaya Dashami*), Bose received an invitation to the main Chettiar temple in Singapore. The Chettiars were a small but wealthy community of south Indian (usually Tamil) origin specializing in mercantile activities and Bose's movement needed their financial support. Yet 'Netaji [Bose] brusquely refused the invitation, saying he would not step over the threshold of a place which even some Hindus, not to speak of other Indians, were not permitted to enter'. The notoriously dogmatic Chettiars then relented and Bose visited the temple accompanied by hundreds of INA officers and civilian colleagues of various caste origins and all religious backgrounds – Hindu, Muslim, Sikh and Christian. In his speech, Bose said,

> I have always denied that there is communalism [religious enmity] among the Indian masses, as asserted by the imperialists and some self-seeking Indians serving their cause. We are one [nation] whatever our individual religion. I congratulate the priests of this temple for giving us the opportunity to demonstrate that today.[10]

---

10  Abid Hasan, 'Netaji and the Indian Communal Question', 45. Hasan, one of Bose's closest associates in both wartime Europe and Southeast Asia, was an eyewitness to this

This spirit carried over into independent India and its secular state. Even prior to the proclamation of the Republic in January 1950, the government of the (then) province of Bombay had passed a temple-entry act in 1947. That prompted members of the Swaminarayan sect, a puritan order of Vaishnavite Hinduism founded in the early nineteenth century by followers of a preacher called Swaminarayan, to approach the judiciary in 1948 for exemption from the act. They apprehended that 'untouchables' would try to enter their temples pursuant to the passage of the legislation. The Swaminarayan order's devotees were mostly in the present-day State of Gujarat – Gandhi, Vallabhbhai Patel and Narendra Modi's region of origin – which was then part of the sprawling Bombay province, a colonial-era administrative unit (the order is still influential among some Gujaratis as well as their diaspora – Neasden, a suburb of north-west London, is well-known for its ornate Swaminarayan temple, inaugurated in 1995). After the Indian Constitution came into effect, the order's legal suit cited its freedom to manage its own affairs – a case of clutching at straws, since that freedom was subject to the state's jurisdictional oversight. Even more implausibly, the order claimed to be distinct from Hinduism, and therefore not covered by the Constitution's provisions on equal access to Hindu religious sites. The 1955 Untouchability (Offences) Act however specifically named the Swaminarayan *sampradaya* (community) as a Hindu sect. Then in 1956, the State of Bombay passed a supplementary law which clarified and strengthened its 1947 legislation. After a lengthy and convoluted legal process in lower courts, the Bombay High Court ruled in 1958 that the 1956 legislation was consistent with the Indian Constitution and applied to the order's temples. The order appealed the decision and the case was reviewed by India's Supreme Court in 1966.

The Supreme Court's judgment, written by the chief justice P. B. Gajendragadkar with the concurrence of four other judges, was scathing, even brutal. It said that the sect's twenty-year legal battle to protect its temples from polluting outcasts was 'founded on superstition, ignorance and complete misunderstanding of the true teachings of the Hindu religion' and indeed 'of the real significance of the tenets and philosophy taught by Swaminarayan himself'. In a lengthy exposition on the essence of Hinduism, the judgment exalted its polytheism and (purported) lack of dogma, and positively compared

---

and many other historic events.

these characteristics with the 'narrow ... features' of other world religions (which were not named). The judgment commented that the faith did have 'certain broad concepts which can be treated as basic' such as the acceptance of the ancient Vedas as the ultimate source of religious doctrine and philosophical wisdom, a cosmological view of the universe, and the realization that there are many gods and numerous paths to salvation. While celebrating Hinduism's apparently inherent diversity and elasticity, the judgment also waxed lyrical about its underlying unity, 'There is a kind of subtle, indescribable unity which keeps them [all Hindus] within the sweep of the broad and progressive Hindu religion'. The judgment concluded that given its uniqueness among the world's faiths, Hinduism 'may broadly be described as a way of life' rather than a religion like any other. In the court's view, the Swaminarayan order's conduct represented a disgraceful deviance from the 'true', 'real' and 'progressive' nature of Hinduism.

In a 1971 article, the scholar Marc Galanter noted 'the paradoxical character of the interventionist stance' exemplified by the Supreme Court's judgment. The judges set themselves up as the authoritative interpreters of the essence of Hinduism. Galanter asked, 'Is the Supreme Court a forum for promulgating official interpretations of Hinduism? Is it a Supreme Court of Hinduism? What equips judges to prescribe the nature and content of Hinduism?' He pointed out that since the Constitution's Articles 25 and 26, read in this instance together with Article 17, 'establish the primacy of public interests over religious claims and provide a wide scope for governmentally sponsored reforms', the Supreme Court simply needed 'to authorize state use of this power' in the Swaminarayan case. For that, 'it was necessary only to construe the scope of this power. It was not necessary to consider the nature of Hinduism *per se*'. But the court instead adopted an approach of 'active reformulation of Hinduism in the name of secularism and progress'. In doing so, the apex judiciary of the Indian secular state seemed to be flying 'the banner of "true" Hinduism' rather than that of "secular modernism".' Galanter warned that this 'use of religious justifications is not without danger[s]'.[11]

The warning was prescient. In 1966, the Indian secular state appeared secure. Three decades later, in 1995, as it faced a rapidly growing anti-secular

---

11 Marc Galanter, 'Hinduism, Secularism, and the Indian Judiciary', in *Secularism and its Critics*, ed. Bhargava, 268–293.

challenge represented by the rise of Hindu nationalism from the margins to the centre-stage of Indian politics, the Supreme Court delivered another landmark judgment to do with Hinduism. Drawing heavily on the 1966 judgment's view of Hinduism, this one read:

> No precise meaning can be ascribed to the terms 'Hindu', *'Hindutva'*, and 'Hinduism', and no meaning in the abstract can confine it to the narrow limits of religion alone, excluding the content of Indian culture and heritage ... The term *'Hindutva'* is related more to the way of life of the people in the subcontinent. It is difficult to appreciate how the term *'Hindutva'* or 'Hinduism' *per se* can be assumed to mean and be equated with narrow fundamentalist Hindu religious bigotry, or be construed to fall within the prohibition in sub-sections (3) and (3A) of Section 123 of the R.P. Act ... these terms are indicative more of a way of life of the Indian people.[12]

The judgment used very contorted reasoning to overturn the cancellation by the Bombay High Court of the election to the Assembly of Maharashtra State in western India of a senior leader of the Shiv Sena, a nativist regional party of Maharashtra allied to the BJP, who had declared in an election speech in Bombay's (now Mumbai) Shivaji Park in 1990 that 'the first Hindu State will be established in Maharashtra'. The Bombay High Court had viewed this as a breach of the prohibition on appeals to religion in election campaigning included under Section 123 of the Representation of the People (R.P.) Act of 1951, voided the result and cancelled his membership of the State legislature (exculpated by the Supreme Court, the politician served as Maharashtra's Chief Minister from 1995 to 1999). The author of the 1995 judgment, Justice J. S. Verma, was a highly regarded jurist who had been appointed to the Supreme Court in 1989. He retired in 1998 after a year as its chief justice and went on to serve in the early 2000s as the chairperson of the Government of India's National Human Rights Commission (NHRC) as an appointee of the 1999–2004 BJP-led coalition government in New Delhi.

The judgment's most obvious flaw was that it blithely conflated 'Hinduism', an ancient faith, with 'Hindutva', the political ideology of Hindu nationalism born in the mid-1920s. An essential distinction between the two, 'religion-

---

12 Gary J. Jacobsohn, *The Wheel of Law: India's Secularism in Comparative Constitutional Context* (Princeton and Oxford: Princeton University Press, 2003), 200–202.

as-faith' versus 'religion-as-ideology', has been made by the Indian scholar Ashis Nandy. While religion-as-faith is 'definitionally non-monolithic and operationally plural', religion-as-ideology seeks to 'homogenize co-believers into proper political formations' and represents a strategy of 'political mobilization' with the goal of capturing state power. Nandy argues that Hindu nationalism, far from being 'a retrogression into primitivism or a pathology of traditions', is in fact 'a by-product and pathology of modernity'.[13] Hindutva, the political ideology of Hindu nationalism born less than a century ago, is extensively discussed in Chapters 4 and 6 of this book, as well as in Chapter 7.

The 1995 Supreme Court judgment was greeted with jubilation by Hindu nationalists, ascendant in Indian politics (in May 1996, as narrated in Chapter 1, the BJP became India's single largest party for the first time following elections to the Lok Sabha). In December 1995, the RSS's English journal *Organiser* triumphantly declared that 'the Supreme Court has put its seal of judicial imprimatur on the Sangh ideology of Hindutva by stating that it is a way of life or state of mind and that it is not to be equated with religious fundamentalism'. Like Turkish Islamists, India's Hindu nationalists have always held theirs, and not the 'secular' version of the founding state elite, to be the authentic form of Indian nationalism. The BJP declared in 1999,

> Every effort to characterize Hindutva as a sectarian or exclusive idea has failed as the people of India have repeatedly rejected such a view, and the Supreme Court, too, finally endorsed the true meaning and content of Hindutva as being consistent with the true meaning and definition of secularism.[14]

The RSS office in Delhi published a celebratory booklet titled *Supreme Court Judgment on Hindutva: A Way of Life* in 1995, which went into its fourth printing in 2015.[15]

The American scholar Gary Jacobsohn has correctly noted that while Justice Verma's (untenable) conflation of 'Hinduism' and 'Hindutva' is the judgment's most obvious flaw, it is the 'benign depiction of *Hinduism* [emphasis in the original] as a way of life that has deeper implications for ...

---

13  Nandy, 'The Politics of Secularism and the Recovery of Religious Toleration', 321–344.

14  Jacobsohn, *The Wheel of Law*, 201, 203.

15  M. Rama Jois, ed., *Supreme Court Judgment on Hindutva: A Way of Life* (New Delhi: Suruchi Prakashan, 2015).

Indian secularism'. Verma told Jacobsohn that 'secularism in the constitution is merely a reaffirmation and continuance of this … Indian way of life' and 'the aim of the constitution is the same as the aim of Indian society from time immemorial'.[16] This view was directly derived and indeed quoted from the view of Hinduism expressed in the 1966 Supreme Court judgment. Starting from this basis, the 1995 judgment went on to conflate Hinduism with Hindutva and both with 'the way of life of the Indian people'.

◆

This raises the vital question of whether the Indian concept of state-secularism – the equal status and treatment of all religious faiths – has been based ever since the inception of the secular state after independence on the virtue of tolerance said to be inherent in the nation's majority faith, rather than on a genuinely neutral view of all religions found in India. In other words, has the secular Indian Republic always been a soft Hindu state, rather than a religiously impartial state in the true sense of the term? On 16 January 1999, with the BJP in power in New Delhi at the head of a coalition government, the Congress Working Committee (CWC), the highest committee of the founding party of India's secular state, adopted a resolution which stated that it was a 'basic truth' that 'Hinduism is the most effective guarantor of secularism in India'. The resolution strongly endorsed a speech made a few days earlier, 12 January, the birth anniversary of the philosopher and social reformer Swami Vivekananda (1863–1902), by Sonia Gandhi, the party's President since early 1998. In the speech Sonia Gandhi, Indira Gandhi's daughter-in-law and the Italian-born widow of Rajiv Gandhi, had said, 'India is secular primarily because Hinduism, both as a philosophy and as a way of life, has been based on what our ancients said: *ekam satyam, vipraha bahudha vadanti* [Sanskrit: "truth is one, the wise pursue it variously"]'. The speech went on to accuse the Hindu nationalists of 'spreading the politics of hate and antagonism, of rejecting the secular foundations of our ancient civilization, and of distorting the very message of Hinduism—tolerance, harmony and understanding of different faiths'. She also accused them of trying to appropriate Vivekananda, whose teachings have in fact been a point of reference for both secular Indian

---

16 Jacobsohn, *The Wheel of Law*, 202, 207.

nationalists and Hindu nationalists, past and present – the radically secular Subhas Chandra Bose was much inspired by Vivekananda, but Narendra Modi also cites the Swami as an inspiration. A BJP vice-president responded to the Congress's resolution as follows:

> The resolution has correctly stated that 'Hinduism is the most effective guarantor of secularism in India' ... for the Congress, secularism has been a matter of electoral expediency. Its so-called secularism, essentially targeted against the majority community, has always been mortgaged to vote-bank politics [a reference to the Hindu nationalist allegation of Congress's chronic 'appeasement' of Muslims in return for their votes] ... The BJP hopes the CWC resolution marks a genuine change of heart.[17]

The notion that the Indian secular state is the institutional embodiment of Hinduism's ethos of tolerance of other religions has in fact been a staple of state-secularist discourse since the Nehru era. On 31 January and 1 February 1966, All-India Radio broadcast nationwide a two-part talk on 'Secularism in India'. The speaker was M. C. Setalvad, who had served from 1950 to 1963 as the Nehru governments' Attorney-General, the state's top legal officer. Setalvad's talk was that year's Sardar Patel Memorial Lecture, in honour of the Congress leader and India's first Deputy Prime Minister/Home (interior) Minister who passed away in end-1950 (and like Setalvad, was Gujarati). The full text of the lecture was subsequently released as a booklet titled 'Secularism' for nationwide dissemination in 1967 by the publications division of the Government of India's Ministry of Information and Broadcasting. Setalvad said,

> The Hindu view of life necessarily makes for toleration ... [this is] highlighted in the history of India, which has for centuries permitted communities of Jains and Buddhists, Jews, Christians and Zoroastrians to live in India unmolested. Indeed for hundreds of years [?] before Muslims invaded India in the eleventh century, numerous Muslims had lived peacefully in the country. Unlike Buddhism and Islam, Hinduism has not been a missionary religion. The Hindu State [sic] never attempted to

---

17 Ibid., 201–202. The episode is also discussed in Rasheed Kidwai, *24 Akbar Road: A Short History of the People Behind the Fall and Rise of the Congress* (Delhi: Hachette India, 2013). The full text of the BJP's response can be found on the website of the Hindu Vivek Kendra, self-described as 'a resource centre for the promotion of Hindutva'.

impose a particular religion upon its people. Various creeds were permitted to practise and even propagate their faiths, build their places of worship and live in their own way. Thus ancient India could well be said to have a tradition of secularism ... the essential spirit of Indian culture is Hindu.

Setalvad's views on the subcontinent's other great religious tradition during the second millennium CE are equally instructive:

Islam, the religion of over 10 per cent of the population of India, is based on a totally different philosophy. It approaches with intensity the mission of establishing a divinely revealed religion and social order. The very existence of religions other than Islam would seem to be forbidden by it.

Setalvad could have been queried on how the Indian subcontinent remained a solidly Hindu-majority society, and with a multiplicity of other faiths, after nearly a millennium of Muslim rulerships. He could also have been asked how the Sunni Muslim Ottoman Empire tolerated religious diversity, even institutionalizing that policy through the *millet* system which granted confessional and cultural autonomy to non-Muslim communities.[18]

The binary distinction between tolerant Hinduism and intolerant Islam has always been a core feature of Hindu nationalist discourse. But it has also recurrently appeared in state-secularist discourse, sometimes in an implicit form (as in Sonia Gandhi's 1999 statement) and at other times explicitly, as in M. C. Setalvad's narrative of Indian history. To Indian Muslims this is obviously troubling, for two reasons. First, it effectively demeans their religion as inferior to that of India's majority faith. Second, it suggests that the Indian secular state has perhaps been a soft-Hindu state in which Muslims have been tolerated on the sufferance of the majority.

The Indian state has in fact shown partiality towards certain agendas pushed by orthodox Hindus since the Nehru era. In the Constituent Assembly (1947–49) a demand was raised, by some Congress members as well as others, that a total, nationwide ban on the slaughter of cows, sacred in Hindu orthodoxy, be incorporated in the Constitution. Nehru and Ambedkar eventually gave in, but did ensure that a religious justification was not cited

---

18 M. C. Setalvad, 'Secularism in India', in *Aspects of Democratic Government and Politics in India*, eds. K. R. Bombwall and L. P. Choudhry (Delhi: Atma Ram & Sons, 1968), 39–63.

for the protection of cows. Thus a 'Directive Principle of State Policy' (as for the UCC, Article 44) was incorporated as Article 48 of the Constitution: 'The state shall endeavour to organise agriculture and animal husbandry on modern and scientific lines and shall, in particular, take steps for preserving and improving the breeds, and prohibiting the slaughter, of cows and calves and other milch and draught cattle'.

This partial victory, and the dry scientific rationale cited for it, did not satisfy the champions of the cause of the holy cow. In 1955, an Indian Cattle Preservation Bill was tabled in parliament. It was rejected by a wide margin when put to vote, although most Congress members absented themselves and a few actively defied their party whip and voted in favour of the bill along with the handful of Hindu nationalist MPs. But the Nehru government's victory in parliament proved pyrrhic. The same year, the Congress government of the giant northern State of Uttar Pradesh appointed an expert committee to enquire into cow welfare. The committee's report described the cow issue as 'the biggest that confronts the nation' and recommended a blanket ban on the slaughter of cows and calves. The recommendation was passed into law amid acclaim in a joint session of the two chambers of the State legislature (where the Congress held a commanding majority). Following the example of Uttar Pradesh, identical laws were rapidly enacted by the Congress governments of other north Indian States – Bihar, Madhya Pradesh and Rajasthan—and cow slaughter became illegal across northern India.

Mahatma Gandhi, who had before his death by assassination a decade earlier so strongly opposed the demand for banning cow slaughter based on his own religious and political perspective (as described towards the end of Chapter 2), would have been horrified. Some disaffected Muslims went to court to challenge the ban. The legal recourse did not work. In one case, M. H. Qureshi v/s the State of Bihar, which came before the Supreme Court in 1958, the plaintiffs claimed that the law infringed both their freedom of religion guaranteed under Article 25 of the Constitution (citing the custom of sacrificing a cow in the religious celebration of *Bakr-Eid*) and their right as persons engaged in the butcher trade to carry on an occupation, trade or business guaranteed under Article 19. The apex judiciary of the secular state rejected their complaint and upheld the law. The judgment quoted the Koran and other Islamic texts to argue that sacrificing a cow was not essential, as a goat or even a camel would suffice, and that while the law did restrict occupational freedom there was no bar on the slaughter of bulls and buffaloes in addition to sheep and goats. The Supreme Court ruled the restriction 'reasonable' citing the 'sentiment' of Hindus on the issue.

Donald Smith's otherwise highly sympathetic account of the Indian experiment in secularism asserts that the State laws, reinforced by the judicial verdict, 'must be viewed primarily as attempts to impose the taboos of one religion on all citizens' including Muslims and Christians, and as 'certainly contrary to the spirit of the secular state'.[19] In fact, the taboo on eating beef does not apply uniformly across the 79.8 per cent of the population classified in the census (2011) as Hindus. The consumption of beef is prevalent in many Adivasi (tribal) and Dalit communities, and also among some caste-Hindus who do not subscribe to religious orthodoxy. Nonetheless, six decades after the proscriptions on cow slaughter came into effect, the issue, like the matter of the UCC, is still a flashpoint. In 2015, a middle-aged Muslim man in a village in western Uttar Pradesh, not far from the national capital Delhi, was lynched in his own home by a mob of locals on suspicion of storing beef in his refrigerator; the victim's son was seriously injured in the attack but survived. In 2016, a few young Dalit men of a very poor background were stripped and beaten in public in Gujarat, Prime Minister Narendra Modi's home State, by a vigilante band of *gau-rakshak*s (cow-protectors), ostensibly for skinning the hide of a deceased cow for sale as part of their efforts to earn a livelihood. Since the BJP government's ascension to office in New Delhi in mid-2014 such activity by vigilante groups, almost always targeting Muslim individuals and communities, has been occurring in several BJP-ruled States including Haryana, Jharkhand and Rajasthan.

Prime Minister Modi's criticism of the Uttar Pradesh incident in which the Muslim, Mohammad Akhlaq, was killed was belated and tepid. By contrast, he promptly and strongly condemned the violence against Dalits in his home State. Yet vigilante violence in the name of the cow continued unabated. In 2017, Rajasthan emerged as a leading laboratory of this form of Hindutva politics. In April 2017, five Muslim men who were transporting a few milch cows (and calves) they had purchased, in a perfectly legal transaction, at a cattle fair in Rajasthan's capital, Jaipur, to their village in Haryana in two

---

19  Smith, *India as a Secular State*, 489.

pick-up trucks were intercepted on a national highway by a *gau-rakshak* gang numbering in the dozens. The gang allowed one pick-up's driver, a Hindu, to leave and then set upon the Muslims, beating and kicking them. The brutal assault left all the victims injured; one, Pehlu Khan, in his mid-fifties, subsequently died of his injuries in hospital. A dairy farmer, he supplied milk for a living. It was a clear case of public lynching.[20] A fortnight before this lethal incident in Rajasthan, a Muslim-owned hotel in Jaipur was attacked by a mob after spurious rumours that beef was being cooked there. The police arrived and instead of acting against the perpetrators, closed down the hotel. Forensic tests on samples of seized meat found them to be chicken, but two months after the attack the hotel had still not been allowed to re-open despite its owner obtaining an order to that effect from a local court. Meanwhile, cow vigilantism spread to the sensitive, Muslim-majority northern State of Jammu and Kashmir. In April 2017, a Muslim family belonging to a community of nomadic pastoralists (*Bakerwals*) were set upon and assaulted by a gang in the State's multi-religious Jammu region while travelling with their herd of livestock to summer pastures. A girl aged nine was among several people badly injured in the attack.

As Smith noted more than fifty years ago, 'for some' the cow issue is not simply a matter of religious belief but a means of asserting 'Hindu dominance',[21] and it continues to feature prominently in the repertoire of issues of the early twenty-first century Hindu nationalist movement. The current RSS *sarsanghchalak* (supreme chief), Mohan Bhagwat (b. 1950), is an expert on cow-related matters. In March 2017, he was awarded an honorary doctorate by a university in Nagpur – the city in the western State of Maharashtra where the RSS was founded in 1925 and where its national headquarters is located – for research on the cow, including the therapeutic effects of consuming moderate amounts of cow urine on human ailments such as kidney disease and joint pains. Prime Minister Modi attended the conferral ceremony. In April 2017, Bhagwat called for a national law banning cow slaughter during a speech in New Delhi. The fact that cow slaughter has for decades been illegal in the majority of India's States – the notable exceptions being West

---

20 'Five Men Assaulted by Gau-rakshaks in Alwar, One Dead', *The Indian Express*, 5 April, 2017, 1.

21 Smith, *India as a Secular State*, 489.

Bengal in the east, Kerala in the south, and a few small States in the north-eastern border region which have large Christian populations – clearly does not suffice for the RSS.

The early proclivity of the Indian secular state to show partiality towards certain kinds of agendas and demands typically raised by Hindu nationalist groups became a character trait of the state during the 1980s, and a serious problem for India's largest religious minority. During that decade the ostensibly secular, Congress governments led by Nehru's daughter Indira Gandhi (from 1980 to 1984) and then her son Rajiv Gandhi (1984–89) pursued a slippery-slope strategy, aimed at electoral gain, of pandering to and even actively promoting majoritarian Hindu politics. Rajiv Gandhi, inept and blundering compared to his cynical but politically-skilled mother, stirred the cauldron further by a capitulation to the demands of Muslim conservative elements on the rights of Muslim women, which lent traction to the perennial Hindu nationalist claim that Congress-style 'pseudo-secularism' was nothing more than 'appeasement' of Muslims with the purpose of getting their votes in elections ('vote-bank politics' in the Hindu nationalist vocabulary). Through the 1980s and into the early 1990s, India saw a steady rise in Hindu–Muslim tensions and escalating 'communal riots' – major incidences of Hindu–Muslim violence, in which Muslim communities were hit hardest due to the usual complicity of the local police and bureaucracy with the other side, especially in Uttar Pradesh but also in other large, populous States like Bihar in the north and Maharashtra in the west. The spiral culminated in an orgy of communal violence in 1992–93, by which time the Hindu nationalists had decisively emerged from marginality to become the principal opposition in Indian politics and were well on the way to winning state power. The contradictions and anomalies of the Indian secular state had, nearly, come full circle.

All that and more is discussed in Chapter 4. A quarter-century on, in the era of Narendra Modi's premiership, Hindu nationalist politics has assumed a distinctly twenty-first century articulation which may be described as *Hindutva 2.0*: a relatively more sophisticated and potentially more effective version of the brute majoritarianism of the first half of the 1990s. Yet, while twenty-first century Hindu nationalism has evolved since the 1950s into a comparatively more modulated, adaptable and in some ways, even apparently 'progressive' form, to keep in step with India's social and political evolutions as a country, its basic character remains as before. The debates over 'intolerance' and 'nationalism' which animate educated middle-class citizens in India today reflect the divide between those who see themselves as secularists and those who do not. Caught in the middle, India's Muslim citizens have proved to be the only segment of the Indian population immune to the charismatic aura of the Modi premiership. They vote in elections overwhelmingly for the party or parties, mostly regional (State-specific) parties, which present the strongest competition to the BJP in their geographical location. They probably don't have a choice anyway. None of the BJP's 282 Lok Sabha MPs is Muslim, whereas one of every seven Indians is Muslim. In elections to constitute the State legislature and government of Uttar Pradesh in early 2017, the BJP contested 380 of the 403 single-member constituencies, leaving the rest to minor allied parties. None of its 380 candidates was Muslim, although UP's population of 210 million is 19 per cent Muslim. By comparison, the two major regional parties of UP, the Samajwadi Party (Socialist Party, SP) and the Bahujan Samaj Party (Party of the Social Majority, BSP) had candidate lists that were respectively 21 per cent and 24 per cent Muslim.

♦

In Turkey, the heyday of state-enforced secularism lasted a quarter-century, from the mid-1920s until the end of the 1940s. In a landmark national election in 1950 the CHP, the founding party of the Republic, was defeated by the Democrat Party (DP), which had been established in early 1946 by several high-profile CHP leaders who broke away from the CHP. The DP's victory in Turkey's first genuinely competitive election in 1950 brought single-party rule to an end and ushered in a two-party system. Until Turkey's first military coup in 1960, the country was governed by the DP, which defeated the CHP in two further elections in 1954 and 1957. Adnan Menderes, the DP's charismatic leader, served as Prime Minister from 1950 to 1960. The DP's mass base lay predominantly in rural Turkey, among the nation's peasant majority, and the party's rise and consolidation represented a popular pushback against the bureaucratic, Ankara-centred regime of the CHP.

As a party founded and led by a breakaway group of senior CHP politicians, the DP largely agreed with, and preserved, the secular basis of the Kemalist state. But its rise to power, and its victory in three consecutive elections – it polled 53 per cent, 57 per cent and 48 per cent respectively of the nationwide votes in 1950, 1954 and 1957, compared to 40 per cent, 35 per cent and 41 per cent for the CHP (with consistently high turnouts, for example, 89 per cent of the eligible electorate in 1950) – reflected not just a general fatigue with one-party authoritarianism but also a reaction among Turkey's traditionally pious and Sunni peasant majority against the draconian state-secularism of the CHP era. So the new ruling party rolled back a few of the most unpopular edicts of Kemalist secularism; for example, the very first legislation of the DP government upon assuming office in 1950 was to reinstate the Arabic *ezan* (call to prayer) instead of a Turkish version compulsory since 1933. As a symbolic gesture, the law was passed by the Grand National Assembly where the DP held a huge majority, 396 of the 487 seats, on the eve of the commencement of the holy month of Ramazan. In the 1930s and 1940s, 'mosque attendance dropped off sharply in cities. Many mosques were deserted and not maintained'.[22] During the 1950s, public religiosity returned with a vengeance. An American scholar reported in the mid-1950s,

> Old and new mosques are being used regularly, even in the new residential quarters of Ankara, where none existed five years ago but where over a dozen have been put up or are under construction now. From the [northern] Black Sea coast near Samsun to Antalya on the Mediterranean [in the south], from Thrace and Istanbul [in the west] to the eastern cities of Erzurum and Diyarbakir, in fair weather and foul, overflow crowds of worshippers jam mosques, courtyards and even adjacent squares and streets for the Friday prayers.[23]

Alongside the resurgence of mosque attendance, the tradition of folk Islam popularized by Anatolian mystics since the thirteenth century also reappeared in public. In December 1954, on the death anniversary of Mevlana Rumi (d. 1273), a commemoration of the Sufi saint was held at his tomb-cum-mausoleum in the west-central Anatolian city of Konya for the first time since the shrine's forced closure in 1925. The whirling dervishes, banned since 1925, appeared in their robes and conical hats not just in the Konya shrine

---

22  Yalman, 'Islamic Reform and the Mystic Tradition in Eastern Turkey', 47.
23  Reed, 'The Religious Life of Modern Turkish Muslims', 115.

but also in parallel celebrations in Istanbul, Ankara and other major cities. In some provincial towns, reading circles devoted to studying the works of the Islamic thinker Said Nursi (1876–1960), who was hounded by the secular state's authorities during the latter half of his life, came out into the open.

Of course, mass religiosity, and public manifestations thereof, are not necessarily incompatible with a secular state. If so, India could never have been a secular state. But in the case of Turkey, the public revival of religiosity in the 1950s, after a quarter-century of repression, signalled the beginning of a long and tortuous trajectory that culminated in the decisive rise of anti-secularist forces to the helm of the secular state a half-century later.

A striking fact of this trajectory is its extreme instability. In less than forty years, there were no fewer than four military interventions – two outright coups in 1960 and 1980 (of which the second coup was violently repressive) and two less direct but no less purposeful interventions in 1971 and 1997. A period of relative political liberalization under the military's watchful eye in the 1960s was followed by a turbulent decade in the 1970s, as coalition governments came and went in a revolving-door fashion (quite extraordinarily, Turkey had 65 cabinets between the Republic's formation in 1923 and 2016, which means that governments were reconstituted every 1.4 years on average). By the end of the 1970s, street violence between radical leftist and far-right nationalist groups reached grave proportions in Turkey's cities and towns, much like Germany in the early 1930s, and the economy – chronically weak and sometimes precarious almost throughout the Republic's existence – went into a tailspin similar to the meltdown of 2001. The competitive party system was gradually restored after 1983, but the civilian polity remained weakly institutionalized and ultimately subordinate to the military's supervision and diktats. In the meantime, a Kurdish nationalist insurgency against the state that began in 1984 gradually intensified and spread across the predominantly Kurdish eastern and south-eastern parts of the country. By the end-1980s the conflict reached civil war proportions and peaked during the first half of the 1990s, with thousands killed and hundreds of thousands of rural Kurds forcibly displaced, their villages razed, by army operations. The conflict militarily died down by 1999 with the insurgency largely exhausted, by which time around 40,000 guerrillas, civilians, soldiers and police had been killed. Apart from the human toll, the conflict led to about a dozen provinces being governed under emergency regulations (effectively martial law) from 1989, and the stifling of dissent and rights of free speech across the country. This further retarded the weak prospects of democratization in Turkey. Mustafa Kemal's Republic evolved by the end of the century into a profoundly troubled country polarized between secularists and Islamists, leftists and rightists, Turks and Kurds, and Sunnis and Alevis, the cleavages intersecting with each other in complex patterns. It also evolved into a country deeply divided on the sources of its basic identity, and thoroughly unsure and insecure about its place (if any) in the wider world. The seeds of long-term dysfunctionality of state and society had been sown during the formative period, when authoritarian Kemalism was the unchallengeable ideology.

The model of the Turkish secular state which tightly controlled and comprehensively regulated the religious sphere also had consequences over time, surely unforeseen by the Kemalist founders, for the prospects of secularism in Turkey. Once the authoritarian enforcement of Kemalist secularism weakened from the early 1950s onwards, the framework of state *control* of religion paradoxically evolved, by the 1970s, into one of state *sponsorship* of religion – in the Sunni (and mostly Hanefi) variant of the country's majority of ethnic Turks. The *Diyanet* or Directorate-General of Religious Affairs, established in 1924 with vast powers over the religious domain and attached to the office of the Prime Minister, its head to be appointed by the President of the Republic on the recommendation of the Prime Minister, became by the 1970s a vehicle for the promotion of this majority version of the Islamic faith. Serif Mardin observed in 1977 that 'clerical personnel in the higher reaches of the General Directorate of Religious Affairs' saw their role 'as a golden opportunity to establish solid foundations for *Sunni* Islam on a national scale' (emphasis in the original).[24] Nur Yalman had noted a paradox in 1969:

> [An] effect of the [state's] anti-*tarikat* policy has been to give renewed power and opportunity to orthodoxy ... The Sunni practitioners of religion [of the Ottoman era] have been officially reinstated as a State department [the Diyanet] ... but the opportunity to challenge their views, which had always been one of the theological roles of the [banned]

---

24  Serif Mardin, 'Religion in Modern Turkey', *International Social Science Journal* 29, no.2 (1977): 280.

Sufi orders, has been lost. The result has been an increasing rigidity in the teaching and practice of Sunnism, precisely the opposite of what had been intended.[25]

Lutfi Dogan, the man who headed the *Diyanet* from 1968 to 1971, was one of the core group mobilized in the late 1960s by Mehmet Zahid Kotku, the Naqshbandi sheikh of Istanbul, to launch the nation's first explicitly Islamist political party (from which Erdogan's AKP, the Justice and Development Party, is descended). Mardin has observed that although 'the Naqshbandi are usually described as a Sufi order', the brotherhood and its offshoots in fact stand for and propagate a formalist version of Sunni Islam based on 'strict observance of the divine law and the normative example of the Prophet'. The modern Turkish form of the Naqshbandi sect has among other major influences the Indian Naqshbandi tradition developed by Ahmad Faruqi al-Sirhindi (1563–1624), who sought

> to combat the religious eclecticism of the Mughal emperor, Akbar. Sirhindi felt that Akbar's tolerance of Indian civilization and religion was sweeping away the distinct characteristics of Islam, duping Muslims into becoming idol-worshippers and destroying the central Muslim belief in the unicity of God.

Akbar, the Mughal monarch of India from 1556 to 1605, indeed went to the extent of starting a short-lived court religion called *Din-i-Ilahi* which propounded a syncretistic merger of Hinduism and Islam. Sirhindi countered this imperial idiosyncrasy with a *mujaddedi* (revivalist) response intended 'to revive the straight path of prophetic guidance' and 'establish the reign of Sunni morality'; he also opposed Sufi mysticism. Kotku (1897–1980), or Zahid Efendi as he was respectfully addressed and referred to by his numerous admirers, 'witnessed the closing of religious orders in 1925, in his youth' and in 1952 became the head of the clandestine Naqshbandi community in Istanbul.[26] His dream and mission, as noted in Chapter 1, was 'the restoration of the Ottoman-Islamic identity' he believed to constitute the core identity

---

25 Yalman, 'Islamic Reform and the Mystic Tradition in Eastern Turkey', 59.

26 Serif Mardin, 'The Naqshbandi Order in Turkish History', in *Islam in Modern Turkey: Religion, Politics and Literature in a Secular State*, ed. Richard Tapper (London and New York: IB Tauris, 1991), 121–142.

(*kimlik*) and moral character (*kisilik*) of the Turkish nation, which he felt had been deeply wounded by state-secularism, and the establishment of a political order based on 'an Islamic sense of justice'.[27] In addition to inspiring the formation of Turkey's first overtly Islamist party in January 1970 led by Necmettin Erbakan, who was to briefly become Prime Minister in 1996–97 after serving as a Deputy Prime Minister in 1970s coalition governments, Zahid Efendi also encouraged his followers to establish a daily newspaper, *Sabah*, launched in 1968 to promote this alternative conception of the Turkish nation and state.

Kotku would surely have been thrilled had he lived to see Turkey's military-dominated regime in the 1980s propagate a 'Turkish-Islamic Synthesis' as the ideological framework best suited to unite an increasingly fractured and fractious country. This was strange as the military hierarchy simultaneously presented themselves as the ultimate guardians of Kemalist secularism. The men in uniform combined this permissiveness towards Islam with ringing rhetoric of their unshakeable commitment to upholding Kemal's secular ideals as the basis of the state, and indeed implemented harsh 'secularist' measures such as enforcing the ban on women wearing headscarves in universities. Following the 1980 coup, the junta formed a Council of Higher Education (YOK) to tightly supervise the nation's universities, which had bred both leftist and rightist radicalism during the 1970s. The YOK started expelling headscarf-wearing students from 1982 onwards. The military's muddled policy of tolerating and even sanctioning Islam as part of a reformulated state/nation ideology (ostensibly to counter a much exaggerated threat of radical leftism to internal stability, Turkey being a NATO member-state and an American ally), uneasily combined with professions and practices of dogmatic secularism, is similar to the contradictory, double-edged politics and policies of India's avowedly secular Congress governments during the 1980s mentioned a little earlier in this chapter. This paradox of the secular state is discussed further in Chapters 4 and 5. In both countries, the accommodations made by the leaders of the secular state with anti-secular tendencies during the 1980s paved the way for the rise of such forces to the political centre-stage during the 1990s and beyond.

---

27  Yavuz, *Islamic Political Identity in Turkey*, 207.

◆

The creeping Islamization of the Turkish state that took off in the 1970s and picked up pace with the military-dominated regime's collusion in the 1980s had, like its Hindutva counterpart in India, a deeply ingrained majoritarian-nationalist thrust. This was about bringing back the Hanefi–Sunni identity of the country's ethnic Turk majority – most of Turkey's Kurds, usually estimated to be about 20 per cent of the population, are also Sunni but follow the Shafi school of jurisprudence – to the heart of the self-definition of Turkish nationalism. The *Diyanet*, set up by the original Kemalist secularists as a powerful watchdog to control and regulate the practice of religion, turned by the late twentieth century into a vehicle for the promotion of the majority faith. In 2005, a group of representatives of the country's main confessional minority, the heterodox Alevi community, complained to Prime Minister Erdogan that the *Diyanet* had, ever since its inception, recognized and financially supported only Sunni (and Hanefi) Islam, in contravention of the secular state's principle of impartial treatment of all denominational communities. Receiving no satisfactory response, they took the matter to court. In 2010 Turkey's constitutional court, the apex judiciary, rejected their complaint. They then approached the European Court of Human Rights, which sits in the city of Strasbourg in France. In 2016 the ECHR bench ruled by a majority of sixteen to one that the Alevis, due to being denied state recognition and funding, were indeed discriminated against by the Turkish state (as with Kurds, whose collective identity was denied to even exist in the Kemalist Republic, it is not precisely known what proportion of Turkey's population is Alevi, as they are not officially recognized as a distinct group and therefore not counted in censuses. Most estimates put Alevis at 15–20 per cent of the total population of 80 million; among the Alevis, the usual estimated ethnic breakdown is about 70 per cent Turks and about 30 per cent Kurds). Welcoming the ECHR verdict, an Alevi spokesman pointed out that

> everybody in Turkey pays taxes, but these taxes are only used for a part of the population, for instance for building [Sunni] mosques. If the *cemevi* [Alevi prayer halls] are not recognised as places of worship, of course that's unjust. Recognising them is the first step—then the Diyanet could support them as well.

Turkey currently has around 110,000 state-supported mosques. Another Alevi spokesman emphasized exactly how much the state exclusively supports the majority version of Islam:

> The Diyanet's budget in 2016 is two billion euros but they only serve the Sunni community in Turkey, not one euro goes to the Alevi community. If you add the 600 mid-level [religious, *imam-hatip*] schools, the university [theological] faculties, the media [dedicated to Sunni religion] and all the other projects with state support, this would be up to five billion euros annually.[28]

The validation of the Alevis' case by the ECHR was no more than a token victory, unenforceable in Turkey and simply ignored by the Turkish state. Another longstanding Alevi grievance is that the religious education classes compulsory in all Turkish schools teach only a standard Sunni version of the faith, with no reference whatsoever to any other tradition(s) of Islam. In the words of a typical Alevi parent of school-going children, in the state-approved textbook used for religious instruction across Turkey 'there is nothing about our beliefs ... from A-Z, nothing'.[29] These compulsory lessons were introduced by the military-dominated regime of the 1980s as part of the promotion of its 'Turkish–Islamic Synthesis' agenda. During the past ten or so years, Alevi parents have gone to court to get their children exempted from these classes and have won favourable judgments both in Turkey and at the ECHR. The rulings have been ignored by the Turkish state's Ministry of National Education. As for state recognition of *cemevis*, the prayer houses-cum-community centres where Alevis congregate across Turkey, Erdogan unequivocally ruled that out during a dinner with a small number of the community's leaders while campaigning to become Turkey's first President by direct, popular election in 2014. 'I don't see *cemevis* as places of worship', he said, underlining that for Muslims, worship could only be in a mosque. This stance was not surprising, as a survey had just shown 99 per cent of Erdogan/AKP voters to be Sunnis (and very largely Sunni Turks).[30]

---

28 'Turkey Discriminates against Alevi Faith, ECHR Rules', *Deutsche Welle*, 26 April 2016.

29 'Turkey Election: AKP Courts the Alevi Minority Vote', *BBC News Online*, 4 June 2011.

30 'Turkey's Alevi Minority Fear Future under Erdogan Presidency', *Financial Times*, 27

Erdogan won the August 2014 presidential election in the first round, as noted in Chapter 1, gaining an absolute majority (52 per cent) of the nationwide vote. In the parliamentary election of June 2015, his AKP did not nominate a single Alevi among its 550 candidates, much as Modi's BJP did not nominate a single Muslim among its 380 candidates for the crucially important Uttar Pradesh State election in early 2017 (and still won a massive four-fifths majority in the State's legislature with a strong plurality share, 40 per cent, of the vote). In the 2011–15 Turkish parliament, just one of the AKP's 327 deputies was Alevi. A Turkish commentator observed in mid-2015 that

> even taking into account traditional Alevi under-representation in Turkish politics, the AKP's rule since [late] 2002 represents a near-total Alevi marginalization that is unique in Turkey's modern history. There are no Alevis in the governing party's leadership or among the 26 cabinet ministers. More significantly, there are no Alevis among the 81 provincial governors, 81 provincial police chiefs, and 26 [cabinet] undersecretaries— all key bureaucratic positions filled by central government appointment ... The ongoing alienation has led many Alevis to oppose the AKP through street protests and demonstrations. For example, large numbers of them took part in the liberal Gezi Park movement of [summer] 2013, organizing rallies and establishing NGOs".[31]

In contrast to Turkey's rigidly unitary and highly centralized state structure, India's devolved, quasi-federal structure, in which non-BJP regional (State-specific) parties still govern numerous States, does not permit such exclusion of Muslims – although Muslims' share of public offices and socioeconomic opportunities is still far from proportionate in almost all States and nationally. Still, the parallels between the Erdogan regime's attitude to Turkey's Alevis and the Modi regime's attitude to India's Muslims are clearly evident. Both are regimes which subscribe to a concept of national identity built on a political ideology of religious majoritarianism. In this framework, the Muslim and Alevi minorities, who constitute a similar proportion of the population in the two countries have no place, except as the 'Other'. The anger and despair of Alevis was indeed manifested in their large-scale participation in the anti-

---

July 2014.

31  Soner Cagaptay, 'An Alevi Tide Headed for Turkey's Parliament', briefing of the Washington Institute for Near East Policy, 6 May 2015.

Erdogan street demonstrations which occurred in numerous Turkish cities in the summer of 2013, and almost all of the eleven people killed during the protests were Alevis.

Yet the nature and biases of the Erdogan regime have a long back-story in the nature and biases of the secular state established by Mustafa Kemal. In 1924 the Turkish Grand National Assembly adopted a citizenship law for the new Republic, which was incorporated into the Constitution as Article 88. Its principle was equal citizenship for all persons living in the country, a typically republican approach used from revolutionary France to independent India. Participating in the debate, Celal Nuri, a deputy representing Gallipoli (the place of World War I fame, Canakkale in Turkish), made a most penetrating and prescient comment. He stated that while he agreed with the ostensibly neutral, territorially-based concept of citizenship being proposed, it was universally known that the 'real' citizens of Turkey were Sunni Muslims of the Hanefi school who spoke Turkish.[32] Celal Nuri, incidentally, was among the most ardent secularists, Europeanists and Westernizers of the Kemalist group, and had been associated under Ottoman rule with the journal *Ijtihad*, a mouthpiece of that line. His candid statement foreshadowed not just substantive inequality but often acute discrimination and violent oppression in the Turkish Republic for the tiny non-Muslim minorities such as Greek Christians and Jews, non-Turkish speakers such as the large rural Kurdish population of eastern and south-eastern Anatolia, non-Hanefi Sunnis such as the Sunni Kurds who adhere to the Shafi school, and the non-Sunni heterodox community of Alevis, comprising of majority Turk and minority Kurd segments. The Turkish scholar Kemal Kirisci has shown that the Turkish state's immigration policy, a barometer of its *actual* as distinct from formal principles of citizenship, consistently 'reveals a striking preference for admitting immigrants of a Sunni and Hanefi religious background',[33] and mainly from Balkan countries such as Bosnia, Albania and Bulgaria, consistent with the state's Europhile orientation. This policy drew on a 'Law of Settlement' enacted in 1934, known as Law 2510. The contents and implications of Law 2510, which classified the Republic's population into

---

32 Kemal Kirisci, 'Disaggregating Turkish Citizenship and Immigration Practices', *Middle Eastern Studies* 36, no.3 (July 2000), 18.

33 Ibid., 3.

three categories and its territory into three regions, based on 'Turkishness' or lack thereof as perceived by the state, are markedly in contrast to the equal citizenship law of ten years earlier.

The institutionalized discrimination and *de facto* second-class status that Alevis complain about have thus been present for most and perhaps all of the Republic of Turkey's existence. Its chief symptoms – denial of state recognition and support, lopsided religious instruction in schools, gross under-representation in high politics and high administration – have simply grown more blatant since the rise to state power of Sunni Islamists after 2002. Yet in the eight decades prior to that rise, the Alevi presence in Turkish parliaments averaged between 3–5 per cent, a fraction of their proportion of the national population.[34] Howard Reed noted in the mid-1950s that while the Sunni-oriented festivals of *seker bayram* and *kurban bayram* (at the end of the Ramazan fasting month and the *hajj* pilgrimage period, respectively) were state holidays in Kemalist Turkey, the most important events in the Alevi calendar – the holy month of *Muharram* and the observance of *asure*, which commemorates the martyrdom of Hasan and Hussein, the sons of Imam Ali, the Prophet's nephew and son-in-law – were not. A community leader in the Alevi-populated district of Okmeydani in Istanbul said in 2011, 'Throughout the history of the Ottoman Empire, we suffered repression and massacres. After the Republic was established in 1923, we expected to get equal rights. But that didn't happen'.[35]

The Alevis' situation and dilemmas are starkly revealing of the paradoxes, contradictions and anomalies of the Turkish secular state. They were indeed ostracized and persecuted during the Ottoman centuries. In the early sixteenth century, the Ottoman ruler Selim 'the Grim' ordered mass killings of members of the sect as heretics. The naming of the third bridge across Istanbul's Bosphorus Strait, opened in August 2016, after this sultan by the Erdogan regime was seen by many Alevis as a calculated slight (the inauguration of this new bridge shortly followed the naming of the well-known 1970s bridge a few miles to its south as the '15 July Martyrs' Bridge', to commemorate the approximately 250 people who died during the failed coup against the Erdogan regime in July 2016). Partly as a result of their historical experience, the Alevis

---

34 Cagaptay, 'An Alevi Tide Headed for Turkey's Parliament'.
35 'Turkey Election: AKP Courts the Alevi Minority Vote'.

very largely remained withdrawn in their rural settlements in the deep interiors of Anatolia until the 1960s. Their main areas of traditional habitation are a swathe of central Anatolia extending into eastern Anatolia, where the ethnic Turk majority yields to a predominantly Kurdish population. In the 1970s large-scale rural-to-urban migration started, and gained increasing momentum over the next two decades. By the 1990s Turkey's cities were dotted with numerous *gecekondus* or shantytowns inhabited by these masses of migrants seeking jobs and improved lives. Large numbers of Alevis were part of this influx of peasant society into cities and towns, and distinctively Alevi neighbourhoods sprang up in Istanbul and other urban agglomerations. Alevis also constitute a significant minority of the Turkish diaspora in Europe.

The Alevis' eclectic form of faith diverges from Sunni orthodoxy in numerous ways. Alevism exalts Ali, the Prophet's nephew and son-in-law, as well as Ali's sons Hasan and Hussein. Praying five times daily is regarded as ritualistic and unnecessary. The main religious text is not the Koran but the *Buyruk*, which is said to have been written by Cafer, the sixth Imam of Shiism. Fasting, if at all, is during the month of Muharram rather than Ramazan. No particular importance is attached to the pilgrimage to Mecca. Mosques and mosque attendance are not part of the Alevi faith. Instead, a local Alevi community congregates in a colourfully decorated prayer house of distinct architectural design known as a *cemevi*, where the weekly day of congregation is Thursdays rather than Fridays. Both men and women attend, and there is no physical separation of the sexes as in mosques. Alevi women normally wear colourful headscarves during worship sessions, but in public they appear and live with their hair uncovered. Alevism regards the formal rules of Islam as the most superficial level of engagement with the religion. This level, referred to as *seriat*, is considered by them to be typical of most Sunnis, whereas most Alevis are said to be at the next higher level (*tarikat*), where they have acquired a degree of true spirituality beyond the rules and rituals. *Tarikat* is also the term for religious brotherhoods common among Turkish Sunnis but in the Alevi understanding, the term signifies something much deeper and more complex. The major devotional ritual of Alevism is an elaborate annual ceremony called the *cem*, traditionally conducted only by a *pir* or *dede* – learned elder, literally 'grandfather' – a man descended from a holy lineage (although the role and influence of these figures has steadily declined as more and more Alevis have left their rural roots). Both genders participate, the full version includes the sacrifice of a ram whose meat is eaten in a communal feast, and the ceremony ends with the *sema*, a slow collective dance performed jointly by men and women. The ceremony, and Alevi community life more generally, involves not just dance but poetry and minstrel music, all in Turkish, descended from the thirteenth-century folk poet Yunus Emre. Alevis do not have any prohibition on alcohol (or cigarettes); indeed, drinking and smoking are integral parts of bonding in the community. And Alevis have their own pantheon of saints. The central figure is the thirteenth-century mystic Haji Bektash Veli, who is said to be a descendant of Ali; Haji Bektash's shrine-cum-mausoleum in central Anatolia is a sacred place of pilgrimage for most Alevis. Another important figure is Pir Sultan Abdal, a sixteenth-century folk poet executed by the Ottomans, whose verses are sung with the *baglama* (or *saz*), a popular stringed instrument. By the 1990s, many urbanized, young Alevis began to define their identity as a culture – *Alevilik*, meaning 'Aleviness' or 'being Alevi' – rather than as a religious faith *per se*.

It is not surprising that numerous Sunni Turks of a traditionally pious disposition do not regard the Alevis as fellow-Muslims but as a deviant tendency. The social prejudice and stigma attached to them during the Ottoman centuries endured in the Kemalist Republic, often with crude sexual connotations. When the anthropologist Nur Yalman was conducting fieldwork in a Kurdish Alevi village in eastern Anatolia in the late 1960s, he occasionally visited the nearby town of Elazig. There he was 'often told that [he] should not live with the Alevi because they are dirty'. When he asked the (Sunni) owner of a coffeehouse to explain, he was informed, 'They are filthy; they do not wash themselves after sexual intercourse'.[36] This was a reference to the Koranic injunction that men must bathe from head to foot after intercourse to purify sexual pollution before doing their prayers. The Alevi villagers, living in a cold highland climate with a very limited supply of water, could not possibly do this even if they wanted to. In the early 1990s a British anthropologist happened to visit, with a male Alevi friend, the local chief of the Motherland Party (ANAP), a prominent right-of-centre party of the time, in a provincial town close to the Turkish Alevi village of central Anatolia where he was engaged in field research. In a room filled with favour-seeking supplicants, the petty official declared that there were no Turkish–

36  Yalman, 'Islamic Reform and the Mystic Tradition in Eastern Turkey', 53.

Kurdish divisions in Turkey, and that everyone was a 'Turk' (a standard Kemalist dogma). At the time, a war was intensifying between the forces of the Turkish state and the Kurdish nationalist insurgents of the Workers' Party of Kurdistan (PKK) across eastern and south-eastern Turkey. Then he said, 'But some people are Alevi. That is the real division [in Turkey]. Alevi women sleep with anyone, they are untrustworthy, isn't that so?'[37]

It is equally unsurprising that Alevis generally supported and indeed strongly identified with the secular state instituted by Mustafa Kemal. In 1925, Kurdish Alevi tribes in the Diyarbakir area of south-eastern Turkey helped government forces suppress a revolt against Kemal's regime which was led by a local Kurdish leader of the (Sunni) Naqshbandi order, Sheikh Said. This revolt was an important event in the formative period of the Republic and deepened the regime's authoritarianism. In the second half of the 1930s, the hammer-blow of Kemalist authoritarianism fell on Kurdish Alevi tribes in the area of Dersim (officially renamed as Tunceli) in eastern Turkey after some among them resisted intrusions by the central government on their turf. The rudimentary Turkish air force bombed the remote, mountainous area from the air, and the army perpetrated massacres of men, women and children on the ground. The massacres, and forced deportations of the survivors to other parts of Turkey, became a major reference point for the Kurdish nationalist revolt led by the PKK which developed from the 1980s. But these episodes of state terror did not undermine the identification of most Alevis, over two-thirds of whom are ethnic Turks and not Kurds, with the secular state. During the 1960s and 1970s, many young Alevis were attracted to leftist and radical-leftist political groups which emerged in Turkey.

During the same period, majoritarian Sunnism was making gradual but steady advances in the political sphere, encroaching on and eroding the secular state. Serif Mardin noted in 1977 that this was being seen by 'Shii-Alevis as a threat to their religious identity'.[38] Their fears soon came true, as violence between right-wing Turkish nationalist and radical-leftist groups – in which Alevis were disproportionately represented – escalated in the late 1970s. In end-1978 more than one hundred Alevis, both Turks and Kurds, were killed in a massacre by the 'Grey Wolves', a far-right youth group affiliated

---

37  Shankland, *The Alevis in Turkey*, 27–28.
38  Mardin, 'Religion in Modern Turkey', 280.

to the ultranationalist Nationalist Movement Party (MHP), in the south-central Anatolian town of Kahramanmaras. In mid-1980, another pogrom perpetrated by the Grey Wolves in the north-central town of Corum killed 57 ethnic-Turk Alevis. State complicity was widely suspected in these attacks, as the Grey Wolves were known to be deeply connected to elements of the police as well as parts of the military.

The military coup of September 1980 violently restored order and the pogroms ceased, but as the decade progressed the Alevis faced a new problem. Alevi villages in the Anatolian countryside experienced unwelcome visits from army officers, carrying instructions from the regional military command to forthwith build mosques.[39] This was a part of the 'Turkish–Islamic Synthesis' ideology, alluded to a few pages earlier, which was promoted by Turkey's military-dominated regime during the 1980s. The mosques were duly built, and stayed deserted, their state-appointed Sunni *imams* politely ignored by the villagers.

The decade of the Turkish–Islamic Synthesis paved the way for the meteoric growth of anti-secular forces in Turkish politics during the 1990s. The pogrom returned. In 1993, an Alevi cultural festival held in honour of Pir Sultan Abdal in the martyred sixteenth-century folk poet's hometown Sivas, in east-central Anatolia, was targeted by a mob. The venue of the festival, a hotel, was set on fire and three dozen attendees, among them many leading members of the Alevi intelligentsia, were burned to death. Once again, police complicity was strongly suspected. Alevi nerves were still raw from this traumatic incident when two years later, in 1995, gunmen riding a hijacked taxi opened fire on three cafes and a bakery in a working-class Alevi neighbourhood of Istanbul. The two dead included a community elder (*dede*), and several others were seriously injured. Angry protests broke out in this and other Alevi areas of Istanbul and spread to other cities including Ankara. For a few days, it seemed that Turkey was on the brink of being engulfed in large-scale violence between Sunnis and Alevis. The protests were suppressed by heavy-handed police action, which left two dozen Alevis dead. The Istanbul violence happened exactly a year after the Sunni–Islamist Welfare Party (RP), the predecessor of the AKP, won power in about 300 cities and towns across the country in municipal elections, including

---

39 David Shankland, *Islam and Society in Turkey* (Huntingdon, England: Eothen Press, 1999), 145.

both Istanbul and Ankara. The RP's top young leader, Recep Tayyip Erdogan, had taken charge as Istanbul's mayor in 1994. He did try to soothe Alevi anger and fear, by making statements such as 'if Alevi means being a follower of Ali, I too am Alevi'. But the verbal balm was not convincing to Alevis since Erdogan's administration also closed down one of Istanbul's biggest *cemevi*s.

Like India's Muslims, who too bore the brunt of steadily escalating violence through the 1980s and into the early 1990s, Turkey's Alevis have always preferred and continue to prefer the flawed secular state to the religious-majoritarian alternative. During the periods when Turkey has had a multiparty system, which is almost the entire time since 1950, Alevis have consistently voted for secularist parties of a nominally left-of-centre orientation, mostly the Kemalist CHP and at times for its offshoot and breakaway parties. Today the two main parties opposed to Erdogan's AKP, the CHP and the mainly Kurdish HDP (People's Democratic Party) have strong Alevi support, among Alevi Turks and Alevi Kurds respectively. Likewise, India's Muslims mostly voted for the Congress when that party dominated Indian politics, until the end-1980s, and a lesser but significant proportion for secularist opposition parties. Since that time, the Congress has gradually withered and is now on the brink of political extinction, and Muslims across India largely vote for secularist regional (State-specific) parties which oppose the BJP's Hindutva ideology. But just as there is substantial truth to the Hindu nationalist claim that the Congress used Muslims as a 'vote bank' while doing very little for their political representation or socioeconomic advancement, Sabahat Akkiraz, a popular female folk singer who was a CHP member of parliament from Istanbul from 2011 to 2015, pointed out in 2012 that although '75 per cent of Alevis tend to support her party in elections, the CHP's leadership has long taken them for granted, and few of its deputies are Alevi'.[40] There are distinct parallels between the situations of the largest confessional minorities of the two countries.

By the 1990s, the secular states of India and Turkey, burdened by their strikingly similar paradoxes, anomalies and contradictions examined in this chapter, had reached a crossroads. The stage was set for the anti-secularist ascendancy.

---

40 Cagaptay, 'An Alevi Tide Headed for Turkey's Parliament'. The CHP's leader since 2010, a colourless ex-bureaucrat called Kemal Kilicdaroglu, is an Alevi of Dersim/Tunceli origin.

4

# INDIA: THE ANTI-SECULARIST ASCENDANCY

> *The danger to India, mark you, is not Communism. It is Hindu right-wing communalism.*
>
> —Jawaharlal Nehru, Prime Minister of India,
> speaking to officers of the Indian Foreign Service in 1959[1]

A wintry day in December 1992 is etched in independent India's history. On 6 December 1992, a disused 464-year-old mosque was razed in northern India by thousands of Hindu nationalist militants in a frenzied assault which lasted several hours. After an initial wave of activists climbed on the mosque's parapets and domes and triumphantly raised saffron flags – saffron being the traditional colour associated with Hinduism – a vast mob from amongst the tens of thousands who had gathered close to the mosque for a show of strength used axes, hammers, grappling hooks and other implements to completely demolish the structure. They had clearly come thoroughly prepared to launch the attack. The site was the small but famous pilgrimage town of Ayodhya, located in the eastern part (*purvanchal*) of India's most populous State, Uttar Pradesh (Northern Province), which is a gigantic sprawl across the Indo–Gangetic plain.

According to ancient Hindu mythology, Ayodhya is the birthplace of the deity Lord Ram, a prince who is the central character of the Sanskrit epic known as the *Ramayana*; hence its holy status. The town's mosque was built in 1528 CE by a general of the army of Babur, a warrior of Turkic

---

1 Godbole, *Secularism*, 1.

Central Asian origins who in 1526 founded the subcontinent's Mughal Empire, which lasted for over three centuries until its formal liquidation by British colonial power in 1857. The zenith of Mughal power was from the late sixteenth century – the reign (1556–1605) of the dynasty's greatest monarch Akbar, who combined martial exploits with religious eclecticism, promoting a synthesis of Hinduism and Islam as his court religion – until the late seventeenth century. Thereafter the Empire gradually declined, and from the mid-eighteenth century onward the Mughal monarchy had a largely nominal existence, while the British gradually took over the subcontinent. Babur claimed descent from two previous founders of empires: the Mongol warrior Genghis Khan and the Turkic–Mongol warrior Timur ('the lame'). Babur wrote a detailed autobiography, the *Baburnama*, in a hybrid of his native Turkic dialect and Persian; this was published shortly after his death in 1530. Like Timur's empire, which was established in the late fourteenth century, the dynasty Babur founded in India was rooted in Persian culture and the Mughal Empire used Persian as its official and court language throughout its existence. Mughal rule also gave rise to a distinct spoken language, Urdu or Hindustani (Indian), a hybrid of Persian and Sanskrit which used the Arabic script (the word 'Urdu' is derived from *ordu*, the old Turkish word for 'army', reflecting the language's origins in the interactions of Mughal convoys with the population). This language survived the demise of the Mughal Empire and over time spawned a very rich literary tradition which endured into the twentieth century.

According to the Hindu nationalist narrative of the second half of the twentieth century and the early twenty-first century, Ayodhya's *Babri Masjid* (Babur's Mosque), built in 1528 and named in honour of the Mughal founder, was constructed on the exact birthplace of Lord Ram (*Ramjanambhoomi*) after demolishing a temple dedicated to the ancient deity which had existed on that site. The twin-claim that Lord Ram was born exactly in that spot and that a temple dedicated to him had existed there until the early sixteenth century is impossible to either verify or falsify.

The Ayodhya controversy has existed throughout India's existence as an independent country. In December 1949, the *mahant* or head priest of a Hindu *math* (shrine complex) in Gorakhpur, a sizeable town located in the same eastern region of Uttar Pradesh as Ayodhya, organized a devotional ceremony dedicated to Ram in the immediate vicinity of the Ayodhya mosque. The head priest, Digvijay Nath, was simultaneously a leading member of the Hindu Mahasabha (Great Hindu Forum), an organization which became a political party in 1937 with Vinayak Damodar (V. D.) Savarkar, the pioneer ideologue of Hindu nationalism as a political doctrine, as its President. N. C. Chatterjee, the Bengali Brahmin lawyer from Calcutta who passionately opposed the reform and codification of Hindu personal and family laws in the mid-1950s on the floor of India's parliament, as recounted in Chapter 3, was elected to the Lok Sabha from the eastern Indian State of West Bengal on this party's ticket in India's first general election in 1952. Mahant Digvijay Nath, too, enjoyed a reasonably successful political career, and was elected to the Lok Sabha from the Gorakhpur parliamentary constituency in 1967. The 1949 ceremony at *Ramjanambhoomi* he organized involved the chanting of prayers and hymns for over a week, during which unknown persons, probably participants, sneaked into the mosque and placed idols of Ram lala (Ram as a child) and his consort Sita inside the Babri Masjid. Rumours were then spread that a miracle had happened and Ram had reappeared in his birthplace. To prevent a deluge of pilgrims to the site, the Indian central government headed by Nehru asked the Uttar Pradesh government headed by Govind Ballabh (G. B.) Pant – a very conservative provincial Congress leader inclined to Hindi linguistic chauvinism and Hindu majoritarian views, both in tune with Hindu nationalist politics – to remove the idols from the mosque. Pant's government pleaded its inability to do so, on the grounds that the district's administrative authorities had advised that communal (meaning Hindu–Muslim) peace would be endangered. Nehru's government did not press further, and the district's administrative head – the district magistrate or DM, a post known as 'collector' since the nineteenth century, when its holders acted as the grassroots enforcers of British rule across India – later emerged as an activist of the Hindu nationalist movement. However, the Babri Masjid site's gates were locked and the mosque fell into disuse from that time. This *status quo* endured for three and a half decades, until 1986, when the dormant issue and the dilemma it represented for India's secular state revived with a vengeance.

The Rashtriya Swayamsevak Sangh (National Volunteer Organization, RSS) emerged as the core of India's Hindu nationalist movement from

1950s onward, displacing and marginalizing other groups such as the Hindu Mahasabha. The RSS was founded in 1925 as a strictly hierarchical and all-male militia-style outfit with local *shakhas* (branches) in various parts of the country forming its grassroots units, and it was a stand-alone organization until the time of India's independence. Its members, about 600,000 by 1947, were major participants in the massive violence that accompanied India's partition, when hundreds of thousands of Hindus, Muslims and Sikhs were slaughtered and tens of millions became refugees. The RSS also carried out relief and rehabilitation work in northern India among Hindu refugees from western Punjab and other parts of Pakistan. It was briefly banned after Mahatma Gandhi's assassination in Delhi in early 1948 – his killer, a former RSS member, was a Maharashtrian Brahmin from western India like the bulk of the early RSS's leaders and cadre. After independence and partition, the RSS grew beyond its Maharashtrian Brahmin roots, recruiting mainly from among Punjabi Hindu refugees who re-settled in and around Delhi, although its national headquarters remained in the city of Nagpur in west-central India. In independent India, the RSS also shed its status as a stand-alone organization and grew to become the core of a *sangh-parivar*, a family of organizations comprising the Hindu nationalist movement. Its first affiliate, formed in 1948, was the Akhil-Bharatiya Vidyarthi Parishad or ABVP (All-India Students' Council), reflecting the RSS's emphasis on recruiting and indoctrinating youth. This was followed by the formation of the affiliated political party, the Bharatiya Jan Sangh (BJS), in late 1951, on the eve of India's first general elections. The BJS was renamed as the Bharatiya Janata Party (BJP) in 1980. As the family developed, more affiliates were born. These included the Bharatiya Mazdoor Sangh (Indian Workers' Organization, BMS), the labour wing, in 1955, and the Vishwa Hindu Parishad or VHP (World Hindu Council), responsible for religious matters, in 1964. The VHP's brief, as the name suggests, was to organize among Hindus globally, but of course through activities focused on India. Since the 1980s, the VHP has developed a reputation of being the most rabid face of the RSS-led *sangh-parivar*. The western State of Gujarat, where Prime Minister Narendra Modi is from, has a particularly extensive VHP presence and its members were widely implicated in pogrom-like attacks on Gujarat's 10 per cent Muslim minority in 2002, which occurred four months into Modi's eventual tenure of twelve and a half years as the State's Chief Minister (until he became India's Prime Minister in May 2014). This episode remains, to date, the one large-scale outbreak of religious violence in twenty-first century India. The VHP also has numerous overseas units, with a well-established presence among the Gujarati diaspora in particular, most notably in the United States. The *parivar* has other longstanding constituents, such as a wing that has worked since the 1950s among India's *Adivasi* (tribal) communities, as well as a network of schools across the country with several million pupils. This collective of activist formations built around the RSS makes up the *sangathan* (organizational apparatus) dedicated to spreading the movement's ideology of *Hindutva* (being Hindu).

In April 1984, the VHP, at the time a relatively obscure arm of the Hindutva movement, announced the launch of a campaign to reclaim Ram's birthplace in Ayodhya. The timing of the announcement was probably linked to the approach of India's eighth general election, due by the end of 1984. Atal Behari Vajpayee (b. 1924), a relative moderate who was to go on to become India's first Hindu nationalist Prime Minister (briefly in 1996 and then from 1998 to 2004), was then the BJP President. His line was to abjure radicalism, distance the BJP from its image of representing an extremist fringe in Indian politics and reposition it as a responsible right-wing party. This, however, was easier said than done given the basic nature of the movement that had produced the BJP and of which it was, and is, an integral component. Vajpayee's political socialization in the RSS had been tempered by nearly three continuous decades in parliament – he was first elected to the second Lok Sabha in 1957 and rapidly established a reputation as an outstanding speaker and dignified politician, resolute but not rabid. Vajpayee's preference for a moderate strategy caused much unease in the party and in the larger movement, most importantly in the movement's fount, the RSS.

The VHP's move in 1984 was probably motivated by the desire of the RSS leadership to counter Vajpayee's moderate line and reassert a hardline approach. The VHP had become increasingly active since the early 1980s, organizing a series of so-called *virat Hindu sammelan*s (massive Hindu gatherings) in cities across India. One such event, held in Delhi in late 1981, was presided over by Karan Singh, son of the last Maharaja of the erstwhile princely state of Jammu and Kashmir and a Congress politician. The princely state ruled by Karan Singh's forebears from 1846 to 1947, as an autonomous principality of the British Raj, imposed a strict Hindu regime on a largely (over three-quarters) Muslim population. Most Muslim subjects lived as peasant serfs mired in poverty and illiteracy, and were not permitted to join the state's police, military, or civil administration as officers. In the princely state, cow slaughter was punishable by death until 1920, later reduced to hefty prison terms under British pressure. In 2017, the BJP-ruled western State of Gujarat passed a law making cow slaughter punishable with a minimum sentence of ten years and a maximum of life in prison; this tightened a 2011 law, passed under Narendra Modi's Chief Ministership, which had stipulated a prison term of three to seven years.[2] The BJP has been continuously in power in Gujarat, Mahatma Gandhi's region of origin, since 1995. In this century Gujarat has emerged as the laboratory of the Modi brand of Hindutva, which combines majoritarian nationalism with a more broadly appealing discourse of socioeconomic development and responsiveness to aspirations of upward mobility. Today, of all of India's 29 federal units, Gujarat comes closest to the vision of the ideal *Hindu rashtra* (Hindu state) the RSS-led movement would like India as a whole to become.

Until its emergence as the battering ram of the *Ramjanambhoomi* agitation in the second half of the 1980s, the VHP's activities focused mainly on protesting conversions among low-caste Hindus to other religions. In 1981, several hundred desperately poor Dalit villagers in the southern State of Tamil Nadu had converted *en masse* to Islam, setting off a national debate and rousing great alarm in the RSS. Preventing such conversions has traditionally been a central concern of the RSS. In Nagpur, the city where the RSS has been headquartered since its inception in 1925, Dr B. R. Ambedkar, the Dalit leader who was one of the framers of India's Constitution, converted to Buddhism in the 1950s, towards the end of his life, along with a large number of his followers. Soon after the VHP's announcement about Ayodhya, a new group called the Bajrang Dal (Monkey Force, in honour of Hanuman, the monkey-god who is Ram's sidekick in the epic) was launched in the summer of 1984 to act as the storm-troopers of the envisioned agitation. Led by an ABVP/RSS activist who became a BJP member of parliament from Uttar

---

2   'Hundreds of Cases, but Only One Conviction Since 2011 under Gujarat Cow Law', *The Indian Express*, 3 April 2017, 1.

Pradesh in the 1990s, it recruited from among lumpen youths and developed a reputation for lawlessness within a few years.

◆

The beginnings of the *Ramjanambhoomi* agitation were however not simply linked to the internal politics of the Hindutva movement, but to much broader developments in Indian politics in the mid-1980s.

Indira Gandhi (1917–84), Nehru's daughter and political heir, was the dominant figure of Indian politics from 1969 – when she achieved nearly full control of the Congress party – until her death by assassination on 31 October 1984. Mrs Gandhi was India's Prime Minister from early 1966 until her death, except for a period of less than three years between March 1977 and December 1979. Although Prime Minister from 1966, Indira came into her own politically in 1969, when she decisively won a struggle for control of the Congress from old-guard leaders left over from her father's era. In India's first elections after Nehru's death in 1964, held in 1967, Congress had been returned to power but with a significantly reduced parliamentary majority, and for the first time the hegemonic party lost power in a number of States across the country to various opposition parties. From 1969, Mrs Gandhi embarked boldly on a two-pronged strategy to revitalize the Congress and consolidate her own leadership of the party and the nation. The Nehru era had bequeathed a legacy of relative stability and political pluralism, but in the 1950s and 1960s the Congress had also mutated from a national liberation movement to a party representing the interests of dominant and privileged groups in society and a conservative social *status quo*. Twenty years after independence, the party's hold over the people was clearly weakening, much like the situation the African National Congress faces two decades after South Africa's liberation from apartheid. Mrs Gandhi decided that a major renovation of Congress's image and strategy was needed. In the second half of 1969 her simmering conflict with the old-guard conservatives (known as the 'Syndicate') who dominated the party in numerous States came to a head, and ended with a decisive victory for Indira and her younger and more progressive-minded cohort of loyalists. At the same time as she took firm control of the party, Mrs Gandhi's politics took a markedly populist left-wing turn. In headline moves, her government nationalized India's banking sector, and abolished state allowances given since independence to the former ruling families of over 500 princely states which had existed until 1947 under the umbrella of the British Raj.

In general elections held in the spring of 1971, Mrs Gandhi's Congress campaigned on a simple slogan which resonated across the country: *Garibi Hatao!* (Eliminate Poverty!). The slogan's effectiveness was telling, in a country where desperately poor people comprised the majority of the population. Mrs Gandhi was re-elected Prime Minister with a commanding (nearly two-thirds) parliamentary majority, and by early 1972 the Congress regained power in all States lost in 1967 except one, Tamil Nadu in the deep south. Her deft handling of the subcontinental conflict that resulted from the terminal crisis of Pakistan's unity in 1971 further fortified her popularity. That crisis unfolded between March and December of 1971 and ended with the total victory of Indian forces in a two-week war in December; Pakistani forces in erstwhile East Pakistan were routed and unconditionally surrendered, and sovereign Bangladesh became a reality. Atal Behari Vajpayee, the Hindu nationalist leader, hailed Mrs Gandhi as 'Durga', a ten-handed goddess who symbolizes *stree-shakti* (female power). In 1972, Indira Gandhi's national and international stature was at its peak.

Her fall from the pedestal of popular adulation was equally dramatic. The main problem was that the much-hyped promise of social transformation failed to materialize. As discontent grew, opposition parties renewed their challenge vigorously in 1974–75. A young generation of anti-Congress activists, many of them university students, gathered around the septuagenarian socialist Jaya Prakash (J. P.) Narayan, a long-time opponent of the Congress who had been an anti-colonial freedom fighter. Narayan mobilized opposition to Indira's government with a call for *sampoorna kranti* (total revolution). A nationwide railway workers' strike organized by George Fernandes, a firebrand socialist leader, rattled Mrs Gandhi in 1974, while large-scale student protests broke out in the western State of Gujarat. By 1975, opposition activities were drawing a massive response in Narayan's home base, the large northern State of Bihar. Increasingly beleaguered and paranoid, Indira Gandhi responded by clamping a nationwide 'Emergency' in mid-1975 on grounds of internal unrest, abusing a provision of the Constitution that empowered the President of the republic to declare such an Emergency. The occupant of this largely ceremonial post was a handpicked loyalist of hers and readily complied.

The Emergency lasted nineteen months until January 1977 (it was formally lifted in March 1977). During that time, India was ruled by fear, as tens of thousands of leaders and activists of opposition parties – spanning the diverse spectrum from the Hindu nationalist Jan Sangh to Marxists – were arrested and imprisoned, along with thousands of journalists and intellectuals. The vibrant Indian press was heavily muzzled (the national radio was controlled by the central government, as was the limited television service). Most were detained under a so-called Maintenance of Internal Security Act or MISA, passed by the Congress-dominated parliament. The opposition State governments in Gujarat and Tamil Nadu were summarily dismissed. The Emergency, during which a cabal around Mrs Gandhi led by her younger son Sanjay did as they pleased, was ostensibly intended to foster a disciplined and orderly environment in which rapid socioeconomic development could be implemented. All that materialized was repression, on a scale which shocked and alienated the country. Surrounded by sycophantic politicians and obsequious bureaucrats, the Prime Minister became more and more disconnected from the popular mood, to the extent that she called a general election in early 1977 (a year behind schedule) in the expectation of winning a fresh mandate. Instead, the Congress was severely defeated. It was virtually wiped out across Hindi-speaking northern India and suffered serious losses in western and eastern India as well; the party survived as a sizeable bloc in parliament only because it did well in the States of southern India, where the excesses of the Emergency had been milder and welfare schemes for the poor implemented by Congress's State governments paid off.

Nonetheless, thirty years of continuous Congress rule since independence came to an end in 1977. A broad opposition coalition which called itself the Janata Party (People's Party) won a parliamentary majority and formed the national government. The Janata Party was a mainly north Indian phenomenon and it swept that region (although the new Prime Minister, Morarji Desai, 81, was a Gujarati – he was a prominent leader of the conservative Congress faction defeated by Indira in the party's power struggle of the end-1960s). The Janata Party had three major constituent groups: socialist-leaning peasant leaders with a core base among middle-caste farmer communities in north Indian States such as Uttar Pradesh and Bihar; elderly leaders of the conservative Congress faction marginalized by Indira Gandhi's rise, augmented by some younger Congress leaders who had broken with her upon her resort to authoritarianism in the mid-1970s; and the Hindu nationalist Bharatiya Jan Sangh, forerunner of the BJP. The Jan Sangh's Atal Behari Vajpayee became the External Affairs (foreign) Minister in Morarji Desai's cabinet.

The Janata Party and its government imploded spectacularly in the second half of 1979. The causes were a complex admixture of conflicts of personal ambition and factional feuds. One catalyst of disintegration was the concurrent RSS membership invariably held by the leaders of Jan Sangh constituent and its representatives in government, which some of the socialists objected to as they regarded the RSS as a fascist organization. As the Janata Party and its government gradually unravelled, the doughty Mrs Gandhi had not just been biding her time to make a comeback, but had been travelling across India to rally her loyalists in different States. The Janata government's attempts to prosecute her for abuse of power proved clumsy and backfired to her advantage, as she played the victim card with dexterity. After the dissolution of the Janata government, mid-term national elections were held in January 1980. Mrs Gandhi's Congress (Indira) or Congress (I) campaigned on a simple slogan which proved remarkably effective in exploiting the disillusionment with the failed, chaotic Janata interlude: 'Elect a government that works! Vote Congress (I)'. Indira Gandhi stormed back to power on the promise of a stable government, her party winning a two-thirds majority in the Lok Sabha with 43 per cent of the nationwide votes. After the coalition experiment of 1977–79 ended in a shambles, the Jan Sangh resumed its independent existence in 1980, renaming itself as the Bharatiya Janata Party (BJP).

Indira Gandhi's final term as India's Prime Minister became more and more turbulent as it progressed. Her 1980 victory was not the kind of positive affirmation she had received a decade earlier, in 1971, riding on her pro-poor plank. Rather, she had capitalized on public disillusionment with the failure of the Janata experiment, and benefited from the opposition vote being split among two competing factions of the disintegrated Janata Party, an anti-Indira faction of the Congress, communists and several regional (State-specific) parties. The turning point of her last term came at the beginning of 1983, when her ruling party was sensationally defeated in elections to constitute the legislatures and governments of two populous States in southern India, Andhra Pradesh and Karnataka. The winners were a resuscitated State-specific version of the Janata Party in Karnataka and a dynamic, newly formed State-specific party – the Telugu Desam Party (TDP) – in Andhra Pradesh. These two southern States were longstanding Indira bastions and had voted strongly for her even in the post-Emergency national election of 1977. The timing of the defeats in erstwhile impregnable strongholds was ominous for Mrs Gandhi, as they came with the next national election visible on the horizon, just under two years away in end-1984. As a shrewd politician, Mrs Gandhi was surely aware that her party was not secure in northern India; there, especially in the giant States of Uttar Pradesh and Bihar, opposition parties remained a potent challenge. In the populous State of West Bengal in eastern India, meanwhile, regionalist communists were strongly entrenched in government and the Congress's prospects were dim. At stake for Mrs Gandhi was not just her own political future but that of her older son, Rajiv, whom she had been grooming since the early 1980s as her eventual successor. Her younger son Sanjay, the notorious figure of the Emergency, had been killed in a flying accident in mid-1980, a few months after her return to power. The Andhra Pradesh and Karnataka results triggered exactly what Mrs Gandhi feared the most: the vigorous renewal of attempts by a range of opposition parties to build a broadly based anti-Congress alliance for the general election due in late 1984.

Always an audacious and imaginative strategist, Indira Gandhi's response was to resort to a populist counter-strategy with potential appeal to a majority of the electorate across the country, cutting across geographic regions, States, and diverse social groups. The 'Garibi Hatao' slogan that had worked nationwide in 1971 was long exhausted and no longer viable as a strategy. The alternative path to mobilizing an electoral majority Mrs Gandhi pursued was to systematically exaggerate, and to some extent fabricate, dire threats to India's national unity and territorial integrity allegedly emanating from secessionist elements.

There were three such purported threats, all in States bordering neighbouring countries. One was in Assam, by far the most populous State in India's far north-east – a complex region bordered by Bangladesh, Myanmar,

Bhutan and China and prone to ethnic conflicts and insurgencies. Here a nativist agitation led by students from the ethnic Assamese majority had emerged in the end-1970s, raising issues such as illegal immigration from Bangladesh and claims of both neglect and exploitation of Assam by the central government. The agitation led by the All-Assam Students' Union (AASU) resulted in near-paralysis of the State government and lethal inter-group violence, and both problems were gravely aggravated by Indira Gandhi's decision to hold a State election there in early 1983 in defiance of the agitation and the very disturbed conditions. The second case was in the northern State of Punjab, bordering Pakistan. Here Mrs Gandhi's party encouraged a radical fringe of the majority Sikh community in the early 1980s in order to counter a campaign by the Congress's established competitor in the State, a Sikh-based regional party called the Akali Dal (Believers' Party), for enhanced State autonomy and greater recognition of Sikh identity. The radical fringe got out of control by 1983 and spawned an armed separatist group led by a messianic Sikh preacher, who took up residence in Sikhism's holiest shrine, the Golden Temple in the city of Amritsar, and converted it into an encampment bristling with hundreds of militants brandishing lethal weapons mostly supplied from Pakistan. The radical group then started a campaign of assassinating police officers (including Sikhs) and prominent citizens of Punjab's Hindu population (a large minority of about 37 per cent in the State), which rapidly escalated to small-scale massacres of ordinary Hindu citizens. The third and extremely delicate case was the far-north State of Jammu and Kashmir (J&K). This State covers the greater part of the territory and contains most of the population of the larger princely state of the same name which existed until 1947; the rest is under Pakistani control, across a ceasefire line which was established in 1949 and was renamed the 'Line of Control' (LoC) by mutual agreement in 1972. Sovereignty over the former princely state has been disputed between India and Pakistan since 1947, and J&K happens to be the only Indian State with a majority of Muslim citizens (68 per cent according to the 2011 national census). Here a State election held in mid-1983 pitted Mrs Gandhi's Congress against the State's ruling party, a mainly but not exclusively Muslim party based mostly in the Kashmir Valley, the most populous of the State's three sub-regions. This party had had an initially uneasy and then conflictual relationship with New Delhi and the Congress party since the early 1950s because its platform of maximum autonomy for J&K ran up against the central government's policy, enforced since 1953 (i.e., the Nehru era), of the State's integration with the rest of India. But in 1975 the regional party, the Jammu and Kashmir National Conference (JKNC), had unambiguously abandoned its previous platform and made its peace with Indira Gandhi's government.

From early 1983, the JKNC became a participant in cross-party talks aimed at forming an opposition alliance to take on the Congress. In response, Indira Gandhi campaigned energetically in J&K's Jammu region, a Hindu-majority region within the Muslim-majority State, accusing the JKNC of harbouring a secessionist agenda. She delivered a strident message of national unity and national integration. In the process, she appropriated a major theme of Hindu nationalist politics. Since the early 1950s, Hindu nationalists have demanded the formal abrogation of Article 370 of the Indian Constitution, which enshrines Jammu and Kashmir's special autonomous status within the Indian Union, on the grounds that it amounts to 'appeasement' – a key word in the Hindu nationalist vocabulary – of Muslims. In fact, Article 370 simply reflected the terms of the princely state's accession to India in late 1947, as signed by the last Hindu Maharaja, which specified that all matters except defence, foreign affairs and currency would be under the jurisdiction of the J&K government. Moreover, J&K's special autonomy was largely eliminated in substantive terms by the mid-1960s, through a series of centralizing and integrative measures imposed from New Delhi since 1953. Despite this, the formal continuation of Article 370 persisted as a lightning rod for Hindu nationalist propaganda. In the 1990s, the BJP articulated three core demands on behalf of the broader *sangh-parivar*: (a) the construction of a grand Ram temple at the site of the razed mosque in Ayodhya; (b) an uniform civil code for all communities in India, to eliminate the 'pseudo-secular' state's acceptance of the legal validity of Sharia law in personal and familial matters among Muslims; and (c) the removal of Article 370 from the Constitution. But unlike the Ayodhya issue, which was picked up in the 1980s, the question of Article 370 has featured centrally in Hindu nationalist politics since the early 1950s. In 1953, the Jan Sangh's first President, Syama Prasad Mookerjee (a Bengali Brahmin who had strongly advocated the partition of both the province of Bengal and India as a whole a few years earlier), arrived in Jammu and Kashmir to lend heft to an already ongoing agitation in the Jammu region – led by jobless ex-officials of the last Maharaja's administration and Hindu landlords dispossessed by the new J&K government's land reform programme – for 'full integration' of J&K with the Indian Union. He was arrested by the J&K government headed by Sheikh Mohammad Abdullah (1905–82) and taken to Srinagar, the main city of the Kashmir Valley (which lies north of the Jammu region), where he died in detention of apparently natural causes.

Mrs Gandhi's 1983 campaign successfully polarized the electorate of Jammu and Kashmir on communal (i.e., religious) lines. The JKNC, headed by the recently deceased Sheikh's son Farooq Abdullah, swept its traditional stronghold, the Kashmir Valley, which is overwhelmingly Muslim, and was returned to office with a majority in the J&K legislative assembly. But the Congress performed very strongly in the Hindu-majority Jammu region, and won three-fourths of the assembly seats from the region. The result of Indira Gandhi's appropriation of the traditional Hindu nationalist plank was that 'BJP, with a traditional base of support in Jammu, lost every seat it contested ... [because of] a shift of Hindu BJP supporters to Congress'. Around the same time in mid-1983, elections were held to the city government of Delhi, the national capital. Since the 1950s, the Jan Sangh, otherwise marginal in Indian politics, had enjoyed a solid base in Delhi, mainly among Hindu partition refugees from Pakistan and their descendants. Amid rising Hindu–Sikh tensions in nearby Punjab and escalating terrorist activity there, Mrs Gandhi's tough stance against the Sikh extremists – a Frankenstein's monster her party and government had created – paid off in this election as well. The Congress won a majority in Delhi, as 'RSS cadres [in the city] maintained a neutral stance'.[3]

Indira Gandhi's strategy to get herself reelected was rife with Hindu-majoritarian overtones, targeted as it was against religious minorities: Muslims and Sikhs. The pilot experiments in Jammu and Kashmir and Delhi having paid off, she broadened the strategy. As the election year of 1984 dawned, the state-controlled national radio and television incessantly warned Indians against the 'anti-national' forces seeking to break up India with assistance from the 'foreign hand' – a reference mainly to Pakistan but

---

3   Walter Andersen and Shridhar Damle, *The Brotherhood in Saffron: The Rashtriya Swayamsevak Sangh and Hindu Revivalism* (New Delhi: Sage Publications, 1987), 231–232.

probably extending to the United States and China as well. The message was that Indira Gandhi's party and government were essential to protect India from these dark forces. The use of the term 'anti-national' to describe a variety of critics by some members of Narendra Modi's government and other BJP politicians has triggered much debate in India over the past few years. The term entered the political lexicon after being coined by Indira Gandhi's spin-doctors in 1983–84.[4]

With six months to go before the general election, Mrs Gandhi upped the ante. In early June, she ordered the Indian army to retake the Golden Temple from the Sikh radicals encamped there. The operation, codenamed 'Bluestar', turned into a bloodbath over two nights of savage fighting. When it ended, 83 military personnel and at least 492 Sikhs were dead, and the shrine complex including its inner sanctum, the Akal Takht, was badly damaged. The Sikh dead were mostly heavily armed followers of the fanatic preacher Jarnail Singh Bhindranwale (who also died), but a sizeable number of pilgrims caught in the firefight were also killed by army shelling, and there were allegations of summary executions as well. The Indian political scientist Rajni Kothari noted in a book titled *State against Democracy* he published in the late 1980s that after the assault, 'Mrs Gandhi said openly that Hindu *dharma* [faith] was under attack'.[5] Later in June, Mrs Gandhi managed to bring down the Jammu and Kashmir government headed by Farooq Abdullah, which was just one year into a six-year term, by engineering defections from the Kashmiri regional party to the Congress. The Congress-defector combine formed a new State government, causing severe unrest in the Kashmir Valley. Two months later, in August, the same tactic of engineering defections was used in an attempt to unseat the opposition government of Andhra Pradesh elected to a five-year term in January 1983. The regional party governing Andhra Pradesh, the TDP, was led by N. T. Rama Rao (known by his initials, NTR), a popular movie actor turned politician, and it had a three-fourths majority in the State

---

4   A revealing glimpse of Mrs Gandhi's increasingly paranoid state of mind during her last prime ministerial term is contained in private letters she wrote to A. C. N. Nambiar, a longtime friend, between 1980 and 1984. The letters have been published in Vappala Balachandran, *A Life in Shadow: The Secret Story of ACN Nambiar, A Forgotten Anti-Colonial Warrior* (New Delhi: Roli Books, 2016).

5   Rajni Kothari, *State against Democracy: In Search of Humane Governance* (Delhi: Ajanta Publications, 1988), 247.

legislature. Since his meteoric political rise just two years earlier, NTR had emerged as a key player in the efforts to forge opposition unity against the Congress government in New Delhi. The attempt to oust NTR fizzled out after a month because the renegade group failed to muster numbers remotely approaching a majority in the legislature. Had it succeeded, it is very likely that the other opposition government in the neighbouring State of Karnataka would have been targeted next.

Amid all this tumult, the VHP-led campaign to liberate *Ramjanambhoomi* in Ayodhya attracted scarcely any attention.

On the morning of 31 October 1984, Indira Gandhi was shot dead in the garden of her home in New Delhi by two Sikh members of her bodyguard detail. The two men who riddled her slight frame with bullets were avenging what they saw as the desecration of Sikhism's holiest shrine in Amritsar. Over the next three days, about 3,000 Sikhs were murdered across northern India. The worst violence by far was in Delhi, where more than two-thirds of the victims died. At that time, Delhi's 400,000 or so Sikhs made up 6 per cent of the city's population. Citizens of this small minority, mostly adult males, were hunted down like animals in the national capital's neighbourhoods, streets and public transport by marauding mobs led by Congress politicians. Hundreds of victims were set alight and burned alive. The Congress party immediately appointed Rajiv Gandhi, a political greenhorn, as its new leader as well as interim Prime Minister, pending the imminent general election. Asked to comment on the mass slaughter of innocent Sikhs, he replied, 'When a giant tree falls, the earth shakes.'[6]

A nationwide sympathy wave gave Rajiv Gandhi the largest parliamentary majority, unequalled until today, in India's democracy. The Congress won 415 of the 543 seats in the Lok Sabha, and gained 48 per cent of the nationwide polled votes, its highest share ever (by comparison the party, led by Rajiv's grandfather Jawaharlal Nehru, had obtained 45 per cent of the nationwide votes and 364 of the 489 Lok Sabha seats in the first general election of 1952). The Congress won the vast bulk of the (single-member) constituencies in all States – the States' representation in the Lok Sabha are proportional to their

---

6   Sumantra Bose, 'Hindu Nationalism and the Crisis of the Indian State', in *Nationalism, Democracy and Development: State and Politics in India*, eds. Sugata Bose and Ayesha Jalal (New Delhi: Oxford University Press, 1997), 123.

share of the nationwide population – except in Andhra Pradesh, West Bengal, Assam, Punjab and the Kashmir Valley in J&K. One theme dominated the election – the imperative to defend national unity and territorial integrity against the assortment of internal threats, abetted by external enemies. After Indira's gruesome death, the majoritarian–nationalist electoral strategy she had been honing for two years achieved the kind of spectacular success she could only have dreamed of when alive.

The BJP's prospects fell victim to Congress's appropriation of the majoritarian–nationalist card. The BJP did come (a very distant) second to the Congress in the nationwide vote share, polling nearly 8 per cent of the vote in a very fractured opposition spectrum. But this was the same percentage the party (as the BJS) had secured in the third general election in 1962, which meant that the Hindu nationalists – who had always viewed themselves as the natural alternative to the Congress – were completely stagnant. More important, BJP candidates won in only two of the 543 Lok Sabha constituencies, which rendered the party almost invisible in national politics. By contrast, NTR's TDP had as many as thirty Lok Sabha parliamentarians, all elected from Andhra Pradesh, and indeed the JKNC had more Lok Sabha MPs than the BJP after winning all three constituencies in the Kashmir Valley. Even Atal Behari Vajpayee, the veteran parliamentarian and future Prime Minister, failed to be elected, for the first and last time in his political career. The American political scientist Paul Brass observed that the Congress appropriated 'both the Jan Sangh slogan of "One United India" and more than half of the Jan Sangh vote base in northern and central India'.[7] The BJP 'was totally decimated in the Hindi-speaking States [of northern India]', the only part of the country where it had a sizeable base, and there was 'widespread speculation that many RSS cadres had backed the Congress'. Indeed Nanaji Deshmukh, a top RSS leader who served as a general secretary of the confederated Janata Party in the late 1970s, had openly endorsed Rajiv Gandhi. It seemed that 'the view that a solid victory for Rajiv Gandhi was necessary to keep the forces of disintegration in check had a compelling appeal for many RSS members, and for a large part of the BJP's traditional constituency'.[8]

---

7  Paul Brass, *Ethnicity and Nationalism: Theory and Comparison* (New Delhi: Sage Publications, 1991), 208.

8  Andersen and Damle, *The Brotherhood in Saffron*, 234.

◆

From the margins, the Hindu nationalists continued to pursue the Ayodhya issue. In February 1986, in response to a VHP petition on the matter, a judge of the district court with jurisdiction over Ayodhya issued an opinion that a temple had existed at the site prior to the construction of the mosque and ordered that the gates of the site, locked since end-1949, be re-opened to enable Hindu worship. The gates were opened almost instantly. A gaggle of saffron-robed monks and VHP activists gathered at the site then engaged in a noisy, triumphal celebration-cum-prayer session. An intriguing sequence of events occurred just before as well as immediately after the judicial opinion was announced. An Indian journalist who was covering the news story at the time recalled a few years later:

> The [Congress] Uttar Pradesh government precipitated the confrontation. It deliberately stepped into the controversy, and actually took sides. The [Congress] Chief Minister [of the State] visited Ayodhya a few days before the [court] judgment and met VHP members. On 1 February [1986], shortly before the order was announced, a crowd of VHP supporters collected at the site. This was seen as an indication by persons living there [in the town] that they had advance knowledge of the verdict. A Doordarshan [state television] team too was present at the site, as if the [central] government wished to publicize the entire event. The 'victory' celebrations were filmed and telecast on the national network [all-India news] the same evening.[9]

Indeed, as a teenaged schoolboy, I remember watching the evening news at home in Calcutta (now Kolkata) that day and feeling puzzled that a seemingly obscure religious ceremony was leading the nationwide broadcast, as well as by the presenter's gushing language and tone. At the time, and until the mid-1990s, the central government had a monopoly on television broadcasting in India and throughout the 1980s the state television functioned as an embarrassingly crude propaganda tool of the Indira and Rajiv governments. The Indira Gandhi government of 1980–84 put much emphasis on extending

---

9   Seema Mustafa, 'Uttar Pradesh Government Took Sides in Ayodhya Dispute', in *The Babri Masjid-Ram Janambhoomi Controversy*, ed. Asghar Ali Engineer (Delhi: Ajanta Books, 1990), 117.

the reach of television broadcasting beyond the cities to small-town and rural India with precisely this purpose, a policy continued by her son's government.

The behaviour of the Uttar Pradesh government was of course not surprising in historical perspective – the State was, after all, the first in India to enact a law banning cow slaughter in the mid-1950s, as recounted in Chapter 3. Then, too, a 'secular' Congress government, with a similarly huge majority in the State legislature, was responsible. So the structural biases of the Indian secular state were a long established fact, and familiar to Muslims in Uttar Pradesh and elsewhere in India. Nonetheless, the conduct of the Congress Chief Minister, who had been appointed to the post by Rajiv Gandhi just a few months earlier, in September 1985, and served until mid-1988, as well as the use of the lower judiciary and the state-controlled broadcast media constituted an especially blatant violation of the secular state's notional principle of impartiality. The Chief Minister, Vir Bahadur (V. B.) Singh, of upper-caste Rajput/Thakur background and a typical example of the high-caste Congress hierarchy of Uttar Pradesh before and since India's independence, was originally from Gorakhpur, the large town in the same region of Uttar Pradesh as Ayodhya. As narrated at the beginning of this chapter, the *mahant* or head priest of the Hindu *math* (shrine complex) in Gorakhpur, Digvijay Nath, had spearheaded the 1949 agitation which surreptitiously installed idols of Ram and his consort Sita inside the mosque, leading to its closure. That priest-politician's successor as head of the Gorakhpur shrine, Mahant Avaidyanath (1921–2014), emerged as one of the leading lights of the renewed *Ramjanambhoomi* agitation from the mid-1980s onwards and was elected from Gorakhpur to India's parliament as a BJP nominee in 1991 and 1996 (prior to that, he had already won election twice to the Lok Sabha from Gorakhpur and no less than five times to the Uttar Pradesh legislature). Avaidyanath's successor, Yogi Adityanath, carried on the priest–politician tradition and was elected to the Lok Sabha from Gorakhpur five consecutive times between 1998 and 2014. Like his mentor Avaidyanath, Adityanath (b. 1972) is a Rajput/Thakur from a mountainous area called Pauri-Garhwal in the north-western tip of Uttar Pradesh which became part of a new, small State of the Indian Union called Uttarakhand (Northern Land) created in late 2000. In March 2017, after Modi's BJP won a massive victory in Uttar Pradesh State elections, winning a four-fifths majority in its legislature with about 40 per cent of the popular vote, Adityanath, a hardline figure even by Hindu nationalist standards, was appointed as Uttar Pradesh's Chief Minister. During his parliamentarian career of almost two decades (1998–2017), Yogi Adityanath was very active in the Lok Sabha and the issue he pursued most consistently over his five consecutive terms was a national law to ban cow slaughter. He tabled private member's bills in successive Lok Sabhas calling for such a law.

The turn of events in the revived Ayodhya dispute orchestrated in 1986 by Rajiv Gandhi's government in New Delhi and its Uttar Pradesh subordinate caused deep disquiet among Muslims in that State and elsewhere in India, especially in northern India. It seemed that the authorities of the secular state were abandoning all semblance of impartiality and equal treatment of religious faiths, and conniving actively with a far-right Hindu nationalist agenda. A Babri Masjid Action Committee (BMAC) was formed with both clerics and lay Muslims, under the convenorship of Zafaryab Jilani, a lawyer based in Lucknow (the State capital of Uttar Pradesh), to represent the Muslim case. The anxiety and anger roused among Muslims was a political problem for Rajiv Gandhi's party. In Uttar Pradesh, India's most populous and therefore politically weightiest State, Congress had won elections and formed governments since India's independence by getting the bulk of the votes of three social blocs, each constituting nearly one-fifth of the State's population. These were: the upper castes comprising Brahmins, Rajputs/ Thakurs and Kayasths, who, especially Brahmins, dominated the Congress organization in Uttar Pradesh; the Dalits or Harijans, some of whom had benefited from reservations (affirmative action) in national and State representative institutions as well as in government jobs implemented under Congress rule after India's independence; and the Muslims, who looked on the Congress as a minimally neutral and 'secular' party sensitive to their concerns. Nationwide, Muslims, at that time in the late 1980s one of every eight Indians, comprised at least 10 per cent of the electorate in as many as 207 of the 543 parliamentary constituencies, and over 20 per cent in 81 of those.[10] The Congress party and Rajiv Gandhi's government needed to act to recoup faltering Muslim confidence and support, and moved swiftly to do so.

In the late 1970s, Shah Bano Begum, a Muslim woman from a provincial city called Indore in the State of Madhya Pradesh (Central Province) in

---

10 Lloyd Rudolph and Susanne H. Rudolph, *In Pursuit of Lakshmi: The Political Economy of the Indian State* (Chicago: University of Chicago Press, 1987), 194–197.

north-central India, had approached the courts seeking justice. Then in her fifties, Shah Bano came from a poor background (her father had been a police constable) and was not literate (she signed with a thumb impression as she could not write). After nearly four decades of marriage and several children, Shah Bano had been divorced by her husband, Mohammad Ahmed Khan, and turned out of the family home. The husband had divorced her simply by saying the word *talaq* thrice, a legal way (until August 2017, when India's Supreme Court ruled instant *talaq* illegal) for Muslim men to divorce their wives in India, where Muslims may invoke and be governed by Sharia law in personal and familial matters such as marriage, divorce, alimony, custody of children, inheritance of property and adoption. This has been the case since the British colonial government made Muslim personal and familial matters subject to Sharia law in 1937 by enacting a Muslim Personal Law (Shariat) Application Act, supplemented by a Dissolution of Muslim Marriages Act in 1939. Faced with destitution, Shah Bano went to court and pleaded that her former husband be ordered to pay her a monthly maintenance. The lower court ordered him to do so, but the monthly sum specified in the judgment was very meagre and Shah Bano appealed to the State's high court to increase the amount. The high court ruled in her favour and modestly increased the amount. An organization that calls itself the All-India Muslim Personal Law Board (AIMPLB) then appealed, on behalf of the ex-husband, to India's Supreme Court to overturn the judgment, on the grounds that it violated Indian Muslims' right to be governed by Sharia law in personal and familial matters. Despite its official-sounding name, the AIMPLB is no statutory body but a (mainly Sunni) lobbying group which acts as the self-appointed defender of Sharia law. Zafaryab Jilani, the convenor of the Babri Masjid Action Committee in the Ayodhya dispute, has simultaneously been a long-term legal eagle of the AIMPLB. In a landmark judgment delivered in April 1985, the Supreme Court rejected the AIMPLB's appeal and upheld the high court's order.

The courts at all levels ruled in favour of Shah Bano by citing Section 125 of the Criminal Procedure Code (CPC) of 1973, which states that 'if any person having sufficient means neglects or refuses to maintain ... wives, children and parents' who are in need, a court may 'upon proof of such neglect or refusal, order such [a] person to make a monthly allowance for the maintenance'. This provision of the 1973 CPC is directly descended from a colonial-era law enacted in 1872 to prevent 'vagrancy' (a term very expressive of its Victorian England origins). The AIMPLB was formed with a single-point agenda of defending Sharia law in 1973, around the same time the CPC came into effect. The Shah Bano case was not the first instance of a Supreme Court judgment in favour of a Muslim woman who had sought maintenance after being divorced by her husband through the 'triple *talaq*' method; there had been two previous rulings based on Section 125 of the CPC in 1979 and 1980, which the Supreme Court cited as precedents in its Shah Bano verdict.

Nonetheless, it was the Shah Bano judgment that attracted nationwide attention, because a motley crew of self-appointed spokesmen of 'Muslim rights' launched vociferous protests. One prominent critic was a septuagenarian Uttar Pradesh cleric, popularly known as Ali Miyan, who had openly praised the Islamization policies of the regime (1977–88) of the Pakistani military dictator Zia-ul Haq, and also admired the theocratic state of Saudi Arabia. A Hanafi–Naqshbandi theologian of uncompromising anti-secular views, he now claimed that the judgment endangered India's secular state. This twentieth-century descendant of Ahmad Faruqi al-Sirhindi, who in the late sixteenth century opposed the religious syncretism promoted by the Mughal emperor Akbar and whose vision of strictly orthodox Sunnism later influenced the evolution of the Naqshbandi order in Turkey, was then the chairman of the AIMPLB. Another leading figure was Syed Shahabuddin, a maverick opposition politician who managed to win a parliamentary by-election in a heavily Muslim constituency in the northern State of Bihar in December 1985 by agitating on the issue. He defeated the Congress's Muslim candidate. The AIMPLB, described in mid-1986 by Danial Latifi, Shah Bano's lawyer in the Supreme Court case, as a self-appointed 'College of Cardinals of Indian Muslims' and an 'illegitimate Papacy', emerged as the body coordinating the campaign to save the divinely revealed law. Shah Bano herself clearly came under extreme pressure. In November 1985, a statement was published in her name, signed with a thumb impression and attested by four male witnesses, in *Inquilab*, an Urdu paper. In it she disowned the Supreme Court judgment,

> which is apparently in my favour, but since this judgment is contrary to the Quran and the *hadith* [sayings of the Prophet] and an open interference in Muslim personal law, I, Shah Bano, being a Muslim, reject it and dissociate myself from every judgment which is contrary to the Islamic

Shariat. I am aware of the agony and distress this judgment has caused the Muslims of India.

However, there was no sign yet of any government intervention in favour of the Muslim conservatives. Instead, Rajiv Gandhi asked Arif Mohammed Khan, a Congress MP elected to the Lok Sabha from Uttar Pradesh and a junior minister in his government, to make a speech in parliament defending the Supreme Court's verdict. Khan, a young politician in his mid-thirties who had been a student leader at Uttar Pradesh's Aligarh Muslim University (AMU) in the first half of the 1970s, did so to great acclaim both in parliament and the media. The government's stance was very consistent with the liberal, modernizing face Rajiv Gandhi projected during the first year of the premiership he had inherited from his assassinated mother. Any government intervention to nullify the judgment, as demanded by the AIMPLB-led agitators, was in any case contrary to India's constitutional structure, since it would amount to gross infringement of the independence of the judiciary (and the apex court, at that). There were murmurs in the Congress party about a potential loss of Muslim support, but Rajiv Gandhi had very little to fear on that score. The next general election was four years away, in late 1989, and there were no imminent State elections in which a backlash might hurt the Congress (the Congress's Uttar Pradesh government, for example, had been elected in early 1985 and its term ran till early 1990).

The government abruptly changed tack in the early spring of 1986, just after the opening of the Babri Masjid site to the VHP-led agitators. G. M. Banatwala, an Indian Union Muslim League (IUML) parliamentarian elected to the Lok Sabha from the southern State of Kerala, the only State where this party, formed in 1948, has a sizeable base, had tabled a private member's bill seeking to nullify the Supreme Court's judgment (Kerala has the fourth highest proportion of Muslims of India's 29 States, nearly 27 per cent as per the 2011 national census, after Jammu and Kashmir, Assam and West Bengal). Hundreds of private member's bills are tabled in every Lok Sabha and very rarely do any become law. In February 1986, Rajiv Gandhi's government suddenly picked up this particular bill and its law minister tabled it in parliament as the Muslim Women (Protection of Rights in Divorce) Bill. The government-sponsored bill specified that divorced Muslim women would no longer be covered by Section 125 of the CPC. Moreover, upon divorce, the ex-husband would only be obliged to return the *mehr* (dowry) to the woman and pay her alimony for three months (a period known as *iddat*), consistent with Sharia principles. Thereafter, he would have no obligations whatsoever, and the woman's maintenance would be the responsibility of her parents, children and any other members of her natal family who stood to inherit her property. If she did not have such relatives or they lacked the means to support her, she could approach a court to direct that maintenance be paid to her from State *wakf* (Islamic trust) funds.

In March 1986, Rajiv Gandhi personally defended this bill on the floor of parliament in an incoherent speech. In early May, the bill was voted on and passed into law as the Muslim Women (Protection of Rights in Divorce) Act. This was a foregone conclusion due to the Congress's brute majority (nearly four-fifths) in the Lok Sabha; moreover, a three-line whip was issued to all Congress MPs to vote in favour. As the vote took place, a large number of women of various political persuasions and religious backgrounds protested outside parliament. More than one hundred women chained themselves to the wrought-iron railings of the Parliament compound and were arrested. Arif Mohammed Khan resigned immediately from the government; a year later, he left the Congress party and became an opposition politician.[11]

The Hindu nationalists of course objected vehemently as well to the Muslim Women's Bill, as it came to be commonly referred to. Ever since, they have cited it as one of the most blatant examples of the 'pseudo-secular' state's 'appeasement' of Muslims in pursuit of 'vote-bank' politics. While politically motivated, their criticism is substantially true. The 'Directive Principle of State Policy' enshrined as Article 44 of the Indian Constitution says, 'The state shall endeavour to secure for the citizens a uniform civil code throughout the territory of India'. The Muslim Women's Bill represented movement in the opposite direction. As the Hindu nationalists' political fortunes rose exponentially from the end-1980s, the demand for such an UCC became one of the three fundamentals of the BJP agenda, along with the building of a grand Ram temple at the mosque site in Ayodhya and the formal abrogation of Article 370 of the Constitution, which enshrines Jammu

---

11 The quotes on the Shah Bano case in the preceding paragraphs are sourced from Zakia Pathak and Rajeswari Sunder Rajan, 'Shahbano', *Signs: Journal of Women in Culture and Society* 14, no.3 (spring 1989): 558–582. See also Asghar Ali Engineer, ed., *The Shah Bano Controversy* (Hyderabad: Orient Longman, 1987).

and Kashmir's special autonomous status within the Indian Union. What the Hindu nationalists conveniently omit to mention is that what the Rajiv Gandhi government did in 1986 was to reduce Indian state-secularism to the competitive appeasement of the most regressive demands raised in the name of both Hindus and Muslims.

Donald Smith wrote in 1963: 'That Hindus, Muslims and Christians, all citizens of the same country, should be governed by different [religious] laws [in personal and family matters] is an anachronism indeed, and diametrically opposed to the fundamental principles of secularism'.[12] Three decades after the Shah Bano case became a *cause celebre* across India, this glaring anomaly of the Indian secular state is starker than ever, and a very live issue in contemporary politics. As noted in earlier chapters, the Narendra Modi government initiated a nationwide public consultation on the issue of the Uniform Civil Code in late 2016, and its legal officials have represented to the Supreme Court that the practices of triple *talaq*, *nikaah-halala* (whereby a Muslim woman divorced by *talaq* has to first consummate a marriage with another Muslim male before she can be remarried to the original husband) and polygamy (up to four wives at one time) allowable to Indian Muslim men under the law are unconstitutional.[13] In the meantime, more 'Shah Bano' cases emerged in twenty-first century India, and a growing Muslim women's movement took up their cause. The matter of separate laws, it should be stressed, pertains not just to Muslims and Muslim women, as it is usually framed, but to Christians and Christian women as well. The reaction from Muslim conservatives, led by the ever-active AIMPLB, has been more or less what it was in the 1980s. Their tune is echoed by politicians of various 'secularist' political parties, which lends further traction to the Hindu nationalists' charge of 'pseudo-secularism'

---

12  Smith, *India as a Secular State*, 497.

13  The ban on polygamy has its origins in the Indian Penal Code (IPC), enacted in 1860 by the British colonial regime. A century and a half later, the IPC remains India's criminal code with few changes. Under the British, the classification of polygamy as a criminal offence in Sections 464 and 465 of the IPC applied only to Christians. The prohibition was extended to Hindus, Sikhs, Jains and Buddhists as part of the reform and codification of Hindu personal and family law that took place under Nehru's government in 1955–56, specifically in the Hindu Marriage Act. Muslims and communities classified as Scheduled Tribes (ST) are exempt. These two populations add up to 23 per cent of India's people (14.2 per cent and 8.6 per cent).

and 'minority appeasement' in the expectation of gaining votes. I return to the contemporary debate in the concluding chapter (Chapter 7) of this book.

♦

Rajiv Gandhi's government degenerated into a shambles from 1987 onwards. The causes were various but mutually reinforcing: inept governance, poor decision-making, corruption scandals, reliance on cronies rather than seasoned politicians, etc. Rajiv Gandhi, a neophyte politician pitchforked into politics as heir-apparent after his younger brother Sanjay's sudden death in 1980, and into the premiership after his mother's equally sudden assassination, was simply unable to cope with the many challenges of leading a large and complex country. As his blundering government's crisis deepened during 1988–89, efforts at opposition unity found a focal point in Vishwanath Pratap (V. P.) Singh, a Congress politician from Uttar Pradesh who had been the State's Chief Minister in the early 1980s and then a senior minister in Rajiv's cabinet, but been expelled from the party in mid-1987. By 1989, the government had become so unpopular that it was clear that if a substantial degree of opposition unity could be forged, Congress's defeat in the general election due before the end of the year was very likely. In the run-up to the November 1989 election, a so-called National Front came into being with V. P. Singh as its main face. It grouped the regional opposition parties of the north (who had constituted the Janata alliance of the late 1970s) and the south (the TDP of Andhra Pradesh, the Dravida Munnetra Kazhagam or DMK of Tamil Nadu) in an umbrella coalition. This pre-poll alliance in turn coordinated with the largest communist party, strong in West Bengal and Kerala, and the BJP, a party with a sizeable base in several States of northern and western India (mainly Rajasthan, Madhya Pradesh and Gujarat). Thus, the Congress faced a single opposition candidate in the large majority of parliamentary constituencies, as Indira Gandhi had in 1977.

As the polls approached, the VHP and its storm-trooper formation, the Bajrang Dal, sharply stepped up the *Ramjanambhoomi* agitation. In a highly effective initiative from September 1989, hundreds of thousands of people of various castes and classes travelled to Ayodhya from villages and towns across northern India, carrying bricks for the proposed Ram temple. The already delicate communal (Hindu–Muslim) dynamic deteriorated gravely in northern India. In October, poor Muslim communities in Bihar's Bhagalpur district, on the eastern edge of that northern State, were targeted in a spate of horrific attacks. Nearly 2,000 Muslims were massacred there in gory violence, their villages razed and mosques as well as shrines of Sufi saints destroyed. According to the findings of an official commission consisting of retired judges of the Bihar High Court which probed the pogrom, 1,852 persons (overwhelmingly Muslims) were killed over several weeks starting on 24 October 1989 and 11,550 homes were damaged or destroyed along with 68 mosques and thirty *mazars* (tombs of Sufi saints). The local silk-weaving trade which provided many Muslims with their livelihood was badly hit as some 600 power-operated looms and 1,700 handlooms were destroyed. Bihar had a Congress government at the time.

As the mutilated or charred corpses of Muslim men, women and children stacked up in Bhagalpur, Rajiv Gandhi kicked off the Congress's election campaign in Ayodhya, where he promised to establish *Ram Rajya* (the mythical kingdom of Ram, embodying good and enlightened rule) in India if re-elected. A fortnight before the election, the VHP received permission from the Uttar Pradesh government, which would do nothing without the approval of the central Congress leadership, to conduct a *shilanyas* or foundation-laying ceremony for the proposed Ram temple at the Ayodhya site. The Congress then claimed that 'the interests of the majority and minority communities [had been] successfully harmonized' – 'harmony', incidentally, is a deceptively benign catchword of the Hindu nationalist vocabulary – and the Home (interior) Minister in Rajiv Gandhi's cabinet was reported to have suggested to the VHP that 'the prime minister should be allowed to lay the foundation stone' (the request was turned down).[14]

Rajiv Gandhi's desperate and cynical attempt to piggyback on Hindutva majoritarianism to retain power failed. The Congress won just 197 seats (of 543) in the Lok Sabha elected in November 1989, compared to the 415 seats it had in the 1984–89 parliament. The Congress remained the single largest party, but Rajiv's *bete noire* V. P. Singh became India's new Prime Minister. Singh fronted the Janata Dal (People's Party), cobbled together

---

14 A. G. Noorani, 'Congress Agreed to Ram *Shilanyas*', in *The Babri Masjid-Ramjanambhoomi Controversy*, ed. Engineer, 151.

from the north Indian factions which had comprised the Janata Party of the late 1970s, minus the Hindu nationalist constituent of that anti-Indira coalition. The Janata Dal won in 142 constituencies, mostly in northern India, and V. P. Singh was able to form a government with 'outside support' from two strong performers on its right and left flanks – the BJP, which secured 86 seats, and the communist-led bloc, which got 53. The BJP and the communist-led bloc did not join the government, but agreed to support it from outside so V. P. Singh would have a working parliamentary majority. Together (142+86+53) they had 281 MPs in the Lok Sabha, above the majority threshold of 272.

The November 1989 general election – India's ninth since the first Lok Sabha was constituted in 1952 – was a watershed in the evolution of Indian democracy. It marked the definitive end of the long era (42 years, 1947–89) of Congress's hegemony, and the beginning of a new phase in the country's politics.[15]

A prime legacy of the last decade (1980–89) of Congress's hegemonic rule of India was the political space opened up for the rise and advance of Hindu nationalism from the early 1990s, through the complicity and connivance of the avowedly secular Indira and Rajiv governments with Hindutva majoritarianism. Chapter 3 has recounted how a similar process unfolded in Turkey, as the 'Turkish–Islamic Synthesis' ideology promoted by the military hierarchy – the self-declared guardians of the secular state – during the 1980s had the effect of facilitating the ascendancy of the alternative Islamist-majoritarian conception of nation and state during the 1990s (and beyond). That is discussed in further detail in the latter part of the next chapter (Chapter 5). In both countries, the structural contradictions and embedded anomalies of the secular state explained earlier in this book were exacerbated by the policies of those at the helm during the crucial decade of the 1980s.

A major consequence of the erosion of the Turkish secular state was that the heterodox Alevi community, the principal confessional minority accounting for 15–20 per cent of the nation's population, found themselves

---

15 A detailed account of the origins, evolution and end of the Congress era (1947–89) of India's politics can be found in Sumantra Bose, *Transforming India: Challenges to the World's Largest Democracy* (Cambridge, MA and London: Harvard University Press, 2013), Chapter 1.

increasingly beleaguered. Chapter 3 has described how Alevis were subjected to pogrom-like violence during the disturbed period of 1978–80, and then again in the 1990s. The perpetrators were organized groups of thugs usually linked to the far-right Nationalist Movement Party (MHP), who targeted the non-Sunni, 'heretical' Alevis because of the liberal and leftist orientations prevalent among them. But police complicity was very often evident in the attacks. This was not surprising, for two reasons. First, police forces in Turkey have for several decades harboured significant elements, including men in command positions, with either Sunni–Islamist or far-right loyalties – both hostile to Alevis. Second, the 'deep state' in Turkey – a term used for police and intelligence networks frequently linked to organized crime syndicates – has since the late 1970s used fascist thugs as its mercenaries and hitmen. This nexus became particularly evident during the 1990s, when the 'deep state' waged a dirty war against Kurdish nationalists in Turkey's east and south-east regions.

As India's secular state was compromised by those in power through the 1980s, Indian Muslims, like Turkey's Alevis the essential 'Other' of religious-majoritarian nationalists, found themselves increasingly vulnerable to pogrom-like violence in certain locales. 'Communal riots', as Hindu–Muslim violence is referred to in India, had erupted periodically in various parts of the country even before the 1980s. But the 1980s surpassed the previous three decades. In late 1980, violence broke out in Moradabad, a large town in western Uttar Pradesh, a region with a significant concentration of Muslims. It lasted for several weeks and there were several hundred fatalities, mostly Muslims. This was towards the end of the first year of Indira Gandhi's last term as Prime Minister. In mid-1984, as her premiership neared its cataclysmic end, severe violence gripped Bhiwandi, a large town known for textile production close to Bombay (now Mumbai) in the State of Maharashtra. Maharashtra, like Uttar Pradesh, was ruled by a Congress government. The Bhiwandi riots left several hundred dead, again mostly Muslims.

During Rajiv Gandhi's term, the complicity of police and other state officials in violence directed at Muslims became starker. In May 1987, communal disturbances flared in Meerut, a provincial city in western Uttar Pradesh located just 80 kilometres (50 miles) from Delhi. An unit of the Provincial Armed Constabulary (PAC) – a State police force whose name reveals its origins as an enforcer of British rule in late-colonial India, raised in the late 1930s almost exclusively from among so-called 'martial' communities of Hindus in the 'United Provinces', as Uttar Pradesh was known until independence – entered Hashimpura, a Muslim neighbourhood of Meerut. The PAC had been implicated in summary executions of scores of Muslims during the Moradabad riots of late 1980. The unit that entered Hashimpura picked up 43 young Muslim men and took them in a truck to the edge of a canal in the neighbouring district of Ghaziabad, which borders Delhi. There the captives were raked with gunfire as they emerged from the truck and their bodies were dumped in the canal. Five men survived with bullet injuries; the other 38 men died. Vibhuti Narain Rai, who was then the superintendent of police (SP) of Ghaziabad, the district's top police officer, found the corpses, and the survivors, a few hours after the massacre. In 2016, he published a detailed account of the massacre and its immediate as well as long-term aftermath.[16] It is a chilling account, not least because it suggests that the then Congress Chief Minister of Uttar Pradesh, Vir Bahadur Singh – the same man who had played a dubious role in opening up the Babri Masjid site in Ayodhya to the Hindu nationalist agitators a year earlier – was directly involved in the attempt to cover up what had happened. The day after the Hashimpura men were taken away to be killed, another PAC unit entered Maliana, a Muslim village on Meerut's outskirts, accompanied by a mob from adjacent Hindu villages. The PAC fired indiscriminately on the Maliana villagers, while the accompanying mob, armed with sharp weapons and stocks of kerosene, hacked and burned others to death. The death toll was 72 – and it included men and women of all ages.[17]

Rajiv Gandhi's Prime Ministership began with the massacre of Sikhs, in Delhi and elsewhere, and ended with the carnage of Muslims in Bihar's Bhagalpur district.

◆

V. P. Singh's government lasted just under a year. It collapsed in November 1990 when the BJP withdrew its outside support, causing the government to

---

16 Vibhuti Narain Rai, *Hashimpura, 22 May 1987: The Forgotten Story of India's Biggest Custodial Killing* (Delhi: Penguin Books, 2016).

17 'Maliana's Victims Lose Hope', *The Hindu*, 30 March 2015.

lose its working parliamentary majority. Although short-lived, Singh's tenure, and one decision he made in particular, had a far-reaching impact on the trajectory of Indian politics, especially in northern India.

In the first half of August 1990, Singh announced – first in parliament and then in the customary Prime Minister's address to the nation from the Red Fort in Delhi on Independence Day (15 August) that his government would implement the main recommendation made a decade earlier by the Second Backward Classes Commission. This five-member commission had been constituted in 1978 by the Janata Party government to identify ways of improving the socioeconomic condition of the 'other backward classes' (OBCs), a vast and heterogeneous layer of castes sandwiched between the upper castes and the Dalits (who are classified as the Scheduled Castes or STs). It is known in India as the Mandal Commission after its chairman, B. P. Mandal, who was a politician from Bihar and a Yadav, an OBC caste. The Mandal Commission submitted its report in 1980, by which time Indira Gandhi had returned to power, and she and then her son's government kept the report in cold storage for the next decade. The report had claimed that OBCs comprised the majority of India's population, 52.1 per cent (43.7 per cent Hindu OBCs and 8.4 per cent Muslim, Sikh and Christian OBCs). Its main recommendation was that 27 per cent of all levels of jobs in the Union government and in institutions of higher education supported by that government be reserved for OBCs. Since the SCs and the Adivasis or tribal communities (Scheduled Tribes or STs) had been respectively entitled since the formation of the Republic in 1950 to 15 per cent and 7.5 per cent reservations in higher education and government jobs, this would extend the reserved quota to one-half (49.5 per cent) of the total.

V. P. Singh (1931–2008) was himself of upper-caste background – a Rajput (or Thakur) from a family that owned a small feudal estate in Uttar Pradesh. However, the Janata Dal, the conglomerate of factions based mostly in Uttar Pradesh and Bihar he had led into the November 1989 general election, drew its support predominantly from OBC groups. Since the 1960s, opposition (anti-Congress) politics in the two huge north Indian States, Uttar Pradesh and Bihar, had been predominantly driven by support from middle castes, while the Congress had been dominated by upper-caste interests, and also drawn the bulk of Dalit and Muslim votes.

Singh's announcement triggered a visceral reaction from upper castes in north India. As an American scholar observed in the early 1990s, due to

> a complex of changes that [gradually] undermined the forward castes, the demand for reservations in educational institutions and government posts by the backward classes was a signal for all-out struggle ... At issue is the age-old privileged position of the upper castes on all fronts: social status, economic strength, educational advantages, high-prestige occupations, and political power.[18]

Upper-caste college and university students, typically of lower middle-class background, led the furious anti-Mandal agitation that erupted across urban north India after Singh's announcement. In September, a hunger-striking Brahmin student at Delhi University set himself on fire. He survived with serious burns, but a few days later a young Rajput succeeded in burning himself to death. He was the first of 63 protesters to commit suicide by self-immolation, of a total of 151 such attempts. Police firing killed another 58 anti-Mandal protesters, 51 in north Indian States, of which the largest numbers were in Uttar Pradesh and Bihar (sixteen and twelve, respectively).

The caste conflict that gripped the nation, acutely so in northern India, posed a great dilemma for the Hindu nationalist movement. The movement's political appetite and ambition had been whetted by the 86 seats the BJP had secured in the Lok Sabha in late 1989, by far the party's best performance in any general election since independence. Founded and principally led by Brahmins since its inception in the 1920s, and rooted in a traditional Brahminical view of Indian history and society, the Hindu nationalist movement has always been uncomfortable with the topic of caste divisions and oppression, which contradicts its ideology of a solidary, united Hindu nation. The RSS has always been, in principle, opposed to caste-based affirmative action ('reservations' in the Indian terminology). As recently as late 2015, the current RSS supreme chief, Mohan Bhagwat, who has headed the RSS since 2009, embarrassed the Modi government (Modi himself is of OBC origin) and damaged the BJP's chances in a vigorously fought election to constitute Bihar's legislature and government by speaking negatively about caste-based

---

18 Francine Frankel, 'Middle Classes and Castes in India's Politics', in *India's Democracy: An Analysis of Changing State–Society Relations*, ed. Atul Kohli (New Delhi: Orient Longman, 1991), 255, 259. See also Christophe Jaffrelot, *India's Silent Revolution: The Rise of the Lower Castes in North India* (London: Hurst and Company, 2003).

reservations. The BJP lost this State election to a renewed alliance of two factions which had comprised the Janata Dal in Bihar in the early 1990s. But Bhagwat, whose father Madhukar Rao Bhagwat was a pioneering RSS activist, was simply expressing the long-established RSS view on the awkward matter of caste. Mohan Bhagwat's trailblazing predecessor Madhav Sadashiv (M. S.) Golwalkar, RSS chief from 1940 to 1973 and like the Bhagwats a Maharashtrian Brahmin, wrote in the late 1960s that while in the twentieth century 'the caste system has degenerated beyond all recognition', the hierarchy had 'in fact served as a great bond of social cohesion for thousands of years of our glorious national life'.[19]

However, it was not possible for the *sangh-parivar* to directly oppose the Mandal recommendation of 'social justice', given the movement's ultimate goal of Hindu unity. So it chose a different path of responding to the crisis precipitated by V. P. Singh's announcement.

Until 1990, the RSS had been content to let the VHP, its affiliate with responsibility in religious matters, take the lead in the *Ramjanambhoomi* agitation. That changed on 25 September 1990 when L. K. Advani, the BJP's national President, got on a minibus decked up to resemble a *rath* (ancient chariot) and began a *yatra* (journey) from a place called Somnath, in the western State of Gujarat, to Ayodhya – a distance of some 2,000 kilometres (1,250 miles). Advani, born in the city of Karachi in undivided India's Sindh province in 1927, joined the local RSS there aged fifteen and migrated to India after the 1947 partition when Sindh became part of Pakistan (Karachi is Pakistan's largest city today). The choice of Somnath was deliberate, as it is the site of a famous Hindu temple which was repeatedly vandalized or destroyed by a succession of Muslim conquerors between the eighth and eighteenth centuries, and repeatedly rebuilt by Hindu rulers. The ruins underwent a controversial restoration just after India's independence in 1947 at the initiative of Sardar Vallabhbhai Patel, Nehru's Home (interior) Minister and Deputy Prime Minister until his death in December 1950, who was a conservative Congress leader from Gujarat. Advani himself would go on to serve as India's Home Minister in two BJP-led coalition governments from 1998 to 2004, and was elevated to become Atal Behari Vajpayee's Deputy Prime Minister from 2002 to 2004.

19  M. S. Golwalkar, *Bunch of Thoughts* (Bangalore: Vikram Prakashan, 1968), 18, 108–110.

For the next four weeks, Advani's *faux* chariot travelled through the north Indian heartland, stirring communal tensions and eruptions of Hindu–Muslim violence on the way. His convoy evoked a massive response from emotionally charged crowds along the route. Cries of *Jai Shri Ram* (Victory to Lord Ram), *mandir wahin banayenge* (we will build the temple there, no matter what), *garv se kaho, hum Hindu hain* (say it with pride, we are Hindu) and *aur ek dhakka do, Babri Masjid tor do* (give it another push, and the Babri Mosque will fall) rent the air, as Advani brandished swords presented to him at frequent stops on the journey to redeem *Ramjanambhoomi*.

The canny strategy of deflecting caste conflict by stoking Hindu–Muslim antagonism and polarization had a recent precedent. In 1985, the then Congress government of Gujarat had proposed to nearly triple OBC reservations, from 10 per cent to 28 per cent, in the State's administrative apparatus and public educational institutions. This sparked rioting by upper castes, which initially targeted public transport and government buildings. But the *sangh-parivar* then succeeded in preventing the escalation of inter-caste conflict by encouraging lethal attacks on the State's 10 per cent Muslim minority, especially in the largest city, Ahmedabad, which had a history of communal violence including a major episode in 1969.[20] The strategy of Hindu consolidation against the 'internal Enemy' worked. The BJP grew rapidly in Gujarat from that point. When a mid-term national election took place in 1991, the party won 20 of Gujarat's 26 Lok Sabha constituencies. In 1995, the BJP won a two-thirds majority in the State legislature, decisively outpolling the Congress in all parts of the State and among all social groups (even tribals, in whose communities the RSS had been active since the 1950s) except one – Muslims. The BJP has been in power in Gujarat ever since, and is poised to win again in State elections due in Narendra Modi's home State in December 2017.

The BJP President's Ayodhya mission was aborted on 23 October 1990, when he was arrested and taken into police custody for inciting public disorder and breach of peace during a logistically unnecessary but politically strategic detour through Bihar. Policing is under the jurisdiction of States in India, and the order for his arrest was given by Lalu Prasad Yadav (b. 1948), the Janata

---

20 See Ornit Shani, *Communalism, Caste and Hindu Nationalism: The Violence in Gujarat* (Cambridge: Cambridge University Press, 2007), 77–88.

Dal Chief Minister of Bihar elected in early 1990, who had earned his political spurs in the anti-Indira movement in Bihar led by Jaya Prakash Narayan in the mid-1970s and been jailed during the Emergency. Despite Lalu's decapitation strike, a large mob of Hindu nationalist zealots tried to storm the Ayodhya site a week later, on 30 October 1990. The Janata Dal Chief Minister of Uttar Pradesh, Mulayam Singh Yadav (b. 1939), also elected in early 1990, ordered the State police to disperse the mob, and several dozen were killed as the police opened fire. Mulayam Yadav had joined politics in the 1960s inspired by Ram Manohar Lohia (1910–67), an anti-colonial freedom fighter and post-independence socialist leader of Uttar Pradesh who was a strident critic of Nehru's regime in the 1950s and 1960s. The BJP withdrew its outside support to V. P. Singh's fragile government in New Delhi after this fiasco. In end-1990, Hindu–Muslim violence gripped swathes of India from the town of Aligarh in western Uttar Pradesh to the city of Hyderabad in southern India, leaving scores dead.

The Babri Masjid's respite proved temporary. Two years later, the Hindu nationalist movement extracted its revenge, as its activists razed the mosque. By that time, Uttar Pradesh was run by a BJP government, elected in 1991 in a mid-term poll, riding on the fervour generated by the *Ramjanambhoomi* issue. Until then, the BJP and its predecessor, the Jan Sangh, had been a relatively marginal political force in Uttar Pradesh. Its base had been largely restricted to urban centres in an overwhelmingly rural State, and within those urban centres, to the middle-caste *bania* community (shopkeepers and petty traders) and some elements of the upper castes. In 1991, the BJP won a majority in the Uttar Pradesh legislature (221 of the 425 seats) with one-third of the polled votes, as the Congress's upper-caste base defected *en masse* to the BJP. The State police naturally did not intervene when the Hindu nationalists launched their final offensive on the Babri Masjid in December 1992. Paramilitary troops under the authority of the Union government's Home Ministry were also posted at the site. The Union government was then run by the Congress, which had emerged as the single largest party, but short of a parliamentary majority, in the mid-term general election held in May–June 1991. Rajiv Gandhi had been assassinated by Sri Lankan Tamil terrorists during the campaign, and a seasoned Congress politician and erstwhile Indira Gandhi aide from the southern State of Andhra Pradesh, P. V. Narasimha Rao, was the Prime Minister from mid-1991 to mid-1996. The paramilitary troops under the Union government's control were either unwilling or unable, or perhaps a combination of both, to take on the vast, fevered mob that attacked the Ayodhya mosque in December 1992.

The BJP leaders who looked on with thrilled faces as the mosque was demolished included Advani and Murli Manohar Joshi, an Uttar Pradesh Brahmin who had succeeded him as BJP's national President in 1991. Joshi (b. 1934) had undertaken his own nationalist *yatra* in January 1992 to Srinagar, the main city of the Kashmir Valley in India's Jammu and Kashmir State. The Kashmir Valley had erupted in an uprising against Indian rule in 1990, and Srinagar was then dominated by pro-independence and pro-Pakistan insurgent groups. This had lent further traction to Hindu nationalist propaganda, and Joshi went there and raised the Indian tricolour in the centre of Srinagar on India's Republic Day, 26 January 1992. He was accompanied by Narendra Modi, then a BJP organizer deputed to the party by the RSS. Hindu–Muslim violence erupted in cities and towns across India after the Babri Masjid's demolition; at least 2,000 people were killed. The single worst episode was in Bombay (Mumbai), where members of the Shiv Sena, a thuggish nativist Maharashtrian party allied to the BJP, went on a murderous rampage, abetted by elements of the police, against the city's large Muslim minority. In April 2017, India's Supreme Court ordered that Advani, Joshi and a dozen others accused of criminal conspiracy to destroy the Babri Masjid be tried in a specially constituted Uttar Pradesh court within a two-year time frame. The Supreme Court observed that 'crimes which shake the secular fabric of the Constitution of India have allegedly been committed almost 25 years ago' but 'the accused persons have not been brought to book'.[21]

As Chapter 6 elaborates, Hindu nationalism is not a form of atavistic 'religious fundamentalism' at all. It is a very modern and political formulation of Indian nationalism which originated in the 1920s. It represents an alternative form of Indian nationalism to the 'secular nationalism' of the Congress-led independence struggle, which was hegemonic in India until the

---

21 '25 Years after Demolition, Advani, Joshi, Bharti to Face Babri Trial', *Indian Express*, 20 April 2017, 1. Six of the other prime accused have died and a seventh – the then Chief Minister of Uttar Pradesh – currently has immunity from prosecution as he is serving as the State Governor (a largely ceremonial role) of Rajasthan.

end of the 1980s. The Hindutva movement has always used, and continues to use, religious symbolism and emotions in an instrumental way, to power strategies of political mobilization which have a very concrete purpose and end-goal – capturing state power.

The *Ramjanambhoomi* campaign was instrumental in turning the Hindutva movement from a minor to a major force in Indian politics, 65 years after the birth of the RSS and a full four decades after the formation of the movement's political party, the Bharatiya Jan Sangh, in 1951. The Jan Sangh's best performance in a national election was in 1967, when the party gained 9.4 per cent of the nationwide vote and won in 35 of the 520 parliamentary constituencies comprising the Lok Sabha. All its 35 seats came from northern India, the bulk from Uttar Pradesh (12) and Madhya Pradesh (10), followed by Delhi (six) and Rajasthan (three). In 1967, the Congress suffered a jolt and opposition parties of various shades and stripes made gains across India, the Hindu nationalists included. The geographic limits of Hindu nationalist influence were evident in the late 1989 election as well, which the BJP contested as an adjunct of the main opposition alliance formed around V. P. Singh – 74 of its 86 MPs were elected from the north (Madhya Pradesh, Rajasthan, Uttar Pradesh, Delhi) and the west (Gujarat, Maharashtra). In the mid-term national election of May–June 1991, the BJP, emboldened by the response to the *Ramjanambhoomi* agitation, struck out on its own. The party put up candidates in no less than 468 of the 543 Lok Sabha constituencies (for comparison, the Jan Sangh had contested less than half, 251, of the 520 constituencies in 1967). The BJP polled 20.1 per cent of the nationwide votes and won in 120 constituencies, an impressive achievement. But nearly half of those wins, 51, were in one State, Uttar Pradesh, where the *Ramjanambhoomi* campaign had made a strong impact. Nonetheless, the BJP had emerged as the India's largest opposition party.

The onward march of Hindu nationalism continued. In the 1996 national election, as recounted in Chapter 1, the BJP emerged as India's single largest party, winning 161 of the 543 Lok Sabha constituencies and pushing Congress into second place. It was a historic breakthrough. But the sense of triumph quickly turned into bitter disappointment. As Chapter 1 has described, although the BJP was (rightly) given the first chance to form a government as the single largest party, it abjectly failed to muster support from other non-Congress parties, almost all with a regional (State-specific) base, and the government headed by Atal Behari Vajpayee resigned after 13 days rather than face a vote of confidence in the Lok Sabha, which it was certain to lose. The experience was a wake-up call for the BJP, as it underlined the party's isolation in national politics. As long as the party remained identified solely with dogmatic anti-secularism – as expressed in its core three-point charter about the Ram temple in Ayodhya, the uniform civil code or UCC, and the removal of Article 370 regarding Jammu and Kashmir from India's Constitution – it was destined to remain the pariah of Indian politics, its advances notwithstanding. The limits of political growth powered by *Ramjanambhoomi* had been reached.

It was at that point that the party, and the broader Hindutva movement, truly re-discovered the utility of Vajpayee, whose civil personality and style contrasted with the harsh, polarising politics represented by Advani. Despite his seniority, Vajpayee had been sidelined in the party after the mid-1980s, and he had, wisely, stayed away from the *Ramjanambhoomi* campaign. The party put him forward as its prime ministerial nominee in 1996, in realistic acknowledgment that an Advani candidacy would be a complete non-starter. But playing the Vajpayee card was in itself not enough. In order to forge the electoral alliances with various regional, mostly secularist parties needed to access state power at the 'Centre' (New Delhi), that would otherwise remain out of reach, the BJP was forced to formally put in abeyance its three-point anti-secular agenda. The strategic compromise – much short of renunciation – caused great chagrin among the Hindutva movement's purists, such as the leaders of the VHP. But it enabled the BJP to lead two successive coalition governments at the centre under Vajpayee's premiership, first in 1998–99 and then from 1999 to 2004, in partnership with an array of regional parties mostly based in eastern and southern Indian States, where the BJP was weak. In the mid-term national elections of both spring 1998 and autumn 1999, the BJP won exactly one-third (182) of the 543-seat Lok Sabha, and gained working parliamentary majorities with the support of its regional allies. The Congress, meanwhile, declined from the 141 seats it had won in both 1996 and 1998 to 114 seats in 1999 under its new leader, Rajiv Gandhi's Italian-born widow Sonia. Both L. K. Advani and Murli Manohar Joshi, advocates of hardline Hindutva, were rewarded with the fruits of office – the former as Home (interior) Minister from 1998 to 2004 (and from 2002 also Deputy Prime Minister), and the latter as Human Resource Development Minister from 1998 to 2004, in which capacity he tried to promote the RSS's 'saffronization' programme in education and culture.[22]

The failure of the BJP-led alliance to win a majority in the mid-2004 general election, despite Vajpayee's personal popularity and the decent governance record of the coalition government was a lesson in the complexities and uncertainties of Indian politics. One factor that contributed to the defeat was the pogrom of Muslims which occurred in Gujarat under Narendra Modi's watch in 2002. The first (and only) major outbreak of communal violence since the BJP assumed the reins at the centre in 1998, the pogrom deeply frightened Muslims across India, who feared what might happen if the BJP returned to power in 2004. A sizeable section of the electorate in many States, they voted *en masse* for anti-BJP parties in 2004, and some of the ruling alliance's regional party constituents such as the Trinamool Congress in West Bengal – who unlike the BJP enjoyed support among Muslims – suffered greatly from the backlash. Many Hindu middle-class voters across the country were also disturbed and alienated by the Gujarat episode. The Gujarat violence had an Ayodhya connection. The pogrom took place over several days after a few compartments of a train travelling to Ahmedabad were engulfed in fire close to the station in Godhra, a town in Gujarat with a slight (51 per cent) Muslim majority. The train had originated in Varanasi, the famous pilgrimage centre in eastern Uttar Pradesh, and on that day was packed with people returning from a VHP event at the *Ramjanambhoomi* site

---

22 A Member of Parliament who strongly opposed the attempts to promote the RSS's view of Indian history, society and culture through state organs was my mother, Krishna Bose. A university academic and author, she was initially elected to the 11th Lok Sabha in 1996 from West Bengal as a Congress candidate. When the Congress in West Bengal split in end-1997, she joined the Trinamool (Grassroots) Congress, a strong regional party floated by a fiery young Congress leader of the State, Mamata Banerjee. Political circumstances and compulsions meant that the staunchly secularist Trinamool Congress was allied to the BJP from 1998 to 2004. Krishna Bose was re-elected to the 12th (1998–99) and 13th (1999–2004) Lok Sabhas as a Trinamool Congress candidate, and served as the chairperson of the parliamentary standing committee on external (foreign) affairs from 1999 to 2004. Although an MP of the ruling alliance, she regularly criticized the BJP and the broader Hindutva movement on specific issues, such as the anti-Muslim pogrom in Gujarat in 2002.

in Ayodhya. The train was probably targeted by some local Muslims, although there are different versions of the incident. A total of 59 persons, including 27 women and ten children, were burned to death.

The 'hung' (fractured) Lok Sabha thrown up in 2004 enabled the Congress to stitch together a coalition government with a few regional parties and outside support from the communist-led bloc in parliament (the Congress and the BJP had won an almost equal number, 145 and 138 respectively, of the 543 Lok Sabha seats, with regional parties holding the rest). By the time the 2009 general election came around, the BJP's 1998–2004 alliance network had largely disintegrated, and Vajpayee had retired from politics due to ill-health in old age. The disorganized BJP failed to put together an appealing campaign, and its prime ministerial candidate, L. K. Advani, did not evoke much popular confidence. The Congress-led alliance was returned to power. The BJP retained its position as the main opposition party, with 116 Lok Sabha MPs.

The Congress-led coalition government became deeply unpopular as its term progressed, plagued by weak leadership, corruption scandals and general misgovernance. By 2014 it was comprehensively discredited. The BJP capitalized on this with a message of purposeful leadership and effective governance delivered in charismatic style by its next-generation leader, Narendra Modi of Gujarat, who was declared the party's prime ministerial candidate in mid-2013. In May 2014, the BJP won a majority in the Lok Sabha, 282 of the 543 parliamentary constituencies, powered by a Modi landslide in the States of northern and western India. Its share of the nationwide votes was 31.3 per cent, an all-time high for the party. This was the first time in thirty years, since the sweeping Congress victory in the December 1984 election just after Indira Gandhi's assassination, that any party won a Lok Sabha majority. With a few allied regional parties, the new Modi government's majority was even stronger – 336 seats, with 37 per cent of the nationwide votes. The Congress won in just 44 constituencies, eight per cent of the Lok Sabha; its share of the nationwide votes was 19 per cent.

Since the end of the era of Congress's hegemony in Indian politics in the watershed general election of November 1989, two sets of forces have vied to fill the void left by the Congress's decline, which has now entered its terminal stage. One is the Hindu nationalist movement and its political party, the BJP.

The other is the diverse and disparate spectrum of regional (State-specific) parties which have proliferated since the 1990s and continue to command mass support in numerous States across the Indian Union.[23] In the age of Narendra Modi, the BJP's explicit ambition is to emerge and establish itself as a pan-Indian hegemonic party, equalling or even surpassing what the Congress was in its prime. It does face significant challenges in realizing that ambition, especially as it is still weak in most of the States of eastern and southern India. But the ambition has been making progress since Modi's 2014 victory. As of end-2017, the BJP runs 18 of India's 29 State governments, covering over 60 per cent of India's population, either on its own (14) or in coalition with allied local parties (four). During 2017, due to a string of victories in State elections, it emerged as the single largest party, though still far short of a majority, in the upper chamber of India's parliament, the Rajya Sabha (House of the States). The Rajya Sabha's 238 members (plus twelve members nominated by the party in power in New Delhi, making a total of 250) are elected by the members of State legislatures, which means that its composition reflects the relative strength of parties across the Indian Union. In contrast, the dying Congress – controlled by Sonia Gandhi and her son Rahul, a miserably failed politician – has a government in just one of India's large States, Karnataka in the south (whose capital, Bangalore/Bengaluru, is India's main IT hub), where it faces a serious BJP challenge in a State election due in the late spring of 2018.

In March 2017, the BJP won an overwhelming four-fifths majority in the legislature of India's most populous State, Uttar Pradesh, with a strong plurality, about 40 per cent, of the polled votes. The Congress won in seven of the Uttar Pradesh legislature's 403 constituencies, and polled 6 per cent of the State-wide votes. This was not novel. Since the 1990s, the Congress has been near-extinct in Uttar Pradesh, as the three social blocs whose support underpinned its dominance there until the 1980s have predominantly voted for other parties: the upper castes for the BJP; the Muslims for the Samajwadi Party or SP, a regional party formed by Mulayam Yadav's Janata Dal faction in October 1992, two months before the Babri Masjid's demolition; and Dalits for the Bahujan Samaj Party or BSP, a party formed in 1984 to advance Dalit rights and empowerment which succeeded in developing a mass base

---

23 For a detailed account of the transformations in Indian politics between 1990 and 2013, see Bose, *Transforming India*, Chapter 2.

only in Uttar Pradesh. In the 2017 State election, the Congress, which is almost non-existent on the ground in Uttar Pradesh, made a last-minute alliance with the SP, headed by Mulayam Yadav's son and successor Akhilesh Yadav, the outgoing Chief Minister. The alliance was simply steamrolled by the Modi/BJP juggernaut, which skilfully combined the old anti-Muslim Hindutva message (Muslims are 19 per cent of Uttar's Pradesh's population) with Modi's signature discourse of good governance and socioeconomic development. The BJP campaign was managed, as was its successful national campaign in 2014, by Amit Shah, a hardline Hindu nationalist from Gujarat handpicked by Narendra Modi to serve as BJP's national President after the mid-2014 triumph which elevated Modi to India's premiership. The BJP, whose fortunes in Uttar Pradesh had declined since the end-1990s, once the *Ramjanambhoomi* fervour abated, returned to power in the State for the first time in fifteen years; since 2002, Uttar Pradesh had been alternately governed by the BSP and the SP. The decisive victory in India's most populous State whetted the BJP's ambition of pan-Indian hegemony, and it launched an all-out propaganda offensive against regional party State governments ideologically opposed to Hindutva and its concept of a *Hindu rashtra* (Hindu state), with Mamata Banerjee's Trinamool Congress government in the populous eastern State of West Bengal at the top of the hit list.

In April 2017, Modi by his side, Amit Shah told a top-level party conference that the BJP aimed to dominate India 'from panchayat to parliament' and he would only consider his mission accomplished when 'every State' in India had a BJP government (panchayats are elected village-level bodies). The tone was hyperbolic but the statement is one of serious intent.[24] It expressed the ultimate aspiration of the founders and pioneers of the Hindutva movement – total control of the Indian state. This meeting of the BJP's national executive was held in Bhubaneswar, the capital of the eastern State of Odisha. In panchayat elections in this overwhelmingly rural State in early 2017, the BJP had finished a strong second to the regional party which has governed the State continuously since 2000, pushing the Congress into near-oblivion in distant third place.

The future of India's secular state hangs in the balance.

---

24 'Shah Target: Panchayat to Parliament, and Every State', *Indian Express*, 16 April 2017, 1.

# 5

# TURKEY: THE ANTI-SECULARIST TRIUMPH

*Some countries ... are divided over whether their society belongs to one civilization or another. These are torn countries. Their leaders typically wish to ... make their countries members of the West, but the history, culture and traditions of their countries are non-Western. The prototypical torn country is Turkey. The twentieth-century leaders of Turkey followed in the Ataturk tradition and defined Turkey as a modern, secular, Western nation-state. However, elements in Turkish society have supported an Islamic revival and argued that Turkey is basically a Middle Eastern Muslim society. In addition, while the elite of Turkey has defined Turkey as a Western society, the elite of the West refuses to accept Turkey as such ... Turkey will not become a member of the European Community. Having rejected Mecca, and then being rejected by Brussels, where does Turkey look?*

—Samuel Huntington, American political scientist, in 1993[1]

The unravelling of the Turkish secular state unfolded gradually over more than a half-century. In retrospect, the process of erosion and decline began in the 1950s, but escalated from the 1990s and climaxed in the lasting capture of state power by anti-secular forces in the new century.

The long retreat of state-secularism in Turkey began with the end of single-party rule. As noted in earlier chapters, Turkish state-secularism had two congenital defects, which proved over time to be chronic maladies. The

---

1   Samuel P. Huntington, 'The Clash of Civilizations', *Foreign Affairs* 72, no.3 (summer 1993), 42.

first of the two banes was the imposition of laicism (*laiklik*) on the population by an authoritarian state using extremely repressive methods. The second problem, which compounded the first, was the crudely imitative nature of the Turkish state-secularist concept, derived from the Kemalist vanguard's facile – and ultimately futile – ambition that Turkey be accepted by European peoples and states as a European, equally 'Western' compatriot.

The era of the one-party state lasted nearly a quarter-century. Its end was first signalled by dissent, and then an unprecedented public split, in the ruling Republican People's Party (CHP) just after the end of World War II. Unlike World War I, when the fast-unravelling Ottoman state's membership of the Central Powers had led to the Empire's final demise, the Turkish Republic stayed out of the 1939–45 war, consistent with Mustafa Kemal's policy of caution and circumspection in foreign affairs. At home, the regime led after Kemal's death in November 1938 by his successor as President, Ismet Inonu, continued on the authoritarian path established by the Republic's founding leader (Inonu was one of Kemal's closest comrades). The regime's hidebound nature eventually became suffocating for a small minority in the CHP's upper echelons. As the war ended, they raised the banner of revolt. In June 1945, four senior CHP figures submitted a memorandum to the CHP's parliamentary party (of which they were members) calling for political reform and greater pluralism. The call was rejected by the party-state's leadership, upon which the group of high-profile dissidents quit the CHP and formed the Democrat Party (DP) in January 1946.

The DP's four founders were Celal Bayar, Adnan Menderes, Fuat Koprulu and Refik Koraltan. Bayar (1883–1986) was the senior-most figure; he had been minister of the economy from 1932 to 1937 and Prime Minister under Ataturk in 1937–38. Koprulu, an accomplished historian, was the group's intellectual member. But the man who rapidly emerged as the new party's charismatic face, with mass appeal, was Adnan Menderes (1899–1961), who would dominate Turkey's politics as Prime Minister from 1950 to 1960. Menderes was from a landowning family in Aydin province, in the Izmir region of southwestern Turkey's Aegean coast. This region would remain his personal stronghold until Turkey's first military coup brought his premiership and political career to an abrupt end in 1960. Menderes began his political life in a shortlived 'opposition' party established at Mustafa Kemal's initiative in 1930 to provide a fig-leaf of pluralism to the state. This experiment with a token opposition was terminated by Kemal after three months when the new party, led on Kemal's command by one of the supreme leader's trusted associates, started to show signs of outgrowing its token character by attracting a range of people unhappy with the regime. Following its closure, young Menderes was inducted into the CHP at Kemal's behest and became a deputy in the Grand National Assembly in 1931.

The DP competed against the CHP in Turkey's first multi-party election in July 1946. It was a landmark development by Turkish standards because it marked the first time since the republic had come into existence 23 years earlier that a semblance of political competition was allowed. Nonetheless, this election is generally not regarded as Turkey's first substantively multi-party election because the state machinery throughout the country worked blatantly to ensure a CHP victory and the electoral process was marred by malpractice and fraud. Moreover, the newly formed DP was yet to develop a countrywide network and Inonu called a quick election to exploit the infant challenger's organizational weakness. Indeed, the DP was able to put up only 250 candidates for the National Assembly's 465 seats. Despite all this, the DP was able to establish itself as a serious opposition force, winning 64 seats. The CHP won 395 seats, a huge majority, but the tarnished election of 1946 began the countdown to the end of the one-party state established and nurtured by Ataturk. That came four years later, in May 1950, when the DP swept to power with a huge parliamentary majority.

The DP challenge led by Menderes grew stronger in the late 1940s, fuelled by widespread public discontent with a quarter-century of one-party authoritarianism. Some elements of the regime realized that one significant reason for the discontent and the fledgling opposition party's popularity was the draconian secularism inflicted on Turkey since 1924. So some backpedalling measures were taken during the last two years of one-party rule as part of a damage-control strategy. The government made foreign exchange available to Turkish citizens wishing to undertake the pilgrimage to Mecca, permitted the reinstatement of religious instruction in primary schools (but only as an optional add-on after regular school hours), allowed limited training courses for Muslim clerics (*imam-hatip kurslari*), and even approved the opening of a theological faculty at the University of Ankara, the capital of the Kemalist

Republic. In 1924, the existing *imam-hatip* institutions had been brought under the authority of the state's Ministry of Education, after which their numbers declined until the last such facilities closed down in 1932. Of the 479 *medreses* (seminaries) in existence in 1924, only one, attached to the sixteenth-century Suleymaniye mosque in Istanbul, survived the Kemalist crackdown for a time. It was first converted into the theological faculty of Istanbul University, a secular institution, then downgraded in 1933 into a research centre within the university's humanities faculty, and finally abolished altogether in 1941. A couple of months before the May 1950 election, the government permitted, for the first time since 1925, the reopening to the public of the dilapidated tomb-mausoleums of Ottoman monarchs as well as spiritual figures of Turkish history, such as the shrine of the thirteenth-century Sufi mystic Rumi in the city of Konya.

It was too little, too late. The DP swept to power in 1950, winning 396 of the 487 seats in the Grand National Assembly; the CHP was reduced to 68 seats. The electoral system that translated votes into seats was the same plurality-majority, 'first-past-the-post' system that has been used in India, in both national and State elections, since the early 1950s. This method favours the party with the single largest vote share and often converts relatively slim pluralities of the popular vote into large legislative majorities. The Congress party won parliamentary majorities in seven of India's first eight national elections, between 1952 and 1984, without ever securing a majority (at least 50 per cent) of the polled votes. In Turkey's newly emerged two-party system, however, the DP won a clear majority of the nationwide votes, nearly 54 per cent, while the CHP got 40 per cent (the turnout was 89 per cent of the eligible electorate, up from 85 per cent in 1946). This gave the DP a massive parliamentary majority. President Inonu, who was simultaneously the CHP leader, had apparently thought (or hoped) that the CHP would get the larger vote share and thus a parliamentary majority. He was sadly mistaken. After the DP triumph, Bayar replaced him as the Republic's President, while Menderes became Prime Minister and the nation's most powerful politician. Of the other two DP founders, Koraltan became the speaker of parliament and Koprulu the Foreign Minister. The CHP fared even worse in the next national election in 1954. The DP increased its share of the nationwide vote to almost 57 per cent, while the CHP declined to 35 per cent. This gave the

DP 503 of the 550 seats in the Grand National Assembly, and the CHP was reduced further to just 31 seats.

The DP's dramatic ascendancy was driven by mass support among the religiously pious Sunni majority of Turkey's population. This majority was largely comprised of the Anatolian peasant society Ziya Gokalp (see Chapter 2) had romanticized in the early 1920s; when Menderes was ousted by the military coup of 1960, about 75 per cent of Turkey's people were rural agriculturists. The DP's rise gave a large section of this rural population as well as humble provincial townspeople a winning voice against the bureaucrats and middle-class professionals, based mainly in the metropolitan centres of Ankara and Istanbul, who made up the elite and backbone of the CHP and its regime. The DP–CHP rivalry reflected both a class divide and a rural–urban schism, and the DP unmistakably had the greater numbers in this contest.

The advent of the DP era brought forth a great revival of public religiosity in Turkey during the first half of the 1950s, described in Chapter 3. In the mid-1950s, it was clear to an American scholar that 'from birth to death, the life of the majority of Turks today continues to be punctuated and illumined by Islam'. He also noted that among the 'hospitable peasant Turks, the tremendous sway which [Anatolian] folk Islam exercises over them is constantly apparent', as well as the very important fact that Turkey's Muslims, '98 per cent' of the population, 'are split into orthodox [Sunni] and heterodox [Alevi] groups'.[2] During the DP decade (1950–60), at least 5,000 new (Sunni) mosques were built in Turkey, and several thousand existing ones which had fallen into disrepair since the 1920s were renovated by state funding provided through the *Diyanet*, the central government's Directorate of Religious Affairs. In February 1960, just three months before the DP era came to an end, *The Times* (London) ran a story headlined 'Turks Turn Again to Religion'.[3] Along with the renewed public manifestations of the majority's Sunni faith, the more private observances of religion also returned, as increasing numbers of state employees started keeping the Ramazan fast and families in provincial towns revived the practice of having suitably learned men teach the Koran to their children.

---

2  Reed, 'The Religious Life of Modern Turkish Muslims', 119–120, 126, 135.

3  Walter F. Weiker, *The Turkish Revolution, 1960-1961: Aspects of Military Politics* (Washington, DC: The Brookings Institution, 1963), 9.

The DP regime's apex leadership, however, had no anti-secular agenda. They were breakaway elements of the Kemalist establishment and had no wish to undo the secular state established by Ataturk. They wanted to distance themselves from the draconian state-secularism practiced between the mid-1920s and the late 1940s, and no more. The DP's programme accepted five of the so-called 'six arrows' or slogans of Kemalism which had comprised the CHP-run state's dogma: republicanism, nationalism, populism, reformism and laicism. The only element not endorsed was statism/*etatisme* – meaning state control, direction and regulation of the economy, which the DP proposed to liberalize through encouragement of private entrepreneurship. Only one of the 87 points in the DP's 1950 election manifesto dealt with Kemalist laicism, and its tone was measured: 'Our party rejects the erroneous interpretation of secularism as enmity towards religion, and recognizes religious freedom like all other freedoms as a sacred human right'.[4] The DP's moderate line on the secular state was helped by the fact that in 1948, a conservative, pro-clericalist DP faction had split off and formed a separate party. This party, the Nation Party (*Millet Partisi*, MP), made no more than a marginal impact in the electoral politics of the 1950s. Freed of the pro-clericalist element, the DP simply defined religious freedom as one of numerous basic freedoms, 'provided it did not violate the [state's] principle of secularism'. Celal Bayar, soon to be President, stated rather wearily and with an undertone of sarcasm in 1949, 'The Turkish nation is Muslim. It will stay Muslim. It will reach its God as Muslim. Religious education is entirely a technical matter'.[5]

A segment of the DP's local units and grassroots base did want an assertive anti-secular policy. Thus a resolution passed by the DP unit in Konya in 1951 called for the outlawing of the top-hat made compulsory for Turkish men in the mid-1920s and the reintroduction of the *fez*, veiling of women, the restoration of the Arabic script banned in the late 1920s, and the re-legalization of polygamy.[6] Konya, a graceful city in west-central Anatolia, is best known for the mausoleum of the Sufi saint Mevlana Rumi, but it has also been a centre of orthodox Sunnism throughout the Turkish Republic's existence and was the base of Necmettin Erbakan, Turkey's leading Islamist

---

4   Rustow, 'Politics and Islam in Turkey, 1920–1955', 91.

5   Karpat, *Turkey's Politics: The Transition to a Multi-Party System*, 233.

6   Ibid., 287.

politician from the late 1960s to the late 1990s. But the stance of the DP regime's apex leadership prevailed over the local idiosyncrasies. The first, symbolic act of the DP government elected in 1950, as noted in Chapter 3, was to reinstate the Arabic prayer call (*ezan*) which a Kemalist fiat had replaced with an unpopular Turkish version in 1933. A few months later, in the autumn of 1950, Menderes's government slightly modified the delivery of religious instruction in primary schools, reinstated by the predecessor CHP government from 1949. Instead of being an optional, add-on session conducted after regular school hours, religion (meaning standard Sunni Islam) classes were incorporated into regular school hours, but pupils would still be excused from attending these classes if their parents so requested.

The DP regime's tinkering with the edifice of the secular state ended there. Based on the results of the 1950 and 1954 national elections, the American scholar Dankwart Rustow classified Turkey's population into three categories in 1957: 'Secularists' (supporters of Kemalist laicism), 'Moderates' (broadly accepting of the secular state but sceptical of dogmatic Kemalist secularism), and 'Clericalists' (religious conservatives opposed to the secular state). He estimated that 55–60 per cent of Turkey's people were Moderates, 35–40 per cent Secularists, and a mere 5 per cent Clericalists, whilst cautioning that 'the lines are fluid' and cut across party loyalties.[7]

◆

The DP regime was not undone by any secular/anti-secular divide, a potentially explosive issue it straddled with considerable dexterity. It was undone by descent into authoritarianism, which destabilized Turkey's infant political pluralism and produced a blowback, in the form of a military intervention in 1960, whose legacy had a retarding effect in the longer run on the country's prospects of evolving into a stable democracy. One major consequence of the derailing of the nascent trajectory of democratic development was that the place of secularism as a principle of the state could not be debated and negotiated in a framework and atmosphere of pluralism. Instead, the extremely authoritarian (and culturally inauthentic) Kemalist form of the concept continued as a rigid dogma for the next four decades,

---

7   Rustow, 'Politics and Islam in Turkey, 1920–1955', 101–105.

until the end of the twentieth century, even as social change and political turbulence slowly but steadily eroded the capacity of the secular state to enforce the compliance essential for the Kemalist concept's survival. The sporadic attempts to coopt anti-secular opposition such as the 'Turkish–Islamic Synthesis' doctrine promoted during the largely military-dominated decade of the 1980s, following the third military coup (of 1980) in the space of just two decades, simply aggravated the long-term legitimacy problem of authoritarian secularism. In the early twenty-first century, as the political tables turned decisively in favour of anti-secular forces commanding the loyalty of a vast social constituency, such enforcement of state-secularism was no longer possible and the Kemalist secular state unravelled in all but name – only to be replaced by an equally authoritarian anti-secular model of nation and state.

The unravelling of DP rule began, ironically enough, with its smashing second consecutive victory in the national election of mid-1954 – 57 per cent of the nationwide vote and 503 of the 550 seats in parliament. The triumph, and its scale, 'made the DP leadership, starting with Menderes, dizzy with success' and intoxicated with 'the illusion of unlimited power'.[8] The inordinately intoxicating effect was due to the extremely incipient, shallow nature of political pluralism in Turkey. Menderes and his colleagues were products of the founding Kemalist era of 1923–45 and were deeply infected with its authoritarian ethos, which had demanded unquestioning obedience to those at the helm of the state. Debate, dissent and opposition were considered deviant and often treated as outright criminal. Despite the emergence of a competitive two-party system in the 1950s, the political culture of Turkey as shaped during the first three decades of the republic was thoroughly dominated by this authoritarian legacy. Menderes and his associates had been politically socialized in that environment and their behaviour in power replicated the attitudinal frame of the founders of the Republic led by Mustafa Kemal, who in turn were products of the violent authoritarian tendency increasingly dominant in the CUP movement during the first two decades of the twentieth century (see Chapter 2). Moreover, the state-sponsored personality cult of Mustafa Kemal which appeared in the 1920s and developed

---

8   Cem Erogul, 'The Establishment of Multi-Party Rule, 1945–1971', in *Turkey in Transition: New Perspectives*, eds. Irving Schick and E. Ahmet Tonak (New York and Oxford: Oxford University Press, 1987), 111.

in the 1930s provided an unhealthy model for later, and lesser, leaders to emulate. Menderes's increasing megalomania evident during the latter half of his decade-long (1950–60) leadership of the Turkish state was the first example of this syndrome. The leader cult around Recep Tayyip Erdogan that appeared in the first decade of the twenty-first century and developed to ever more morbid proportions during the second decade is also directly descended from the Ataturk cult of the secular state, mixed in Erdogan's case with the absolutist tradition of the Ottoman sultanate. These foundational anti-democratic traits – the cult of the God-like supreme leader and intolerance of difference, dissent and opposition – have endured as the defining features of the DNA of the Republic of Turkey. By comparison, the Republic of India's complex inheritance from the formative Nehru period of the 1950s and 1960s included a basic commitment to values of social and cultural diversity and political pluralism. This legacy, ingrained in India's political culture by the 1970s, defeated his daughter's attempt in 1975–76, as described in Chapter 4, to turn India's democratic polity into a dictatorship.

Intra-party discord appeared in the DP during Menderes's second term as Prime Minister (1954–57), catalyzed by the growing concentration of power in the hands of Menderes and his closest associates. In September 1955, the remnant Greek communities of Istanbul and Izmir were subjected to a pogrom with the probable complicity of elements of the DP government. During the early 1920s, about one million Greeks living in different parts of Anatolia had fled as Mustafa Kemal's forces repelled Greece's invasion of Anatolia, and around half-a-million more left Anatolia as well as eastern Thrace (geographically the only 'European' area of the Turkish Republic established in 1923) for Greece later in that decade as part of a population transfer agreement between Turkey and Greece, which brought about 400,000 Turks from Greece to Turkey.[9] This was the Greco–Turkish equivalent of the massive, violent population transfers that accompanied the partition of India in 1947. The attack on the small Greek communities of Istanbul and Izmir (Smyrna in Greek) in 1955 was sparked by a crisis on the island of Cyprus, an Ottoman possession from 1571 to 1878 and then a British colony until 1960. Cyprus, located just fifty nautical miles south of

---

9   See Bruce Clark, *Twice a Stranger: How Mass Expulsion Forged Modern Greece and Turkey* (London: Granta Books, 2006).

Turkey's Mediterranean coastline, was about four-fifths Greek and one-fifth Turkish. In 1955, a section of Greek Cypriots launched an insurgency there to evict the British and unite Cyprus with Greece. This *enosis* (union with Greece) campaign made the Turkish Cypriot minority feel direly threatened and aroused consternation in Turkey.[10] The 1955 attacks on the tiny Greek communities of Istanbul and Izmir were not the first instance of targeting of non-Muslim minorities in the Turkish Republic. In 1942, the one-party CHP regime headed by Ismet Inonu, Ataturk's successor, had imposed a punitive tax on the Republic's Armenian, Greek and Jewish citizens which drove many families from those communities – together just 2 per cent of Turkey's population – into penury. The measure was reminiscent of the *jizya/cizye* tax sometimes inflicted on non-Muslim subjects by Muslim rulers in medieval and early modern times (including in India), and starkly revealed the ostensibly secular Turkish Republic's atavistic approach to religious minorities. It was particularly cruel on the Republic's remnant Armenian population because hundreds of thousands of central and eastern Anatolia's Armenians had perished during World War I under the CUP-dominated regime in massacres, as well as during brutal deportations across Anatolia and to present-day Syria and Iraq. But because Menderes's regime had presented itself as a democratic departure from Turkey's dark history of the first half of the twentieth century, the 1955 anti-Greek pogrom blotted its reputation and almost brought Menderes's premiership to an end amid a crescendo of criticism from within his own party and its representatives in parliament. Menderes barely survived by agreeing to reconstitute his cabinet.

The autocratic behaviour of the Menderes government steadily worsened through the second half of the 1950s. It systematically harassed and persecuted the press, the judiciary, the civil service, the trade unions, university administrators and academics, and the only significant opposition party, the CHP. Even leaders of small opposition parties were vindictively pursued. The objective seemed to be two-fold: to subordinate state organs to party control, and to punish and silence all critical voices in civil society. Of course, the CHP had run its party-state in precisely this manner for over a quarter-century,

---

10 On the Cyprus conflict, which remains unresolved today, see Sumantra Bose, *Contested Lands: Israel–Palestine, Kashmir, Bosnia, Cyprus, and Sri Lanka* (Cambridge, MA and London: Harvard University Press, 2007), Chapter 2.

but the DP's replication of that approach was inappropriate in the (weakly) plural post-1950 environment and ran contrary to the party's founding aim of democratizing Turkey. The DP regime's degeneration was similar to the Indira Gandhi government's authoritarian turn in the mid-1970s (see Chapter 4). In 1957, the Menderes government decided to hold a general election ahead of its scheduled date in mid-1958 in the hope of consolidating its position with a fresh mandate, much as Indira Gandhi attempted (and failed) in 1977 to win a popular mandate for her authoritarian rule. Three weeks before this early election was held in September 1957, Fuat Koprulu, one of the DP's four founders, resigned from the government and the party, much as some Congress leaders who had been attracted to Indira Gandhi's pseudo-progressive populism during 1969–71 were to quit after she imposed the Emergency in mid-1975. In his resignation statement, Koprulu condemned 'a man [Menderes] aiming to revive the single-party, single-leader system' established by Mustafa Kemal and continued under Ismet Inonu.[11]

Unlike Indira's 1977 gamble, the snap election of 1957 seemed to pay off for Menderes. The DP was returned to power with 48 per cent of the nationwide votes, while the CHP got 41 per cent. The DP's support had fallen significantly from its 1954 result (57 per cent) and was also lower than the 54 per cent it had secured in 1950, but its base had not collapsed. It was still decisively ahead of the CHP, which got 41 per cent, up from 35 per cent in 1954 and about the same level (40 per cent) it had polled in 1950. The discontent with the Menderes government was strongest among the educated urban class – the elite of civil bureaucrats, white-collar professionals and military officers spawned by the Kemalist order who were mostly CHP supporters anyway – and the Prime Minister still commanded much support among the peasantry in the countryside as well as among working-class people in the cities and towns. The DP's vote share gave it a two-thirds parliamentary majority (424 of the 610 seats), reduced since 1954 but still a commanding advantage over the CHP's 178 seats.

The DP's third successive electoral victory was soon overshadowed by a severe economic crisis which hit Turkey in 1958. This had been in the making since the mid-1950s, as the first DP government's (1950–54) policy of freeing the economy from the pervasive state control of the CHP era and encouraging

---

11 Erogul, 'The Establishment of Multi-Party Rule, 1945–1971', 115.

private commerce and entrepreneurship gave way to a renewed emphasis on state control in tandem with the turn to political authoritarianism. Under the third DP government elected in 1957, inflation ran out of control and shortages of essential goods became routine. In August 1958, the Turkish lira had to be severely devalued and an austerity regime was imposed on the country. Between 1960 and 1980, Turkey developed a pattern of generating a military coup every ten years. Likewise, the economic crisis of the late 1950s set a pattern of economic collapse every twenty years – this recurred in the end-1970s, just before the third military coup, and then again in 2001. That economic meltdown, as narrated in Chapter 1, was instrumental in the rise of Erdogan's AKP to power in late 2002.

The CHP, already emboldened by its relatively good result in the 1957 election, seized the opportunity. The CHP chairman, Ismet Inonu, embarked on a tour of the country in spring 1959 to mobilize opinion against the government. The DP responded with thuggish attacks by its activists on Inonu's rallies, which simply deepened the growing sense of crisis, economic and political. When Inonu renewed his campaign in the spring of 1960, the government ordered army units to block his tour. This was a serious miscalculation. Inonu, like Mustafa Kemal a career military officer before the birth of the Turkish Republic in 1923, was widely respected in the armed forces because of that background and especially for his contributions as a commander in the 1919–22 war of independence. The army personnel sent to block Inonu's travels ended up kissing his hand, saluting and allowing him to pass. Then, in April 1960, the government established a commission made up of fifteen DP parliamentarians to 'investigate' the CHP as well as the minor opposition parties. This commission was given virtually unlimited powers, in a law passed by brute majority in the Grand National Assembly, to hound the political opposition and the government's critics in the press and among university academics. Major student demonstrations against the government immediately broke out, at the end of April, in Istanbul and Ankara Universities. The government declared martial law in both cities and military units were sent to join the police in pitched battles with student protesters. In a telling sign of what was about to come, some junior officers leading those units refused orders from their superiors to use force to disperse the agitating students. Large numbers of students were however arrested, and the two universities were closed for a month. The rumour-mill ran berserk as newspapers were prevented from reporting the repression and responded with blank columns on their pages, as some Indian newspapers were to react to their forcible muzzling during the Emergency of 1975–76. On 20 May 1960, one week before the end of the Menderes regime, Prime Minister Jawaharlal Nehru of India arrived in Ankara on a scheduled state visit. He had apparently been 'deaf to the Turkish government's private requests for a postponement'. As he travelled in convoy through Ankara with Menderes after arrival at the airport, crowds on the streets jeered the Turkish Prime Minister. Anti-Menderes sentiment was strongest in the Turkish capital, a bastion of the Kemalist elite. During a press conference the next day, Nehru was pointedly asked whether he was in the habit of jailing journalists in India, and 'parried the question'.[12]

On 27 May 1960, a statement was broadcast over radio on behalf of the Turkish armed forces to 'honourable fellow countrymen': 'Owing to the crisis into which our democracy has fallen ... and in order to prevent fratricide, the Turkish armed forces have taken over the administration of the country'. The statement went on to promise 'just and free elections, to be held as soon as possible'. It further asserted that 'our initiative is not directed against any person or class', and pledged that 'our administration will not resort to any aggressive act against personalities'. 'All personalities of the [Menderes] Cabinet' were 'requested to take refuge with the Turkish armed forces, their personal safety [being] guaranteed by law'. The statement concluded with a mention of 'the great Ataturk' and undertook to uphold his 'ideal [of] peace at home, peace in the world'.[13]

Turkey's first military junta, which ran the country until October 1961 (i.e., nearly one and a half years) styled itself the National Unity Committee (NUC). The 1960 coup was different in one respect from the three succeeding military coups – the slightly less direct 'coup by memorandum' (an ultimatum to the elected civilian government to resign in March 1971); the outright seizure of power in September 1980 which lasted until 1983; and the 'soft coup' of February 1997 that led to the fall of the shortlived coalition government headed by the (Islamist) RP and its leader Necmettin Erbakan (see Chapter

12  Weiker, *The Turkish Revolution, 1960–1961*, 18–19.
13  Ibid., 20–21.

1). The latter three coups were all coordinated by the central command of the Turkish Armed Forces: the chief of the general staff and the commanders of the army, air force, navy, and gendarmerie (*Jandarma*, a force used for internal security purposes which is nominally under the Interior Ministry but is the fourth constituent of the Armed Forces). The 1960 coup, by contrast, was led by a group of 38 senior, mid-ranking and junior military officers who named themselves the NUC after seizing power. Their ranks varied from full generals to captains. The oldest, a general, was 65; the youngest, a captain, was just 27. The oldest member, Cemal Gursel, who had been the commander of Turkey's land forces until early May, when he was sent on leave after publicly criticizing Menderes, became the NUC chairman.

Most of the promises made in the statement announcing the coup proved to be specious. The DP was banned and in October 1960, more than four hundred leaders of the party, taken into 'protective custody' after the coup, were put on trial at a specially constituted tribunal which conducted its proceedings on one of the small islands off Istanbul, in the Sea of Marmara. Earlier, in August 1960, over 5,000 officers suspected of DP sympathies were forcibly retired in a massive purge of the army, air force, navy and the gendarmerie. Those purged ranged from generals and admirals of various grades of seniority to colonels, lieutenant-colonels and majors. In October 1960, 147 university professors suspected of pro-DP views were summarily dismissed by the NUC regime. The NUC, composed solely of military men, held and exercised all power until October 1961, although a day after the coup it appointed a seventeen-man civilian 'cabinet', composed almost entirely of technocrats, to run various ministries. Almost as quickly, the junta brought over a group of seven law professors from Istanbul University to Ankara and constituted them into a commission, headed by the rector of Istanbul University and later augmented with several Ankara University professors, to write a new constitution as well as a new electoral law. These developments, which both happened a few days before the names of the 38 NUC members were made public, showed that the coup against Menderes had been carefully planned.

The commission of experts initially charged with writing a new constitution and framing a new electoral law was replaced by a so-called 'Constituent Assembly' in January 1961, which delegated the job to a sub-committee of twenty members chaired by an Ankara University professor who headed the university's Institute for the History of the Turkish [i.e., Kemalist] Revolution. This body completed its tasks in a matter of months and the results of its labours were publicized with fanfare on 27 May 1961, the first anniversary of the coup. The new constitution was put to a nationwide referendum in July 1961 and passed with a 61 per cent 'Yes' vote; the turnout was 81 per cent of the eligible electorate. Nearly 40 per cent of those who turned out voted 'No' even under military rule, including majorities in many DP strongholds across the country.

The 1961 Constitution is often described as the most 'liberal' of the Turkish Republic's three constitutions, and that in a purely literal sense is probably true in comparison to both the original Kemalist Constitution of 1924, and the 1982 Constitution which was enacted under the extremely violent and repressive military regime which took over the state in 1980. Yet the 'liberal' characterization is also highly misleading. The main legacies of the 1961 Constitution for Turkey's subsequent political trajectory were two new institutions it established, both of which were retained and strengthened in the 1982 Constitution. One was the National Security Council, comprised of roughly equal numbers of military men and civilians – the chief of the general staff and the commanders of the four wings of the armed forces on the one hand and the Prime Minister and his senior cabinet members on the other, with the President of the Republic as the chair. This body gave the military hierarchy a direct role in the governance of the state. The other was the Constitutional Court, empowered to rule on the constitutionality or otherwise of legislation passed by the parliament, and to ban political parties it deemed to violate the Constitution's principles. From the 1980s, these two extra-parliamentary and unaccountable institutions became the powerful watchdogs of rigidly authoritarian state-secularism, with consequences described later in this chapter. Moreover, the 1961 Constitution extended the term of the indirectly elected President of the Republic to seven years (also retained in the 1982 Constitution), as opposed to four years for the popularly elected Grand National Assembly. Although the President elected by the National Assembly had limited powers, this gave the military further political influence because the presidency was continuously occupied by a succession of military men, including the coup leaders of 1960 and 1980, from 1961 until 1989.

In a speech to a party conference in September 1960, the CHP leader Ismet

Inonu stated that a new parliament should be elected by October 1961 at the latest. The NUC however was split between a majority, mostly comprising senior officers, who favoured a return to civilian rule as soon as possible, and a large minority of mostly mid-ranking and junior officers who wanted a protracted period of military rule. The latter group was led by Colonel Alparslan Turkes, who had been born in Cyprus in 1917 and came to Turkey with his family in 1932. A detailed study of the 1960–61 military regime published in 1963 by an American who was based in Turkey during that time described Turkes as:

> represent[ing] ... probably the most ardent Kemalism among an intelligentsia whose Kemalism is its prime common characteristic. In his speeches [after the coup] he constantly repeated that Turkey [must] return to the rapid and drastic reform policies of secularism, populism and revolutionism ... of the period when Ataturk guided the nation.[14]

In November 1960, the NUC purged 14 members of its radical faction led by Turkes, who were sent off on diplomatic assignments to Turkish embassies in capitals around the world ranging from New Delhi to Ottawa.

One task remained before Turkey could be returned to civilian rule. In September 1961, the nine-member tribunal appointed by the junta pronounced its verdicts on 581 persons under trial since the previous October for complicity in the misdeeds of the deposed regime. Four defendants – ex-President Bayar, ex-Prime Minister Menderes, and Menderes's Finance and Foreign Ministers at the time of the coup – were sentenced to death by unanimous vote of the tribunal's judges after being found guilty of a range of offences including abuse of power, high treason and personal misconduct. Eleven other men were sentenced to death by majority vote; they included the DP co-founder Koraltan, who had been the speaker of the Grand National Assembly from 1950 to 1960, and the chief of the general staff of the Turkish Armed Forces at the time of the coup, who had stayed loyal to the Menderes government. Thirty-one defendants were sentenced to life in prison, and another 402 defendants received prison terms ranging from two to twenty years, while 133 others were acquitted. Three of the death sentences were speedily carried out. Menderes and his two cabinet ministers were hanged. Bayar's death

---

14  Ibid., 126.

sentence, also passed by unanimous vote of the judges, was commuted by the NUC to life imprisonment. Had he not been spared, both the President and the Prime Minister of the first multi-party decade of the Turkish Republic (1950–60) would have died on the gallows. Bayar was released in late 1964 on compassionate grounds – he was 81. None of the eleven death sentences passed by majority vote were carried out. Menderes and his two executed cabinet ministers were symbolically rehabilitated in 1990.

◆

Multi-party politics returned to Turkey a month later, in October 1961, curiously on the exact timetable Inonu had called for a year earlier. His CHP was widely believed to hold a decided advantage in the national election held that month, with the DP's leader executed and hundreds of other DP leaders in jail. Two parties representing rival factions of the dissolved DP formed prior to the polls and were allowed to enter the fray. The military junta and its allies in the staunchly Kemalist civil bureaucracy were realistic enough to understand that an electoral process would be meaningless if the DP's social constituency was excluded, and would probably lead to a mass boycott. The major DP faction called itself the Justice Party (*Adalet Partisi*, AP) and the minor faction the New Turkey Party (*Yeni Turkiye Partisi*, YTP). The peculiar phenomenon of banned parties reappearing under new names became a feature of Turkey's surreal politics for the rest of the twentieth century. In the 1990s, for example, four parties representing Kurdish aspirations appeared in quick succession, starting with the People's Labour Party (HEP) in 1990. Banned by the constitutional court in 1993, it re-formed as the Democracy Party (DEP). The DEP was banned by the constitutional court in 1994 and immediately re-emerged as the People's Democracy Party (HADEP). The HADEP was targeted for closure in 1996 and reappeared as the Democratic People's Party (DEHAP) in 1997. In this bizarre cat-and-mouse game, there was no question of 'Kurdish' being part of any of these parties' names, because a Kurdish identity was not recognized to exist in Kemalist Turkey (see Chapter 6 for more on this).

The late 1961 election turned out to a keen contest between the CHP, which won 37 per cent of the nationwide votes, and the AP, which got 35 per cent. The second, smaller ex-DP faction, the YTP, also polled respectably at 14 per cent, as did (for the first time) the party of the conservative right, the Republican Peasants' Nation Party (also 14 per cent). This party was the successor to the Nation Party, founded in 1948 as the right-wing splinter group of the DP. The Nation Party had been closed down in 1953 for its anti-secular leanings, re-emerged as the Republican Nation Party in 1954, and merged in 1958 with an even smaller party, the Peasants' Party, to form the Republican Peasants' Nation Party. The result meant that the two factions of the erstwhile DP had together polled almost one-half of the nationwide votes (49 per cent), much higher than the CHP's 37 per cent. The CHP had failed to pull off a decisive victory even with the dissolved DP's leadership and organization in complete disarray in the wake of the coup. Indeed, a *very* revealing fact of Turkey's electoral history is that the CHP, the party established by Mustafa Kemal in the early 1920s and ever since then the main standard-bearer of Kemalism in general and its doctrine of secularism in particular, has never won an election under competitive conditions (i.e., 1950 onwards) – whether in Kemalist Turkey (1923–2002) or post-Kemalist Turkey (2003–present). This applies both to the CHP contesting under its own name and two significant offshoot parties which existed towards the end of the Kemalist era – the Social Democratic Populist Party (SHP) from 1985 to 1994, and the Democratic Left Party (DSP), which operated from 1985 until the late 2000s. The SHP was led for most of its existence by Erdal Inonu, a professor of physics and a son of Ismet Inonu, and the DSP by Bulent Ecevit (1925–2006), a very prominent politician who was the CHP's leader from 1972 to 1980. By contrast, the Congress, the main standard-bearer of India's state-secularism, did win parliamentary majorities in seven of India's first eight general elections (between 1952 and 1984), and was the single largest party in the parliament in four of the next eight elections (in 1989, 1991, 2004 and 2009).

The new electoral law enacted in 1961 at the behest of the military junta had replaced the plurality-based, 'first-past-the-post' (FPTP) system with the proportional representation (PR) method. The reform was intended to prevent the huge single-party parliamentary majorities of the kind that the DP enjoyed during the 1950s, which had enabled and encouraged Adnan Menderes's drift into autocratic rule – though the DP would have won (smaller) parliamentary majorities even under a PR system in 1950 and 1954 because it won clear majorities, 54 per cent and 57 per cent respectively, of the popular vote. Unlike the FPTP method, which is used in India and disproportionately favours the party with the plurality (single largest) share of the popular vote, the PR method allocates seats to parties on the basis of the popular vote received. So the late 1961 election produced a fractured (in Indian terminology, 'hung') Grand National Assembly in which no party had a majority. Of the 450 seats, the CHP got 173, the AP 156, the YTP 64, and the Republican Peasants' Nation Party 54 seats. The two parties born of the DP were together very close to a majority (220, AP's 156 plus YTP's 64), and a decisive majority (63 per cent) of the voters had supported parties other than the Kemalist–secularist CHP.

Nonetheless, as the leader of the single largest party, Ismet Inonu headed three coalition governments as Prime Minister between late 1961 and early 1965. The first, an ambitious 'grand coalition' between the CHP and the AP, lasted six months; the second, a CHP–YTP–Republican Peasants' Nation Party coalition, survived for under a year and a half. The CHP-led coalitional possibilities exhausted, Inonu's third and final government was a minority CHP government supported by some independent members of a weak upper chamber (senate) of parliament that had been introduced under the 1961 reforms. This lasted just over a year, until February 1965. Thereafter, a caretaker government headed by an independent senator and supported by all the non-CHP parties in the National Assembly took charge until the election of autumn 1965. The leader of the 1960–61 military junta, Cemal Gursel, was elected by the reconstituted National Assembly in late 1961 to become the fourth President of the Turkish Republic for a seven-year term. He died in 1966, five years into his term, and was replaced by Cevdet Sunay, who had succeeded him as commander of Turkish land forces in May 1960 and then became the chief of the general staff of the Turkish Armed Forces (the apex position) from August 1960. Sunay served out his full term as Turkey's President, until 1973.

In attempting to rid the polity of the risk of tyranny posed by governments with large parliamentary majorities, the military junta and its allies in the civil bureaucracy and the Kemalist sector of the academic intelligentsia had created a problem for government formation *per se*. The merry-go-round of four governments in four years (1961–65) illustrated the problem. The problem was resolved in the October 1965 election when the AP won 53 per cent of the nationwide votes and, under the PR system, secured a clear parliamentary majority – 240 of the 450 National Assembly seats.

That the erstwhile DP base was not only intact, but consolidating behind the AP, had become evident when the AP performed very strongly in local elections in late 1963. In the autumn 1965 national election, the YTP's challenge to the AP for the DP's mantle collapsed and the AP gained the vast bulk of the former DP voters, as well as the support of a part of the electorate that had supported the Republican Peasants' Nation Party in 1961 (two competing factions of this party gained a total of 8 per cent of the vote, down from the 14 per cent the united party had obtained in 1961). The AP's emergence as the successor to the DP legacy was emphatic, and so was its victory over the CHP, the preferred party of the Kemalist-secularist military hierarchy and its allied civilian elite. The CHP got just 29 per cent of the nationwide votes in 1965 – down from 37 per cent in 1961 and only a little over half of the AP's vote share (53 per cent). This gave the CHP 134 seats in the 450-member National Assembly, still a sizeable opposition.

The Justice Party's (AP) first chairman (1961–64) was a military man, Ragip Gumuspala. An army commander, he was promoted to chief of the general staff of the Turkish Armed Forces after the 27 May 1960 coup but forcibly retired just two months later, in the massive purge of the officer corps of all four wings of the military that took place in August 1960. He was the senior-most of the 5,000-plus serving officers of the army, air force, navy and gendarmerie who were ejected from the military. From 1961, he became a focal point for the re-grouping of DP activists in the AP. Upon his death in mid-1964, the leadership of the AP became vacant. In late 1964, Suleyman Demirel, a hitherto obscure technocrat, unexpectedly won the contest for the leadership of the AP against a much more politically-experienced rival candidate. Aged just forty, Demirel, a hydraulic engineer by training and profession, was not even an elected parliamentarian at the time and it is possible that his surprise accession to the AP leadership had the tacit support of the military hierarchy. Of modest, non-elite provincial origins typical of the fast-rising AP's politicians, Demirel (1924–2015) conspicuously lacked the popular charisma that had made the late Adnan Menderes such a threat to the Kemalist military hierarchy and its civilian allies. He became Prime Minister after the AP's victory in the October 1965 election and proved to be one of several resilient dinosaurs of Turkish politics in the latter third of the twentieth century, ending his public career as the President of the Turkish Republic from 1993 to 2000.

For a few years after the autumn 1965 election, it seemed that Turkey was stabilizing politically. There was a government with a stable parliamentary majority, but balanced by a large parliamentary opposition of which the CHP was by far the largest constituent. There was a reasonable degree of political pluralism – the smaller parties represented in parliament spanned the ideological spectrum from the conservative right (the two Nation Party factions) to the socialist left. All varieties of socialist and communist thought had been banned in the Kemalist state from 1925, when a draconian 'Law for the Maintenance of Order' was promulgated, and left-wing members of the intelligentsia were relentlessly persecuted from then on. Turkey's finest poet of the twentieth century, Nazim Hikmet (1902–63), was sentenced to ten years in prison under the CHP's single-party regime because of his communist inclinations. He was released in a general amnesty of political prisoners after the first DP government came to power in 1950 and subsequently fled to the Soviet Union, where he died in Moscow in 1963. Another gifted writer, Sabahattin Ali (1907–48), best known for his romantic novel *Madonna in a Fur Coat*, was repeatedly jailed for socialist beliefs and his criticism of Kemalist authoritarianism and was eventually killed while trying to flee to Bulgaria, the country of his birth. By Turkish standards, it was thus a sign of real democratic progress that a small socialist party, the Workers' Party of Turkey (TIP), which emerged mainly in Istanbul in the 1960s at the initiative of some trade unionists and like-minded intellectuals, was allowed to compete in the 1965 election and sent a small number of deputies to the National Assembly after getting 3 per cent of the votes. It was also during this phase of relative pluralism in the late 1960s that a group of Sunni Islamists gathered around Mehmet Zahid Kotku (a.k.a. Zahid Efendi), the leader of Istanbul's Naqshbandi community and *imam* of the city's Iskenderpasha mosque, moved to establish 'a party where Muslims could feel at home' after becoming 'tired of being used by the [existing] centre-right parties', in the words of the then head of the *Diyanet*, who was one of the men involved in the initiative (see Chapters 1 and 3).[15] At Kotku's urging, Necmettin Erbakan left the AP and was elected to the National Assembly in the 1969 parliamentary election as an independent candidate from Konya, a city where religious conservatism had a strong influence. A few months later, in January 1970, the Turkish Republic's first explicitly Islamist party, the National Order Party (*Milli Nizam Partisi*, MNP) was launched under Erbakan's leadership. This was the first incarnation of the Welfare (*Refah*) Party that rose meteorically during the 1990s and most of whose members subsequently joined the AKP, which was formed in mid-2001 and has been Turkey's ruling party since late 2002. As pluralism bloomed, the Turkish scholar Nur Yalman referred in an article published in 1969 to the emergence of 'a free political system' after decades of Kemalist authoritarianism and repression.[16]

In fact, Turkey's democratic development was still very superficial. The fundamental problem was that the country manifestly lacked any significant ideological tradition(s) of democratic thought that could provide an alternative path to the deeply authoritarian legacy of Kemalism which pervaded its political culture. The problem persists today, nearly fifty years later, in the post-Kemalist state thoroughly dominated by anti-secularists. By 1969, Turkey's nascent experiment in a plural polity that accommodated the diversity of views and tendencies in its society was already in the process of unravelling.

In the 1969 national election, the AP was returned to power. Its vote share fell from 53 per cent in 1965 to under 47 per cent but the party still secured a comfortable parliamentary majority (256 of the 450 seats) because a modified system of weighted PR adopted in allocating seats favoured parties with large vote shares, starting with the frontrunner, at the expense of parties with small vote shares. This weighted PR system is still used in Turkish elections along with an additional requirement, introduced in the 1980s, that a party or alliance must receive 10 per cent of the nationwide votes to be allocated seats in parliament. The CHP showed no signs of resurgence and declined further to only 27 per cent of the popular votes (143 seats), a disappointing result which caused much frustration among the Kemalist elite groups. The

---

15  Yavuz, *Islamic Political Identity in Turkey*, 207.

16  Yalman, 'Islamic Reform and the Mystic Tradition in Eastern Turkey', 42.

standout feature of the election was the abnormally low voter turnout, just 64 per cent. Since 1946, the national elections had seen a turnout of 80–90 per cent, and high voter turnout is the norm in Turkish parliamentary elections – 84 per cent and 86 per cent voted in the two most recent elections held in the space of five months in 2015. The sharply diminished turnout seemed to signal growing public apathy towards competitive party politics instead of enthusiasm for the pluralism it had fostered.

The public's growing wariness was not entirely misplaced because the relatively permissive environment of the late 1960s was, in a country with extremely weak if not nearly non-existent democratic traditions, facilitating political polarization rather than the development of a durable, tolerant pluralism. A toddler cannot bear the responsibilities of adulthood, or even of adolescence, and so it was with Turkey, a country at the toddler stage of democratic evolution almost a half-century after Mustafa Kemal's authoritarian state came into being with its rigid ideology, which suffocated all democratic potential and stifled all manifestations of social, cultural and ideological diversity.

A prime symptom of the problem was the rise of hyper-active forces on the extreme left and the extreme right. As the TIP descended into factional feuds between social-democrats and dogmatic Marxists in the end-1960s, a section of leftist university students and other youth influenced by the global climate of anti-imperialist campus radicalism and Guevarism formed militant urban groups to pursue the cause of revolution. To the dismay of the civilian government and the horror of the military brass, these groups started targeting American military personnel stationed in or passing through Turkey, an important constituent of the US's anti-Soviet alliance since the country's entry into NATO in 1952. Meanwhile the ex-colonel Alparslan Turkes, the leader of the radical-Kemalist NUC faction in the 1960 coup, had returned to Turkey in the mid-1960s from his enforced diplomatic assignment abroad, and commenced a full-fledged political career. In 1965 he took over the small and drifting Republican Peasants' Nation Party, which was suffering from a leadership void, and retooled it over the next few years into a far-right Turkish nationalist party, which was renamed as the Nationalist Movement Party (*Milliyetci Hareket Partisi*, MHP) in 1969. The MHP survived Turkes's death in 1997 to remain a significant force in Turkish politics; it has a devoted core following and in two parliamentary elections within the last twenty years, in 1999 and June 2015, the party won as much as 18 per cent of the nationwide votes. In the late 1960s, Turkes's outfit established so-called 'idealists' hearths' (*ulku ocaklari*), local cells designed to attract and indoctrinate students and youth. This recruitment gave rise to the 'Grey Wolves', a fascist militia affiliated to the MHP which engaged their radical-left adversaries in violent battles on university campuses and on the streets in 1970–71.[17] The violence created the impression that the Demirel government had lost control and was unable to maintain law and order, the basic duty of the state. In 1970, Demirel was also beset with discord and dissidence in the AP and its parliamentary delegation; some AP politicians had never reconciled to his abrupt rise to the party's leadership in the mid-1960s and viewed him as an upstart at best and usurper at worst. Although he won a vote of confidence in parliament, the middle-of-the-road AP's organizational apparatus witnessed an exodus of some members to the newly formed, highly ideological rightist parties: Turkes's fascist MHP and Erbakan's Islamist MNP.

At 1 pm on 12 March 1971, a short but unequivocal statement was broadcast on national radio on behalf of the leadership of the Turkish Armed Forces. It asserted that 'parliament and the government have driven our country into anarchy, fratricidal strife, and social and economic unrest ... [and] have destroyed the hope of reaching the level of contemporary civilization, which Ataturk set as our goal'. It went on, 'It is essential that a powerful and credible government be set up ... in the spirit of Ataturkism'. Then came the chilling threat, 'If this is not speedily undertaken, the Turkish Armed Forces, carrying out the duty given to them by law to protect and preserve the Turkish Republic, are determined to take over the administration directly'.

The grim ultimatum was very different in tone from the deceptively mild, almost apologetic wording of the statement that had announced the 1960 coup against the Menderes government. At 5pm, Prime Minister Demirel sent President Sunay, a former chief of the general staff of the Turkish Armed Forces, a letter of resignation after holding an emergency cabinet meeting. The letter stated, 'It is impossible to reconcile the memorandum with the

---

17 A myth of Turkish folklore has it that a grey wolf (*bozkurt*) guided the migratory Central Asian tribes that settled in Anatolia in the journey to their new home.

constitution and the principle of the rule of law'.[18] Nonetheless, Demirel clearly did not want to risk following Menderes to the gallows.

The Kemalist military-bureaucratic complex had struck for the second time in a decade, and with a vengeance. The architects of the 1971 'coup by memorandum' were doubtless genuinely concerned and horrified by the 'unrest', 'fratricidal strife' and 'anarchy' bred by the political pluralism that had developed in the second half of the 1960s, which is the most democratic period in the Turkish Republic's nearly one-century existence alongside 1950–54 (the first DP government), and 2003–07 (the first AKP government). The inevitably conflictual consequences of democratic pluralism offended not just the intrinsic military preference for order and discipline. It violated the obsession with homogeneity and uniformity, to be enforced at all costs, which constitutes the essence of Kemalism. Speaking in Izmir in 1923, on the occasion of the formal establishment of his People's Party (renamed the Republican People's Party or CHP a year later), Mustafa Kemal had outlined its purpose with his characteristic clarity,

> The aim of a people's organization as a party is not the realization of the interests of certain classes over those of other classes. The aim is rather to mobilize the entire nation, called People, including all classes and excluding none, in united action towards genuine prosperity which is the common objective of all.[19]

◆

The 1971 military intervention pushed the fragile democratic polity into an abyss of dysfunction and chaos. Over the following nine and a half years, until the next military coup of September 1980, there were eleven governments that came and went in a revolving-door fashion.

Unlike the 1960 coup, and the subsequent 1980 coup, the military did not directly take over the state in 1971 and form a junta to rule the country. The coup-makers instead tried to rule indirectly, using civilian proxies. After forcing Demirel's resignation, they got the President to appoint a handpicked

---

18 William Hale, *Turkish Politics and the Military* (London and New York: Routledge, 1994), 184–185.

19 Berkes, *The Development of Secularism in Turkey*, 463.

civilian to lead a new government. The appointee, Nihat Erim, was an Ankara University professor who had enjoyed a long political career, since 1946, as a CHP parliamentarian and had also been a minister in CHP-led governments in the late 1940s and the first half of the 1960s. On being appointed Prime Minister in March 1971, he resigned his nearly lifelong membership of the Kemalist party.

The military hierarchy's stentorian ultimatum had talked about the urgent need for 'reforms' without specifying their nature and content, to be implemented by 'a powerful and credible government'. The two so-called governments Erim led from March 1971 to April 1972 were, needless to say, neither credible nor powerful. The proxy civilian regime's main function was to provide a cover for military repression. The Erim cabinets were composed of a combination of technocrats and politicians drawn from both the CHP and the AP. The inclusion of politicians, especially from the deposed AP, made no sense from the ultimatum's viewpoint that 'parliament and the [AP] government' had fostered anarchy and destroyed Ataturk's dream of Turkey achieving the level of contemporary (meaning Western) civilization. The purpose was probably to co-opt a part of the political class and divide and weaken the two major parties. This did not happen because Demirel and most of the AP remained sullenly aloof while Bulent Ecevit, the rising star of the CHP, took a strong stance against the military intervention, unlike Ismet Inonu in 1960. In May 1972, Ecevit defeated the aged Inonu in a contest for the party leadership and became the CHP's new leader. The only agenda the peculiar hybrid regime of military masterminds and its civilian collaborators pursued coherently was repression. In the months after the *de facto* coup, thousands of people, mostly leftists, were rounded up in mass arrests. The vast majority had no involvement in violent activities and the detainees included leaders of the trade union movement as well as eminent academics such as Tarik Zafer Tunaya and Mumtaz Soysal (both professors of constitutional law and political science). Martial law was imposed in large parts of the country including the three biggest cities: Istanbul, Ankara and Izmir. Under martial law regulations, strikes were banned and press freedom severely curtailed. Two political parties – the socialist TIP and the Islamist MNP – were closed down on charges of violating Kemalist taboos by the powerful constitutional court which had been established at the behest of the previous military regime in 1961. The TIP was banned for speaking about the existence of Kurdish identity in Turkey, a subject strictly prohibited since 1925, and Erbakan's MNP for propagating anti-secular heresy. The MNP was however allowed to re-open just a year later, in 1972, as the National Salvation Party (*Milli Selamet Partisi*, MSP). No action was taken against Colonel Turkes's ultranationalist MHP, whose 'Grey Wolves' storm-troopers had been the prime source of the street and campus violence of 1969–71.

The facade of civilian government operating under the military's tutelage was simply unworkable. Erim departed in April 1972 and was replaced as Prime Minister by Ferit Melen, who had been the Defence Minister in Erim's cabinets. A member of a small party formed by a breakaway right-wing faction of the CHP, he enjoyed the confidence of the military brass. Melen's government, also a hotchpotch of technocrats and reluctant party politicians, proved as ineffectual as his predecessor's and collapsed in April 1973. Just before its demise, a retired admiral who had headed the Turkish navy from 1957 to 1960 was elected as the Republic's President for a seven-year term, the third consecutive military man to assume that mostly ceremonial but not powerless post. Thereafter, an entirely lame-duck caretaker administration took office, pending a national election to restore a popularly elected government in October 1973.

That election, unlike those in 1965 and 1969, returned a fractured or hung parliament in which no party won a majority. The weighted PR system favoured the larger parties and especially the frontrunner, exactly as in 1965 and 1969. But the leading vote-getter, Ecevit's CHP, obtained just 33 per cent of the nationwide votes and its 185 seats left it forty short of a majority in the 450-seat National Assembly. The AP slipped to second place with a 30 per cent vote share and 149 seats; it was hurt by a splinter-group which polled almost 12 per cent of the total votes. The modest resurgence of the CHP was due to the strong anti-military stance of its new leader, Ecevit, and the party would have done better had a rebel CHP faction not polled 5 per cent of the votes. The most significant development, however, was the emergence of Erbakan's MSP as the nation's third largest party, with 12 per cent of the votes and 48 parliamentary seats. It was an impressive electoral debut for the almost new-born Islamist party.

After three months of wrangling during which a 'grand coalition' between the CHP and the AP failed to materialize, the CHP finally formed an unlikely coalition government with the MSP as the junior partner. It was a strange alliance between the founding party and standard-bearer of Kemalist secularism, then fifty years old, and the three-year-old anti-secular entrant to the Turkish political scene. In a meteoric personal rise, Erbakan became Ecevit's Deputy Prime Minister, and the MSP received six of the 23 ministerial posts. The ministries gained by the MSP were all important ones: interior, justice, agriculture, trade, industry and technology, and religious affairs. The implausible cohabitation of ideological opposites lasted ten months before collapsing in November 1974. It would probably not have lasted that long had Turkey's civil–military and partisan divisions not been temporarily effaced by a crisis that gripped the island of Cyprus in July–August 1974. That crisis precipitated a Turkish military invasion of Cyprus in defence of the island's Turkish–Cypriot minority, and the invading force captured and occupied the north of the island (37 per cent of Cyprus's land area) to carve out a de facto Turkish–Cypriot statelet, a status quo which endures more than four decades later. The statelet proclaimed its sovereignty in 1983, an act not recognized by any country except Turkey.

After another four-month hiatus during which negotiations to put together an alternative coalition government took place, Suleyman Demirel returned in March 1975 to the prime ministership he had been forced to abdicate exactly four years earlier. He headed a multi-party coalition government of his AP, Erbakan's MSP, Turkes's MHP, the breakaway CHP faction, and some of the parliamentarians of the breakaway AP faction. Together, this unwieldy coalition, which was styled the 'Nationalist Front', mustered a slight parliamentary majority. Erbakan again became Deputy Prime Minister, as did Alparslan Turkes, the MHP chief. The MSP got eight of the thirty ministerial portfolios, and two of the three MHP parliament deputies became ministers (Turkes included). This government 'managed to survive for 27 months, until June 1977, but was hardly able to do anything else'.[20] It was paralyzed by distrust and feuding between its multiple constituents and their leaders. But thanks to its paralytic existence for more than two years, both the Islamists and the fascist fringe got access to state offices and the patronage resources that offered. The circus ended when Demirel gave up and decided, with Ecevit's consent, to go for elections in June 1977, a few months before schedule.

---

20 Hale, *Turkish Politics and the Military*, 220.

The June 1977 election threw up another hung National Assembly, although the CHP came tantalizingly close to a parliamentary majority, gaining over 41 per cent of the nationwide votes and 213 of the 450 seats, just thirteen short of a majority. This stands out as the Kemalist-secularist party's best ever performance in a competitive election, and represented the high point of Bulent Ecevit's leadership and political career. Ecevit, an unusually cosmopolitan person by Turkey's extremely insular cultural standards, had a personal Indian connection – he learned Sanskrit and Bengali while studying in London in his youth and subsequently translated some works of Rabindranath Tagore, India's famed poet-laureate, from Bengali to Turkish. The AP finished a strong second, with 37 per cent of the votes and 189 seats. The breakaway AP and CHP factions disintegrated as their voters returned to the parent parties. The third largest party was once again Erbakan's MSP. Its vote share declined to 9 per cent from 12 per cent in 1973; some Islamist voters, particularly the *Nurcu*s (followers of Said Nursi, the fundamentalist philosopher who died in 1960), were angry with the MSP for having forged the 1974 coalition with the CHP, whose one-party secular state had persecuted Nursi during his lifetime. But though the MSP's parliamentary presence halved from 48 to 24 seats, the party was still the third largest in the National Assembly.

As the leader of the single largest party, Ecevit was asked to form the government by President Koruturk, the retired naval admiral. The rivalry between Ecevit and Demirel ruled out a grand coalition of the two largest parties. Ecevit was reluctant to repeat the alliance with Erbakan's Islamists, and as a semi-progressive politician could not contemplate seeking support from the fascist MHP which had doubled its vote from three to six per cent and improved its parliamentary presence from three to 16 seats. So he took the gamble of forming a single-party cabinet. The *Hurriyet* daily, a staunchly secularist paper, headlined its front page: 'Thank God, a government without Erbakan'.[21] The jubilation was ephemeral as Ecevit failed to win a vote of confidence in the National Assembly and resigned within a month. Demirel seized the chance and put together a second version of the so-called Nationalist Front, a coalition government of the AP with the MSP and the MHP, which mustered a razor-thin parliamentary majority (229 of 450). Erbakan and Turkes once again became Deputy Prime Ministers. The MSP received eight

---

21 Ibid., 229.

of the 30 ministerial posts and the MHP five. Over the next few months, ten AP parliamentarians resigned from the party and formed an independent bloc in protest against Demirel's pandering to the Islamists and worse, the MHP fascists. Recognizing that he had lost his parliamentary majority, Demirel resigned in January 1978. His government had lasted barely six months. Ecevit then put together a government of the CHP, the AP defectors, and three parliamentarians elected from the now tiny CHP and AP breakaway parties, which just reached the majority threshold of 226.

This was the penultimate act of the increasingly absurd game of musical chairs between Demirel and Ecevit, which was reducing Turkey's politicians to an international laughing stock and discrediting the legitimacy of democratic politics within the country. Over the next two years, until its ignominious end in October 1979, Ecevit's fragile government unravelled as an economic crisis of unprecedented proportions engulfed Turkey and, in parallel, murderous political violence between left-wing radicals and the far right took on epidemic proportions.

The economic crisis of the end-1970s had been in the making for several years. The first 'oil shock' of 1973–74, when Arab petroleum-exporting countries restricted oil exports, led to a spiral in global crude oil prices. Turkey, totally dependent on oil imports for its needs, was severely affected and its balance-of-payments situation drastically worsened during the second half of the 1970s. The state became heavily indebted, and by 1979 debt-interest payments were 40 per cent of the total earnings from exports and remittances sent home by the significant population of Turkish workers in western Europe. The paralysis of government throughout the 1970s left the growing crisis unaddressed, and in the late 1970s it grew to unmanageable proportions. Inflation climbed to 44 per cent in 1978 and reached 68 per cent in 1979. The second, smaller oil shock of 1979 (due to the Iranian Revolution) made matters worse. 'Working-class families faced a desperate struggle to make ends meet' and 'in the harsh winter of 1979, people shivered in their homes for lack of heating oil'. Shortages of everyday goods became common, the black market thrived, and 'power cuts became a daily fact of life, constantly disrupting work in offices and factories'.[22] The collapsing Turkish currency, the lira, was devalued by the Ecevit government in 1979.

---

22  Ibid., 223–224.

As the economic crisis deepened, political violence between leftist and rightist extremist groups reached epidemic levels. The number of deaths in that violence rose from 231 in 1977 to 832 in 1978 and 898 in the first nine months of 1979. Ordinary citizens feared going out after dusk. In 1971, the military command had cited extremist violence as a major reason for deposing the elected civilian government. At the end of the decade, during which Turkey's polity had been thoroughly destabilized by effects originating in the 1971 coup, and its economy nearly ruined as well, the problem reappeared on a far greater scale. Moreover, the spate of killings had grave implications for the country's social equilibrium because of a strong sectarian dimension. The far-left groups involved had large numbers of Alevis, students and youth belonging to the heterodox minority community, whereas their far-right adversaries in the Grey Wolves and *ulkuculer* (idealist) groups affiliated with the MHP were all drawn from the Sunni majority. Several massacres of Alevis occurred during 1978–80, recounted in Chapter 3. Beyond radicalism on university campuses, where both sides had a significant presence, the violence ravaging urban Turkey was linked to the villages-to-cities migration that began in the 1960s and picked up in the 1970s, as Turkey transitioned from being a largely agricultural country to a partly industrialized economy (the migration escalated further in the 1980s and 1990s and was a major factor in the Islamist political surge, discussed later in this chapter). By the end of the 1970s, *gecekondus* (shantytowns) housing migrants from the countryside had already sprung up in Turkish cities, and many youth in these impoverished slums became recruits for both the radical left and the radical right.

After Ecevit submitted his government's resignation in October 1979, Demirel took his final turn as Prime Minister. He formed a minority AP government in November with outside support from the MSP and the MHP. It tenuously lasted ten months.

Inflation officially rose to 107 per cent in 1980. The economy had already contracted by 0.4 per cent in 1979; in 1980 it contracted a further 1.1 per cent. Between October 1979 and September 1980, there were 2,812 deaths reported in political violence, an average of eight a day. One of those victims was Nihat Erim, the military-appointed Prime Minister of 1971–72, who was assassinated by left-wing militants in July 1980. The police were increasingly affected by polarization between leftist and rightist unions, Pol-Der and Pol-Bir.

Since 1979, there had been rumblings of a military coup in the offing. By 1980, it was only a matter of time. It finally happened on 12 September 1980, after several months of discussions, planning and preparation at the highest levels of the military's officer corps. The detailed plans already in place, the final provocation came from the MSP leader Necmettin Erbakan's 'open defiance of secularism'. On 30 August, a national holiday that commemorates the victory of 1922 in the 1919–22 war that established the Turkish Republic, Erbakan refused to attend the parade in Ankara and pay obeisance at Ataturk's mausoleum, *Anitkabir*, a requirement of all the country's senior political and military leaders. A week later, on 6 September, he led a huge demonstration in Konya, a MSP stronghold, 'at which open calls for the establishment of an Islamic state were made'.[23]

On 12 September 1980, the high command of the Turkish Armed Forces took over the country, 'to protect and look after the Turkish Republic'.[24] All activities by political parties were banned and the senior leadership of the four major parties (CHP, AP, MSP and MHP) were immediately arrested, to be followed by thousands of lesser politicians. Martial law was proclaimed nationwide and a massive, protracted crackdown was launched against a wide range of suspect elements, from trade unionists and liberal and leftist intellectuals to Kurdish activists, and even some of the far-right gangs. Over the next couple of years, the number of arrests ran into the hundreds of thousands and brutal torture of detainees was endemic.[25] The junta's apex leadership were the five military members of the National Security Council – *Milli Guvenlik Kurulu* or MGK, established in 1961 after the first military coup – headed by General Kenan Evren, the chief of the general staff, and comprising the commanders of the army, air force, navy, and gendarmerie (the other five members of the NSC being the President, an office successively occupied by four military men between 1961 and 1989, plus the Prime Minister

---

23  Ibid., 237–238.

24  Ibid., 246.

25  The bleakness of post-coup Turkey in the early 1980s is portrayed in a riveting movie, *Yol* (The Road), released in 1982 and written and directed by Yilmaz Guney in collaboration with his associate Serif Goren. Guney, an actor and filmmaker of working-class origins, was a Turkish Kurd and a radical leftist. *Yol* won the Palme d'Or at the Cannes film festival in 1982.

and the ministers of interior, defence and foreign affairs). The junta took over all legislative and executive powers and ruled the country with an iron fist for over three years, until November 1983. It gave a cabinet of 27 ministers, appointed a week after the coup, responsibility for running the day-to-day administration. The cabinet was headed by a recently retired commander of the navy and included five other former military officers; the rest were civilian technocrats.

♦

The three years of direct military rule threw up the civilian leader who would dominate Turkish politics for a decade, from end-1983 to 1993. Turgut Ozal served as Prime Minister for six years, from November 1983 to October 1989, when he became Turkey's eighth President, only the second man of a non-military background after Celal Bayar (1950–60) to occupy the post. His seven-year presidential term was cut short midway by his sudden death in April 1993. The Ozal decade was crucial in Turkey's transition from a state governed, nominally at least, by the Kemalist conception of secularism to a country in which anti-secular politics decisively emerged – over the decade after Ozal's death – from the margins to prominence and then captured state power through democratic means.

Turgut Ozal was of ordinary, non-metropolitan origins and had partial Kurdish parentage. He was born in Malatya in eastern Anatolia in 1927 and grew up in towns in eastern Anatolia (Mardin) and central Anatolia (Kayseri) before graduating in electrical engineering from the Istanbul Technical University in 1950. Over the next three decades he worked mainly in the State Planning Organization, the equivalent of India's Planning Commission and similarly responsible for preparing five-year strategies of socioeconomic development and resource allocation, and had a stint at the World Bank in Washington, DC in the early 1970s. His first foray into politics was in the mid-1977 national election, when he stood as a candidate for Erbakan's MSP. Twenty-four MSP candidates were elected to the National Assembly but he was not among them; he had contested from Izmir on Turkey's western coast, where the Islamist party's base was weak. The politician in the family was Turgut's younger brother, Korkut Ozal (1929–2016). Korkut Ozal, like Turgut a graduate (1951) in civil engineering from Istanbul Technical University, was one of the inner circle of Mehmet Zahid Kotku, the Naqshbandi leader of Istanbul and the *imam* of the city's Iskenderpasha mosque, who was the brain and the inspiration behind the launch of the MNP as the Turkish Republic's first explicitly Islamist party in 1969–70. Korkut was elected to the National Assembly in both 1973 and 1977 as a candidate of the MSP – the renamed MNP formed in 1972 – from Erzurum in eastern Anatolia. The younger Ozal, a MSP vice-chairman during the 1970s, served as a minister in all the three governments in which the MSP leader Necmettin Erbakan was a Deputy Prime Minister in the 1970s. He was the minister of food, agriculture and livestock in the Ecevit-led coalition government of 1974 and the Demirel-led one of 1975–77, and then minister of the interior in the shortlived Demirel-led coalition government of the second half of 1977. After his 1977 defeat, Turgut reverted to his technocrat career and upon taking charge as Prime Minister yet again in late 1979, Demirel tasked him with devising a policy to cope with the economic crisis, especially runaway inflation. Ozal's emergency measures included another sharp devaluation of the lira, by 50 per cent, in January 1980.

In the civilian government established by the military junta in September 1980, Turgut Ozal became a Deputy Prime Minister with special responsibility for macroeconomic policy. He served in this position for nearly two years, until he resigned in mid-1982 due to tensions with some of his ministerial colleagues. During those two years, Ozal gained widespread popularity as the architect of policies which reduced inflation. Shortages also eased and the rampant black market diminished. The volume of Turkey's exports rose significantly, improving the trade balance, and the economy returned to a modest level of growth after the contractions experienced in 1979 and 1980. Ozal's achievement was no more than a repair job – the economy continued to rest on shaky structural foundations, a condition which persists to this day, and inflation remained high by international standards for the rest of the 1980s and beyond. But the relative improvements of the early 1980s brought direly needed relief to the suffering middle and working classes, and the formerly faceless technocrat became a household name across Turkey.

In autumn 1982, two years after the military takeover, the junta put together a new Constitution, which was drafted by a team of handpicked civilian 'experts' and then scrutinized and revised by the (then all-military) NSC before being submitted to a nationwide referendum. The referendum produced a 91 per cent affirmative vote on a 91 per cent turnout. Of course, there was no question of a 'No' campaign. Demirel and Ecevit were cooling their heels in their Ankara residences, the former in silence and the latter subjected to occasional arrests and brief detentions for writing articles and giving interviews critical of the military dictatorship in foreign, mainly Western newspapers and magazines. Turkes and Erbakan were on trial, the former for fomenting terrorism and inciting civil war and the latter for violating the constitutional principle of secularism as well as Section 163 of the penal code, under which calling for an Islamic state was illegal. Both were convicted and sentenced to prison terms but were released in 1985, Turkes on health grounds and Erbakan after being acquitted on appeal. So for the time being, the civilian political elite was out of the picture. In October 1981, the junta had summarily dissolved all political parties. A year later, the Constitution ratified by referendum included a provision which banned all politicians who had held senior posts in the dissolved parties from any role or participation in politics for a period of ten years. General Evren, the junta's leader, got himself sworn in as Turkey's seventh President after the referendum, and occupied that position for a seven-year term until November 1989 (when Ozal replaced him). A key article of the Constitution (Article 118) ensured the military hierarchy's position as the ultimate arbiters of the state, by stipulating that decisions made by the National Security Council for 'the preservation of the state' would have to be given 'priority consideration' by an elected civilian government. This meant that the NSC – in which the military had six (including President Evren) of the ten members from late 1983 to late 1989 and five of the ten members thereafter, throughout the 1990s – would oversee the state and intervene as necessary. The NSC's overweening authority over the state was not diluted until 2001 when, under constitutional reforms conducted by a government headed by Bulent Ecevit as part of the very preliminary stages of Turkey's accession process to the European Union – a process which has fizzled out completely since – the NSC's composition was altered to include a majority of civilians and, more important, its powers downgraded. Under the 2001 amendment, Deputy Prime Ministers and the Justice Minister also became NSC members and the NSC's remit was changed to conveying views rather than issuing directives for implementation. The council of ministers would have to discuss the views conveyed but would no longer have to give them 'priority consideration'.

Nonetheless, as in 1960, the junta upon seizing power in September 1980 had promised a return to elected civilian government once a new Constitution had been prepared and enacted, and new laws on the electoral system and political parties put into effect. In 1983, this agenda accomplished, the junta busied itself with this next step in its strategy. In mid-1983, it sponsored the formation of two entirely new parties, headed respectively by a retired general and a retired civil bureaucrat who had had strong CHP connections. The former was intended to serve as the new party of government after a two-party national election, and the latter as the opposition. The political class responded by floating new parties in the summer of 1983 – Demirel's loyalists, some CHP leaders (though without Ecevit's endorsement), and associates of both Erbakan and Turkes announced new parties. In July 1983, some of Erbakan's associates formed the Welfare Party *(Refah Partisi,* RP), the name Turkey's Islamist party would carry till its closure by the constitutional court in 1998 on the charge of promoting anti-secular politics, after a 1997 intervention by the NSC to protect the secular state led to the demise of Erbakan's year-long premiership in 1996–97 at the head of a RP-led coalition government. In 1983, the military regime had no intention whatsoever of letting these reincarnated versions of the banned parties compete in the national election it planned for late 1983, and prevented them from doing so. Some politicians of the outlawed AP (Demirel included) and CHP were placed in detention for a few months as an additional precaution. Ozal, who was spending most of his time in his holiday home on the southern Mediterranean coast, recounted in 1988 that he visited General Evren and asked if he could form a party to run in the election. According to Ozal, Evren told him he was free to do so, since intelligence reports suggested that a party led by Ozal would garner no more than 5 per cent of the votes. Evren's memoirs don't confirm this, but does say that he warned Ozal not to fill a new party with MSP Islamists, in which case there was no chance it would be allowed to run, and that Ozal committed not to reincarnate the MSP.[26]

Armed with this dismissive endorsement/conditional permission, Ozal floated the Motherland Party (*Anavatan Partisi,* ANAP) in mid-1983. A few

---

26 Hale, *Turkish Politics and the Military,* 265, 274.

months later, in early November, the ANAP won 45 per cent of the polled votes in a three-party race (the turnout was 92 per cent), which the weighted PR system translated into a slim but clear majority of 212 seats in the 400-member National Assembly, and Turgut Ozal became Prime Minister. The party the junta had intended to take charge of the government finished last. It was evident that large numbers of voters of the banned AP, MSP and MHP had consolidated behind Ozal's new party and upset the junta's game-plan. Four years later, in the national election of November 1987, Ozal won a second mandate, in a much more plural and competitive field. Prior to this election, Ozal sponsored a constitutional amendment which did away with the ten-year ban on his political rivals. The amendment was first approved in the National Assembly by the required two-thirds majority and then put to a nationwide referendum, in which it passed with a wafer-thin majority. Thus, the ANAP competed in late 1987 against the True Path Party (*Dogru Yol Partisi*, DYP), which was the reconstituted pre-1980 Justice Party (AP) and led once again by Demirel; two parties born of the CHP led respectively by Erdal Inonu and Bulent Ecevit; and the Islamist RP whose leading figure, as before, was Necmettin Erbakan. The ANAP got a plurality vote share (36 per cent) but this gave it a commanding majority in the National Assembly – 292 of the 450 seats – because under the revised electoral law in operation since 1983 a party needed to win at least 10 per cent of the nationwide votes to gain parliamentary representation. Only two other parties, Demirel's DYP and the party led by Erdal Inonu, crossed this qualifying threshold and gained the required number of seats. In late 1989, as General Evren's seven-year presidential term came to a close, Ozal decided to run for the presidency and was duly elected by the National Assembly. The ANAP continued to run the government for the next two years; two other ANAP leaders successively served as Prime Ministers during this period. In the next national election of October 1991, ANAP was beaten into second place by the DYP and Demirel became Prime Minister after reaching a post-poll coalition agreement with the third largest party, led by Erdal Inonu, who became the Deputy Prime Minister. Nonetheless, President Ozal remained Turkey's dominant political figure until his death in April 1993.[27]

27 In the October 1991 election, Erbakan's RP and Turkes's MHP formed a one-time pre-poll alliance to make sure to cross the 10 per cent threshold. The alliance was not popular with many members and voters of both parties. The joint list's 17 per cent vote share

Turgut Ozal's relationship with the military hierarchy was one of uneasy co-existence and co-operation. He proved to be no puppet or pawn of the generals, and the relationship was regularly marked by tension and friction. Yet the relationship survived. The military had failed to create a puppet civilian leadership that it could install as the government, and was allergic to the prospect of the banned politicians returning to public life. That left Ozal as the only option for the commanders' approach of restoring civilian government whilst retaining control and pulling strings as needed, and they were compelled to tolerate the political upstart and his fledgling party. During the second half of the 1980s, the balance of power shifted in Ozal's direction as his stature grew and the late 1987 election, in which he competed against the just unbanned established politicians and their parties, showed that he had the largest popular base of any politician in the country. The initially uneasy, nearly accidental and rather unequal relationship between the domineering generals and Ozal evolved into a stable and more equal partnership in the latter half of the 1980s. That it did suggests a strategic convergence that was deeper than mere calculations of mutual need and convenience.

Turgut Ozal can be accurately characterized as a 'soft Islamist', deeply ambivalent towards the Kemalist secular state. However, he was not a dyed-in-the-wool ideological Islamist like his brother Korkut. Nor did he carry the ideological baggage that made Necmettin Erbakan a suspect in the eyes of the staunch Kemalists who dominated the military hierarchy. Erbakan's political career had developed from his stewardship of the *Milli Gorus Hareketi* (National Outlook Movement, MGH), which proposed an explicitly ideological alternative rooted in Turkey's Ottoman–Islamic heritage to the Westernizing model of Kemalist secularism as the basis of Turkish nationhood and the Turkish state. The *Milli Gorus* ideology, articulated in party politics first by the MNP (1970–71), then the MSP (1972–80) and finally the RP after the restoration of competitive elections in late 1987, directly challenged the second of 'the two basic pillars of Kemalist

---

gave it 62 of the National Assembly's 450 seats. In May 1993, Demirel was elected by the National Assembly to the presidency left vacant by Ozal's death with the support of his own DYP, the party led by his coalition partner Erdal Inonu, and the MHP element of the RP–MHP parliamentary bloc. The prime ministership relinquished by Demirel was filled by Tansu Ciller, a female DYP politician, who to date is Turkey's only woman Prime Minister. There have been no female Turkish Presidents.

ideology – the [homogenously] national and unitary state and the principle of secularism'.[28] Such an overtly ideological articulation of a radically different conception of nation and state to the Kemalist dogma was unacceptable to the military high command. But at the same time, the generals were in search of an ideological framework which might be able to provide a formula of national unity. Their overriding objective in mounting the 1980 coup was to rescue and reinstate the core Kemalist goal of national homogeneity from the depths of division and disunity plaguing Turkey. With the original Kemalist vision of a laicist state more than three decades past the hegemonic dominance it had once enjoyed under the single-party authoritarian regime, the best hope of preserving the first pillar of Kemalism lay in giving space and rein to the Sunni–Hanefi identity of the country's majority population of ethnic Turks, but without fundamentally compromising the second pillar. Ozal was the ideal civilian partner in the execution of such a strategy of re-mooring Turkish nationalism in the Sunni–Hanefi majoritarian tradition, without jettisoning the secular state. A man of strong Sunni–Islamic connections and leanings, he was at the same time not overtly ideological and made a virtue of pragmatism. The awkward strategic convergence of Ozal's civilian regime and the military guardians of the Turkish state coalesced around the latter's 'dual-track policy of co-optation and containment'[29] of the Sunni–Hanefi identity of Turkey's majority.

The new Turkish Constitution imposed by the military junta in late 1982[30]

---

28 Ergun Ozbudun, 'The Turkish Constitutional Court and Political Crisis', in *Democracy, Islam, and Secularism in Turkey*, eds. Kuru and Stepan, 156.

29 Yavuz, *Islamic Political Identity in Turkey*, 213.

30 This Constitution is still valid today but has been subjected to major amendments over the years, mostly in the twenty-first century. A wave of amendments in the early through mid-2000s aimed to eliminate numerous draconian provisions incompatible with liberal democracy, which made it impossible to progress Turkey's EU accession process. This followed the EU's decision to give candidate status to Turkey in December 1999, twelve years after it formally applied to join in 1987. Another significant set of amendments was sponsored by the second AKP government in 2010, ostensibly in the interests of democratization. After being adopted by majority vote in the National Assembly, the amendments passed with a 58 per cent affirmative vote in a nationwide referendum. The most recent amendments in 2017 transformed Turkey's polity by instituting a nearly all-powerful executive presidency that emasculates parliament and the council of ministers. After clearing the required threshold of a three-fifths majority

contained strong provisions to protect secularism. Articles 2 and 4 reiterated the principle of *laiklik* as a core tenet of the state, and these articles were declared unamendable. Article 68 prohibited political parties from acting 'against the principles of the secular Republic', and Article 69 provided that any parties which deployed religious symbols and arguments or otherwise sought to appeal to religious sentiments 'shall be banned'. These provisions were cited in the 1998 constitutional court decision that closed down the RP, by then the country's most popular party. This happened in early 1998, seven months after the RP-led coalition government headed by Erbakan was forced to step down after only a year in office (June 1996–June 1997) following an ultimatum to the government from the NSC, delivered at the initiative of its military members in February 1997, that 'the principle of secularism should be strictly enforced' (the ultimatum is generally regarded as Turkey's fourth military coup in four decades). In 1982, the same year the military-approved Constitution came into effect, the Council of Higher Education (YOK) established by the junta to strictly monitor and supervise universities, practically all of which were public or state institutions at the time, began to ban female students who wore headscarves from campuses. There was no law as such prohibiting these students from accessing higher education but another state body, the Council of State, ruled in 1984 in response to a petition from a barred student that,

> some of our daughters who are not sufficiently educated wear headscarves under the influence of their social environments, customs and traditions ... showing that they adopt the ideal of a religious state ... [and] a world-view that opposes ... the fundamental principles of our Republic. The decision to expel the plaintiff from the university does not contradict the laws. She is so against the principles of the secular state that she resists removing her headscarf even when she comes to university for higher education.[31]

Of the eighteen directives issued to Erbakan's government by the NSC at the behest of its military members (the chief of the general staff and the

---

in the National Assembly, the amendments were put to a nationwide referendum in April 2017 and narrowly passed with a 51.4 per cent affirmative vote (the turnout was 85 per cent). The amendments were designed to formalize and strengthen President Erdogan's despotic power.

31 Kuru, *Secularism and State Policies Toward Religion*, 188.

commanders of the four wings of the armed forces) on 28 February 1997 – Prime Minister Erbakan and three senior cabinet colleagues were also on the NSC and the meeting was chaired by President Suleyman Demirel – the thirteenth point stipulated that 'practices which violate the attire law and may give Turkey a backward image must be prevented'.[32] The ban on women students wearing headscarves in all of Turkey's universities – the public ones as well as new private universities that had emerged in the 1990s – was strictly enforced after this ultimatum led to the forced resignation of Erbakan's government.[33]

On the other hand, however, the 1982 Constitution emphasized the importance of inculcating 'religious culture and morals' (Article 24) in the population, and especially among the younger generation. For the first time, religious instruction – in the basic and standard Sunni version – became a compulsory part of the curricula in all primary and secondary schools. Article 24 also stipulated that 'no one shall be allowed to exploit religion ... for even partially basing the social, economic, political or fundamental legal order of the state on religious tenets'.[34] Nonetheless,

> as prime minister [1983–89], Ozal pursued a policy of putting Islam in the educational system. His education minister Vehbi Dincerler, a

32  The full text of the ultimatum is reproduced as an appendix in Yavuz, *Islamic Political Identity in Turkey*, 275–276.

33  While teaching summer school at Istanbul's Bogazici (Bosphorus) University in 1999, I met a very intelligent young woman who had been banned from attending classes for wearing a headscarf. She told me that a Turkish professor in the university's department of political science and international relations had said to her that she looked like a member of the Ku Klux Klan, the white-supremacist group in the United States. Bogazici University originated as Robert College, a private institution of higher education founded by American missionaries in 1863. Over the next one hundred years, it taught and graduated numerous students who became members of Turkey's social, political and intellectual elite, and was converted into a public (state) university in 1971. As the campus is situated in a hilltop location overlooking the Bosphorus strait that divides Istanbul into 'European' and 'Asian' parts – on the 'European' side– the renamed institution was called Bogazici University. At the time of my summer-school stint there nearly two decades ago, it was regarded as Turkey's most prestigious university. The young woman had qualified to study there after performing very well on a national university entrance examination. The majority of Turkish women already wore some form of the headscarf in public at the time; currently, about two-thirds do.

34  Ozbudun, 'The Turkish Constitutional Court and Political Crisis', 152; Kuru, *Secularism and State Policies Toward Religion*, 169.

member of a Naqshbandi order [*tarikat*, formally banned since the mid-1920s], prepared a new curriculum on national history and culture which constantly used the term *milli* or nation in its religious sense.[35]

Since the 1990s, this compulsory religious education has drawn criticism from three very different quarters: some Kemalists, who feel it undermines secularism; some hardline Islamist conservatives, who feel the provision does not go far enough; and some Alevis, who argue that their children are forced to imbibe a Sunni religious curriculum which completely ignores their distinct tradition. At the same time, 'the generals attached importance to building relations with Muslim countries such as Pakistan'.[36] The Turkey–Pakistan nexus dates to the 1950s, when both countries joined the US-led bloc in the superpower conflict and became members of military alliances aimed at 'containment' of the Soviet Union's geopolitical influence. Building on those roots, the Turkish military hierarchy of the 1980s clearly felt a special affinity with Pakistan because this friendly state was ruled during that decade (until 1988) by a military junta headed by General Zia-ul Haq, who was implementing a sweeping program of Islamization of Pakistan's legal system and social mores, derived from his conviction that emphasizing the shared bond of Islam was the only means of holding Pakistan – what remained of it after the departure of East Pakistan (Bangladesh) in 1971 – together. The affinity with Pakistan has endured in the very different political era dominated by Erdogan, who openly identifies with Pakistan as a fellow Muslim country founded on the basis of religion. A 'Turkish–Islamic synthesis that combined Turkish nationalism with a Muslim identity'[37] became the *de facto* official ideology of the Turkish 'third republic' born in 1982 through military intervention. The mutation horrified diehard Kemalists and deeply alarmed Alevis, who sensed their community's further marginalization (described in Chapter 3), as military personnel started visiting remote Alevi villages to ensure the construction of mosques to be run by state-appointed (Sunni) *imams*.

Ozal's political party, the Motherland Party or ANAP founded in mid-1983, was composed of several distinct elements but it was definitely not of a

---

35  Yavuz, *Islamic Political Identity in Turkey*, 213.

36  Kuru, *Secularism and State Policies Toward Religion*, 229.

37  Ibid.

secularist orientation. The party's provincial and local leaders and its grassroots networks were largely comprised of religious Sunni Turks, augmented by Turkish ultranationalists of the MHP variety (contesting under a slightly different name, the MHP got under 3 per cent of the votes in the late 1987 national election as its base mostly supported ANAP). These two elements were colloquially known as the 'holy alliance'. At ANAP's annual convention in 1988, the holy alliance gained a majority on the party's top body, the executive board.

As Turkey's dominant civilian leader, Ozal managed to abolish Section 163 of the penal code, which criminalized expressions of political Islamism and had been used for six decades to persecute and jail anti-secularists. Its last prominent victim was Necmettin Erbakan, who was charged, tried and convicted after the 1980 military coup but acquitted on appeal in 1985. Ozal also got Sections 141 and 142 repealed; these had criminalized communism and been used over the decades to persecute and jail intellectuals and activists suspected of such beliefs. He was supportive of *imam-hatip* schools, a small segment of the state-school system in which religious subjects are taught in addition to the regular curriculum. These schools, co-educational since 1976, have for decades been a lightning rod for secularist paranoia and were particularly targeted after the *de facto* coup of 1997. As the 'Turkish–Islamic Synthesis' ideology gained legitimacy during the Ozal-military partnership, the number of such schools rose from 374 in 1980 to 612 in 1997, and in the latter year the schools had over 500,000 pupils (almost half girls), accounting for about 10 per cent of total enrolment in secondary and higher secondary education.[38]

---

38 As part of the secularist crackdown of the late 1990s ordered by the military hierarchy, *imam-hatip* graduates were made ineligible for jobs in the police (they were already barred from all wings of the armed forces). It also became nearly impossible for them to gain university places, except in theology departments whose intake was reduced by 90 per cent at the direction of YOK, the state body supervising higher education, and the sixth to eighth grades of *imam-hatip* schools were eliminated by increasing compulsory general education from five to eight years. Enrolment in 536 *imam-hatip* schools collapsed to under 65,000 in 2003. The first AKP government's attempts in 2004–05 to alleviate the nearly non-existent higher education and career prospects of these students were vetoed by President Sezer and then by the Council of State. Ibid., 193–196. However, things changed thereafter with the decisive anti-secularist ascendancy in Turkish politics. In 2015, President Erdogan proudly noted that almost

Even more boldly, Ozal attempted to end the ban on women students wearing headscarves in universities enforced since the early 1980s. In November 1988, the ANAP majority in the National Assembly passed a parliamentary bill to permit any form of dress at universities. The President, General Evren, vetoed the legislation two days later for being contrary to the spirit of 'Ataturkism'. Three weeks later the National Assembly passed another, slightly modified bill which called for 'modern dress and appearance' but permitted religious students to cover their neck and hair with a headscarf. Evren then approached the constitutional court to annul the legislation. In March 1989, the constitutional court ruled the law unconstitutional, arguing that 'the dress issue is limited by the Turkish Revolution and Ataturk's Principles' and that 'attending classes in anti-modern attire has no relevance to freedom or autonomy'. Only one judge dissented from the verdict, which quoted from the Council of State's 1984 decision: 'Secularism is a transformation of mentality. It is a must for a modern, healthy society ... Anti-modern dresses that contradict the Laws of Revolution cannot be seen as appropriate'. This did not end the tussle, however. In October 1990, the ANAP-dominated parliament passed yet another law which stated that 'as long as they do not violate existing laws, dress codes are free at universities'. By this time Ozal was President and he promptly approved the law. The largest opposition party represented in parliament – the bigger of two factions of the erstwhile CHP – then approached the constitutional court to annul the legislation. In its ruling delivered in April 1991, the court did not annul the law outright but interpreted it as disallowing headscarves because wearing headscarves in universities conflicted, according to the court, with the bedrock constitutional principle of secularism (even though no existing law explicitly forbade the headscarf in universities). The result of this tit-for-tat battle was that 'universities did not pursue a consistent policy towards headscarves until the 1997 [de facto] coup [which toppled the government led by Erbakan]. Even in the same university, some departments enforced the ban while others did not, depending on the personal opinions of deans and heads of departments'.[39] The prohibition was strictly enforced nationwide – in all universities, public

---

a million boys and girls were studying in *imam-hatip* institutions, the vanguard of a new 'pious generation' as he called them.

39 Kuru, *Secularism and State Policies Toward Religion*, 188–190.

and private – after the February 1997 'soft coup' orchestrated by the military hierarchy through the NSC specifically directed that 'attire … that may give Turkey a backward image must be prevented'.

Turgut Ozal did not prevail in the battle with the Kemalist secularists on the headscarf front – the single most emotive issue on both sides of Turkey's secular/anti-secular divide. In 2003, in response to the arrival in power of the first AKP government, President Ahmet Necdet Sezer – who had prior to becoming President in 2000 chaired the constitutional court from 1988 and been the pivotal player in its judgments on the headscarf issue in the end-1980s and early 1990s as well as in the ruling which closed down the RP, the AKP's predecessor, in 1998 – appointed a hardline secularist to head YOK, the Council of Higher Education established by the military junta in the early 1980s. This appointee extended the ban to wigs, which some religious students had taken to wearing in order to cover their real hair. In 2004, Prime Minister Erdogan proposed to retain the headscarf ban in state universities but lift it in private ones, but the proposal was stiffly opposed by the secularist alliance comprising the military hierarchy, the constitutional court, and the political opposition.

Twenty-five years after Ozal first challenged the secularists' headscarf taboo, the anti-secularists won the long war of attrition on the issue with their much-weakened secularist foes. As recounted in Chapter 1, in late 2013 the third AKP government was able to pass legislation in the National Assembly which allowed women to wear headscarves except for those working in the courts, the police and the military. It was Erdogan's last major act before he stepped down as Prime Minister in mid-2014 to run for – and win – the first direct election by popular vote to the Turkish presidency. As mentioned in Chapter 1, in 2016–17 the AKP government also legalized headscarves worn under caps or berets for women serving in the police and the military, provided they matched the colour of uniforms and were unobtrusive.

♦

The legacy of the Ozal decade (1983–93) had profound and far-reaching effects on Turkey's political transformation in the twenty-first century. Rather oddly for a late-bloomer politician who had spent his professional career until his fifties working as a cog in the notoriously bloated and hidebound state bureaucracy – or perhaps because of that experience over three decades – Ozal proved to be a determined proponent of private entrepreneurship and commerce. The first DP government of 1950–54 had also promised to liberate the Turkish economy from the shackles of state ownership and regulation, but its fitful efforts in that direction had not gone very far. More than 30 years later, Ozal acted on that agenda. He switched the focus of the economy from import-substituting industrialization run primarily through state enterprises to an export-oriented approach driven mainly by private firms. Until the 1980s, the non-state sector of Turkey's economy was thoroughly dominated by a handful of crony capitalists, based mainly in Istanbul, who were closely linked to the loose military–bureaucrat–politician alliance at the heart of the Kemalist state. This bunch of state-connected metropolitan oligopolists operating so-called 'holding companies' organized a chamber of big business in 1971 called the Turkish Industrialists' and Businessmen's Association (TUSIAD) to protect and lobby for their interests. The paradigm shift Ozal pursued led during the 1990s (and beyond) to the rise of a far larger and much more diversified class of entrepreneurs running manufacturing firms and other businesses from among the petty-bourgeoisie in dozens of cities and towns across the Anatolian heartland. This class of new private capitalists in provincial Anatolia were the engine of Turkey's relative economic recovery and reasonable growth in the first ten or so years (2003–13) of AKP rule, after the economic collapse of 2001 (described in Chapter 1) which spelt the death-knell of politicians and parties of various hues tied to the Kemalist state. This class, composed mainly of religious non-metropolitan Sunni Turks, has been a solid bulwark of support over the past fifteen years for the AKP regime and its supreme leader, Tayyip Erdogan. In May 1990, six months after Ozal relinquished his prime ministerial tenure of six years and became Turkey's first civilian (non-military) President since 1960, this emergent class of middle and small-scale business owners and entrepreneurs established an umbrella organization called the Independent Industrialists' and Businessmen's Association (MUSIAD). In 1997, MUSIAD's membership consisted of 2,897 companies of which 1,318 had been established post-1983, and as many as 580 in the 1990s.[40]

---

40 Yavuz, *Islamic Political Identity in Turkey*, 93.

The last few years of the Ozal era, before his sudden death in office in 1993 at the age of 65, saw other significant reforms which spurred Turkey's political evolution away from the Kemalist secular state. Until the early 1990s, state control of the broadcast media and the university system was absolute. Just as India's All India Radio (AIR) and Doordarshan (DD, the state television), both controlled by the central government, held a monopoly over broadcast rights until the mid-1990s, so did the Turkish equivalent – Turkish Radio and Television (TRT) – until the early 1990s. Thus, until the early 1990s, Turkey had a 'one-channel public TV, [one] public radio station, and public [state] universities'.[41] This changed dramatically after the early 1990s due to Ozal's policy, near-revolutionary by Turkish standards, of permitting private radio and television broadcasting as well as private universities. The end of the TRT monopoly led to a proliferation of private radio and television media through the 1990s and into the new century. In keeping with the political climate in which the Turkish–Islamic Synthesis had *de facto* displaced Kemalist secularism as the official ideology of the state, many among this plethora of new broadcast media articulated religiously based outlooks and orientations. In parallel, the print media also diversified, and numerous newspapers and periodicals promoting a variety of Islamist stances and their critiques of the secular state came into existence. Islamist public intellectuals such as Ali Bulac (b. 1951) and Abdurrahman Dilipak (b. 1949) became household names, their writings and commentaries widely circulated and read. The Kemalist media remained influential – in 1996 'the TUSIAD and its media networks, the Dogan and Sabah publishing conglomerates', campaigned hard to prevent the formation of the RP–DYP coalition government headed by Necmettin Erbakan. During the 1997 military intervention which toppled the Erbakan government, 'the military worked very closely with major media cartels such as the Dogan group [owned by a family of the same name], the publisher of the *Hurriyet* and *Milliyet* dailies, and with leading university administrators'.[42] But the mass media was no longer overwhelmingly dominated by the state-secularist perspective and the impact was both limited and transitory.

Some of the first private universities were established by crony-capitalist families tied to the secularist establishment, such as Koc University (founded

---

41  Kuru, *Secularism and State Policies Toward Religion*, 230.
42  Yavuz, *Islamic Political Identity in Turkey*, 240, 246.

1993) and Sabanci University (1994). But even these universities, which sought to imitate the American liberal-arts paradigm of pedagogy, promoted freer and more liberal thinking compared to the recycling of Kemalist slogans and dogmas then prevalent in the state universities. Because of the authoritarian, enforced nature of Kemalist state-secularism ever since its inception in the 1920s, and the fact that only a substantial minority of the population subscribed seven decades later to its fantasies of Turkey becoming and being accepted as an 'European' country and joining 'Western civilization', it was absolutely essential for the secularists to maintain their dominance of public discourse. That dominance unravelled through the 1990s, and so did the secular state. In the late 1990s and early 2000s, some commentators openly used the term *laikcilik*, roughly translatable as secularist fundamentalism, to describe the increasingly desperate stratagems of the state-secularist establishment to defeat and destroy the growing anti-secularist challenge to its hegemony. The appellation was justified. In its 1998 decision closing down the RP by a 9–2 majority vote of its eleven judges (the two dissenting judges had both been appointed by President Ozal in the early 1990s), the constitutional court described secularism as the inviolable 'way of life' of Turkish society. The wording was identical to the Indian Supreme Court's characterization of Hindutva – the political ideology of majoritarian Hindu nationalism – in a controversial 1995 judgment which was discussed in Chapter 3.[43]

◆

By the mid-1990s, the rising Islamist counter-elite was in a position to mount a serious challenge for state power to the secularist elite comprised of high-ranking military officers, civil bureaucrats, establishment politicians and the Kemalist urban intelligentsia. The political vehicle for the challenge was the *Refah* (Welfare) Party or RP, still led by Erbakan and his associates from the older generation of Islamist activists but increasingly driven by the energy and dynamism of a younger generation of rising leaders including Abdullah Gul (b. 1949) and Recep Tayyip Erdogan (b. 1954). The RP's breakthrough moment came (as related in Chapter 1) in nationwide municipal elections in the spring of 1994, when the party won control of some 300 cities and

---

43  Ibid., 247.

towns, including 29 large urban centres. The metropolis of Istanbul and Ankara, the national capital and bastion of the Kemalist elite, both elected RP administrations. Erdogan, the party's most charismatic young face, became Istanbul's mayor.

The RP's 1994 breakthrough was highly significant, and mortally threatening to the secularist elite for two reasons. First, Turgut Ozal had strengthened local governments to the limited extent possible under Turkey's rigidly centralized state structure by expanding their budgets and giving them greater authority over everyday governance. Second, Turkey had become a predominantly urbanized society by the 1990s, after three decades of rural-to-urban migration. In 1960, when the first military coup occurred, just six million of Turkey's 28 million people lived in urban locales. The proportion steadily increased from then on and by 1990, the urban population outstripped the rural population. In that year, 31 million of Turkey's 56 million citizens were classified as urban dwellers. By 1995, 38 million of the country's 62 million people lived in urban centres and agglomerations (in 2005, 49 million of 71 million citizens did so).[44]

The masses of migrants included large numbers of Alevis (Turk and Kurd) and Kurds (Sunni and Alevi). But consistent with the overall demography of the country, the majority consisted of Sunni Turks. These recent or new urbanites of rural origins were (and are) typically of a pious, God-fearing disposition whose lives and outlooks Kemalist state-secularism had barely touched, if at all. The bulk of the migrants lived (at least initially, and many for long periods) in *gecekondu*s, sprawling shantytowns which became a prominent feature of Turkey's urban landscape. Many, probably most, struggled to cope with the pressures of urban life and the challenges of making a livelihood and educating children, particularly in the big cities, and more generally to adjust to their new surroundings. The deep religiosity typical of migrants made many such Sunni Turk individuals and communities (and some Sunni Kurds too) fertile terrain for Islamist political mobilization.[45] The challenges of material

---

44 Heper and Criss, *Historical Dictionary of Turkey*, 357.

45 The same pattern of a pro-AKP Sunni Turk majority is discernible among the largest Turkish migrant communities in Europe. People of Turkish origin settled in Europe can vote in Turkey's national elections and referendums as long as they have retained Turkish citizenship. The population of Turkish origin in Europe is diverse: there are

existence made the quest for a moral framework to guide life and community even more important than in settled rural locales. In Turkish society, 'moral questions and values ... have largely been articulated in Islamic terms because the Kemalist cultural revolution did not produce an alternative, shared moral language, and Islamic references and idioms remained the depository for the moral debate'.[46] Throughout the 1990s, the RP used *Adil Duzen* (Just Order) as its main political slogan. The concept was vague but nonetheless appealing in its invocation of a just society based on Islamic values – precisely what the Naqshbandi leader Zahid Kotku had told his followers (see Chapters 1 and 3) the majority of the Turkish people wanted when he urged them to form a political party in the late 1960s.

The RP's ideological framework continued to evolve during the 1990s, principally at the initiative of Abdullah Gul, the party's most intelligent ideologue. Gul would become Turkey's first AKP Prime Minister, serving from November 2002 to March 2003 – when he relinquished the premiership to Erdogan upon the lifting of the latter's ban from political life imposed in 1999 – and would go on to serve as Turkey's President from 2007 to 2014 (when Erdogan succeeded him as President). Perfectly aware of changing times and new opportunities, 'Gul rejected the idea that the RP represented only the "needy and little man" of society, a notion that the MNP and MSP [the RP's predecessor parties] had publicized in the 1970s'. Instead, in the mid-1990s, Gul called for the RP to become the representative and mobilizer of a far broader cross-section of society 'linking the Anatolian bourgeoisie,

---

large numbers of Kurds, many of whom support the Kurdish nationalist Workers' Party of Kurdistan (PKK), as well as Alevis, who are almost unanimously opposed to Erdogan and the AKP. But the majority consists of Sunni Turks whose first generation came to Europe as cheap labour in the 1960s and 1970s to escape poverty in Turkey. Their social profile mirrors that of the religious Sunni Turk majority of the home country's population. The largest (by far) migrant community is in Germany and 60 per cent or higher of those who have voted in Turkish national elections in the twenty-first century have supported the AKP. About 1.4 million people of Turkish origin living in Germany were eligible to vote in the 2017 referendum on creating a nearly all-powerful executive presidency in Turkey, and 63 per cent voted in favour (although the turnout was low, under 50 per cent). Even higher majorities supported Erdogan's 2017 power-grab in two other countries with sizeable Turkish populations: France (65 per cent) and Holland (71 per cent).

46  Yavuz, *Islamic Political Identity in Turkey*, 220.

Sufi orders, neighbourhood associations and [religious] foundations' in a social and political Sunni–Islamic coalition.[47]

This was the beginning of the ideology of 'conservative democracy' (discussed in Chapter 1), based on empowering the vast 'periphery' of Turkish society marginalized by the Kemalist 'centre', that the AKP deployed as Turkey's ruling party during the first decade of the twenty-first century. In mid-2000, Gul narrowly lost a contest for the leadership of the Virtue Party (FP) – the renamed RP, which had been banned by the constitutional court in 1998 – to an elderly loyalist of Necmettin Erbakan (the FP was in turn banned by the constitutional court in mid-2001 for being a 'centre of anti-secular activities'). But in the longer run, the younger generation prevailed. Two parties emerged from the FP immediately after its forced closure. The old-guard loyal to Erbakan formed the Felicity Party (SP) in July 2001, while the younger generation formed the Justice and Development Party (AKP) in August. In the watershed parliamentary election of November 2002, the SP polled 2.5 per cent and the AKP 34.3 per cent of the nationwide votes. The pattern continued in the subsequent elections of 2007 (SP 2.3 per cent, AKP 46.7 per cent), 2011 (SP 1.2 per cent, AKP nearly 50 per cent) and June 2015 (SP 2 per cent, AKP 41 per cent).[48] In the 1990s, Erbakan's speeches divided Turkey's society and polity into two diametrically opposed categories: *batil* (the cultural imitators of Europe and political tools of the United States) and *hak* (followers of the authentic path rooted in the Turkish form of Sunni Islam). This was a crude inversion of the primitive Kemalist dichotomy between Oriental 'backwardness' and Western/European 'civilization'. The AKP's ideological framework was relatively more sophisticated and elastic. Until about 2005, the first AKP government cultivated a positive relationship with the EU, whose requirements of democratization of the Turkish state and the removal of various constitutional provisions and draconian laws incompatible with liberal democracy in order to progress Turkey's candidacy for EU membership

---

47  Ibid., 213.

48  Two edited collections which focus on the AKP's emergence as Turkey's leading party and its first government of 2002–07 are M. Hakan Yavuz, ed., *The Emergence of a New Turkey: Democracy and the AK Parti* (Salt Lake City: University of Utah Press, 2006) and Umit Cizre, ed., *Secular and Islamic Politics in Turkey: The Making of the Justice and Development Party* (London and New York: Routledge, 2008).

helped in its struggle for supremacy with the still potent and dangerous state-secularist establishment. But the AKP's *modus vivendi* with the EU, motivated by this tactical imperative, dissipated as the party consolidated its power in the second half of the first decade of the twenty-first century and then neutralized the residual threat from the state-secularist bloc by the first years of the current decade. As the 2010s progressed, Erdogan's hegemonic and harshly authoritarian AKP regime gradually reverted to the Europhobic and anti-Western stance and rhetoric Erbakan voiced in the 1990s.

The RP's breakthrough in the 1994 local elections helped the party to grow its influence. The public generally found the RP's local administrations to be less corrupt and better at delivering basic services compared to other parties. The RP's reputation at the time for relative probity mattered because in the second half of the 1990s, the top leaders of the other two major (and nominally secularist) conservative parties – Tansu Ciller (DYP) and Mesut Yilmaz (ANAP) – became mired in corruption scandals. The relative efficiency of RP administrations in cities and towns was in turn rooted in the party's grassroots approach to politics. When over 5,000 citizens in 24 urban centres were surveyed six months after the RP's victory in the spring 1994 local elections, many favourably noted the accessibility of local RP officials and their respectful behaviour towards people regardless of social status.[49] In fact, through the 1990s the RP developed a formidable grassroots machinery unique among Turkey's political parties, which the AKP inherited after its formation in 2001. The RP executive committee in each of Turkey's 81 provinces had 33 members, after the 33 beads in the Muslim rosary. But the party's real source of strength stemmed from its attention to grassroots organization and mobilization:

> Each neighbourhood or *mahalle* had an organizer, who in turn appointed representatives to collect information about the age, ethnicity, religious origin and place of birth of the residents in each street. At the [sub-province] district level, inspectors reviewed the work of neighbourhood organizers every week. In addition to the inspector, each district had a party *divan* or committee of 33 members. None of the other parties was organized to communicate in this way with neighbourhoods, the basic unit of Turkish society.

---

49  Yavuz, *Islamic Political Identity in Turkey*, 219.

The meticulous work ultimately focused on elections; the RP's grassroots network regularly conducted 'voter registration drives' and then organized 'free transportation' to polling stations for reliable voters.[50]

In addition to organizational prowess, the RP's – and much more decisively, the AKP's – trump card was the emergence of the charismatic leader with mass appeal, in the person of Recep Tayyip Erdogan. Born in Rize, a town in the eastern part of Turkey's sprawling northern Black Sea (*karadeniz*) coast, Erdogan grew up in a migrant family in a working-class neighbourhood of Istanbul (on the 'Asian' side) and graduated from an *imam-hatip* school. His life-story resonated with the masses of similarly ordinary and religiously devout Sunni Turks. The military-led secularist elite's attempt to banish him from politics in the end-1990s, and his imprisonment for several months in 1999 after being convicted of anti-secular activity, simply turned him into an iconic symbol of the *mazlum* (oppressed) for most of the Sunni Turk majority of Turkey's society. The state-secularist establishment birthed the Erdogan personality cult. Fully aware of Turkey's political history, Erdogan represented himself as the successor to both Adnan Menderes and Turgut Ozal. Throughout the era of multiparty politics which properly began in 1950, the majority in Turkey have supported parties either ambivalent or hostile towards the secular state conceived and imposed by Mustafa Kemal. In the late 1991 national election, the first to be held in reasonably 'normal' conditions after the 1980 military coup, 68 per cent of the electorate supported parties such as the DYP (descended from Menderes's party of the 1950s, it secured 27 per cent of the votes), Ozal's ANAP (24 per cent) and the overtly Islamist RP, in an one-time alliance with the far-right MHP (17 per cent). After 2002, DYP and ANAP disintegrated and disappeared from Turkey's political landscape and the bulk of the country's Sunni Turk majority, augmented by some Sunni Kurds, consolidated behind Erdogan's AKP. Only the MHP, with its distinctive brand of Turkish ultra-nationalism, has been able to preserve a base of its own.

◆

The crisis-ridden circumstances that propelled the AKP's victory in the

---

50  Ibid., 217, 227–228.

November 2002 general election have been described in Chapter 1. But until at least 2008, it was not clear if the anti-secularist ascendancy in Turkish politics would prove durable, or be rolled back. The first AKP government

> had to face not only the [Kemalist CHP] parliamentary opposition but the opposition of many state institutions: [the arch-secularist] President Sezer until the end of his term in August 2007, the military [hierarchy], the Constitutional Court and the higher judiciary in general, and YOK [the Council of Higher Education, the secularists' vanguard in the headscarf battle].[51]

The turning point in the war of attrition between Turkey's secularist and anti-secularist forces came in 2007–08.

As Ahmet Necdet Sezer's seven-year term as Turkey's President neared its end in the spring of 2007, the AKP government nominated Abdullah Gul to succeed him. Sezer, the chairman of the constitutional court from 1988 until his election to the presidency in 2000, was an ardent Kemalist and champion of the secular state. As President, he resumed the war he had waged on anti-secular forces during his constitutional court career after the AKP came to power in November 2002, and clashed continuously with Erdogan's government. Sezer was known to be close to Deniz Baykal, the opposition CHP's leader till 2010 and a fellow-secularist. Gul, in 2007 a Deputy Prime Minister and Minister of Foreign Affairs in Erdogan's cabinet, was the AKP's suave face and a less divisive figure compared to the mercurial Erdogan. Nonetheless, the prospect of a top AKP leader replacing a staunch secularist as the President of the Republic – a mostly ceremonial but not powerless post – alarmed and enraged the secularist segment of the population, who were already chafing under AKP rule. In April 2007, more than a million pro-secular protesters marched in Turkey's largest cities against Gul's nomination, and a sense of crisis gripped the country. The secularist media was particularly outraged by the prospect of a headscarf-wearing First Lady. Gul's wife, whom he married when she was fifteen and he thirty, wore the headscarf in public.

Under the rules, the President had to be elected by a vote in parliament, the Grand National Assembly (TGNA). A successful candidate needed to

---

51 Ozbudun, 'The Turkish Constitutional Court and Political Crisis', 156.

receive a two-thirds majority in either the first or the second round, and if this did not happen, a simple majority (50 per cent plus one) in a third round would suffice. The AKP, which had secured 365 of the TGNA's 550 seats in November 2002 with a plurality of 34 per cent of the popular vote due to the peculiarities of Turkey's electoral system detailed in Chapter 1, was just short of the two-thirds threshold (367). The CHP, the only other party represented in parliament with 178 deputies, decided to boycott the presidential election. In the first round, 361 parliamentarians were present and Gul received 357 votes. The CHP then approached the constitutional court with the argument that a quorum of two-thirds of the parliamentarians was required and asked for the first round to be cancelled on that basis. Simultaneously, the military high command posted a grim statement on the Turkish Armed Forces' website warning it might intervene to end the crisis, in a move that came to be known as 'e-coup'. Had the threat been carried out, it would have been Turkey's fifth military coup in five decades. The constitutional court accepted the CHP's dubious argument and ruled the first round invalid. Two of the eleven judges, both appointed by President Ozal in the early 1990s, dissented from the majority verdict.

The AKP responded to the secularist offensive by advancing the parliamentary election due by November 2007 to July. In that election, the AKP's share of the nationwide votes jumped from 34 per cent to almost 47 per cent, and the party was returned to power with a commanding albeit slightly reduced parliamentary majority – 341 of the 550 seats. This was because in addition to the CHP (21 per cent vote share, 112 seats) a third party, the fascist MHP, also crossed the 10 per cent national vote-share threshold required to obtain representation in parliament; it got 14 per cent of the votes and secured 71 seats. The secularist campaign against Gul lost momentum after this election outcome and in August 2007, three months after Sezer's term had expired, Gul was duly elected President by the new parliament, the CHP's continuing boycott rendered ineffective by the TGNA's changed composition.

This was not the end of the face-off between the secularist and anti-secularist forces, however. The showdown entered its climactic phase in 2008. The flashpoint issue was, yet again, the headscarf ban in universities. In January 2008, the TGNA passed two constitutional amendments on the matter by a vote of 411 to 103, the AKP and MHP parliamentarians voting in favour. The crucial phrase read: 'No one can be deprived of his or her right to higher education for reasons not openly mentioned by laws' (there being no law as such banning headscarfed female students from universities). President Gul promptly approved the amendments and the new head of YOK (the university system's supervisory body), a man appointed by Gul, issued a circular to all universities, public and private, to permit all forms of dress amongst students. The CHP approached the constitutional court, which in June 2008 annulled the amendments, once again by a 9:2 majority vote, for being contrary to the constitutional principle of secularism and the Kemalist ideals of 'Renaissance, Reformation and Enlightenment'. Secularist street demonstrations hailed the judgment for preventing the Republic of Turkey from becoming a clone of the Islamic Republic of Iran, where it is compulsory for women to cover their hair in public. The Iranian spectre had also featured in the forced departure of the government headed by Erbakan a decade earlier, in 1997. Erbakan, a Sunni Islamist, had chosen the largely Shiite Islamic Republic for his first foreign trip as Prime Minister, and this was seen by the military hierarchy and the rest of the state-secularist establishment as evidence of intent to convert Kemal's Republic into a theocracy. In April 1997, two months before Erbakan threw in the towel and resigned, the high command of the Turkish Armed Forces had formally identified Islamic reaction (*irtica*) as the foremost threat to the state, downgrading the Kurdish insurgency of the PKK in the country's east and south-east to second position.

As the headscarf furore unfolded in the first half of 2008, the high judiciary's chief public prosecutor approached the constitutional court to close down the AKP for anti-secular activity and ban Prime Minister Erdogan, President Gul, Bulent Arinc (the speaker of the TGNA from November 2002 to July 2007) and 68 other AKP leaders from politics on the same charge for five years (although Gul, as the duly elected President of the Republic, could only be charged with treason under the constitution). The case spawned another addition to the lexicon of Turkish politics: 'judicial coup'. The judicial coup almost succeeded, as six of the eleven constitutional court judges voted to ban the AKP in July 2008. It failed only because a three-fifths rather than a simple majority was required to close down a political party, which meant that the assent of seven judges was needed. However, the constitutional court did find the AKP guilty of anti-secular activity by a 10:1 majority vote and penalized it by cutting its annual state funding by one-half.[52]

The drama of 2008 – extraordinary by even the bizarre standards of Turkey's politics – was the last stand of the Kemalist secular state and its authoritarian watchdogs against the anti-secularist ascendancy. The state-secularist tyranny yielded thereafter to the tyranny of the new, anti-secular masters of the Turkish state.

---

52 On the events of 2007–08, see Kuru, *Secularism and State Policies Toward Religion*, 183–187, and Ahmet T. Kuru and Alfred Stepan, '*Laicite* as an 'ideal type' and a continuum: Comparing Turkey, France, and Senegal', in *Democracy, Islam, and Secularism in Turkey*, eds. Kuru and Stepan, 109–111. On the 1997–98 crisis, see Yavuz, *Islamic Political Identity in Turkey*, 243–248.

# 6

# SECULAR AND ANTI-SECULAR
# AUTHORITARIANISMS

*We are openly nationalist. Nationalism is the only cause that keeps us together.
Except for the Turkish majority, none of the other elements shall have any
impact. We shall, at any price, turkicize those who live in our country, and
destroy those who rise up against the Turks and Turkdom.*

—Ismet Inonu, the first Prime Minister (1923–37) and Mustafa Kemal's
successor as the second President (1938–50) of the
Republic of Turkey, speaking in 1925[1]

*The non-Hindu people of Hindustan must either adopt the Hindu culture and
language [sic], must learn and respect and hold in reverence the Hindu religion,
must entertain no idea but the glorification of the Hindu race [sic] ... or [they]*

---

1   Inonu was addressing a meeting of the *Turk Ocaklari* (Turkish Hearths) in Ankara.
This organization, initially established in 1912, was dedicated to promoting Turkish
nationalism and – after the formation of the Republic in late 1923 – the tenets of
Kemalism. Until its formal disbandment in 1949, local branches existed in all cities
and towns, schools, and public bodies in the Republic of Turkey. Its organizational
structure and ideological mission are reminiscent of India's RSS, the core and fount
of the Hindu nationalist movement. Inonu's statement can be found in Martin van
Bruinessen, 'Genocide in Kurdistan? The suppression of the Dersim rebellion in
Turkey (1937–38) and the chemical war against Iraqi Kurds (1988)', in *Conceptual and
Historical Dimensions of Genocide*, ed. George Andreopoulos (Philadelphia: University
of Pennsylvania Press, 1994), 141–170. Prior to becoming Turkey's President upon
Mustafa Kemal's death in November 1938, a post he then held for twelve and a half
years, Inonu served continuously as the Republic's Prime Minister from its inception in
late 1923 until 1937, except for three months between late 1924 and early 1925.

*may stay in the country, wholly subordinated to the Hindu nation, claiming*
*nothing, deserving no privileges, far less any preferential treatment.*
--Madhav Sadashiv Golwalkar, *sarsanghchalak* (supreme chief)
of the Rashtriya Swayamsevak Sangh (RSS) from 1940 to 1973,
writing in the late 1930s[2]

The rhetorics of Ismet Inonu and M. S. Golwalkar are strikingly – and chillingly – similar. Inonu (1884–1973) was, of course, one of the founding leaders of the Turkish secular state. A key lieutenant of Mustafa Kemal, he served as chief of staff of the Turkish Armed Forces in 1920–21 and was referred to as *milli sef,* or national chief, during his long tenure as President of the Turkish Republic (Kemal was referred to after his death as the *ebedi sef,* or eternal chief, among other honorifics). Inonu returned as Turkey's Prime Minister later in life, from late 1961 to early 1965, to lead three shortlived coalition governments after Turkey's first military coup in 1960. He headed the Republican People's Party (CHP), the staunchly secularist party born of Kemal's politics and associated with the eternal chief's legacy, from the time of Kemal's death in late 1938 until 1972, shortly before his own death in 1973.

Unlike Ismet Inonu, Madhav Sadashiv Golwalkar never wielded state power. He was a dissident in India's secular state. But although far removed from state power, Golwalkar's political importance can hardly be overstated. He is probably the single most important figure of the Hindu nationalist movement, and the most influential voice of its creed of anti-secularism, since the movement's inception in the 1920s. If Vinayak Damodar Savarkar (1883–1966) was the pioneer ideologue of the late-modern political doctrine called *Hindutva* developed in the 1920s and 1930s, and Keshav Baliram Hedgewar (1889–1940) the founder of the RSS, which would take the ideology forward in independent India, Golwalkar (1906–73) occupies a unique position in the pantheon of Hindu nationalist leaders as the builder of the RSS and the practitioner who gave political relevance to Savarkar's formulations. A Maharashtrian Brahmin from western India like Savarkar and Hedgewar – the background of almost all of the RSS's pioneers – he was nominated, as a young man of thirty-four, to lead the RSS by his mentor Hedgewar before the

2  M. S. Golwalkar, *We, or Our Nationhood Defined* (Nagpur: Bharat Prakashan, 1947), 55–56. This tract, a key early manifesto of Hindu nationalism, was first published in 1938.

latter's death in 1940. He discharged that role for the next 33 years, until his own death in 1973. His is a profound and lasting influence on the development of India's Hindu nationalist movement. The top leaders of Hindu nationalist politics from the 1970s until the first decade of this century, Atal Behari (A. B.) Vajpayee (b. 1924) and Lal Krishna (L. K.) Advani (b. 1927), both of whom joined the movement through the RSS in the 1940s, always referred to him by the honorific *Shri Guruji* (revered teacher). Narendra Modi, the next-generation (b. 1950) leader and India's current Prime Minister, joined the RSS as a *pracharak* (fulltime volunteer preacher of Hindutva values) at the beginning of the 1970s, under Golwalkar's leadership. Exactly like Golwalkar, Modi was attracted to monastic life in early youth and briefly joined a monastery (*ashram*) in Bengal before discovering his life's mission in the RSS. Deendayal Upadhyaya (1916–68), an Uttar Pradesh Brahmin, was from 1953 to 1968 the top organizer of the Jan Sangh, BJP's predecessor political party formed in 1951, and developed his own distinctive thesis on Hindu nationalism in the 1960s. A bust of Upadhyaya stands at the entrance of the BJP office in New Delhi, and in 2016 a flagship scheme of the Modi government which provides cooking gas connections to poor women nationwide was dedicated to him on the occasion of his birth centenary. Upadhyaya, too, was mentored by 'Guruji' Golwalkar in the RSS.[3]

Despite these differences, the secularist Inonu and the anti-secularist Golwalkar subscribed to and advocated the same type of political creed: authoritarian and majoritarian nationalism. The political transformation of

---

3  An extremely romantic history of the RSS written by a senior insider is K. R. Malkani's *The RSS Story* (New Delhi: Impex India, 1980). Malkani (1921–2003) joined the RSS in 1941 in his home city, Hyderabad in Sindh. He migrated to Delhi after Sindh became part of Pakistan in 1947. One of the founding members of the Bharatiya Jan Sangh in 1951, he was for decades a leading publicist of the Hindu nationalist movement. He edited the RSS's English weekly, *The Organiser*, from 1949 until the 1980s. Malkani's biography of the RSS is an exaltation of its founders and pioneers and their ideological vision. He presents the RSS down the decades as a uniquely virtuous organization motivated by selfless idealism, and seeks to debunk all accusations of proto-fascism. Many anecdotes cited in his account appear fantastic, and others just strange. But his book is still a revealing insight into the nature of the RSS as a tightly disciplined organization united around a messianic belief-system. Malkani wrote the book under the auspices of the Deendayal Research Institute, the RSS think-tank established in Deendayal Upadhyaya's memory after he died suddenly in 1968.

Turkey in the twenty-first century has meant that Ataturk's secularist legacy has proved to be not so eternal after all, while his legacy of snarling, vicious authoritarianism pervades the state – now decisively taken over by anti-secularist forces. That has turned out to be Mustafa Kemal's lasting legacy to the Turkish Republic and its people. In India, successive generations of the Guruji's disciples have moved since the 1990s from the margins of political life to the helm of a definitely democratic (and federal) state, whose secular future is now unclear as the Hindu nationalist movement's political party, the BJP, strives to emerge as the hegemon of Indian politics in the era of Narendra Modi.

The example of Turkey during the twentieth century shows that there is no intrinsic connection between secularism and democracy, contrary to what many secularists in India reflexively believe. In the Kemalist Republic, an official creed of secularism was partnered with a state which – even when superficially 'democratic', as it has been for most of the time since 1950 – has always been defined by a trait of deep authoritarianism. In the Indian case, as this book has shown, secularism as a principle of the state has been partnered with the development and consolidation of a democracy. But, as in the Turkish case, what I call the 'really existing' Indian secular state – which I distinguish from an *ideal* of secularism as an ethic of equality and co-existence of different faiths, an ethic deeply rooted in Indian history and tradition – has been marred by anomalies, contradictions and paradoxes. Moreover, as this book has argued, and as this chapter shows, that really existing Indian secular state has not been free of the temptation and practice of authoritarianism. The contest between secularist and anti-secularist visions of national identity and statehood is now largely decided in semi-authoritarian Turkey, in favour of the latter model. The question that looms large is whether an anti-secular form of democracy is possible in the Indian context. My answer to that question, developed and explained in the next, concluding chapter of this book, is no.

## The Case of Kemalism

A striking fact about 'Kemalism' – the official ideology of the Turkish state and hegemonic for eight decades after the republic's formation in 1923, until the beginning of this century – is its paucity of a doctrinal basis. As M. Sukru

Hanioglu has observed, Kemalism was distinguished by 'the lack of a coherent philosophy' and was neither based on nor subsequently produced 'a major book' or any 'guiding text'. The publicist-poet Ziya Gokalp's (1876–1924) articles and essays, gathered together and published from Ankara in 1923 as *The Principles of Turkism*, probably comes closest to such a text but, as discussed in Chapter 2, Gokalp's ideas were selectively appropriated by 'Kemalism' and diverged in important respects, including the role of Islam in Turkish national identity, from 'Kemalist' practice. Gokalp died a year after the proclamation of the Turkish Republic and had he lived longer, he may or may not have remained a devotee of Mustafa Kemal, whom he hailed in his writings as 'a great genius' and 'our great saviour'. Mustafa Kemal, a career military officer until he led the founding of the Turkish national state following the final demise of the Ottoman Empire after World War I, was a man of action and not a thinker, let alone an ideologue; he never pretended or aspired to be so. In late 1927, he made a lengthy speech to the nation, delivered over six days, known as the *Nutuk*. But consistent with his personality and style, this was not an ideological manifesto *per se* but rather 'a long description of the Turkish war of independence [1919–22] and major events in its wake, [told] from the vantage point of the new leader of Turkey'. It was quickly elevated to the status of a seminal statement of the new Turkish state's origins and rationale – which it is, albeit from the partial and self-interested perspective of Kemal justifying his own actions and policies, especially from 1924 onwards – and published from Ankara, 'supplemented with hundreds of documents reproduced to support Mustafa Kemal's narrative'. The result resembled 'a hybrid of a historical monograph and a memoir' and did not substantively compensate for the absence of a 'major treatise to serve as the basis of an ideology'.[4]

In an attempt to redress this ideological void, the ruling elite formulated six principles or 'arrows' (*alti ok*) to define the essence of Kemalism. The process started in 1931 and the six arrows were formally adopted by the CHP, the single party of the Republic, as the foundation of its political philosophy and praxis at its fourth 'grand congress' in May 1935. The resolution asserted that these 'fundamental ideas' were already 'evident in the acts and realizations which have taken place from the beginning of our Revolution until today' and

4  Hanioglu, 'The Historical Roots of Kemalism', 32–33.

the intent was to codify them 'in a compact form ... the fundamentals [which] constitute *Kamalism* [Kemalism]'. The resolution asserted the indivisible unity and territorial integrity of 'the Fatherland, the sacred country of our present political boundaries', and defined the nation as being 'composed of citizens bound together by the bonds of language, culture, and ideal'. It then declared, 'Turkey is a nationalist, populist, *etatist*, secular and revolutionary Republic'. The six arrows thus were republicanism (*cumhuriyetcilik*), nationalism (*milliyetcilik*), populism (*halkcilik*), statism or etatisme (*devletcilik*), secularism or laicism (*laiklik*), and revolutionism or reformism (*devrimcilik*).

The resolution went on to briefly outline the meaning and significance of each of the six bedrock concepts. 'The Republic is the form of government which represents and realizes the ideal of national sovereignty', it stated, while nationalism was 'essential to preserve the special character and entirely independent identity of the Turkish social community in the sense explained' – as defined by the shared bonds of language, culture and ideal (there is no reference to religion as a binding factor, although presumably 'culture' could include bonds of faith). Elaborating on populism, the resolution asserted that 'it is one of our main principles to regard the people of the Turkish Republic as not composed of different classes but as a community divided into different professions according to the requirements of the division of labour'. It added that 'the functioning of each of these [occupational] groups is essential to the life and happiness of the others and of the community' and that 'our Party aims, with this principle, to secure social order and solidarity instead of class conflict and to establish harmony of interests'. This organic-corporatist view of society is virtually identical to that espoused by Hindu nationalist ideologues. Savarkar wrote in the 1920s that in the 'Hindu State' he envisioned, 'the interests of both capital and labour will be subordinated to the interests of the Nation as a whole' and the 'same principle' would apply to peasant and landlord in the agrarian economy. Golwalkar wrote in the late 1960s that 'disparity [between social classes] is a part of nature and we have to live with it'. An RSS publication of the late 1980s described how the Hindu nationalist movement's labour wing, the Bharatiya Mazdoor Sangh or BMS (Indian Workers' Organization, founded in the mid-1950s), operates in accordance with the 'Bharatiya' (Indian) concept of the 'industrial family', in which 'the capitalist, the labourer and the managerial staff form a 'harmonious' whole. It added that the movement 'rejects the theory of class conflict' as well as the 'idea of collective bargaining by workers', because such notions 'ill-fit this integral concept' and encourage a 'separatist labour consciousness' at the expense of the 'welfare of the nation'. It further stated that the 'concept of the agricultural family and the concomitant spirit of harmony among the several limbs of agricultural production' guides the activities of the RSS's peasant wing, the Bharatiya Kisan Sangh (Indian Farmers' Organization, BKS), thereby 'eliminating class conflict and other socially self-destructive propaganda'.[5]

Elaborating on the concept of statism/etatisme, the CHP's 1935 resolution asserted that:

> although considering private work and activity to be a basic idea, it is one of our main principles to interest the State actively in matters where the general and vital interests of the nation are in question, especially in the economic field, in order to lead the nation to prosperity in as short a time as possible.

It added that 'the interest of the State in economic matters is to be an actual builder, as well as to encourage private enterprise and regulate and control the work being done [by the private sector]'. This arrow of Kemalism is virtually identical to the paradigm of state-led economic development and close state regulation of private enterprise adopted by the founders of the Indian secular state at the beginning of the 1950s (discussed in Chapter 2), with the essential *caveat* that they, unlike the Kemalist pioneers, acknowledged and upheld political pluralism, as well as the Indian nation's social and cultural diversity.

On the principle of *laiklik*, the resolution held that 'the Party considers ... [that] the administration of the State' must be 'in conformity with ... the fundamentals and methods provided for modern civilization by Science and Technique [sic]'. It continued: 'As ... religion is a matter of conscience, the

---

5   V. D. Savarkar, *Hindu Rashtra Darshan* [The Vision of the Hindu State] (Bombay: Veer Savarkar Prakashan, 1984), 109–111; M. S. Golwalkar, *Bunch of Thoughts* (Bangalore: Vikram Prakashan, 1984), 18, 108–110; H. V. Seshadri, ed., *RSS: A Vision in Action* (Bangalore: Jagaran Prakashan, 1988), 242–248. The same arguments can be found in K. R. Malkani, *Principles for a New Political Party* (Delhi: Vijay Pustak Bhandar, 1951), which enumerated the fundamentals of the ideology of the Bharatiya Jan Sangh, the forerunner of the BJP.

Party considers it to be one of the chief factors in the success of our nation in contemporary progress to separate ideas of religion from politics and from ... the State'. The references to 'modern civilization' and 'contemporary progress' making secularism an absolute imperative derive, as this book has shown, from the simplistic and inferiority complex-driven Kemalist fixation with making Turkey an 'European' country and a member of the 'Western' community of nations. This motivation contrasts, I have argued, with the rationale cited by the architects of the Indian secular state, who invoked deeply rooted indigenous traditions of tolerance, mutual respect and co-existence, and emphasized the sheer political necessity of a state not based on a singular religious identity in a multi-religious country. Moreover, as this book has shown, the actual Kemalist paradigm of secularism did *not* separate religion from the state, but rather entangled the state deeply and irretrievably with religion as a regulating and controlling authority. That defining feature of the Kemalist secular state is very similar to the paradigm of the Indian secular state and lies at the root of the dilemmas and problems of both the secular-state projects, as discussed in Chapter 3.

The elaboration of the sixth arrow – revolutionism/reformism – is the most cryptic and indeed vacuous element of the seminal 1935 formulation of the fundamentals of Kemalism. It merely asserts that 'the Party does not consider itself bound by ... evolutionary principles in its administration of the State' and 'holds it essential to remain faithful to the principles born of the revolutions our nation has made with great sacrifices, and to defend those principles'. The implication is that the 'revolutionary' content of Kemalism simply means the defence of the principles of nationalism, populism, statism/etatisme and secularism/laicism underpinning Kemal's Republic.[6]

The crucial line of the 1935 charter of Kemalism reads: 'The form of administration of the Turkish nation is based on the principle of the unity of power ... The Party is convinced that this is the most suitable of all State organizations'. It is not clear what precisely is meant by the phrase 'unity of power'. It could mean the CHP's single-party dictatorship, and it could also be an allusion to the all-powerful President of the Republic – Mustafa Kemal, by then the object of a grotesque state-sponsored cult of hagiography and

---

6  *Program of the People's Party of the Republic* (Ankara: Republican People's Party, 1935), English version of *CHP Programi* (Ankara: Cumhuriyet Halk Partisi, 1935).

mass worship as Ataturk (Father of the Turks), the surname/title he assumed in 1934. It could also mean the rigidly monolithic concept of national identity promoted by the Kemalist Republic and its institutional concomitant, the unitary and centralized state with power concentrated in the hands of the supreme leader and his associates and administered on a day-to-day basis by an ever-growing and ponderous bureaucracy. The phrase probably sought to incorporate and express all of these mutually reinforcing elements of the edifice of authoritarian rule. The Kemalist definition of Turkish national identity was, as we have seen in Chapter 3, *pseudo-civic* – it was in fact implicitly majoritarian, tilted towards Turkish-speaking Sunni-Hanefi Muslims. It did not substantively include the remnant non-Muslim minorities (Christian Greeks and Armenians, and Jews), whose communities were reduced to penury through deliberately targeted punitive taxation in the first half of the 1940s and subjected, in the case of the Greeks, to pogrom-like violence in the mid-1950s. The Kemalist secular state also effectively marginalized the large minority of heterodox Alevis, who realized by the late twentieth century that Kemalist secularism had failed to deliver equality to them as a distinct group of citizens of the Republic. And the Kemalist concept of national identity not only did not accommodate but gave absolutely no quarter to the large Kurdish population of eastern and south-eastern Anatolia, a mix of majority Sunnis (Shafi, not Hanefi as with ethnic Turks) and a significant Alevi component, most of whom did not know or speak Turkish in Kemal's lifetime and many for several decades afterward. Kurdish identity was not just not recognized but harshly suppressed and criminalized under Kemal's presidency in the 1920s and 1930s, a policy and state of affairs that continued until the end of the twentieth century, for six decades after Kemal's death in 1938 and five decades after the end of the CHP's one-party regime in 1950. Throughout the twentieth century, the Kemalist state – actually built around 'the Turkish majority', as Ismet Pasha (Inonu), Ataturk's successor as President until 1950 and leader of the CHP until 1972, candidly declared in 1925 – indeed concentrated on trying to 'turkicize' those 'other elements', especially Kurds, who did not fit into its definition of Turkishness.

Around the time Inonu succeeded the deceased founding deity of the Turkish Republic as its second President in late 1938, the fiery young RSS leader Madhav Sadashiv Golwalkar published his book *We, or Our Nationhood*

*Defined* in India. This was the second seminal text of Hindu nationalism's ideological doctrine after Vinayak Damodar Savarkar's pioneering *Hindu Rashtra Darshan* (The Vision of the Hindu State), which was published in the mid-1920s. The generic resemblance of the mindset of the Kemalist founders of the Turkish state such as Inonu and the thought of early Hindu nationalists such as Golwalkar is evident from the epigraphs at the beginning of this chapter. Not surprisingly, Golwalkar's thought also shared the early, and abiding, Kemalist preoccupation with the 'unity of power' in the organization of the state. After three decades as the supreme chief of the RSS, a role he assumed in 1940, the mature Golwalkar published his magnum opus, titled *Bunch of Thoughts*, in the late 1960s. In this lengthy treatise, which has been required reading for the RSS's middle and upper ranks ever since its publication, Golwalkar wrote:

> The most important and effective step will be to bury for good all talk of a federal structure, to sweep away the existence of all autonomous and semi-autonomous states within Bharat [India] and proclaim: 'One Country, One State, One Legislature, One Executive!' with no trace of fragmentational [sic], regional, sectarian, linguistic or other types of pride being given scope for playing havoc with our integrated harmony! Let the Constitution be redrafted, so as to establish this Unitary form of Government![7]

The scholar Bernard Lewis noted in the early 1960s that the Kemalist conception of the state is 'imbued with a spirit of authoritarian centralism'.[8] Indeed, (secular) Turkish nationalism and (anti-secular) Hindu nationalism are kindred ideological spirits in fundamental ways.

In the late 1960s, Golwalkar was particularly upset with the emergence of Nagaland, in India's far north-east, as the sixteenth State of the Indian Union (which today has 29 autonomous States). The State of Nagaland, carved out on the India–Burma border from the much larger extant State of Assam, took in most though not all of north-eastern India's Naga people and its creation was intended to assuage a secessionist insurgency waged by a section of the Naga population since the 1950s. Golwalkar's objection in the

---

7    M. S. Golwalkar, *Bunch of Thoughts*, 437–438.

8    Lewis, *The Emergence of Modern Turkey*, 204–205.

late 1960s was that the newly formed State had an overwhelming Christian majority; most Nagas are Christian and according to India's 2011 national census, 88 per cent of Nagaland's two million people are Christians. He saw the creation of Nagaland – a State with less than 0.2 per cent of India's vast population – as encouraging an ongoing Western project to turn India into a Christian-majority country (Christians of diverse ethnolinguistic groups and various denominations, scattered across India, are currently 2 per cent of India's 1.3 billion people). He wrote in *Bunch of Thoughts*: 'The creation in Assam of "Nagaland" is a glaring example [of misguided state policy] ... The open rebellion in the Naga Hills is all engineered by Christian missionaries'. He continued in a more general vein,

> What is the fate of all those lands colonized by these so-called disciples of Christ? Wherever they have stepped, they have drenched those lands with the blood and tears of the natives and liquidated whole races. Do we not know the heart-rending stories of how they annihilated the natives in America, Australia and Africa? Are we not aware of the atrocious history of Christian missionaries in our own country? ... There is the story of 'Saint' [Francis] Xavier, who used to experience the highest joy when he saw the new converts trampling on their former gods and goddesses, razing their temples and insulting their parents and elders who remained Hindus.

Golwalkar grimly noted that 'there is already a demand for another Hill State around Shillong [town] in Assam inspired by the Christian missionaries. They are also carrying on an agitation for a separate 'Jharkhand' [State] in Bihar'.[9] In fact, the campaign for a 'Hill State around Shillong' achieved fruition in 1972 when another State of the Indian Union – Meghalaya (Abode of the Clouds) – was created. Meghalaya's three million people are three-fourths Christian, of several tribal identities and denominational affiliations. In 2000, a BJP-led coalition government in New Delhi granted the formation of the State of Jharkhand on the eastern edge of north India from the southern region of the extant State of Bihar, in response to a protracted campaign led mostly by leaders of the one-quarter of Jharkhand's population who belong to tribal communities known as *Adivasis* ('Scheduled Tribes' in the Indian constitutional classification). Jharkhand's population of about 35 million is

---

9   Golwalkar, *Bunch of Thoughts*, 232–265.

however just 4 per cent Christian and Muslims, at 15 per cent, comprise the State's largest religious minority.

Golwalkar's acute antipathy to Christian missionary presence partly reflected an ongoing tussle in many of India's Adivasi communities, which continued into the early twenty-first century, between Christian missionaries and RSS activists working to turn Adivasis living in remote and often forested areas into self-conscious Hindus, loyal to the ideology of Hindu nationalism. But at a deeper level, it reflected an ideological revulsion to the structuring of India as a moderately decentralized Union of self-governing States, which recognized that the Indian nation contained and was built upon many different identities and gave an institutional frame to that mosaic of diversity.

Golwalkar's lifelong advocacy against autonomous States and federalist formulas followed in the trail set by Savarkar, the pioneer ideologue of Hindu nationalism. Savarkar wrote in the 1920s that 'the [independent] Hindustan of tomorrow must be an internal[ly] centralized state, from Kashmir to Rameshwaram [on India's southern tip] and from Sindh to Assam'.[10] This conviction about what independent India's state structure should be stemmed from his explicitly majoritarian concept of Hindutva (Hinduness) as the defining trait of Indian national identity; that is discussed in detail later in this chapter.

Savarkar and Golwalkar never got the opportunity to put their ideas into practice. Savarkar died in relative obscurity in his eighties in 1966, having spent the second half of his life as a marginal politician and polemicist. Golwalkar left a robust institutional legacy in the form of the *sangh-parivar*, the family of organizations grouped around the RSS built under his leadership in independent India. But when he died in 1973, the Hindu nationalists were a minor force in Indian politics, and remained so for another 15-plus years. When Golwalkar passed away, winning state power was a distant dream for the Hindu nationalist movement, nearly a half-century after the formation of the RSS (1925) and a quarter-century after the birth of its affiliated political party, the Bharatiya Jan Sangh (1951). The Jan Sangh could not realistically aspire to winning an election and forming the government in any of India's States, let alone at the national level. The same was true of the BJP, its slightly re-labelled successor party, during the 1980s.

---

10  Savarkar, *Hindu Rashtra Darshan*, 7, 196.

By contrast, the Kemalists, having seized control of the Turkish state, made it into a one-party monopoly and enjoyed a free hand to impose their vision as the sole legitimate path for Turkey. The 'six points' of Kemalism were elevated to the status of a sacred dogma which endured as the state's official ideology until the long Kemalist era was eclipsed by the rise of the Islamist alternative from the beginning of the twenty-first century. The early Kemalist leadership, particularly Mustafa Kemal himself, did have a degree of popular legitimacy from their role in the 1919–22 war of independence. But their monopoly of political power could only be sustained by draconian authoritarianism. In late 1924, an assortment of elements unhappy with Kemal's leadership and policies formed a 'Progressive Republican Party' to act as an opposition. Twenty-two members of the Grand National Assembly joined the new party, which was led among others by Kazim Karabekir (1882–1948), a military hero of the independence war who had commanded the crucial eastern Anatolian front. The party's statutes asserted that 'liberalism and democracy constitute our principal program' (Article 2), called for multiparty elections with universal adult franchise (Article 8), and advocated a decentralized state structure (Article 14).[11] The PRP lasted barely six months and was shut down in mid-1925 by Kemal's regime. Karabekir suffered persecution and imprisonment and was not politically rehabilitated until after Kemal's death.

Karabekir's fall was fairly typical of the fate suffered by relatively liberal elements of the Republic's founding elite, including those who did not raise their head above the parapet. One such notable whose career is illustrative of the nature of Kemal's regime and state was Ali Fethi Okyar (1880–1943). Okyar was briefly made Prime Minister by Kemal in late 1924, replacing Ismet Inonu, as Kemal initially responded to the challenge of the PRP by appointing a relatively moderate, conciliatory figure to head his council of ministers. Okyar was sacked by the President three months later for allegedly failing to take a sufficiently punitive approach to a localized armed revolt against the state's authority, led by a Kurdish Naqshbandi sheikh, that erupted in early 1925 in the province of Diyarbakir in Turkey's largely Kurdish southeast. Inonu was reinstated as Prime Minister and the bloodcurdling quote which is the first epigraph of this chapter is from a speech he made in Ankara

---

11  Stephane Yerasimos, 'The Mono-Party Period', in *Turkey in Transition*, eds. Schick and Tonak, 83.

in the immediate aftermath of the suppression of this revolt, which is known as the 'Sheikh Said' revolt after the name of its leading figure. Okyar was sent into political exile as ambassador to France. After five years, in mid-1930, he was recalled from Paris by Kemal and entrusted with a new task by the President. According to Okyar's memoirs, published in Turkish from Istanbul in 1980, Kemal told him: 'Our present appearance is that of a dictatorship. The institutions I will leave behind are totalitarian [in nature]. I do not wish to leave this legacy and enter history as such'. Okyar was then asked to form a political party to function as a loyal opposition. Once he assented, 'Mustafa Kemal took charge of the rest'. The President chose the name of the new party (Free Republican Party), personally supervised the drafting of its programme, and selected a bunch of CHP members of the one-party Grand National Assembly 'to be transferred to the new party'. Kemal then proceeded to personally dictate their letters of resignation from the CHP, addressed to him. The controlled experiment in party pluralism lasted three months. In November 1930 Kemal asked Okyar to dissolve the party as it 'attracted all those dissatisfied with the regime, of whom there were many, and grew like an avalanche over a few months'.[12] The hapless Fethi Bey, as he was known, duly complied. In 1934, he was sent into political exile once again as ambassador in London.

The formal adoption in 1935 of the six-arrows distillation of 'Kemalism' as the official state ideology happened after some debate and division in the Kemalist camp during the first half of the 1930s. One group of youngish writers and intellectuals organized around a journal called *Kadro* (Cadre), which started publication in 1932, tried to formulate Kemalism as an anti-capitalist and anti-imperialist ideology. This quasi-Marxist interpretation also sought to give an internationalist cast to Kemalism, arguing that the 'Turkish revolution' could and should serve as a model for anti-colonial struggles in Asia and Africa. Mustafa Kemal, a very typically insular Turk, was not interested in any such role of global anti-imperialist champion, and the suggestion of his 'revolution' becoming a reference point for Asian and African movements challenging European imperialist domination sat very uneasily with his regime's precept that Europe/the West represented the sole form of civilized modernity. In 1935, the regime acted to curb this group of enthusiasts; the

---

12 Ibid., 87–88.

*Kadro* periodical was closed by government action and its editor was posted as ambassador to Albania.

A second group of interpreters of Kemalism emerged around another periodical called *Ulku* (Ideal), which started appearing from 1933 as the official journal of the 'People's Houses' (*halk evleri*), established in 1932 in cities and larger towns to educate the common people in the principles of the 'revolution' led by Kemal (in 1940 'People's Rooms', *halk odalari*, were set up in smaller towns and rural areas with the same purpose of mass indoctrination). This group was influenced by German Nazism and Italian Fascism. Its main figure was Mehmet Recep Peker (1889–1950), a former military officer who had held a series of important ministerial portfolios from 1924 to 1930 and served intermittently as the CHP's Secretary-General between 1923 and 1936. A hardline Turkish nationalist, he believed that the response to the Kurdish 'Sheikh Said' revolt of 1925 had not been sufficiently harsh. Peker wanted the CHP to emulate Hitler's NSDAP and Mussolini's Fascists, and also fancied himself in a potential Stalin role to Kemal's Lenin. Kemal did not particularly like the references to the two European parties because he believed in the singularity of the Turkish context – which made his prescription of joining European/Western civilization lock, stock and barrel all the more incoherent – and was sceptical of such comparisons and parallels. More important, he was alarmed by Peker's overweening ambition and removed him from the post of CHP Secretary-General in 1936. Nonetheless, it was very largely the Peker/*Ulku* line that found expression in the manifesto that became the state's ideological framework in 1935. That framework was '[pseudo] scientist, [socially] corporatist, [politically] *etatist*, and [nationally] solidarist',[13] built around the personality cult of Ataturk, christened as the 'Eternal Chief' after his death. This was also the time that various pseudo-theories of the Turks' racial and linguistic origins such as the 'sun-language theory' and the 'Turkish history thesis', mentioned in Chapter 2, were being circulated with state patronage. Recep Peker's political career was far from over; he once again joined the government as Interior Minister in 1942–43, and in August 1946 he became Turkey's Prime Minister after elections contested, for the first time in the Republic, between the CHP and the nascent political opposition represented in the new-born Democrat Party or DP (see Chapter

---

13 Hanioglu, 'The Historical Roots of Kemalism', 36.

5). As Prime Minister, he did his best to roll back the growing momentum for political pluralism. He waged a bitter but losing struggle and resigned as Prime Minister after a year, in September 1947. Peker's last stand was a failed challenge for leadership of the CHP he mounted at the party's congress in 1948 against Ismet Inonu who, unlike Peker, reluctantly resigned himself to the end of the one-party system by the late 1940s.

The six arrows constituting Kemalism were incorporated into the Turkish Constitution in 1937, at the same time that the Republic was formally declared to be a 'laicist' state (following on from the deletion in 1928 of the 1924 Constitution's Article 2: 'The religion of the Turkish state is Islam'). Over the next six decades, until the end of the century, Kemalism/Ataturkism was constantly reaffirmed, much like the monotonous chanting of a holy *mantra*, as the unchangeable and indeed unchallengeable core of the identity and ideology of the Turkish state. Thus a 1989 constitutional court ruling, which by a 10:1 majority of the eleven judges struck down parliamentary legislation passed at the behest of Turgut Ozal's government to allow headscarf-wearing women students to attend universities, cited the inviolable sanctity of the 'Laws of Revolution' and 'Ataturk's Principles'.[14] Any discussion of the historical role of Ataturk himself was very difficult if not impossible because even a whiff of criticism of the demi-god could attract charges of sedition – one of the eighteen points in the ultimatum issued by the military hierarchy to Necmettin Erbakan's civilian government in 1997 through the mechanism of the National Security Council directed that 'the law (no. 5816) defining crimes against Ataturk, including acts of disrespect, must be fully implemented'.[15]

The transcendental status accorded to the creed of Kemalism as a secular analogue of divinely revealed law easily survived the end of the one-party era. The DP's winning election manifesto of 1950 differed, mildly, with only one of the six principles – statism or *etatisme*, i.e., the paradigm of state-led economic development. The DP promised to relax state control and regulation of the economy and encourage private entrepreneurship and commerce, but its governments during the 1950s accomplished very little in that direction and the agenda was retrieved and purposefully pursued decades later, under Ozal's

14  Kuru, *Secularism and State Policies Toward Religion*, 189.

15  Yavuz, *Islamic Political Identity in Turkey*, 276.

leadership in the second half of the 1980s and early 1990s. The 'People's Houses' and 'People's Rooms' set up across Turkey under the one-party regime to disseminate Kemalism to the adult masses were closed down by the DP government in 1953, but the indoctrination of young generations continued for decades afterward through the school system and the network of public (state-run) universities. The second and third Turkish Constitutions, enacted at the behest of the military guardians of the state in 1961 and 1982 after the coups of 1960 and 1980, strongly reaffirmed Kemalism as the ideological bedrock of the Republic, with minor variations in the emphasis on the different constitutive principles in the two cases. Indeed, the greater the magnitude of the crisis, the more Kemalism was invoked as the stairway to salvation. The 1982 Constitution, enacted in a context of deep and interlocking economic, social and political crises which had engulfed the country in the end-1970s, stressed on 'social peace' through 'national solidarity', referred to the state 'always with a capital S', consistent with the 1930s practice, and designated the thus capitalized state as 'Sublime' (*Yuce*) in a tone of messianic devotion. The Constitution also constantly invoked 'Ataturk's principles and reforms' in its text.[16]

The Kemalist CHP is today Turkey's largest opposition party and got one-quarter of the votes cast nationwide in the two most recent parliamentary elections – in June 2015 and the snap poll of November 2015. The party's emblem still features six white arrows on a red background. However, the most authentic legatee of the original Kemalism of the 1930s in contemporary Turkish party politics is probably the far-right MHP, whose ideology blends a fervent, militaristic brand of Turkish nationalism of strong Sunni-majoritarian (but not overtly Islamist) overtones with worship of the tradition of authoritarian, centralized state power. Its adherents often describe their political faith as *ulkucu* (idealist). The party, Turkey's third largest in vote share, was founded by the ex-colonel Alparslan Turkes in the end-1960s, who led it until his death in the late 1990s. Turkes, *basbug* (chief) to his followers, was one of the core group of officers that carried out the first military coup in 1960. In the early 1960s, a detailed study of the coup and its protagonists by a knowledgeable American observer described Turkes, then still a serving

---

16 Ozbudun, 'The Turkish Constitutional Court and Political Crisis', 152–153.

military officer, as 'represent[ing] ... probably the most ardent Kemalism' among the coup-makers.[17]

In sum, Turkey's chronic instability, political dysfunctionality and susceptibility to authoritarian rule are deeply rooted in and derive from the nature of its foundational ideology, 'Kemalism', which has shaped the country that exists today. The legacy of the hegemony of the hidebound Kemalist framework for eight decades after the Republic's formation, until the first years of this century, is that Turkey's political culture is weakly democratic and infused with fundamentally illiberal attributes. The democratic traditions are weak and the authoritarian traditions strong – 'paradoxically despite more than sixty years of competitive, multiparty politics [since 1950]', as the senior Turkish political scientist Ergun Ozbudun (b. 1937) noted at the beginning of the present decade. 'The principal reason for this', he correctly argued, is that 'the founding philosophy of the Turkish Republic' has 'features which are incompatible' with the development of 'a truly pluralistic political system'.[18] As Hakan Yavuz observed in 2000,

> Kemalism has been [only] superficially Western in form while remaining rigidly authoritarian and dogmatic in substance. It continues to stress republicanism over democracy, homogeneity over difference, the military over the civilian, and the state over society ... guaranteeing, ironically, Turkey's failure to make the transition to a Western-style liberal democracy.[19]

It is this legacy of deeply embedded authoritarianism that the new, Islamist ruling elite of the early twenty-first century has taken over and moulded to its preferences. In a historic change, the military has yielded to civilian supremacy and ceased to be the arbiter of the polity, but the coercive and repressive character of the state is unchanged. Secularism, obviously, is no longer emphasized as a core tenet of the state. But otherwise, the continuity of post-Kemalist Turkey with Kemalist Turkey is remarkable, including the zero-sum, winner-take-all approach to politics and power typical of authoritarian countries and the cult of the leader around Erdogan.

---

17  See note 14, Chapter 5.

18  Ozbudun, 'Turkey: Plural Society and Monolithic State', 61.

19  M. Hakan Yavuz, 'Turkey's Fault Lines and the Crisis of Kemalism', *Current History*, 99, no. 633, 33–38.

Commenting on the West/Europe-fixated nature of Kemalism, from which – as this book demonstrates – its secularizing agenda was derived, the Turkish scholar Nilufer Gole wrote in 1995:

> The irony is that the Turks, who for centuries symbolized Muslim and barbarian – the 'other' for Europe – now tried to enter the circle of the 'civilized'. Even more ironically, [the Kemalist state] invented its own 'barbarians', those considered as obstacles to [achieving its definition of] civilization – the [pious] Muslims and the Kurds.[20]

In the twenty-first century, representatives of those pious Muslim Turks – the *de facto* second-class citizens of the Kemalist era – have captured state power, consolidated their dominance, and taken over Ataturk's Republic. Their policy towards the Kurdish movement for recognition and rights shows that the anti-secular form of Turkish nationalism now hegemonic is – the differences in 'civilizational' perspectives notwithstanding – of the same authoritarian gene as its secularist precursor.

◆

As Chapter 2 noted, Mustafa Kemal frequently used the rhetoric of Islamic solidarity to mobilize the Anatolian population during the 1919–22 military and political struggle. A major reason was that it was vital to secure the support of the Kurds of Anatolia, concentrated in the eastern and south-eastern regions, where they comprised the majority across extensive areas. So 'during the … war of independence, the terms "Turkishness" or "Turkish nation" were hardly ever pronounced'. Instead, 'in the declarations of the Erzurum and Sivas congresses as well as in the National Pact', the population on whose behalf the struggle was being waged was defined as 'all Muslim elements' and the 'Muslim majority' of Anatolia. In his address on 1 May 1920 to the newly constituted National Assembly in Ankara, Kemal said:

> The persons who compose your sublime Assembly are not only Turks, only Circassians, only Kurds, only Laz, but a sincere community composed of all Muslim elements. The aims of your sublime body are not limited to one Muslim element. Certainly, the nation whose defence and

---

20  Gole, 'Authoritarian Secularism and Islamist Politics', 23.

preservation we are occupied with is not limited to a single element. Each Muslim element that composes this body are brothers whose interests are entirely common.

In other words, the ethnic and cultural plurality of the Muslims of Anatolia was explicitly recognized. The Erzurum, Sivas and National Pact declarations stressed that these various Muslim elements were joined together by 'real brotherhood', a spirit of 'reciprocal respect and sacrifice', a commitment to 'full partnership in disaster and happiness', and a wish to 'share the same fate'. The declarations spoke of respecting the 'ethnic and social rights' and the particular 'environmental conditions' of the different elements. As Erbudun notes, 'though the meanings of these terms were not clarified, they can be [plausibly] interpreted as a promise of cultural pluralism and a high degree of administrative decentralization', and 'it is no accident that the 1921 [interim] constitution [framed by the National Assembly] adopted a system of broad decentralization never seen in Turkey either before or after that date'.[21] As late as January 1923, with the war won and the proclamation of the Republic imminent, 'Mustafa Kemal still suggested that there might be local autonomy for Kurdish-inhabited areas' at a press conference. When an Istanbul weekly printed the minutes of the press conference in 1988, a furore erupted and the magazine was banned for 'separatist propaganda'.[22]

The policies of Kemal's regime after the formation of the Republic in October 1923 were a study in contrast. All ethnic and cultural diversity was sought to be subsumed and assimilated into a homogenized, monolithic (and implicitly majoritarian) Turkish identity, and a rigidly centralized state emerged under the control of a single party. The Kurdish identity, the second largest 'element' in society, was simply 'defined out of existence' in the Kemalist state.[23] Thus 'on the very day (3 March 1924) that the Republic abolished the Caliphate, it also published a decree banning all Kurdish schools, associations, and publications'.[24] In autumn 1924, British interrogation transcripts of Kurdish officers who had deserted from the Turkish Army reported that the deserters

---

21  Ozbudun, 'Turkey: Plural Society and Monolithic State', 80.

22  Bruinessen, 'Genocide in Kurdistan?', 141–170.

23  Ibid.

24  Christopher Houston, *Islam, Kurds and the Turkish Nation-State* (Oxford and New York: Berg, 2001), 99.

had cited a litany of grievances: the Caliphate had been summarily abolished; the term 'Kurdistan' had been deleted from geography books; the Kurdish language had been banned in schools as well as in courts of law; virtually all senior government officials appointed in the Kurdish-dominated regions were ethnic Turks; and the government was pursuing a 'divide-and-rule' strategy of setting Kurdish tribes against each other. The deserters also feared that the state had intentions to change the demography of eastern and south-eastern Anatolia by deporting large numbers of Kurds to western Turkey and settling ethnic Turks arriving as migrants in the new state, primarily from Greece and elsewhere in the Balkans, in their place. In short, they sensed an existential threat to Kurdish identity in Kemal's Republic.[25]

A localized but fierce armed revolt against the state broke out in early 1925 in a swathe of territory north, west and east of the city of Diyarbakir in south-eastern Turkey. Its main leader was Sheikh Said, a 60-year-old Kurdish religious figure of the Naqshbandi *tarikat* (order). The order had put down strong roots in south-eastern Turkey in the course of the nineteenth century, complemented by a network of *medreses* (seminaries) of the Shafi school of jurisprudence prevalent among Sunni Kurds. The local society was deeply imbued with religiosity and Kurds had not only been active in the war of independence but many (both professional military men and civilians) had played a leading role in deadly violence against (Christian) Armenian communities in eastern and south-eastern Anatolia, which began in the 1890s and culminated in mass murder during World War I under the military-dominated Committee of Union and Progress (CUP) regime. The 1925 rebellion mobilized a significant force of several thousand fighters but was mostly limited to Zaza-speaking Sunni Kurdish tribes among whom Sheikh Said's family had numerous *murid*s or disciples. Sunni Kurdish tribes speaking *Kurmanji* (the other major form of the language among the Kurds of Turkey) participated too but in lesser numbers and, underlining the internal schisms of Kurdish society, Alevi Kurdish tribes not only ignored Sheikh Said's pleas to join the *jihad* but actively assisted government forces in its suppression. The rebels tried hard but failed to take Diyarbakir, then as now the largest city in Turkey's Kurdish-majority territories. The Ankara government declared

---

25 Martin van Bruinessen, *Agha, Shaikh and State: The Social and Political Structures of Kurdistan* (London and Atlantic Highlands, NJ: Zed Books, 1992), 282–283.

martial law in the affected areas in late February and sent in a 35,000-strong military force to quell the rebellion. By April the revolt had been crushed and 'the reprisals were extremely brutal'. Villages that had taken part were razed, there were large-scale killings of non-combatant men, women and children, and 'the population of entire districts were deported to the west [of Turkey]'.[26] In September 1925, Sheikh Said and 47 other captured leaders were publicly hanged in the centre of Diyarbakir after a trial by a special tribunal, and their bodies thrown into an unmarked pit without any of the obligatory religious rituals. The execution site was later converted into a park and a large-size statue of Ataturk was put up at the spot where the gallows had stood.[27]

As Bruinessen writes, 'Sheikh Said's rebellion did not pose a serious military threat to Turkey, but it constitutes a watershed in the history of the Republic. It accelerated the trend towards authoritarian government, and ushered in policies that deliberately aimed at destroying Kurdish ethnicity'.[28] The revolt was the trigger for the blanket ban the regime imposed later in 1925 on all *tarikat*s (religious brotherhoods) including the Naqshbandi, popular among both Turks and Kurds, the proscription of all *tekkes* (dervish lodges) across the country, and the nationwide closure of tomb-mausoleums of revered saintly figures to public pilgrimage. Kemal declared that 'primitive individuals seeking … the guidance of such and such a sheikh despite the enlightenment of science, technology and civilization … should not exist in Turkish society'.[29] With regard to the state's Kurdish policy, the Sheikh Said affair bred an indelible association in the minds of the ruling elite between Kurds and religious reaction, and more generally with ignorance, fanaticism and primitive ways – all in contradiction to the Western/European modernity the Kemalists were determined to inculcate in the population. It made the state's programme of top-down secularization even more expansive and draconian.

Sheikh Said's failed uprising was the first of three major episodes of localized Kurdish resistance to the Turkish state that occurred in Mustafa Kemal's lifetime. In the end-1920s, another significant Kurdish rebellion developed in a remote part of north-eastern Turkey, in the vicinity of Mount Ararat – an area

---

26  Ibid., 290–291.

27  Houston, *Islam, Kurds and the Turkish Nation-State*, 120.

28  Bruinessen, 'Genocide in Kurdistan?', 141–170.

29  See note 12, Chapter 2.

approximating the present-day Turkish province of Agri, bordering Armenia, Azerbaijan and Iran. It began as a revolt among a local tribe against the authorities of the central state, but gradually acquired a Kurdish proto-nationalist character. The rebellion's military organizer was Ihsan Nuri, an officer who had fought in the Ottoman Army, and then in the 1919–22 Turkish war of independence before deserting in 1924. The hostilities peaked in 1930 and ended with the defeat of the rebels. As the revolt was suppressed, Mahmut Esat – one of the pioneers of the secular state, who served as Minister of Justice from 1924 to 1930 and in 1926 tabled the new Civil Code in the Grand National Assembly (see Chapter 2) – told the *Milliyet* (Nation) newspaper: 'The Turks are the only lords of this country, its only owners. Those who are not of pure Turkish stock in this country have only one right: of being servants, of being slaves. Let friend and foe, and even the mountains, know this truth!'[30] (by this time, the word 'Kurd' had become taboo in Turkey and the term 'mountain Turks' had been devised as a code-word to refer to them). The similarity to the pioneering Hindu nationalist M. S. Golwalkar's thinking, as reflected in the second epigraph of this chapter, is very obvious.

The third and final confrontation between Kurds and the Turkish state during Mustafa Kemal's presidency occurred in 1937–38. It happened in Dersim, 'an inaccessible district of high, snow-capped mountains, narrow valleys and deep ravines in central-eastern Turkey'. A sparsely populated area due to its remoteness, forbidding terrain and harsh climate, the local people consisted entirely of Alevi Kurdish tribes, mostly speakers of the Zaza version of the language. Some inhabitants may have been of Armenian origin who gradually assimilated into the heterodox Alevi tradition (which contains crypto-Christian practices). This 'wild' tribal area was 'by the mid-1930s the only part of Turkey that had not been effectively brought under central government control'. Its tribes, who regularly feuded with each other, lived by customary tribal law and recognized only the authority of their chiefs and religious leaders. Police and military officials posted by the central government to the area did not make much headway in asserting the state's authority. In 1935, a special law to bring Dersim's unruly residents to heel was passed by the Grand National Assembly. Presenting the bill to the Grand National Assembly, Sukru Kaya, Interior Minister, noted that its people had 'originally

---

30  Bruinessen, 'Genocide in Kurdistan?', 141–170.

belonged to the Turkish race' but had strayed from their roots and lost their way. In 1936, 'Dersim was placed under military administration, with the express aim of pacifying and "civilizing" it'.[31] The broader juridical framework for the operation was a 'Law on Settlement' enacted in 1934 as Law 2510, which 'divided the population [of Turkey] into three groups and the country into three zones'. The first consisted of people who spoke Turkish and were of Turkish ethnicity, the second of people who did not speak Turkish but were deemed by the state to belong to Turkish culture (such as refugees and immigrants from former Ottoman territories in the Caucasus and the Balkans), and the third of people who did not speak Turkish and were not considered to subscribe to Turkish culture. The last group were targets for enforced 'Turkification', and their areas of habitation were designated as closed, high-security zones by Law 2510. Law 2510's purpose, as approvingly noted by a deputy in the one-party Grand National Assembly at the time of its adoption in mid-1934, was to build 'a country which would speak one single language, think and feel alike'.[32]

The Dersim equivalent of Diyarbakir's Sunni-Naqshbandi Sheikh Said was Seyyit Riza, an Alevi religious leader. In response to the tightening of government control, Riza, who seems to have had the loyalty of only a small section of the population limited to a few of the numerous tribal clans, apparently instigated saboteur actions directed at government buildings, bridges and telephone lines in spring 1937. When the military cracked down and demanded the surrender of the subversives, the tribespeople resisted and the conflict escalated. Punitive military operations intensified in the summer of 1937. In September, Riza was captured with a band of about fifty men and he and ten others were executed after a summary trial. Shortly after the executions, President Ataturk visited the troubled area, and in the spring of 1938 the military operations resumed with greater intensity until Dersim was completely pacified. According to both Kurdish nationalist and Turkish military accounts, the crackdowns of 1937 and 1938 in Dersim were extremely violent.[33] Men, women and children were killed indiscriminately by gunfire, bayoneting and by being burnt alive, and the fatalities ran into thousands.

---

31  Ibid.

32  Kirisci, 'Disaggregating Turkish Citizenship and Immigration Practices', 4–6.

33  Both sets of sources are quoted in Bruinessen, 'Genocide in Kurdistan?'.

Deep caves in which some women and children hid during the fighting simply had their entrances bricked over. Tribes which had not participated in the unrest were victimized as thoroughly as those which had. Sabiha Gokcen (1913–2001), an adopted daughter of Mustafa Kemal's, flew bombing sorties over Dersim as an air force pilot; this role was held up, then and for decades afterward, as an example of the new, emancipated Turkish woman.[34] The Turkish media reported that the 'bandit' (*haydut*) problem plaguing the area had been eradicated. Much of the population that survived the carnage were deported to various places, ranging from central Anatolian provinces such as Sivas to distant eastern Thrace, the only region of Turkey which is geographically part of Europe. Dersim was given the Turkish name 'Tunceli' in 1936. This was part of a state policy of prohibition of Kurdish names in Kemalist Turkey, applicable not just to places but persons, as a result of which numerous avowed Kurdish nationalists of late twentieth-century and early twenty-first-century Turkey have generic Turkish names.

The legacy of these events was that Kurds became *the* taboo topic of Kemalist Turkey. The left-wing Workers' Party of Turkey (TIP) was closed down by the constitutional court after the country's second military coup in 1971 on the grounds that its leaders had mentioned the unmentionable – the existence of a banned and criminalized Kurdish identity. Of course, neither the prosecutorial indictment nor the ruling explicitly mentioned Kurds. The newly formed Islamist party, the National Order Party (MNP), was closed down at the same time on charges of anti-secular politics but was allowed to re-open after a year under a slightly different name – the National Salvation Party (MSP).

The Turkish Republic's policy of assimilating Kurds – who are usually estimated to be about a fifth of the country's population, and about two-thirds Sunni and one-third Alevi – by denying and erasing their identity was a partial success. Numerous Kurds who forsook or concealed their origins and adhered to the unitary, pseudo-civic Kemalist model of citizenship achieved recognition and success over the decades in diverse fields including high-level politics, a variety of professions, the state bureaucracy and even the military. But the homogenization project did not fully prevail and Kurdish identity was

---

34 Istanbul's second airport is named in her honour; the larger airport is named after Ataturk. Aerial bombing and strafing was also part of the campaigns to put down the Sheikh Said (1925) and Ararat (1930) revolts.

not eradicated. A large proportion of Turkey's Kurds continued to privately harbour the forbidden identity, and bitterness at its repression. The latent problem manifested itself from the mid-1980s in the form of a steadily escalating armed insurgency in eastern and south-eastern Turkey, launched and led by an underground organization formed in the late 1970s that called itself the Workers' Party of Kurdistan (*Partiya Karkeren Kurdistane*, PKK).

The PKK's struggle was a rekindling of, but also very different from, the Kurdish uprisings in the first two decades of the Turkish Republic. The organization was an offshoot of radical left-wing politics that attracted sizeable numbers of students in Turkey's universities during the 1970s. Dissatisfied with the Turkish radical left's reluctance to give priority to the question of Kurdish recognition and rights, the PKK's founders constituted themselves as an organization explicitly dedicated to Kurdish national liberation in 1978, but the group retained the imprint of its Marxist–Leninist origins in its ideology and social program. Both these features – the explicit ethno-nationalism and the 'progressive' stance on social issues – differentiated the PKK from the Kurdish rebels who unsuccessfully challenged the Kemalist state in the 1920s and 1930s. The PKK's notional purpose was to act as the engine of the eventual establishment of a Kurdish state across the Kurdish-dominated lands of Turkey, Iraq, Syria and Iran, but its actual struggle focused on the traditional Kurdish habitats of eastern and south-eastern Turkey, which it referred to as 'north Kurdistan', and the emancipation of its people from decades of oppression by the Turkish state. The PKK disavowed and set itself against the traditional tribal structures of east and south-east Anatolia's Kurdish society, the feudal relationships between *agha*s (large landowners) and peasants, the authority of men of religion, and the exclusion of women from the public sphere. In other words, the PKK's ambitious political project sought to confront and change deeply rooted patterns of domination and hierarchy in Kurdish society simultaneously with a war of national liberation against the Turkish state.[35] The movement has attracted and mobilized

---

35 An informed account of the PKK's struggle can be found in Aliza Marcus, *Blood and Belief: The PKK and the Kurdish Fight for Independence* (New York and London: New York University Press, 2007). See also *Programme of the Kurdistan Workers' Party* (Cologne: Wesanen Serxwebun, 1983) and Abdullah Ocalan, *Interviews and Speeches* (London: Kurdistan Information Centre, 1992).

thousands of young Kurdish women as combatants over the past three decades. As one author observed in 2001, the form of Kurdish nationalism the PKK's struggle birthed in the 1980s and 1990s among Turkey's Kurds 'shares some of its tropes with Turkish [statist] nationalism, including a severe secularizing tendency', and more broadly, 'the enlightenment orientation of Kemalism's laicist and evolutionary understanding of history'.[36] Indeed, this enabled the PKK to partially bridge the Sunni–Alevi divide in Kurdish society and it gained numerous members from the sizeable Alevi minority in addition to the Sunni majority. When the PKK's supreme leader, Abdullah ('Apo') Ocalan, was captured by Turkish special forces in Nairobi, Kenya in 1999 after two decades based mostly in Damascus, Syria and brought back to Turkey as a prisoner, 'he praised Ataturk's attempt to create a secular and European state and sharply criticized the Sheikh Said uprising of 1925, as well as the traditional tribal system which promoted despotic *aghas*'.[37] This may have a shrewd strategic turn by a disarmed and helpless captive, but it was consistent with the PKK's ideological orientation and practices.

The PKK's early core of cadres meticulously prepared the groundwork for their insurrection through the first half of the 1980s – during the extremely repressive period that followed Turkey's third military coup in 1980 – before launching their first, modest attacks on Turkish military and paramilitary (*jandarma*) targets in the east and south-east in the second half of 1984. Those first sparks of insurgency did, in the language of Chairman Mao Zedong's operational doctrine of 'protracted people's war', spread a prairie fire of revolt across eastern and south-eastern Turkey over the next few years. The PKK steadily gained strength and momentum in the war-zone during the second half of the 1980s and its armed struggle peaked during the first half of the 1990s. During the second half of the 1990s, however, the tables turned decisively in the war of attrition as the vastly superior Turkish armed forces regained the advantage and pushed the PKK on the defensive. The crucial factor in the change of battlefield fortunes was the Turkish military's calculated destruction of several thousand villages and hamlets across the sprawling rural expanse of the war-zone and the uprooting of their inhabitants, a policy described by the military as 'draining the swamp to eradicate the

36  Houston, *Islam, Kurds and the Turkish Nation-State*, 108.
37  Yavuz, *Islamic Political Identity in Turkey*, 254.

mosquitoes'. The PKK's strategy had been to build a rurally based insurgency that controlled large swathes of the countryside from mountain strongholds, as it generally could not capture and hold cities and towns heavily garrisoned by the Turkish forces. The brutal, forced removal of much of the rural Kurdish population, who became refugees in the urban centres of the war-zone such as Diyarbakir, in cities in other parts of Turkey, or abroad, mostly in European countries, deprived the guerrillas of essential cover and support. Constant attacks by the Turkish air force's fleets of ultra-modern American helicopter gunships and bombers targeted the guerrillas' mountain bases. The Turkish military's local collaborators in the counter-insurgency campaign consisted of a large network of 'village guards'. These men were recruited from among followers of traditional notables threatened by the PKK's social radicalism and its bid for total power over Kurdish society, and from communities that had suffered from PKK violence due to non-support for the cause or some form of perceived collaboration with the Turkish state. A shadowy Kurdish Islamist group known as the Hizbullah, vehemently opposed to the PKK's secularist and socialist ideology, constituted another group of auxiliaries of the Turkish military machine during the 1990s.

By the end of the 1990s, after 15 years of bitter fighting that left about 40,000 civilians, insurgents, soldiers and police dead, the PKK's insurgency was largely spent – a trajectory similar to that of the post-1990 Kashmiri insurgency against the Indian state which is discussed later in this chapter. Its lasting legacy for the twenty-first century, as in the Kashmiri case, was the spread and deepening of Kurdish nationalist consciousness among Turkey's Kurds, especially the younger generations who grew up in the midst of the war of the 1980s and 1990s or in its disturbed aftermath in the new century. After Ocalan's capture in 1999, a body-blow to crumbling rebel morale, most of the PKK's remaining fighting forces abandoned the struggle inside Turkey and retreated across the Turkish–Iraqi border to mountain bases located in the northern Kurdish-populated region of Iraq.

The political and military elites of the Turkish state, and indeed much of the (non-Kurdish) Turkish public at large, were consumed by fear and hatred of the 'separatist-terrorist' menace represented by the PKK. The most common response was to regard the problem purely through the lens of 'terrorism', shorn of any political context. In March 1993, Ocalan, based in his cross-border hideout in Damascus, declared a month-long unilateral ceasefire to start on *Newroz*, the Kurdish new year (public *Newroz* celebrations were not permitted in Turkey until 2000 and during the turbulent 1990s, the day regularly sparked violent confrontations between Kurdish demonstrators and Turkish security forces in cities and towns in the war-zone). He apparently hoped for a favourable response, leading to some form of dialogue, from Turkey's soft-Islamist President, Turgut Ozal, who did not conceal his partially Kurdish parentage and was reputed to harbour sympathy for Kurdish aspirations. Ismet Sezgin, Interior Minister, told the *Milliyet* daily when queried about the possibility of a de-escalation of the intense violence engulfing eastern and south-eastern Turkey: 'The state does not negotiate with bandits'.[38] It was the same terminology, and mentality, as that of state officials of the 1930s. Four weeks later, just after Ocalan extended the PKK's unilateral ceasefire, President Ozal suddenly died, and hostilities resumed with a vengeance the following month. Another common form of denial was to refer to the 'eastern question' or the 'southeast problem', as it was politically incorrect to use the term 'Kurd', and attribute the problem merely to poverty, economic underdevelopment and social 'backwardness' in that region, evading its political content rooted in the nature of the Turkish state. Variants of these two forms of denial are also staples of attitudes towards the Kashmir problem prevalent in India.

In its 1994 ruling closing down the Democracy Party (DEP), a party re-formed in 1993 from an earlier 1990 incarnation (banned in 1993) to provide a political platform and outlet for Kurdish grievances, Turkey's constitutional court observed:

> The Constitution, which is based on the principle of *unitary* state, does not permit *federal* state. Therefore, political parties cannot include federal system in their programs, and cannot advocate such a structure … [moreover] The Constitution is closed to autonomy or self-rule for regions … [furthermore] The recognition of minority status based on differences of race [sic] and language is incompatible with territorial and national integrity … In the Republic of Turkey, there is one state and one nation … It is impossible to give validity to such dangerous aims derived

---

38  Marcus, *Blood and Belief*, 212. In his speeches during World War II, Hitler invariably described resistance fighters in Nazi-occupied countries such as Yugoslavia as 'bandits'.

from certain political causes and foreign factors and intensified by claims to human rights and freedom ... the State is SINGLE, the territory is a WHOLE, the nation is ONE (emphases and capitals in the original).[39]

Even in what turned out to be the last decade of the Kemalist era, during which the nominally secular state was actually 'based on a synthesis between a large dose of Sunni Islam and ethnic Turkishness'[40] fostered by the military hierarchy since the 1980s (see Chapter 5), the Turkish Republic proved completely hidebound in its self-imposed ideological straitjacket.[41] That framework was pithily articulated in 1996 by Alparslan Turkes, ex-colonel and veteran leader of the far-right MHP: 'The Kurds are all of Turkish stock. They are Turks that have become Kurds only through neglect. Turkey is not a cultural mosaic. Everyone in Turkey is a Turk'.[42] He was simply repeating a (then) seventy-year-old dogma of Kemalism.

The battered Kurds had several reasons to feel cautiously optimistic when the Islamist AKP won the November 2002 parliamentary election and assumed the reins of the civilian government. First, both they and the Islamists had been stigmatized as malcontents and deviants and been continuously persecuted by the military hierarchy and its allies in the watchdog apparatus of the Kemalist state, led by the notorious constitutional court. The latest victim of that strategy of relentless harassment was none other than Tayyip Erdogan, who was still banned from politics when the AKP won the watershed election of late 2002, following his conviction and brief imprisonment on charges of anti-secular activity in 1999. He became Prime Minister in March 2003, once the ban was lifted. Second, Islamism in Turkey had deep Kurdish roots and connections. The most influential Islamic thinker of twentieth-century Turkey, Bediuzzaman Said Nursi (1876–1960), was a Kurd from eastern

---

39  Ozbudun, 'The Turkish Constitutional Court and Political Crisis', 157–158.

40  Umit Cizre Sakallioglu, 'Historicizing the Present and Problematizing the Future of the Kurdish Problem: A Critique of the TOBB Report on the Eastern Question', *New Perspectives on Turkey* 14 (spring 1996), 8.

41  For a comparative study of how consistently draconian Turkish state policies radicalized Kurdish dissent, whereas relatively flexible Moroccan state policies ameliorated Berber dissent, see Senem Aslan, *Nation-Building in Turkey and Morocco: Governing Kurdish and Berber Dissent* (New York: Cambridge University Press, 2015).

42  Houston, *Islam, Kurds and the Turkish Nation-State*, 95.

Anatolia. Although he distanced himself from politics after the formation of the Republic, assumed a reticent persona and devoted his time to developing a philosophy of Islam suited to conditions of the twentieth century, he was hounded and persecuted by the state authorities, who continued to see him as a major threat. The perception was not unfounded because his writings were clandestinely circulated throughout Turkey, among both Turks and Kurds, and his significant following came to be known as the *Nur* (Light) movement. Nursi's followers, called *nurcu*s and mostly of the middle and lower-middle classes, could be found in every part of the country but, consistent with Turkey's demography, most were (Sunni) ethnic Turks. In 2000, there were 349 *dershane*s (study circles) devoted to reading and discussing Nursi's works in Istanbul alone, up from 23 such in 1970.[43] Further, the Naqshbandi *tarikat*, formally banned since 1925, had widespread clandestine networks among both Sunni Turks and Sunni Kurds, and throughout the country. In short, there were many bridges connecting the mostly ethnic-Turk Sunni Islamist party that took over the civilian government from late 2002 with the Sunni majority among Turkey's Kurds. This was very different from the metropolitan Kemalist elite of Ankara and Istanbul, who had no such connections and viewed the rural and small-town Kurdish population of the east and south-east as an especially troublesome segment of the unwashed masses of Turkey, at odds with their vision of Turkey as a constituent of Western civilization and Europe.

The overlap was very apparent in voting patterns and party politics. The Islamist political party of the 1970s, the MSP led by Necmettin Erbakan, gained 12 per cent of the nationwide votes in the 1973 parliamentary election and 9 per cent in 1977. It did best in provinces with Sunni Kurdish majorities such as Diyarbakir and Bingol. Its next-best results were in a bunch of east-central Anatolian provinces such as Erzurum, Kahramanmaras, Malatya and Sivas, where Sunni ethnic-Turk majorities lived in tense proximity to large Alevi minorities. In the end-1995 parliamentary election, the MSP's successor the RP, still led by Erbakan, emerged as the single largest party in Turkey's parliament, winning 21.4 per cent of the nationwide votes. Of the 158 RP parliamentarians (of a total of 550 seats in the Grand National Assembly), as many as 35, or 22 per cent, were (Sunni) Kurds. This proportion was

---

43 Yavuz, *Islamic Political Identity in Turkey*, 168.

higher than the estimated Kurdish percentage of Turkey's population, which is usually pegged at a maximum of 20 per cent. One of those 35 deputies was Fuat Firat, a grandson of the legendary Sheikh Said. Firat argued that 'Islamic solidarity' could transcend and heal the Turk–Kurd divide. In 1994, at the height of the Turkish state's war with the PKK, the RP dispatched a 'fact-finding mission' to the war-torn region. Its report, published in August 1994, just after the constitutional court closed down the DEP, 'called on the state to open democratic spaces for Kurdish groups and associations, [by] utilizing religious networks as cross-cutting bonds, allowing education in the Kurdish language, and giving more powers to municipalities [in the Kurdish-dominated territories]'.[44]

In the post-Kemalist context of the twenty-first century, however, a clarion call to renew Sunni-Muslim solidarity across the Turk–Kurd faultline would simply not suffice as a solution to Turkey's Kurdish problem. First, that would not include the Alevi Kurds, nearly a third of the Kurdish population. Sevket Kazan, the head of the 1994 RP fact-finding mission, was subsequently appointed Minister of Justice in Erbakan's coalition government of 1996–1997. Kazan, a lawyer, was also the lead counsel for the defendants in the trial of those indicted for the Sunni mob attack which left 37 leading members of the Alevi intelligentsia dead in Sivas in 1993, described in Chapter 3. Even more important, the political nature of Kurdish identity had been substantially transformed by the secular ethno-nationalist struggle led by the PKK in the 1980s and 1990s. The transformation was apparent in the political evolution of Abdulmelik Firat, another grandson of the martyred Sheikh Said. In 1989 this grandson, who had spent a total of 17 years in detention, told an interviewer, 'Without a doubt, my struggle is for God and the Islamic religion'. Six years later, in 1995, he visited the public park in Diyarbakir – dominated by an Ataturk statue – on the seventieth anniversary of his grandfather's hanging there in September 1925. He prayed and scattered rose petals at the site where his grandfather's body was tossed 'like rubbish' after the execution. He told another interviewer that he then heard his grandfather's voice saying to him, 'Don't be sad. I am not here. I am in the mountains with my friends' (a reference to the guerrillas of the PKK).[45]

---

44  Ibid., 210–211, 231–233.

45  Houston, *Islam, Kurds and the Turkish Nation-State*, 121–122, 162–163.

Abdulmelik Firat came out in open support of the HADEP – the successor to the DEP and similarly viewed by the state establishment as a political front for the PKK – in the end-1995 parliamentary election. He was arrested in 1996 and incarcerated yet again, at the age of 72. Nonetheless, the HADEP and its successor, DEHAP, kept growing in the Kurdish-dominated areas of Turkey. Its share of the nationwide vote in successive parliamentary elections rose from 4.1 per cent in 1995 to 4.7 per cent in 1999 and 6.2 per cent in late 2002. The party could not gain representation in parliament because of the 10 per cent threshold of the nationwide votes required, but by the time Erdogan became Prime Minister, it was easily the strongest party in east and south-east Anatolia, relegating the AKP, the RP's successor, to a fairly distant second position. The crucial question was whether the Erdogan/ AKP regime that consolidated its primacy in Turkish politics during the first decade of the new century, and emerged as its hegemon by the beginning of the second decade, could come to an honourable peace with Kurdish ethno-nationalism, which had developed a mass following among both Sunni and Alevi Kurds.

There was modest progress in that direction during the first two to three years of the AKP's first term in government (2002–07). The new AKP government lifted the state of emergency that had been in force in about a dozen provinces of eastern and south-eastern Turkey since the late 1980s, which had given security forces in that region a virtual *carte blanche* and impunity. There was some leeway given to teaching of the Kurdish language and to Kurdish media. The aggrieved Kurds and the AKP shared a common foe in the military hierarchy and its allies in the 'secular' civilian elite, the forces implacably opposed to both the Islamist political ascendancy and to Kurdish aspirations. Moreover, the EU's criteria for progressing Turkey's candidate status (granted in end-1999) for eventual membership required removal or reform of the Turkish state's panoply of laws, regulations and norms incompatible with liberal democracy. This prominently included the situation of the Kurds and their human and cultural rights. The EU factor was an additional spur to the rudimentary liberalization of the state's approach to and treatment of the Kurdish question under the first AKP government. Many avowed Kemalists lost their (always one-sided) felt affinity with 'Europe' as a result and became bitter critics of the EU. In the post-1999 phase, meanwhile, the focus of Kurdish politics and activism in Turkey moved away from armed struggle for secession to demands for '[substantively equal] citizenship, recognition of cultural rights, [and] the consolidation of local governments [*de facto* grassroots decentralization]'.[46]

The AKP regime's subsequent Kurdish policy was however marked by prevarication, a reluctance to tackle the roots and substance of the conflict, and a 'start-stop' style. Thus a 'Kurdish opening', announced with fanfare by the second AKP government in 2009, was followed by mass arrests of Kurdish politicians and activists. In March 2013, on the occasion of a mass *Newroz* rally in Diyarbakir, a letter to the Kurdish people from the imprisoned PKK leader Abdullah Ocalan was read out in both Turkish and Kurdish versions. The statement called for the permanent cessation of armed struggle. A month later, the PKK operational command based in its mountain redoubt in northern Iraq announced its decision to withdraw PKK fighting units from Turkey. In February 2015, the third AKP government (elected in 2011) and Kurdish politicians held a meeting at Istanbul's nineteenth-century Dolmabahce palace and jointly announced a ten-point agenda for a settlement to the conflict prepared by Ocalan.

A few months later, in the summer of 2015, the worst outbreak of violence since the 1990s flared in eastern and south-eastern Turkey, pitting Kurdish demonstrators and PKK fighters against the vast Turkish military and paramilitary apparatus deployed in the region. The immediate catalyst to the catastrophic relapse was the inconclusive parliamentary election of June 2015, in which the AKP, as described in Chapter 1, failed to win a majority in the Grand National Assembly for the first time since its breakthrough in late 2002. The AKP's setback was because the Kurdish nationalist party, the People's Democratic Party (HDP), formed in 2012 as the latest incarnation of the parties advocating Kurdish rights founded since 1990, crossed the 10 per cent threshold and secured a solid bloc of representation in parliament (80 of the 550 seats). The HDP, in fact, gained over 13 per cent of the nationwide votes. It accomplished this by running on a platform that combined liberal and social-democratic elements with the traditional emphasis on Kurdish identity-politics. The platform amounted to a charter for fundamental democratization

---

46  Yavuz, *Islamic Political Identity in Turkey*, 253.

of the Turkish state and its underlying ideology, and resonated with a sizeable cohort of young, urban and highly educated ethnic Turkish voters in addition to the party's core Kurdish constituency. The HDP's ascendancy was built on its strong grassroots presence in most of the east and south-east, where the party controlled dozens of municipalities and mayoralties won in local government elections.[47] After the setback, Erdogan apparently decided to go for an all-out crackdown in eastern and south-eastern Turkey to consolidate Turkish nationalist opinion against the Kurdish opposition, the perennial 'Other' of the Turkish Republic since its formation. The strategy paid dividends as the AKP regained its parliamentary majority in the snap national election of November 2015, increasing its vote share to 49 per cent from 41 per cent it had secured in June; this was thanks mainly to the defection to the AKP of one-third of voters who had cast ballots for the far-right MHP in June. The MHP's nationwide vote share declined from 18 per cent to 12 per cent between the two elections held in the space of five months in 2015.

Since mid-2015, 'the Kurdish issue has once again become completely securitized and framed not as a problem of democracy and democratization but as one of terror and separatism'.[48] In short, the Erdogan/AKP regime has reverted to the Kemalist approach practiced for eight decades before the Islamists' rise to power in Turkey. In March 2017, the United Nations reported that about 2,000 civilians had been killed and approximately 500,000 displaced or rendered homeless in the country's east and south-east by Turkish security operations between mid-2015 and the end of 2016.[49] Diyarbakir's ancient old-town quarter lies in ruins from shelling to flush out PKK militants, and a number of other towns in the region are heavily damaged as well. In November 2016, in the context of the nationwide state of emergency imposed by Erdogan's regime following the failed military coup of July 2016, the HDP leader Selahattin Demirtas (b. 1973), who got

---

47  For more on this, see Nicole F. Watts, *Activists in Office: Kurdish Politics and Protest in Turkey* (Seattle: University of Washington Press, 2010).

48  Evren Balta, 'The Pendulum of Democracy: The AKP and Turkey's Kurdish Conflict', in *The AKP and Turkish Foreign Policy in the Middle East*, ed. Zeynep Kaya (London: The London School of Economics Middle East Centre, 2016), 19.

49  'Turkey–PKK Conflict: UN Report Tells of 2000 Dead since Truce Collapse', *BBC News Online*, 10 March 2017.

10 per cent of the nationwide votes standing as a candidate in Turkey's first-ever direct presidential election against Erdogan in 2014, was arrested. In February 2017, the prosecutor at his trial called for a 143-year prison sentence for him on charges of terrorism.[50] As of 2017, he remains in gaol along with another eleven of the 59 HDP deputies elected to Turkey's parliament in the November 2015 election, in which the HDP secured 11 per cent of the nationwide votes. The elected HDP mayors of dozens of cities and towns in the east and south-east have been summarily dismissed, and many arrested, by the all-powerful central state exercising its emergency powers during 2017. The dark repression of the 1990s has once again engulfed eastern and south-eastern Turkey. The harsh rhetoric and punitive policies of Erdogan and his regime against the Kurdish opposition have come to replicate those of the Kemalist regimes of the twentieth century.

This turn of events cannot be adequately explained by the AKP's calculations of political expediency, nor by the Erdogan regime's fears at the rise since 2015 of a PKK-aligned Kurdish party and militia in northern Syria as the main force fighting against the Islamic State (IS) movement. The roots lie in the ideological and institutional foundations of the Turkish state. As the autocratic character of the Erdogan regime became ever more pronounced during the tenure of the third AKP government (2011–15) – manifested in its disproportionate and heavy-handed response to citizen protests in Turkish cities in the summer of 2013 – it became clear that the twenty-first-century Islamist rulers of Turkey represent not a departure from but a continuation of the Kemalist tradition of authoritarian state power. They have simply taken over the institutional apparatus of the authoritarian Kemalist state, *sans* the military's dominance and the 'secularism'. The bottle is the same, although the label is different, and its content is just as noxious – intolerant of diversity, dissent and opposition – as the old potion. The Erdogan regime is not likely to be any more successful than its Kemalist predecessors in stamping out the Kurdish 'problem'. Eighty years after the Dersim massacres and deportations of 1937–38, Kurdish identity is very much alive in the remote east-central Anatolian province renamed as Tunceli in 1936. Its small population of fewer than 100,000 voted largely for the HDP in the two 2015 parliamentary

---

50  Sibel Hurtas, 'Turkey's Top Kurdish Politician Faces up to 143 Years in Jail', *Al-Monitor*, 8 February 2017.

elections, and two-thirds of the votes polled there in the presidential election of 2014 went to the Kurdish leader Demirtas.

## The Case of Hindu Nationalism

If Kemalism was an ideology retrospectively constructed in the 1920s and 1930s to provide a framework for the exercise of state power, Hindu nationalism has since its inception in the 1920s and 1930s been an ideology in quest of state power to realize its aims and ambitions.

Vinayak Damodar (V. D.) Savarkar (1883–1966), the prophet of Hindu nationalism, started his political life as an anti-colonial activist. As a student of law in London in the first decade of the twentieth century – a crucial period of anti-imperialist political awakening in India, when sizeable numbers of educated young men were attracted to armed struggle to liberate the country, especially in the eastern province of Bengal – he was part of a circle of Indian students in London drawn to that political cause. The Indian National Congress, founded in 1885, was at the time an elite society largely dedicated to petitioning the British for incremental reform and concessions to Indian rights, and not the mass-based organization it became from the early 1920s onwards under Gandhi's leadership. The appearance of a trend towards armed resistance among a new generation of Indian youth greatly alarmed the colonial authorities, for it rekindled bad memories. In 1857, a large-scale revolt led by *sepoy*s (ordinary Indian soldiers) serving in the British army had broken out across northern and central India. The spate of localized uprisings were suppressed by mid-1858 amid savage British reprisals against the rebels and the Indian population at large after months of heavy fighting, and left a deep-seated fear of armed rebellion by Indians implanted in the British colonialist psyche. The colonial power thus reacted very harshly to sporadic assassinations of British officials by Indian youths that began happening towards the end of the first decade of the twentieth century. The perpetrators of such actions were almost always hanged, and others involved sentenced to very lengthy prison terms, often for life. For the next four decades, until India's independence in 1947, those Indians who advocated, or worse, practiced armed struggle suffered much harsher treatment than adherents of the ideal of non-violent resistance Gandhi preached and tried to uphold.

In 1909, a fellow-student and friend of Savarkar's assassinated a senior British official in London. Savarkar was implicated in the case by the investigation (the perpetrator, Madan Lal Dhingra, was hanged in London's Pentonville prison). Savarkar fled to France but was arrested there by British pursuers in 1910, brought back to England and then taken to India to stand trial. In 1911, he was sentenced to fifty years in prison and transported to the then newly built Cellular Jail – so-named for its distinctive geometric architectural style, derived from the nineteenth-century panopticon concept of detention facilities – located on the Andaman and Nicobar islands, a remote bunch of islands on the southern edge of the Bay of Bengal. The Andamans, as they are commonly known, are one of seven small, lightly populated 'union territories' of India, administered directly by the central government in New Delhi. Distant from the Indian mainland, the islands are closer to the western tip of the Indonesian archipelago than to the subcontinent's land-mass. The British started using these islands, inhabited by aboriginal communities of hunter-gatherers, as a penal colony for rebels captured after the suppression of the 1857 insurrection. In the first decade of the twentieth century, the Cellular Jail was built as a detention facility for Indians who resorted to armed struggle against the Raj. Until the end-1930s, thousands of such Indians were imprisoned there. Transportation to the Andamans and incarceration in the Cellular Jail was considered the most severe form of punishment short of execution for Indian nationalists; only the sixteenth-century Lahore Fort in the north-western Punjab province, also used by the British to detain Indian nationalists deemed especially dangerous, came close to its notoriety. The conditions for Cellular Jail inmates were sub-human – the prisoners were kept in solitary confinement in tiny cells, made to do hard labour, and often died from the continuous torture or due to snakebite (the islands were infested with deadly snakes). Hunger strikes and suicides by inmates were common throughout the four decades the Cellular Jail was in use.[51]

---

51 In 1942, the Japanese overran the Andaman and Nicobar islands. In late 1943, they formally turned over the islands to the authority of the 'Provisional Government of Free India' (*Arzi Hukumat-e Azad Hind*) declared by the Indian nationalist leader Subhas Chandra Bose in Singapore on 21 October 1943. Bose visited the islands in end-December 1943, paid homage at the Cellular Jail, and renamed the Andamans as *Shaheed* (Martyr) and the Nicobars as *Swaraj* (Freedom). My father, Dr Sisir Kumar Bose (1920–2000), experienced solitary confinement in the dungeons of the Lahore

Savarkar was consigned to essentially a life term in this facility at the age of twenty-eight. Remarkably, the ghastly conditions of the Cellular Jail failed to break the spirit and political resolve of the vast majority of the Indians who were sent there over four decades. Savarkar, however, was an exception. In 1911, 1913, 1917 and 1920, he submitted petitions to the British government seeking clemency. The first petition was sent two months after his arrival in the Andamans. In the second petition two years later, he wrote,

> Sir, I have fifty years staring me in the face ... If the Government in their manifold beneficence and mercy release me, I for one cannot but be the staunchest advocate of constitutional progress and loyalty to the English government, which is the foremost condition of that progress ... I am ready to serve the Government in any capacity they like, for as my conversion is conscientious so I hope my future conduct would be. The Mighty alone can afford to be merciful, and where else can the prodigal son return but to the parental doors of the Government?

The lengthy fourth petition of 1920 stated:

> I have publicly avowed my faith in and readiness to stand by the side of orderly and constitutional development ... I am sincere in expressing my earnest intention of treading the constitutional path ... the sweet blessings of home that have been denied to me by myself make me desirous of leading a quiet and retired life for years to come ... The brilliant prospects of my early life, all too soon blighted, have constituted such a painful source of regret to me that release would be a new birth and would touch my heart, sensitive and submissive, to [your] kindness so deeply as to render me personally attached and politically useful in future.[52]

In mid-1921, Savarkar was repatriated from the Andamans and lodged in a jail in his native region in western India – in the present-day Indian State of Maharashtra, which was then part of a larger colonial administrative unit called the Bombay Presidency. He was released altogether from prison in early 1924, with some conditions restricting his movements and prohibiting

---

Fort in 1944–45. His account of that experience can be found in his autobiography of his early life, *Subhas and Sarat: An Intimate Memoir of the Bose Brothers*, edited and with an introduction by Sumantra Bose (New Delhi: Aleph Book Company, 2016).

52  R. C. Majumdar, *Penal Settlements in Andamans* (New Delhi: Department of Culture, Government of India, 1975), 211–213.

participation in active politics for five years. He was never arrested or jailed again under the Raj.[53] In 2002, the airport at Port Blair, the capital of the Andamans, was named after Savarkar at the initiative of the BJP, which then headed a coalition government in New Delhi. A sound-and-light show which presents the history of the Cellular Jail, now a national memorial, to visitors from across India and abroad revolves around Savarkar. In 2003, at the initiative of the BJP's top leadership, a portrait of Savarkar was installed in the Indian parliament building's Central Hall – which functions as an informal common room for parliamentarians and is also used for the rare joint sessions of parliament's two chambers and for occasional addresses by high foreign dignitaries – alongside icons of the freedom struggle and notable leaders of post-independence India. Two days after taking over as India's Prime Minister in mid-2014, Narendra Modi paid his respects to Savarkar's portrait there in a brief ceremony to commemorate his 131st birthday.

By the time Savarkar emerged from his 13 years in captivity (1911–24), India's political context had been transformed by the rise of the mass movement for independence spearheaded by the Indian National Congress under Gandhi's leadership. Inspired by the call to freedom, young men such as Jawaharlal Nehru and Subhas Chandra Bose gave up affluent lifestyles and promising careers and dedicated their lives to the struggle. Bose, who joined the movement in 1921 on returning from England after completing his degree at Cambridge University and declining a post in the Indian Civil Service – the elite bureaucracy that administered India for the Raj – was arrested eleven times between 1921 and 1940, and spent more than half that period either in jail (including two and a half years in Mandalay, Burma in the 1920s) or in enforced exile in Europe (during the 1930s). Nehru was arrested nine times and spent a total of nine years in prison between 1921 and 1945. Nehru served as the President of the Indian National Congress

---

53  Savarkar was arrested in Bombay in February 1948 on suspicion of complicity in Mahatma Gandhi's murder in Delhi on 30 January 1948. Nathuram Godse, the assassin, and the other conspirators were personally known to Savarkar and regarded him as a major inspiration. Savarkar was acquitted on trial for want of credible evidence linking him to the plot. Godse, like Savarkar a Maharashtrian Chitpavan Brahmin, was hanged in November 1949. In the immediate aftermath of Gandhi's killing, furious crowds attacked homes and shops belonging to Chitpavan Brahmins across Maharashtra. Savarkar's home in Bombay too came under attack.

in 1929–30 and 1936–37 and Bose (b. 1897), who was seven years younger than Nehru, in 1938–39. True to the promises of permanent reformation and good, loyal behaviour he made in his mercy pleas, Savarkar stayed totally aloof from both the Congress-led national movement and the armed groups who intermittently fought the colonial regime with assassinations and attacks during the 1920s and 1930s in different parts of the country, especially Bengal but also in northern India and elsewhere. But he did not entirely abjure politics. From the end of his time in the Andamans, he started developing the political doctrine of Hindu nationalism, and formulated its essentials during his subsequent jail time in his native region. In 1937, he became the President of the Hindu Mahasabha (Great Hindu Forum), a vocal but marginal political party, and served as its President for seven consecutive annual terms until 1943. The Hindu Mahasabha – which had in its leadership men such as Syama Prasad (S. P.) Mookerjee, a Bengali Brahmin who after India's independence became the first President of the Bharatiya Jan Sangh, the BJP's forerunner party founded in 1951 – combined staunch loyalty to the British Empire with Hindu nationalist politics and was strongly critical of the Congress-led independence movement.

Savarkar's political rebirth as the founding ideologue of Hindu nationalism probably had its roots in a very influential strand of anti-imperialist politics that emerged in his native Maharashtra around the turn of the nineteenth and twentieth centuries. Its foremost representative was Bal Gangadhar Tilak (1856–1920), a journalist and activist who was the single most prominent voice of Indian nationalism in the pre-Gandhi phase. Tilak, like Savarkar a Maharashtrian Brahmin, was and remains known across India by his honorific title *Lokmanya* (Honourable). For about 15 years before Gandhi took control of the Congress at the beginning of the 1920s and initiated its strategy of nationwide mass mobilization, the Congress was split into two broad tendencies known by the labels 'Moderate' and 'Extremist'. The Moderates essentially advocated continuing the petitioning approach vis-à-vis the British government, whilst the Extremists argued that that approach was obsolete and wanted to confront the colonial power. The leaders of the so-called Extremist tendency took a position of solidarity with the struggle of the Indian youths who resorted to guns and bombs to articulate their defiance of the colonial power. The Extremist camp was especially strong in three disparate regions of India: Maharashtra in the west, where Tilak was its leader; Punjab in the north, where the tendency's main representative was Lala Lajpat Rai (1865–1928); and Bengal in the east, where its major spokesman was Bipin Chandra Pal (1858–1932). The trio were popularly known among the Indian masses as 'Lal–Bal–Pal'. The colonial government regarded Tilak's powerful oratory and print journalism as extremely dangerous. In 1908, he was convicted of sedition and sent to prison for the next six years in Mandalay in Burma, which was part of 'British India' until 1937 (Subhas Chandra Bose was also imprisoned in Mandalay from 1924 to 1927). Under Gandhi's commanding and artful leadership, the Congress papered over the erstwhile Moderate–Extremist divide, but superficially. A new version of the divide surfaced as a rift between Gandhi and Subhas Bose in 1939. Unlike Bose, who was a radical secularist, Tilak's politics invoked Hindu scriptures and devotional practices as the inspirational basis of anti-imperialist struggle. Savarkar's politics from the 1920s onwards drew on the Hindu revivalist aspects of Tilak's political legacy, shorn of the anti-imperialist content.[54]

The emergence of Savarkar's new political *avatar* was triggered by the ripples in India of events in Turkey. The catalyst was the Khilafat Movement, discussed in Chapter 2, which was launched just after the end of World War I by a section of Indian Muslims in solidarity with the defeated Turks and specifically in defence of the Ottoman Sultanate-Caliphate. The Khilafat Movement peaked in 1920–21 and received unequivocal and energetic support from Gandhi, with the strategic purpose of attracting Muslims into the fold of

---

54 Savarkar's Maharashtrian origins profoundly shaped his outlook and his politics. In 1925, he published a book on the Maratha Empire, which grew from modest beginnings in the Deccan under the warrior-king Shivaji in the second half of the seventeenth century to control most of the subcontinent in the mid-eighteenth century. Shivaji is a major historical figure in the Hindu nationalist pantheon of heroes because he waged a tenacious guerrilla resistance to the forces of Aurangzeb, the Mughal emperor. The Marathas' power and dominions expanded as the Mughal Empire declined steeply during the eighteenth century. The Maratha Empire, or the Maratha Confederacy (of warrior clans and chieftains) as it was known from the late eighteenth century, declined after its peak in the mid-eighteenth century and was extinguished in 1818 after suffering a final military defeat by the forces of the English East India Company. A colourful narrative of its rise and fall is in V. D. Savarkar, *The Maratha Movement, Hindu Pad-Padshahi: The Story of the Maratha Struggle to Re-Establish Sovereign Hindu Power and A Review of the Hindu Empire of Maharashtra* (New Delhi: Hindi Sahitya Sadan, 5th edition, 2003).

the anti-colonial struggle. The Khilafat agitation had a strongly anti-British character because of the British occupation of Istanbul and the repressive and manipulative conduct of Britain's representatives in Anatolia. Savarkar, who was transferred from the Andamans to a prison in Maharashtra at a time when the Khilafat Movement was at its peak, had a very different perspective on the agitation. He came into contact with Khilafatist agitators held in the same prison in his native region and was repelled by what he regarded as their pan-Islamist fanaticism. The experience deeply influenced the substance of the doctrine of *Hindutva* he formulated over the next few years, which I outline below.

The Khilafat agitation spawned one particular episode which became a key reference point for Savarkar and other Hindu nationalist pioneers. This was an uprising that took place in the second half of 1921 among Mappillas (or Moplahs), a Muslim community in Malabar, an area on India's south-western coastline extending inland from the sea. Malabar, which today constitutes the northern and central parts of the Indian State of Kerala, was under British rule a district of a huge administrative unit sprawling across southern India called the Madras Presidency. At the time of the rebellion nearly a century ago, Moplahs were a third of the population of Malabar and were most numerous in Malabar's southern zone, where the uprising occurred. The Moplahs of south Malabar (today central Kerala) were mainly converts from Hindu low castes, and most lived in extreme poverty as landless agricultural labourers or as marginal tenants tilling land typically owned by a Hindu high caste (*Namboodiris*). These landlords (*janmis*) were notorious for their oppressive practices, especially arbitrary evictions of their Moplah peasant-tenants, and enjoyed the backing of the police and courts of the British colonial state. Through the nineteenth century, the Moplahs of south Malabar developed a reputation for the *jacquerie*, or 'outrages' as the British called them – small but intense incidents of revolt driven by their social conditions but expressed through the symbols and idioms of their religious faith.

A sizeable section of this impoverished community responded enthusiastically to the call of the Khilafat Movement. From mid-1920 to mid-1921, Moplah mobilization in south Malabar was jointly undertaken by local community leaders and (Hindu) Congress activists as part of the coordinated struggle of the Non-Cooperation Movement launched by Gandhi and the

Khilafatist agitation. In the second half of 1921, however, the situation took a different turn, as an intense insurgency developed among the Moplahs of south Malabar. Its main leader was Ali Musaliar, 'a 60-year-old religious teacher adorned in white robes and red Turkish cap with green turban'. As the peasant uprising intensified, it acquired the character of a millenarian religious movement. Many Hindus in the affected zone, regardless of their social class or caste status, came under attack; there were murders, and about 2,000–2,500 Hindus were subjected to forcible conversion. The Moplah insurgency was suppressed by early 1922 through large-scale British police and military action. According to the official figures, 2,339 rebels who waged guerrilla warfare were killed during the operations and 5,955 captured, and another 39,348 insurgents surrendered as the rebellion declined and then collapsed (government losses in combat were 43 killed, including five British officers). Most of the insurgent leaders died fighting, and those captured were executed after summary trials. In November 1921, 82 of a group of 100 rebel prisoners (97 Moplah and three Hindu men) being transported in a train carriage which lacked ventilation died of asphyxiation.[55]

In the narrative of the Congress-led independence movement, the Moplah uprising was a revolt by oppressed Indians who suffered harsh retribution at the hands of the colonial power, and this is also how the event was mentioned in post-independence school textbooks describing the history of the Indian freedom struggle. The early Hindu nationalists had a very different perspective. They focused exclusively on the violence against Hindus during the insurgency and drew two highly generalized conclusions. First, the Moplahs' behaviour demonstrated the inherent fanaticism and compulsively violent nature of the subcontinent's Muslims, ingrained in their faith. Second, the Congress was deluded to believe in the possibility of joint political action and Hindu–Muslim unity in a shared national movement. These lessons of the Moplah revolt find recurrent mention in the seminal literature of Hindu nationalism, including the writings and speeches of both Savarkar and M. S. Golwalkar, Savarkar's fellow Maharashtrian Brahmin and the builder of the *sangh-parivar* as RSS chief from 1940 to 1973. Golwalkar wrote in the late 1960s in his book *Bunch of Thoughts*:

---

55  Robert L. Hardgrave, Jr., 'The Mappilla Rebellion, 1921: Peasant Revolt in Malabar', *Modern Asian Studies* 11, no. 1 (1977), 57–99.

During the 1920s, in a bid to win the friendship of Muslims, our leaders had called upon the Hindus to take up the Khilafat movement as their own. In Kerala, too, Hindus came forward with men and money to help the movement. But the Muslim wrath against the British soon developed into a *jehad* against the Hindu '*kafirs*' [unbelievers], with all the usual atrocities of Muslim barbarism like killing, burning, molesting, looting, and forcible conversions. When the news of these hair-raising atrocities reached and shocked other parts of the country, an eminent leader came out in open appreciation of these heinous Muslim criminals, calling them 'brave Moplahs'! ... What a marvellous definition of patriotism! Now in Kerala, they openly propagate for an independent 'Moplahland'.[56]

In 1969, to the horror of Hindu nationalists, a coalition government in Kerala led by communists – who became influential in the State from the 1950s – sanctioned a new Muslim-majority district called Malappuram from the area of Malabar with the highest Moplah concentration. The move was in response to a demand by the Indian Union Muslim League, a local party which was a junior partner in the coalition government. To the Hindu nationalists, this was yet another egregious example of the 'appeasement' of Muslims in the Indian secular state.[57]

◆

Vinayak Damodar Savarkar was no religious fundamentalist. He was a convinced atheist (*nastik*) in his personal life and described himself as a 'rationalist'. He was sceptical of the orthodox Hindu predilection for regarding the cow as a holy animal and an object of worship. During the middle and late 1930s, he asserted that while the cow was an 'extremely useful animal' which deserved to be treated with 'affection' and 'gratitude' in a manner 'consistent with the Hindu trait of compassion' and 'in keeping with humanism',

---

56 Golwalkar, *Bunch of Thoughts*, 232–265. Savarkar and Golwalkar's narratives of late modern Indian history are extremely selective. Both men recall the 1857 uprising – which is known in India as the 'First War of Independence' – with admiration, but omit to mention that Hindus and Muslims were equally involved in that struggle against the British colonial occupier.

57 The Kerala Chief Minister whose government created Malappuram was E. M. S. Namboodiripad, a top communist leader hailing from the caste of landlords whose oppression was the root cause of the Moplah rebellion of the early 1920s.

'attributing religious qualities' to it fostered 'a superstitious mindset [which] destroys the nation's intellect', and so 'self-defeating extreme cow protection should be rejected'. He argued that 'without spreading religious superstition, let the movement for cow protection be based and popularized on clear-cut economic and scientific principles', and declared that 'the Hindu nation of tomorrow should not have such a pitiable symbol'. He averred that 'the symbol of Hindutva is not the cow but the man-lion' (*Nrisinha* or *Narasimha*, the fourth avatar of the deity Vishnu, who was half-man and half-lion). According to Savarkar,

> [by] considering the cow as divine and worshipping her, the entire Hindu nation became docile like the cow. It began eating grass. If we are now to found our nation on the basis of an animal, let that animal be the lion … we need to worship such a *nrisinha*. That, and not the cow's hooves, is the mark of Hindutva.

He added that 'the religious fanaticism of those non-Hindus whose religion itself is based on hatred of the cow … is cruel', and 'these non-Hindus should discard their cow hatred and consider cow protection done for economic reasons as their duty'.[58]

Savarkar coined the bedrock concept of Hindu nationalist doctrine – *Hindutva*. He translated the term as 'Hinduness', as distinct from Hindu*ism*, in the presidential address he delivered in English to the annual conference of the Akhil Bharatiya (All-India) Hindu Mahasabha held at 'Karnavati' (the ancient name of the city of Ahmedabad in Gujarat) in 1937. In Savarkar's words:

> The concept of 'Hindutva' is more comprehensive than 'Hinduism'. It is to draw pointed attention to this distinction that I coined the word. Hinduism concerns the religious systems of the Hindus, their theology and dogma. But this is a precisely a matter [Hindu nationalists] leave entirely to individual or group conscience and faith. Hindutva refers not only to the religious aspect [of the Hindu nation] but comprehends their

---

58 These views are reproduced in English translation in the section on Savarkar's rationalism on http://savarkar.org (accessed 10 June 2017), citing mostly Marathi-language sources from *Samagra Savarkar Vangmaya* (Collected Works of Savarkar), published in eight volumes by the Maharashtra Prantik Hindu Sabha from Poona (Pune) between 1963 and 1965.

cultural, linguistic, social and political aspects as well. [It refers] to common affinities – cultural, religious, historical, linguistic and racial – which through the process of countless centuries of association and assimilation moulded us into a homogenous and organic Nation and induced a will to lead a corporate and common National Life. The Hindus are an organic National Being.

Thus, he averred that Hinduism *qua* religion is 'only one' and 'a fraction, a part' of the constitutive elements of Hindutva and described the Hindu Mahasabha as 'pre-eminently a national body'. It was a 'serious mistake' to take it 'for only a religious body', he said. Savarkar formulated Hindutva as a very modern, twentieth-century and explicitly political doctrine of Indian nationalism.

Savarkar asserted that 'everyone who regards this *Bharatbhoomi* [Land of India] from the Indus [river] to the Seas as his Fatherland [*pitrubhu(mi)*] and Holyland [*punyabhu(mi)*]' was a member of the nation in the political and ideological sense of the Hindutva framework. To him, Indian identity was defined by a common bond consisting of 'three essentials': 'nation (*Rashtra*), race (*Jati*) and civilization (*Sanskriti*)'.

The one group Savarkar categorically excluded from the *pitrubhumi/ punyabhumi* framework of Indian identity stands out because he otherwise goes to great lengths and contortions to make it inclusive. His basic premise is that 'the Hindus are bound together by the dearest, most sacred and most enduring bonds of a common Fatherland and a common Holyland … [and so] the National Oneness and homogeneity of the Hindus have been doubly sure'. He claimed that 'the so-called aboriginal tribes [today one in twelve of Indians] are also Hindus, because India is their Fatherland as well as their Holyland, whatever form of religion and worship they follow'. The same applied to the population, today one of every six Indians, stigmatized as untouchables by the caste system. In his presidential address to the annual Hindu Mahasabha conference in Calcutta in 1939, he identified 'Remove Untouchability' as the foremost task of 'the Hindu movement'. He told the delegates,

> [This] will enable you to consolidate … your own brethren who are religiously, culturally, nationally and in every other way as much a part and parcel of Hindudom as any of us can claim to be … To act otherwise is in reality an insult to our common Hinduness.

He added as a *caveat* that 'our *sanatani* [orthodox] brothers may rest assured that ... the Hindu Mahasabha will always refrain from any recourse to law to thrust reform on any sect within the Hindu fold, even in the case of untouchability'. He saw Sikhs and Jains as naturally accommodated by and within the Hindutva concept because they too regarded India as both Fatherland and Holyland, and he emphasized that their distinct religious identities were therefore completely compatible with the ideological frame of Hindutva.

Savarkar's inclusivity extended, albeit in a condescending way, to communities he described as 'the non-Muslim minorities of India'. He thought highly of Parsees, the numerically tiny but high-profile community professing Zoroastrianism, whose ancestors migrated to India from Persia after the latter's conquest by Arabs over a millennium ago. He stated that 'they are no fanatics', 'have contributed their quota of true Indian patriots' such as Dadabhai Naoroji and Madame Cama, and 'nor have they displayed anything but goodwill towards the Hindu Nation which has been the saviour of their race'.[59] 'The Jews', he noted, are 'few in number and not antagonistic'. With regard to the 'Anglo-Indians', the small community of people of hybrid British and Indian parentage which arose in the nineteenth century and was generally known to identify strongly with the Raj, he believed that 'their present arrogance would vanish as soon as England goes out'. About the considerably larger population professing the Christian faith, he observed that their ultimate 'Holyland' was located in Palestine. But he described them as 'less fanatical' and 'civil', sounding only a relatively mild note of warning about proselytizing activity by Christian missionary groups. In sum, he concluded that all these communities 'can be politically assimilated with us' and could be counted on 'to behave ... in an Indian State'.

The one element of India's society Savarkar categorically excluded from his conception of Indian identity and framework of Indian nationhood comprised three of every ten Indians at the time (and one of every seven Indians today). 'In the case of the Mohammedans', he said in his first speech as President of the Hindu Mahasabha in 1937, 'their love for India ... is but a handmaid

---

59 Madame Bhikaiji Cama (1861–1936), who was from Bombay, was a pioneering figure of the Indian independence movement. She sheltered Savarkar in her apartment in Paris when he was on the run from the British police in 1910. Dadabhai Naoroji (1825–1917) was one of the founders in 1885 of the Indian National Congress.

[sic] to their love for their Holyland outside India. Their faces are ever turned towards Mecca and Medina'. In his second presidential address at Nagpur in 1938, he stated that 'the Moslems remained Moslems first, Moslems last, and Indians never!' and cited 'Ali Musaliar, the leader of the Mopla[h] rebellion' as the archetypical example of the fanatic Indian Muslim. 'The fact is that the whole Moslem community is communal, including the Congressite Muslims', he declared. In his 1937 speech, Savarkar said that 'as it is, there are two antagonistic nations living side by side in India', due to 'centuries of cultural, religious and national antagonism between the Hindus and the Moslems'. 'Let us bravely face unpleasant facts as they are', he declared; 'India cannot be assumed today to be a unitarian and homogenous nation but on the contrary there are two nations in the main, the Hindus and the Moslems'. The mirror-version of this argument was to formally become the official line of Jinnah's Muslim League three years later, in 1940. Savarkar's 1938 speech at Nagpur however diverged somewhat and evolved from his two-nation thesis of 1937: 'Yes, we Hindus are a Nation by ourselves. Because religious, racial, cultural and historical affinities bind us intimately into a homogenous nation. Our racial being is identified with India – our beloved Fatherland and our Holyland'. He continued, 'The Germans are the Nation in Germany and the Jews a community. The Turks are the Nation in Turkey and the Arab or the Armenian minority a community. The Hindus are the Nation in India and the Moslem minority a community'.

Stripped down to its fundamentals, the political doctrine of Hindutva has two central and abiding premises: (1) the homogeneity of the 'Hindu nation'; and (2) the blanket, indiscriminate rejection of India's Muslims (before 1947, the subcontinent's Muslims) as fellow-nationals. *Both* are essential and equally important elements of the doctrine and together they form the basis of the ideological outlook and strategic practices of Hindu nationalist politics today, eight or nine decades after the original formulations appeared. The two elements share a monolith fixation. Just as the Hindu nation is homogenous (or should be, and has to be made so through political action if it is not sufficiently so already), the Muslim 'other' is also seen in undifferentiated, monolithic terms. Of course, this is at complete variance with the multi-layered social, cultural and political complexity of India as a country (and of the undivided subcontinent before 1947).

But that did not deter Savarkar from possessing an absolute faith in his convictions, or from asserting Hindutva to be the sole authentic, correct and legitimate formulation of Indian nationalism. To the contrary, he told the Hindu Mahasabha conference in 1937:

> The real meaning of *swarajya* [sovereignty] is not merely the geographical independence of the bit of the earth called India. To the Hindus, the independence of Hindusthan can only be worth having if it ensures their Hindutva – their religious, racial and cultural identity. We are not out to fight and die for *swarajya* at the cost of our *swatva* [self-identity] – our Hindutva! ... *Swarajya* without Hindutva is for us Hindus as good as [sic] suicide.

At almost the same time in the late 1930s, the rising RSS star Madhav Sadashiv Golwalkar, the chief builder of the Hindu nationalist movement in post-independence India, wrote in his book *We, or Our Nationhood Defined*:

> We repeat: In Hindusthan, the land of the Hindus, lives the Hindu Nation ... Consequently, only those movements are truly 'National' as aim at re-building, re-vitalizing, and emancipating from its present stupor, the Hindu Nation. Those only are nationalist patriots who, with the aspiration to glorify the Hindu race [sic] and Nation, are prompted into activity and strive to achieve that goal. All others, posing to be patriots and wilfully indulging in a course of action detrimental to the Hindu Nation are traitors and enemies to the National Cause or, to take a more charitable view if unintentionally or unwillingly led into such a course, mere simpletons, misguided ignorant fools.[60]

A true pioneer, Golwalkar bequeathed this spirit of moral certainty and political mission to the successive generations of Hindu nationalist leaders in post-independence India indoctrinated and socialized in the RSS.

Although slightly less strident in his tone, Savarkar too recurrently uses the term 'pseudo-Nationalistic' to describe the Indian National Congress in his speeches of the late 1930s and early 1940s – prefiguring the term 'pseudo-secular' used to describe the Indian state in Hindu nationalist discourse ever since the 1950s. In his presidential address to the Hindu Mahasabha conference in Calcutta in 1939, for example, he described the Congress as 'a pseudo-Nationalistic nuisance dangerous to the Hindu cause as well as

---

60 Golwalkar, *We, or Our Nationhood Defined*, 21–52.

the Indian National one'. A year earlier in Nagpur, he had asserted that 'the Hindu nationalists, even if they be called communalists, are the only real Indian Nationalists'. At Nagpur, he also claimed to be 'the last man to ignore the benefits reaped from the Indian National Congress movement', which had 'contributed immensely to the consolidation of Hindudom' through its mass mobilizations. But, he added, that contribution had been undone by 'their pursuit of the silly fad of bringing about a Hindu–Moslem unity in India'. The twin-preoccupations with a largely imaginary Hindu homogeneity and the spectre of the Muslim 'other' came together in his 1939 speech in Calcutta, during which he severely criticized Subhas Chandra Bose, whom he sarcastically referred to as *Desh-Gaurav* (Pride of the Nation), for 'proposing from the presidential chair of the Indian National Congress' that the Roman script could be used for official purposes in independent India given the country's diversity of religions, languages and scripts. Savarkar insisted that 'Sanskrit shall be our sacred language and pure "Sanskrit-Nishtha" Hindi, the Hindi that is derived from Sanskrit, our national language' – not the 'Hindustani' hybrid of Hindi and Urdu favoured by Nehru, Azad and Bose. Moreover, he declared, in addition to 'Hindi as the National Tongue of Hindudom' due to its status as 'the tongue of the Hindu people throughout Hindusthan', 'the Nogari [Devnagari, the Sanskritic script] shall be the National Script of Hindudom'. In reality, Hindi was then and still is the 'mother tongue' of only a plurality of Indians and dominant only in northern India; in addition, the Dravidian languages of southern India belong to an entirely different family from the Indo–Aryan languages descended from Sanskrit and have their own, non-Devnagari scripts.

Savarkar was not simply a theorist of identity. He was acutely conscious that the Hindutva vision could be realized only through state power. In Nagpur in 1938, he posed a question, 'How are we to bell the cat? How are we to enable ourselves to shape events in the face of the overwhelming powerlessness in which the Hindu Sanghatanist [organized] movement is stuck today?' He replied, 'Capture the political power that obtains in India today! The Sanghatanists [must] capture the seats allotted to Hindus under the present constitution[61] in Municipalities, Boards and Legislatures [across

---

61  Savarkar is referring primarily to the Government of India Act of 1935, and elections to constitute provincial governments with very limited and circumscribed powers held on

India]'. This was easier said than done, however. The 1937 elections to constitute 11 provincial assemblies across India had resulted in the Congress forming governments – albeit with very limited and circumscribed powers – in eight provinces. Jinnah's Muslim League fared poorly and the Hindu Mahasabha had almost no impact. About the Congress, Savarkar observed that 'the very concept of a Hindu Nation stinks in its nostrils, it has declared the Mahasabha a communal and reprehensible body and ordered millions of Congressite Hindus not to have anything to do with it'. Although Mahasabhaites were able to secure a toehold in some provincial governments, notably in Bengal, after the resignation of the Congress-led ministries in late 1939, the Hindu nationalists remained a marginal force in popular politics. In his presidential speech to the Mahasabha's national conference in Madurai (in India's deep south, in the present-day Indian State of Tamil Nadu) in 1940, Savarkar noted with regret that 'even a year ago there was hardly even a district Hindusabha worth the name throughout this Madras Presidency', and that in 'the municipal election which took place this month in Karnavati [Ahmedabad in Gujarat]' the Mahasabha had 'lost [in] all the seats it competed for'.

The bleak state of affairs did not deter Savarkar from continuously re-emphasizing the strategic direction the Hindu nationalist movement must take in order to increase its strength and influence. In his presidential address to the Mahasabha's national conference in Kanpur in western Uttar Pradesh in 1942, he reiterated: 'Capture all centres of political power from the Central Executive Council [to] Legislatures, Defence Committees and Councils, Municipalities [and] Ministries'. By this time, with war engulfing Asia and the Pacific and Japanese forces on the Burma–India border, he became a vocal proponent of 'responsive cooperation' with the British government and its war-effort,

---

a restricted franchise in 1937. This was part of the British strategy of accommodating nationalist dissent at sub-central levels of government whilst retaining an iron grip on power at the central level. The strategic shift followed the eventual failure of the policy of repression the colonial state pursued during the first half of the 1930s, after Gandhi called a campaign of mass civil disobedience at the start of the decade, to crush the Congress-led national movement. The point about allotment of seats refers principally to the 'Communal Award' made by the British in 1932, whose most important consequences were the creation of a separate Muslim electorate and reservation of seats on religious lines in representative bodies. A fraction for 'untouchables' was also reserved within the 'General' (i.e., non-reserved) seats through a pact between the Congress and the Dalit activist B. R. Ambedkar.

on the grounds that the mass recruitment of Indian soldiers into the British armed forces would enable large numbers of 'Hindus' to gain military training and experience. He exhorted: 'Continue a hundred times more intensely the Hindu Militarization Movement and try to get recruited and enlisted as many Hindus as possible in the Army, Navy, Air Force, Ammunition Factories, [as] War Technicians, etc'. He concluded his speech with a stirring call: 'Hinduise all politics and militarise Hindudom! Hindu Dharm ki jaya, Hindu Rashtra ki jaya!' (victory to the Hindu Faith, victory to the Hindu State).[62] In the same year, Gandhi launched the last mass movement of his political life by calling on the British to 'quit India' at a Congress session held in Bombay in August 1942. The British government immediately arrested nearly all senior Congress leaders, who remained in detention till the end of the war, and launched a massive crackdown on Congress activists and supporters nationwide. Despite the repression, the Quit India movement sparked a popular uprising across India and localized insurgencies gripped several parts of the country. In 1943, meanwhile, Subhas Chandra Bose undertook a perilous three-month journey by submarine from Europe to East Asia, where he assumed the leadership of the Indian National Army and the Azad Hind (Free India) movement in Southeast Asia. The movement and its armed force united men and women from all religious, caste and linguistic backgrounds.[63]

◆

Savarkar never joined the Rashtriya Swayamsevak Sangh, which became

---

62 All quotations from Savarkar are sourced from two compilations: V. D. Savarkar, *Hindu Rashtra Darshan* (Poona: Maharashtra Prantik Hindusabha, n.d.) and V. D. Savarkar, *Hindu Rashtra Darshan* (Bombay: Veer Savarkar Prakashan, 1984). The word *rashtra* can, depending on the specific context of its usage and the meaning intended, be translated as 'nation', 'state', or both (i.e., 'nation-state'). See also V. D. Savarkar, *Essentials of Hindutva*, available on http://savarkar.org; this tract was first published in 1923.

63 Bose explicitly invoked the spirit of resistance of the 'First War of Indian Independence' in 1857–58, in which Hindus and Muslims fought in parallel to rid India of colonial enslavement, in his leadership of the Azad Hind movement and the INA. In 1943, he formed a women's force of the INA, which was called the Rani of Jhansi Regiment in honour of Rani Lakshmibai of Jhansi, the Maratha queen of the principality of Jhansi in north-central India and a legendary figure of the 1857 uprising. Rani Lakshmibai died aged 29 in combat against British forces in June 1858 near Gwalior in central India.

the core and engine of the Hindu nationalist movement after India's independence. However the RSS founder, Keshav Baliram Hedgewar, visited Savarkar in prison in Maharashtra and conferred with him before launching the RSS as an all-male, militia-style organization in autumn 1925. The initial RSS membership consisted of about twenty young men who gathered around Hedgewar in his hometown, Nagpur in Maharashtra (where the RSS has been headquartered ever since), and the organization adopted as its uniform for rallies, drills and parades a 'khaki shirt, [belted] knee-length shorts, and khaki cap with two buttons' with black shoes. The khaki cap was replaced by a black cap in 1930 and later a white shirt replaced the original khaki shirt.[64] The ideological frame of the RSS – and subsequently of the entire *sangh-parivar* which grew around it in post-independence India – was developed by the second RSS *sarsanghchalak* (supreme chief), Madhav Sadashiv Golwalkar, who assumed Hedgewar's mantle upon the latter's death in 1940 and led the organization until his own death in 1973. The seminal RSS text was *We, or our Nationhood Defined*, which Golwalkar published in 1938, two years before he assumed the leadership as Hedgewar's nominated successor at the age of 34.

Golwalkar, revered as *Shri Guruji* (Master-Teacher) by successive generations of RSS cadres and the Jan Sangh/BJP leaders who came from their ranks, dressed in simple white Indian-style clothes (*dhoti* and *kurta*) and sported a long, luxuriant beard which, along with the glasses he wore after his youth, gave him a venerable, monk-like appearance. But Golwalkar was no monk, although he did think about becoming an ascetic in his early youth, prior to joining the RSS at Hedgewar's behest in 1931. In the 1930s he taught zoology at the Banaras Hindu University (whose name has nothing to do with Hindu nationalism as such) in eastern Uttar Pradesh, before dedicating his life to fulltime activism. A Maharashtrian Brahmin like Savarkar and Hedgewar, he was unlike Savarkar in having no anti-colonial activist background and he played no role at any time in India's freedom struggle. The RSS as a body

---

64 Malkani, *The RSS Story*, 1, 15. In 2016, the RSS replaced its signature above-knee khaki shorts with brown trousers. The new-look uniform was designed by an award-winning (male) professional designer of clothes and costumes who comes from a family of longstanding RSS membership. The RSS remains male-only in line with Hedgewar's firm view on the matter but has an affiliated women's organization, the Rashtra Sevika Samiti, established in 1936, which mainly enrols family members of RSS men.

stayed aloof from that struggle led by the Congress, although it did not actively collaborate with the British authorities against independence-seeking nationalists as the Communist Party of India (CPI) did between 1941 and 1945. Golwalkar is more than just a saintly legend in the Hindu nationalist pantheon; his ideological and organization-building legacies pervade the twenty-first-century movement. In 2008, as Gujarat's Chief Minister, Narendra Modi published a book in Gujarati about sixteen men who had inspired or influenced him. All sixteen were members of RSS, which Modi joined at the beginning of the 1970s. The longest of the sixteen sketches is that of Guru Golwalkar. Golwalkar's portrait occupies pride of place in RSS offices and in its local centres (*shakhas*) across India.

Golwalkar's revolutionary outlook made him sceptical of partisan politics. In the end-1930s, he and Hedgewar politely rebuffed Savarkar's overtures to join in the Hindu Mahasabha's political campaigns, preferring to retain the RSS's autonomy. After independence, Golwalkar was initially opposed to the notion of forming a political party from the womb of the RSS to compete in India's emerging democracy. Some young RSS members differed with their supremo; they felt that the RSS should sponsor a party to represent Hindu nationalism in India's elected institutions such as Parliament and the State Assemblies. One such dissenter, K. R. Malkani, wrote in the RSS's English journal *Organiser* in December 1949, a month before the Republic of India's constitution was proclaimed:

> Sangh must take part in politics ... to stop the un-Bharatiya [un-Indian] and anti-Bharatiya [anti-Indian] policies of the Government ... Sangh must continue as it is, as an ashram [monastery] for the national cultural education of the citizenry, but it must develop a political wing for the more effective and early achievement of its ideals.

Golwalkar eventually relented and the BJS, the BJP's predecessor, was formed in late 1951, just before India's first parliamentary election and simultaneous elections to constitute many State legislatures. The new party recruited Syama Prasad Mookerjee, an aristocratic Bengali Brahmin who had been a top Hindu Mahasabha leader since the late 1930s, as its first President. Golwalkar recalled their meeting in Nagpur prior to the announcement of the new party in the *Organiser* five years later, in 1956:

I had to warn him that the RSS could not be drawn into politics, that it could not play second fiddle to any political party because no organization devoted to the wholesale regeneration of the Nation could function successfully if used as a handmaid of political parties.[65]

In this compromise between the exigencies of competitive politics and the long-term agenda of revival and transformation, the RSS developed a policy of seconding its brightest and most committed cadres to the Jan Sangh. In the 1950s and 1960s these included Deendayal Upadhyaya, who worked as the Jan Sangh's General Secretary from 1953 to 1967 and was its President when he died in 1968. Another was Atal Behari Vajpayee, India's first Hindu nationalist Prime Minister (briefly in 1996 and then from 1998–2004), who emerged as the Jan Sangh's outstanding voice in parliament from 1957 onward and succeeded the deceased Upadhyaya as its national President in 1968, to be followed four years later by L. K. Advani, the main figure of the climactic phase of the temple/mosque Ayodhya agitation of the early 1990s described in Chapter 4. The practice became routinized over time and continued after the formation of the BJP as the Jan Sangh's successor in 1980. Men seconded from the RSS occupy key positions both in the BJP's national organizational set-up and in the party's State units – they typically hold posts titled General Secretary (Organization) or Secretary (Organization). In the late 1980s, Narendra Modi was thus seconded to the BJP's organizational apparatus from his fulltime role in the RSS. The formula of RSS–BJS/BJP symbiosis Golwalkar consented to in the early 1950s has enabled the RSS hierarchy to exercise overall control and close supervision of the party that represents it in the political arena down the decades.

In *We, or Our Nationhood Defined*, Golwalkar wrote that 'the National Concept comprises [of] five constituent ideas', which he also called 'the famous five Unities'; these were 'country, race, religion, culture and language'. Of the five, he gave primacy to religion. He wrote that

in our vast country, Hindusthan, the land of Hindus ... Religion is an all-absorbing entity. Based on the unshakeable foundations of a sound philosophy of life, it has become eternally woven into the life of the Race,

---

65 Christophe Jaffrelot, 'The RSS and Politics', in *Hindu Nationalism: A Reader*, ed. Jaffrelot (Princeton and Oxford: Princeton University Press, 2007), 175–177.

and forms its very soul. With us every action in life, [whether] individual, social or political, is a command of Religion. We make war and peace, engage in arts and crafts, amass wealth and give it away, indeed we are born and we die, all in accord with religious injunctions. We are what our great Religion has made us. Our Race-Spirit is a child of our Religion, and our culture is but a product of our all-comprehensive Religion.

He further wrote:

Living in this Country since pre-historic times is the ancient Race – the Hindu Race – united by common traditions, by memories of common glory and disaster, by similar historical, religious, social, political and other experiences, living under the same influences and evolving a common culture, a common mother language, common customs, common aspirations. This great Hindu Race professes its illustrious Hindu Religion, which in its variety is still an organic whole. Guided by this Religion in all walks of life, the Race evolved a culture, which despite the degenerating contact with the debased 'civilizations' of the Musalmans and [then] the Europeans for the last ten centuries, is still the noblest in the world.

He added:

It appears as if the Linguistic unity is wanting, but in fact that is not so. There is but one language, Sanskrit, of which these many 'languages' are mere offshoots. Sanskrit, the dialect of the Gods, is common to all from the Himalayas to the ocean in the south, from East to West ... [and] Hindi is the most commonly understood and used as a medium of expression between persons of different provinces.

The imprint and influence of Savarkar's thought are clearly evident here, but Golwalkar gave the RSS's ideology a distinctive cast within that framework of 'Hindi, Hindu, Hindusthan'. Unlike Savarkar, the RSS guru did mention that a counter-argument existed to his thesis –'At present, there is a general tendency to affirm that Religion is an individual question and should have no place in public and political life. This tendency is based upon a misconception of Religion'. This misconception was that 'Religion concerns itself merely with matters other-worldly – if there be another world, so the sceptic will say – then surely it should have no place in affairs of this world'. But, he argued, in 'Hindusthan' – 'Religion is that which regulate[s] society in all its functions' and

272

[s]uch Religion cannot be ignored in public life. It must have a place, in proportion to its vast importance, in politics. To give it a go-by, or to assign it an insignificant place, would mean degeneration. Indeed politics itself becomes, in the case of such a Religion, a small factor, to be considered or followed solely as one of the commands of Religion and in accord with such commands. We in Hindusthan have been living such a Religion. We cannot give up religion in our National Life.[66]

Although the late Guruji would be horrified to hear it, this formulation is very similar to the totalistic view of faith as the determinant of collective identity and the nature of the polity in influential late modern formulations of political Islam. Golwalkar's resolutely anti-secular argument doesn't explicitly mention the term 'secularism', which is not surprising because, as Chapter 2 noted, the word was very rarely used in the discourse of the independence movement led by the Indian National Congress. The sovereign Indian Republic started to explicitly self-define as a 'secular state' from the beginning of the 1950s. From that point onward, the term 'pseudo-secular' appeared in the counter-discourse of Hindu nationalism as the replacement for the term 'pseudo-nationalistic' Savarkar used in the 1930s and 1940s to describe all non-Hindutva forms of Indian nationalism, whose adherents Golwalkar described in the late 1930s as 'traitors and enemies' or at best 'simpletons' and 'misguided ignorant fools'.

◆

The similarities between Kemalism and Hindu nationalism are overwhelming. They share the obsession with the homogeneity of the nation, the belief that only one form of nationalism (their own) is legitimate, the militaristic ethos, the spurious racialism, and, quite logically given the acute allergy to any form of diversity, the commitment to a unitary and centralized model of state. As we saw early in this chapter, Savarkar was very clear on the last point (see note 10) and Golwalkar was revolted by the moderately decentralized structure the Indian state acquired after independence. In the late 1960s (see note 7), the RSS chief called for 'the sweep[ing] away of all autonomous and semi-autonomous states within Bharat [India]', 'to bury for

---

66 Golwalkar, *We, or Our Nationhood Defined*, 21–52 (Chapters II, III and IV).

good all talk of a federal structure' and for 'the Constitution [to] be re-drafted' to 'establish [an] Unitary form of Government' and 'proclaim "One Country, One State, One Legislature, One Executive!"' The one divergence between the two ideologies is Kemalism's laicism, which derived from the Kemalist elite's aspiration for Turkey to depart the Orient and be accepted as a Western, European country. But otherwise, secular Turkish nationalism bears a sibling resemblance to anti-secular Hindu nationalism. Both ideological frameworks are, in their content, incompatible with a democratic political culture. It is little surprise that deep authoritarianism permeated the state founded and ruled under the Kemalist ideology, which authoritarian legacy dominates the post-Kemalist state of the twenty-first century ruled by anti-secular Turkish nationalists. In India, however, state-secularism has, with all its anomalies and contradictions, been an integral element of a flawed but functional democracy. The crucial question is whether the political hegemony of Hindu nationalism is compatible with that democracy.

Thirty years after he set the ideological frame of post-independence India's Hindu nationalist movement in *We, or our Nationhood Defined*, M. S. Golwalkar published his other major book, *Bunch of Thoughts*. In this late 1960s volume, he reflected at length on India and its problems after 20 years of independence. He had many critical observations to make, and the book's tone is suffused with anger. Golwalkar focused especially on one theme. 'The threat of internal subversion to our national freedom and security', he wrote, is 'very acute and real'. He asserted that 'the hostile elements within the country pose a far greater menace than aggressors from outside', and lamented that 'this first lesson of national security has been consistently ignored ever since the British left this land'.[67] He then proceeded to elaborate on the nature of the internal threat.

That discussion actually has a preamble of sorts in his late 1930s book. There, he wrote that 'the average Hindu mind' is animated by 'the spirit of broad Catholicism, generosity, toleration, truth, sacrifice, and love for all life'. By contrast, 'the spread of Islam' everywhere, from the Arab lands to Iran to India, was 'the same old tale of invasion, with its attendant massacres, devastation, destruction, loot and arson, violating all sacred places, and forced conversion to the faith of the ready executioner, [everywhere] repeated in all its hideousness'. He further wrote in the late 1930s book:

---

67 Golwalkar, *Bunch of Thoughts*, 232.

German race pride has become the topic of the day. To deep up [sic] the purity of the Race and its culture, Germany shocked the world by purging the country of the Semitic Races – the Jews. Race pride at its highest has been manifested here. Germany has also shown how well-nigh impossible it is for Races and cultures having differences going to the root to be assimilated into one united whole, a good lesson for us in Hindusthan to learn and profit by ... To be brief, all the five constituents of the Nation idea have been boldly vindicated in modern Germany and that too, today in the actual present, when we can for ourselves see and study them.

A few pages later, he asserted the stark choice he saw facing 'the non-Hindu people of Hindusthan', which is quoted in the second epigraph at the outset of this chapter. Golwalkar's evident admiration of Nazi Germany's policies did not, however, stem from any anti-Jewish views. To the contrary, both he and Savarkar were very sympathetic to the Zionist movement, and both were avid supporters of the State of Israel after its formation in 1948. Savarkar wrote in the early 1920s that 'if the Zionists' dreams are ever realized – if Palestine becomes a Jewish State – it will gladden us almost as much as our Jewish friends'.[68] This was because he believed that the Zionists were legitimately striving to reconstitute their 'Fatherland' in their ancient 'Holyland'. In December 1947, he hailed the United Nations Special Commission on Palestine's (UNSCOP) partition plan for Palestine which awarded more than half its territory to a Jewish state, and condemned India's vote against the plan in the UN General Assembly (it passed on 29 November 1947 with 33 member-states voting in favour and thirteen against, with ten abstentions). Golwalkar wrote in *We, or Our Nationhood Defined* that 'the children of Israel' are 'exiles from their own country and have no place to call their own', and 'the recent attempts at rehabitating Palestine with its ancient population of Jews are nothing more than an effort to reconstruct the broken edifice and revitalize the Hebrew National Life'. He continued in the next chapter of the book that when Great Britain acquired the 'Mandate' (a hybrid of colony and protectorate) over Palestine under the League of Nations system after World War I,

the British ... began to rehabitate the old Hebrew country, Palestine, with its long-lost children [i.e. Zionist settlers from Europe]. The Jews had maintained their race, religion, culture and language, and all they

---

68  Savarkar, *Essentials of Hindutva*, 52.

wanted was their natural territory to complete their Nationality. The reconstruction of the Hebrew Nation in Palestine is just an affirmation of the fact that Country, Race, Religion, Culture and Language must exist together to form a full Nation idea.[69]

Golwalkar argues in nearly apocalyptic terms that independent India is in constant and dire peril from the presence and activities of a large fifth-column in the country. He does not use the term, but that is the substance of his argument. 'The Muslim menace', as he calls it, is claimed to exist and operate across the country – north, east and south – 'wherever there is a *masjid* [mosque] or a Muslim *mohalla* [neighbourhood]'. These represent, he says, 'countless miniature Pakistans' in India. 'There are sure signs', he writes in the late 1960s,

> that an explosive situation similar to 1946–47 is fast brewing and there is no knowing when it will blow up. Right from Delhi to Rampur [in western Uttar Pradesh] and Lucknow [in central Uttar Pradesh], the Muslims are busy hatching a dangerous plot, piling up arms and mobilising their men and probably biding their time to strike from within when Pakistan decides upon an armed conflict with our country. And when they do strike, it is very likely that even Delhi may be rocked to its foundations unless we wake up in time to nip the mischief in the bud.[70]

Golwalkar does not precisely specify what should be done. But he warns that 'we are sitting on a volcano, feeling all is well with our "secular world"'.

Golwalkar does have a limited point when he speaks of 'Pakistan trying to gobble up Kashmir with the help of powerful pro-Pakistan elements inside

69  Golwalkar, *We, or Our Nationhood Defined*, 21–52 (Chapters II, III and IV). In reality, the Jews of Germany (and Austria) were the best integrated into the broader society of any country in Europe until the Nazis took power in Germany in 1933 and annexed Austria in 1938. In the predominantly Arab and Muslim societies of the Middle East and North Africa, Jews suffered little to no discrimination and were generally a prosperous and thriving community until Israel was formed through the mass expulsion of the Arabs of Palestine in 1948.

70  Uttar Pradesh or UP, India's most populous State, is nearly one-fifth Muslim (19 per cent). It has the fifth largest percentage of Muslims of India's States, after Jammu and Kashmir (68 per cent), Assam (34 per cent), West Bengal (27 per cent) and Kerala (almost 27 per cent). India's second most populous State, Maharashtra, is 12 per cent Muslim and the third most populous, Bihar, is 17 per cent Muslim. The nationwide proportion of Muslims was 14.2 per cent in 2011, 172 million of 1,210,000 people.

Kashmir'– although Pakistan's attempt to seize Kashmir in the 1965 war it initiated with that purpose failed largely because Kashmiri Muslims did not support the Pakistani operation – or when he brings up illegal immigration from (then) East Pakistan into Assam in India's north-east. But he is not talking about specific matters of genuine concern, but a broader problem as he sees it. He argues forcefully that there are literally no '[Indian] nationalist Muslims'. 'For them', by which he means all Muslim citizens of India, 'only those areas in which their unbridled sway is established are "*Pak*", i.e. holy, and the rest of Bharat where they are living and flourishing [too] is "*na-Pak*", i.e. unholy. Can any son, however debased and depraved he may be, call his mother unholy and sinful? And still, we are asked to believe that such elements are the sons of this soil!'

As this chapter has shown, Hindu nationalist doctrine from the time of its inception in the 1920s has had two essential premises: the claim of Hindu homogeneity, where a monolithic identity is said to exist and a common interest is said to be at stake; and the Muslim – defined in absolutely monolithic terms – as the 'other'. It could be reasonably inferred from Golwalkar's late 1960s reflections on 'the case of Muslims' (as he calls it) that he would like the Muslim population of India to be deported wholesale to Pakistan, which still included Bangladesh at the time he wrote the book. But that may not be a correct inference, because Hindu nationalist politics *simply cannot function* without the presence of a significant Muslim minority as the 'other' (three of ten people in colonial India, one of seven citizens of India today). Golwalkar's animus was not limited to Muslims alone. Early in this chapter, I noted the bitter hostility he expressed towards the creation of small States with Christian majorities in India's north-east. But it is the Muslim 'other' which has provided Hindu nationalist politics with its *raison d'etre* ever since the 1920s; it is something the movement simply cannot do without.

This explains why the RSS-led *sangh-parivar* gave such centrality to the agitation, described in Chapter 4, to restore the ancient '*Ramjanambhoomi*' on the site of the sixteenth-century Babri Masjid in eastern Uttar Pradesh in the early 1990s. The agitation deployed the movement's historical narrative of invasion and defilement in the service of the contemporary agenda of capturing state power. The Muslim 'other' remains an indispensable ingredient of the BJP's electoral strategy and its ambition of political hegemony in the era of the Modi premiership, nationally and in populous States from Uttar Pradesh in the north to West Bengal in the east. In the lexicon of Indian politics, this is known as the method of 'polarization' – attempting to consolidate Hindu votes as much as possible by stirring resentment, fear and hatred of the Muslim 'other'.

The Muslim angle has always provided the life-blood of the Hindu nationalist critique of the Indian secular state (and of the Congress-led national movement prior to independence, as this chapter has shown). 'How is it', Golwalkar asked in *Bunch of Thoughts*,

> that they [the Muslims] dare to carry on offensive and anti-national practices openly? ... in practically every place [in India] there are Muslims who are in constant touch with Pakistan over the transmitter [sic] enjoying not only the rights of an average citizen but also some extra privileges and extra favour because they are 'minorities'! ... [and even] as [they] are trying to undermine our very national existence!

He provided the answer himself:

> Everywhere the Muslims are being abetted in their separatist and subversive activities by our own Government, our leaders and political parties ... Not that our leaders do not know it. The secret intelligence reports reach them all right. But it seems they have in view only elections. Elections mean vote-catching, which means appeasing certain sections of people having a solid bloc of votes. And the Muslims are one such solid bloc. Therein lies the root of all this appeasement and consequent disastrous effects.[71]

The terms 'appeasement' and 'vote-bank politics' have been a stock-in-trade of Hindu nationalist politics for at least six decades and continue to be.

In fact, there has never been any uniform Muslim voting in India's democracy, except that in the era of the Hindu nationalist ascendancy in Indian politics since the 1990s they have overwhelmingly supported parties opposed to the Hindu nationalists, with a preference for the strongest such party or parties in the very different State-level contexts that make up the nation's highly complex political landscape. Moreover, Muslims in India have higher than average levels of poverty, unemployment, lack of advanced education

---

71  Golwalkar, *Bunch of Thoughts*, 232–265.

and everyday discrimination. The notion that the Indian secular state has consistently favoured the Muslim minority is a fiction, as this book has shown. Yet, as this book has also shown (see especially Chapters 3 and 4), the Indian version of the secular state has had features and practices which have since the 1990s facilitated the rise of the Hindutva-majoritarian alternative from the margins to the centre-stage. Those conundrums are discussed further in the next, concluding chapter.

As an Indian author acutely observed at the height of the *Ramjanambhoomi* agitation in the early 1990s, described in Chapter 4, the Hindutva movement

> criticizes other religions for being monolithic, but aspires to build a monolithic unity. It glorifies diversity within Hinduism as a mark of its superiority over Semitic religions, but seeks to repress this diversity. It identifies aggressiveness as an evil intrinsic to other religions, but attempts to instil the same quality in all Hindus. It talks of patience and tolerance as innate virtues of Hindus, yet sees these traits as the basis of Hindu weakness. It condemns other religions for their politics of religious repression and temple destruction, but organizes itself around the same politics.[72]

This is a very telling description of the nature of Hindu nationalist ideology, as my discussion of Savarkar and Golwalkar in this chapter has shown.[73] Yet

---

72 Neeladri Bhattacharya, 'Myth, History and the Politics of Ramjanambhoomi', in *Anatomy of a Confrontation: The Ramjanambhoomi–Babri Masjid Dispute*, ed. S. Gopal (Delhi: Penguin, 1991), 131.

73 A third, much lesser ideologue of Hindu nationalism is Deendayal Upadhyaya, the pioneering Jan Sangh leader of the 1950s and 1960s who has been idolized in the movement as the 'perfect' or 'ideal' *swayamsevak* (RSS activist) since his death in 1968. He was a Brahmin from western Uttar Pradesh and joined the RSS aged 21 in 1937. Upadhyaya published a book called *Integral Humanism* in 1965, which took a metaphysical approach lacking the clarity of Savarkar and Golwalkar. He wrote that 'Bharatiya culture is an integrated whole', the nation has a 'soul' (*chiti*) which is both fundamental and eternal, and in '"government of the people, by the people, for the people", "of" stands for independence, "by" stands for democracy, and "for" indicates *Dharma* [literally faith/religion, less literally ethics]'. According to him, 'a government of the people is not enough; it has to be for the good of the people' and 'what constitutes the good of the people, Dharma alone can decide because truth resides with Dharma'. Thus, 'Jana Rajya [rule of the people] must be rooted in Dharma Rajya [rule of faith/ religion/ethics]'. As examples of *Dharma*, Upadhyaya cited 'the old Hindu marriages where a married couple could not divorce even if both parties wished [until the reform

the path of confrontation and polarization the Hindu nationalist movement took to at the start of the 1990s is not only embedded in its ideological DNA, it was the *only* strategy that could overcome the situation the BJP's predecessor, the Jan Sangh, faced during its three decades of existence (1951–80): the Hindu nation seemed to exist 'to a large extent within the party's imagination'.[74] The only way to change that and advance towards state power was to resort to vote-bank politics on the most ambitious scale seen in India's democracy.

◆

Unlike its Kemalist counterpart in Turkey, the Indian secular state has democratic credentials. As Donald Smith wrote in 1963, 'the secular state stands or falls as a basic and inseparable component and fundamental aspect of India's total democratic experiment' (note 44, Chapter 1). The basic concept of a secular state, defined by Nehru in 1948 during the making of the Indian Constitution as 'not tied to any religion' (note 35, Chapter 1) enjoyed widespread popular legitimacy from the Congress-led freedom struggle. Nehru was simply reiterating what a high-level committee appointed by the

---

and codification of Hindu personal and family law in 1955, discussed in Chapter 3], the principle being that their behaviour should be regulated not by their sweet will but by Dharma'. 'The same is the case with the nation', he asserted. So, for example 'if the four million people of Kashmir say they want to secede, all this is against Dharma. Of the 450 million people of India, even if 449,999,999 opt for something which is against Dharma, even then it does not become [the] truth. Dharma is eternal. Since Dharma is supreme, our ideal of the state has been "Dharma Rajya". A state can neither be without Dharma nor can it be indifferent to Dharma'. See Deendayal Upadhyaya, *Integral Humanism* (New Delhi: Bharatiya Jan Sangh, 1965), especially 18–39. In 2016, Prime Minister Modi quoted Upadhyaya on Muslims at a BJP national council meeting: '*Musalman ko na puraskrit kare, na tiraskrit kare, unka parishkar kare* (Neither reward not shun Muslims, clean them instead)'. 'Modi Invokes Jan Sangh Leader in Muslim Outreach', *Hindustan Times*, 26 September 2016, 5. Since the BJP government led by Modi assumed office in 2014, there has been a concerted effort through various ministries to project Upadhyaya as a great Indian thinker, with his birth centenary in 2016 particularly highlighted. The prominence being given to him could partly be because the far more influential figure of Golwalkar is – as yet – still too contentious to be foregrounded.

74 Bruce Graham, *Hindu Nationalism and Indian Politics: The Origins and Development of the Bharatiya Jan Sangh* (New York: Cambridge University Press, 1990), 255.

Congress, which included the young Subhas Bose, had recommended twenty years earlier in 1928: 'There shall be no state religion for the [sovereign] Commonwealth of India' (note 41, Chapter 1). Three years later in 1931, at the height of a nationwide mass campaign of civil disobedience called by Gandhi and led by the Congress against the colonial occupier, a Congress resolution asserted that 'the state [of independent India] shall observe neutrality in regard to all religions' (note 40, Chapter 1). Of course, the regulatory and interventionist form the Indian secular state took (see especially Chapter 2), presaged in Nehru's comment in 1949 (note 35, Chapter 1) that the secular state would 'give protection and opportunities to all [religious communities]' meant that the secular state assumed a very demanding brief of strictly equal treatment of all faiths, a complex challenge which over the decades ever since the 1950s bred anomalies and contradictions of policy (see especially Chapter 3, and also Chapter 4) that contributed to the rise of the Hindutva-majoritarian alternative view from the 1990s onward. Nonetheless, Nehru's observation shortly after the Indian Constitution entered into effect in 1950 that 'the government of a country like India, with many religions ... can never function except on a secular basis' (note 39, Chapter 1), i.e., that the secular path was not simply a choice born of ideological predilection but fundamentally a matter of political necessity in the Indian context, was convincing or at least acceptable across the Indian political spectrum – except to the then marginal Hindu nationalists. Nehru's emphasis on the need for 'tolerance and cooperation' across religious boundaries (note 35, Chapter 1) invoked not just the spirit and commitments of the freedom struggle but a much older aspect of Indian societal tradition down the centuries. These strong indigenous roots and popular resonance meant that the secular state in India, which in contrast to its Kemalist counterpart had nothing whatsoever to do with any desire to imitate the West (see especially Chapter 2), did not have to be forced down the throats of a largely uncomprehending populace by a harshly authoritarian regime as in Turkey. It could become, as it did, a natural and broadly accepted part of a democratic system based on political pluralism and recognition of cultural diversity, the latter above all through the structuring of India as a moderately decentralized Union of autonomous States.

In one case, however, the framework of democracy and devolution has *not* accompanied the Indian secular state. This is the case of the Indian State of Jammu and Kashmir, which covers most (nearly two-thirds) of the area and contains the bulk (currently about 13 million of around 19 million) of the population of a larger territory of the same name which has been the subject of a sovereignty dispute with Pakistan since late 1947. As I noted in the closing pages of Chapter 2, the centrality given to the 'secular' character of the Indian state in official discourse from the early 1950s onward – though the word itself was rarely used in the discourse of the independence movement and was not included in the 1950 Constitution – was motivated by the desire of the political elite, especially Nehru, to distinguish and distance the Indian Republic and its identity from that of Pakistan. Following the first India–Pakistan war of 1947–48 in and over contested Jammu and Kashmir, that territorial dispute emerged as the chief symptom and focal point of the deep, complex India–Pakistan antagonism. 'Kashmir' is a common shorthand for the territory which existed as an autonomous, so-called princely state under the Raj from 1846 to 1947, as one of the largest of over 560 such entities created by the British under vassal Indian rulers during the nineteenth century as the main pillar of their system of 'indirect rule' over nearly half the subcontinent's land area. Kashmir had been an integral part of the idea of Pakistan ever since that idea was first formulated in 1933 as a somewhat vague concept of a Muslim homeland comprising Muslim-majority regions in the northwestern subcontinent. Once Pakistan became a reality in 1947, its founding elite expected all or almost all of the princely state to become part of Pakistan, due primarily to the 77 per cent Muslim majority of the population of the princely state, but also given its greater territorial contiguity to Pakistan than to India and the close transport, trade, commercial and cultural links between the princely state and the Pakistani provinces of Punjab and the North-West Frontier Province (NWFP).

India, by contrast, did not have a clearly elaborated ideological case for ownership of Kashmir until after it became the prime bone of contention with Pakistan from the late 1940s. Such an ideological argument of sufficiently plausible robustness became especially necessary because at the end of the 1947–48 military conflict the bulk of the erstwhile princely state's territory, and an even bigger share of its population, was on the Indian side of the ceasefire line (CFL) which came into being and was renamed the Line of Control (LoC) by an agreement between the governments of the two countries in 1972 (this *de facto* border dividing Kashmir has stayed almost the same as the original line of 1949 over seven decades, through the subsequent India–Pakistan wars of 1965 and 1971 as well as a limited armed conflict initiated by Pakistan on a remote, sparsely inhabited sector of the LoC in 1999). That ideological argument developed *ex post facto* from the early 1950s, and emphasized the convergence of the Indian state's 'secular' identity with the 'secular' nature of Kashmir's society and culture (so-called *Kashmiriyat*). The latter was a politically expedient simplification of a much more complex context. The distinctive cultural character of the Kashmir Valley, which is overwhelmingly Muslim and the most populous of the three regions comprising the Indian State of J&K, indeed has pronounced syncretistic features: Islam as taught by local and non-local Sufi mystics was grafted on to the existing Shaivite Hindu tradition from the late fourteenth century, and even some elements of the previously prevalent Buddhist tradition remained. But this was and is a cultural legacy, and modern mass politics which developed in the princely state from the 1930s was always suffused with and expressed in the idiom of Muslim faith. This was not simply or even primarily due to the demographic fact of a predominantly Muslim society (particularly so in the Valley), but because that Muslim population lived in conditions of profound oppression for a century prior to 1947 under the Hindu rulership of the princely state.

Since 1953, the Indian State of J&K has mostly had unrepresentative or weakly representative governments, installed through either fraudulent or partially flawed elections. The princely state's accession to India in 1947, signed by the last Hindu dynastic ruler, took place under very complicated circumstances and limited the central government's jurisdiction to defence, foreign affairs, currency and communications. This autonomy was a few years later incorporated into the Constitution of India as its Article 370. The article remains in the Constitution, but from 1954 the government led by Nehru in New Delhi embarked on a purposeful strategy of eroding J&K's asymmetric autonomy within the Indian Union by progressively extending the jurisdiction of the central government. A final slew of 'integrative' measures imposed from New Delhi in 1965, shortly after Nehru's death, more or less completed the process of stripping away J&K's asymmetric autonomy and effectively rendered Article 370 dead in both letter and spirit. The strategy of making Article 370 virtually defunct was enabled by the collusion of puppet J&K State governments with negligible popular legitimacy and accountability, installed through farcically rigged elections. From the mid-1950s, a draconian police-state came into being in J&K and over time assumed a permanent form. A colonial-era emergency law called the Defence of India Rules used by the British to imprison Indian freedom fighters (including my own father, Sisir Kumar Bose, in 1944) was used until the mid-1960s against dissidents and activists. This was replaced by a State law called the J&K Preventive Detention Act in the mid-1960s, sometimes used in conjunction with the central Unlawful Activities (Prevention) Act. The Preventive Detention Act was replaced by an equally draconian J&K Public Safety Act in the late 1970s. In 1990, after the eruption of insurgency combined with a popular uprising in the Kashmir Valley, J&K was declared a 'disturbed area' and brought under the purview of the Armed Forces Special Powers Act (AFSPA), which gives the Indian army a virtual *carte blanche* and its personnel immunity from any prosecution. The AFSPA is descended from a colonial emergency regulation which was used by the British to crush the 'Quit India' movement launched by the Congress at Gandhi's initiative in 1942. It was first deployed in independent India by Nehru's government against ethnic Naga rebels in India's north-east in the late 1950s.

Sheikh Mohammad Abdullah (1905–82), J&K's most popular political leader and a virtual icon in the Kashmir Valley in his lifetime, spent almost all of the 22 years from 1953 until 1975 in Indian prisons. In 1968 he said,

> The fact remains that Indian democracy stops short at Pathankot [the last major town in India's Punjab State before the J&K border]. Between Pathankot and the Banihal [a mountain pass which leads from J&K's southern Jammu region into the Kashmir Valley] you may have some measure of democracy, but beyond Banihal there is none. What we have in Kashmir bears some of the worst characteristics of colonial rule.

In a 1968 message to the people of India on the occasion of Republic Day, 26 January, he said,

> Respect for the rule of law, the independence of the judiciary, [and] the integrity of the electoral process are all sought to be guaranteed by the Indian constitution. It is not surprising that many other countries have drawn upon the constitution, particularly the chapter on fundamental

rights. Yet it must at all times be remembered that the constitution provides the framework, and it is for the men who work it to give it life and meaning. In many ways, the provisions of the constitution have been flagrantly violated [in Kashmir] in recent years and the ideals it enshrines completely forgotten. Forces have arisen which threaten to carry this saddening and destructive process further still.[75]

The case of Kashmir is the single worst blot on India's democratic record, as well as on the reputation of Jawaharlal Nehru, the founding statesman of the Indian secular state. Nehru's Kashmir policy, which was continued by the subsequent Congress governments led by his daughter Indira Gandhi (1966–77 and 1980–84) and her son Rajiv Gandhi (1985–89), was rationalized from the 1950s onward by a quasi-official argument, constantly articulated by political leaders, repeated by influential opinion-makers in the intelligentsia and circulated into the public consciousness through mass media, which claimed that the retention of J&K by any means – in order to foil the irredentist aspirations of Pakistan – was essential to protect the secular nature of the Indian state. The argument ran that J&K, being the sole unit of the Indian Union with a Muslim majority, was vital to validating the secular credentials of the Indian Republic. This was a peculiar and dubious argument because the overwhelming majority (nearly 95 per cent) of Muslims in India lived and live in other States of the Indian Union, and their status and treatment could easily serve to validate the secular state. Nonetheless, this argument served as a shibboleth of the state-secularists who constituted the Indian political establishment throughout the second half of the twentieth century. Kashmir was romanticized as the 'jewel in the crown' of the Indian secular state, even as most of its population – the majority of J&K's population is in the Valley – chafed under repression. Thus Sheikh Abdullah, whose strategic alliance with the Nehru government in late 1947 was crucial to turning the first India–Pakistan war over Kashmir in India's favour, could be imprisoned for over two decades because his autonomist tendencies – partly motivated by considerations of maximizing his personal power but rooted in and resonant with the dominant political tradition in the Kashmir Valley – could jeopardize the Indian state's grip over Kashmir. In the process of this

75 *Speeches and Interviews of Sher-e-Kashmir Sheikh Mohammad Abdullah* (Srinagar: Jammu and Kashmir Plebiscite Front, 1968), Vol. 2, 13; Vol. 1, 15–16.

state-secularist fetishization of Kashmir, the Valley and its people became simultaneously the prize exhibits and the prime victims of the Indian secular state and its concept of nationalism. Indian secularists equate the secular state with democracy; in the Kashmir Valley, the Indian secular state is synonymous with authoritarianism and oppression (*zulm*).[76]

Once the Kashmir Valley descended into a maelstrom of violence from 1990, the state-sponsored myth cultivated in India over the previous four decades that secular-minded Kashmiris naturally belonged in the Indian secular state disintegrated. A mixture of lament and condemnation took its place. The new Indian secular-nationalist narrative went that Kashmiri Muslims had betrayed both their own secular ethos and the trust of the Indian secular state and turned 'communal', even 'fundamentalist', and succumbed to the siren call of Pakistan from across the border. The most delusional version of this narrative – blind to the actual experience of Kashmiri Muslims in the Indian state since the 1950s – was and is that these misguided people simply need to rediscover their secular essence and reconnect with India, the secular state. The Hindu nationalists, meanwhile, adopted a smug 'we told you so' posture, equally at variance with reality, that 'appeasement' of Kashmiri Muslims under the secular state (primarily through Article 370) had led to the secessionist outbreak, with the Kashmiri Muslims finally revealing their Pakistani colours. Some perspectives straddled the two narratives. For example, an Indian scholar rued in 1993 that:

> the way to hell is paved with good intentions, and so it has been in Kashmir. Although the state [J&K] has been ruled since 1947 by a succession of governments headed by Muslim chief ministers, and the representation of Muslims in the bureaucracy and the professions has very considerably improved, a secessionist movement has erupted there which has turned violent ... What the turbulent elements are asking for is, in effect, another Partition.[77]

In fact, the predominant definition of *azaadi* (freedom) in the Kashmir Valley since the 1990s has been liberation from both Indian oppression and Pakistani

---

76  See Sumantra Bose, 'An Uneasy Jewel in the Indian Crown: Kashmir and the Fallacy of the Secularism Argument', *Open*, 26 September 2016, 14–17.

77  T. N. Madan, 'Whither Indian Secularism?', *Modern Asian Studies* 27, no. 3 (July 1993), 692–694.

exploitation and manipulation of their predicament. The Pakistani state and its military, operating mainly through the notorious Directorate of Inter-Services Intelligence (ISI), ruthlessly exploited the rage of a new generation of Kashmiri Muslim young men and their willingness to take up the gun against Indian rule by supplying lethal weaponry, training and money to pro-Pakistan Kashmiri armed groups, and from the mid-1990s onwards by sending waves of Pakistani radical Islamists across the LoC to join the fight. But the predominant sentiment in the Valley remained pro-independence rather than pro-Pakistan, and the fact of continuous Pakistani incitement and abetment did not alter the basic reality that this was India's homemade, self-inflicted crisis.

The violence of insurgency and counter-insurgency that engulfed the Valley from 1990 and spread as that decade progressed to some areas of the Jammu region lasted a decade and a half, until the middle of the first decade of the new century, and went through several distinct phases. The traumatization of society by protracted armed conflict was reflected in the creative work of a new generation of Kashmiri writers. Shakeel Shan wrote about a missing friend:

> Who knows where my friend is? Who knows where my friend is hiding? Who knows whether he is scared of the dark night? Who knows whether he is hungry and unable to stand on his feet? Who knows whether the place where he sits is not damp?

He added, 'If I did not write, my heart would explode like a bomb'. Bashir Manzar wrote about fear: 'Break the pen, spill the ink, burn the paper; Lock your lips, be silent, shhh; Say "I saw nothing" even if you did; Or else have your eyes gouged out; Keep humming eulogies, be silent; It is the season of burying the truth'. Another anonymous writer expressed himself or herself thus,

> I can't drink water because I feel it is mixed with the blood of the young men who die up in the mountains. I can't look at the sky because it is no longer blue, it is painted red. I can't listen to the roar of the gushing stream, it reminds me of the wailing mother next to the bullet-riddled body of her only son. I can't listen to the thunder of the clouds, it reminds me of a bomb blast. I feel the green of my garden has faded, perhaps it too mourns. The sparrow and the cuckoo are silent, perhaps they too are sad.[78]

This was the situation the BJP-led coalition government inherited when it

---

78 Sumantra Bose, *Kashmir: Roots of Conflict, Paths to Peace* (Cambridge, MA and London: Harvard University Press, 2003), 5–6, 102.

took office in New Delhi under Atal Behari Vajpayee's premiership in early 1998. As India's Prime Minister until mid-2004, Vajpayee, a lifelong Hindu nationalist, pursued a Kashmir policy anchored in strategic diplomacy. Over a five-year period between early 1999 and early 2004, he undertook a series of diplomatic moves which signalled a conciliatory approach towards the wounded people of Kashmir and a willingness to engage with Pakistan. He persisted in this strategic approach in spite of rude setbacks and grave provocations such as the Pakistani military's cross-LoC incursion in the Kargil district of J&K's Ladakh region in 1999, and a terrorist attack on India's Parliament building in end-2001. Meanwhile, a war of attrition continued between Indian security forces and insurgents, among whom Pakistanis outnumbered Kashmiris by the early 2000s, in stark contrast to the early 1990s, when the insurgency consisted overwhelmingly of local Kashmiris and was dominated by the pro-independence Jammu and Kashmir Liberation Front (JKLF). In end-2002, Indian official sources reported that 1,581 insurgents had been killed in counter-insurgency operations during the first eleven months of the year. Vajpayee's recurrent peace overtures amid the mayhem, and his framing of the Kashmir issue as one of *insaaniyat* (humanity), earned him – uniquely for an Indian politician – a great deal of goodwill and respect among the Valley's people, exhausted and sickened by more than a decade of carnage.

India's Hindu nationalist Prime Minister's diplomacy-based approach was very counter-intuitive because he had spent half-a-century in a party and movement which had called for the formal abrogation of Article 370 throughout that time, regarding it as one of the most blatant examples of the Indian secular state's 'appeasement' of Muslims. During the 1990s, the BJP's political agenda revolved around three key demands: the construction of a grand temple dedicated to the Hindu deity Lord Ram at the site of Ayodhya's sixteenth-century Mughal mosque (razed in mob violence in December 1992); the enactment of an Uniform Civil Code or UCC applicable to all citizens and communities in the country, superseding the right of Muslims to invoke Sharia law in personal and familial matters; and the formal abrogation of Article 370. Indeed, Article 370 was the focus of the Jan Sangh's first major agitation in the early 1950s, when the newly formed party joined an already ongoing agitation in the Jammu region's Hindu-majority southern areas led by former officials of the last Hindu princely ruler's administration and Hindu landlords dispossessed by a sweeping land reform implemented by Sheikh Abdullah's government from 1950 to 1952, which liberated hundreds of thousands of Valley Muslims from generations of serfdom (and also benefited a considerable population of low-caste Hindus in the Jammu region). The slogan of that agitation was *Ek Vidhaan! Ek Nishaan! Ek Pradhaan!* meaning 'One Law, One Flag, One Premier'. This referred to J&K's asymmetric autonomy under Article 370 and the existence of a J&K State Constitution, the existence of a J&K State flag, and the 'Prime Minister' title of the head of the J&K government, which in 1965 was changed to 'Chief Minister' as in other Indian States, at the same time as the decade-long process of *de facto* revocation of Article 370 initiated and pursued by Nehru's government was completed. The Jan Sangh's first President, S. P. Mookerjee, died of natural causes in detention in the Kashmir Valley in mid-1953 after he entered the Jammu region to join the agitation and was arrested by the J&K police. The BJP had put its three core demands in abeyance in early 1998 in exchange for support from a rainbow spectrum of mostly secularist 'regional' (State-specific) parties which enabled it to form a coalition government, and the same compromise enabled Vajpayee to form a second, more stable coalition government after mid-term parliamentary elections in autumn 1999. The J&K BJP nonetheless called for the formal abrogation of Article 370 in its manifesto for elections to the J&K State legislature in autumn 2002, and won only one seat in the 87-member legislature. The RSS went further and campaigned for 'trifurcation' of J&K to create a separate Hindu-majority State of Jammu and 'Union Territory' status for the third region, Ladakh, a high-altitude desert on the western edge of the Tibetan plateau with a small population almost evenly divided between Muslims and Buddhists. L. K. Advani, the Home (Interior) Minister and Deputy Prime Minister in Vajpayee's government, who was the leading figure of the Ayodhya agitation during its climactic phase from 1990 to 1992, however made it clear that the government did not support the trifurcation demand.

Between 1999 and 2004, Vajpayee laid the groundwork for a Kashmir peace process. The BJP-led National Democratic Alliance (NDA) failed to renew its mandate in India's mid-2004 parliamentary election, which produced a 'hung' Lok Sabha. A major reason for the NDA's disappointing performance was the pogrom against Muslims that took place in Gujarat under Narendra Modi's chief ministership in 2002, which enraged Muslims across India and alienated liberal opinion. Vajpayee retired from active politics after the unexpected defeat. The momentum towards a Kashmir peace process was lost during the term (2004–09) of the subsequent coalition government put together after the 2004 election under the leadership of the Congress. A window of opportunity was squandered during this time, when insurgency declined sharply and the Pakistani regime headed by General Pervez Musharraf – who had been behind the Kargil operation of 1999 – seemed amenable to a compromise settlement of the Kashmir dispute.[79]

When the BJP stormed back to power in New Delhi in 2014 under Narendra Modi's leadership, winning a single-party Lok Sabha majority not seen since 1984, its government inherited the unresolved dispute and a situation of simmering unrest in the Kashmir Valley. Two episodes during the decade (2004–14) the BJP was out of power illustrated the fragile and volatile situation. In the summer of 2008, there had been competing agitations in the Valley and the Hindu-majority southern areas of the Jammu region (in which the local RSS played a prominent role), sparked by a dispute centred on an annual Hindu pilgrimage to a famous cave-shrine of the deity Shiva located in the Kashmir Valley. Two years later, in the summer of 2010, a massive stone-pelting agitation gripped the Valley for nearly four months, in the course of which tens of thousands of locals, mostly teenaged boys and young men in their twenties, confronted Indian security forces. The eruption, during which about 120 protesters were shot dead, revealed that a new generation in the Valley were just as alienated from Indian authority as the generation which took to insurgency in the 1990s. The new generation had grown up in a brutalized environment and the stone-pelting epidemic was the latest manifestation of the sense of grievance transmitted from generation to generation in the Valley since the 1950s.[80]

---

79 On the Kashmir conflict, see Bose, *Kashmir: Roots of Conflict, Paths to Peace*, and Sumantra Bose, *Contested Lands: Israel-Palestine, Kashmir, Bosnia, Cyprus, and Sri Lanka* (Cambridge, MA and London: Harvard University Press, 2007), Chapter 4. On the Kashmir Valley's specific context, see Sumantra Bose, *Transforming India: Challenges to the World's Largest Democracy* (Cambridge, MA and London: Harvard University Press, 2013), Chapter 5.

80 See Bose, *Transforming India*, Chapter 5; Sumantra Bose, 'Kashmir: Missed Chances for Peace', *BBC News Online*, 22 August 2008; and Sumantra Bose, 'Kashmir's Summer of Discontent is Now an Autumn of Woe', *BBC News Online*, 21 September 2010.

In end-2014, six months after Modi's ascension to the prime ministership, scheduled State elections were held in J&K. Turnout was good at about 65 per cent, and many areas in the Valley exceeded that State-wide average – although the election was held as the Valley reeled from severe floods caused by torrential early-autumn rain. The outcome was a hung J&K legislature, as in 2002 and 2008. The single largest party was the J&K People's Democratic Party (PDP), which won well over half the seats from the Valley and secured nearly one-third of the total seats. The BJP was close behind due to a very strong performance in the Hindu-majority Jammu region, where it won two-thirds of the seats at stake.

The PDP had been formed in 1999. Its leader, Mufti Mohammad Sayeed, was a veteran J&K politician from the Valley who had spent most of his long political career in the Congress party, as an opponent first of Sheikh Abdullah and then the Sheikh's son and successor Farooq Abdullah. At the end of the 1990s he, along with his daughter Mehbooba, launched the PDP as a regional (State-specific) party which sought to articulate the grievances and aspirations of the people of the blood-soaked Valley through electoral politics, unlike a range of pro-independence and pro-Pakistan groups in the Valley who boycott elections because they do not accept the legitimacy of Indian authority. The PDP made a strong debut in the 2002 State elections and Sayeed served as the State's Chief Minister from late 2002 to late 2005 in a coalition government with the Congress (which was then the strongest party in the Jammu region). During that chief ministerial tenure, he helped in the scarred State's limited recovery from over a decade of intense violence and provided a significant local prop for Vajpayee's conciliation efforts.

The end-2014 outcome threw up the possibility of a pact between Kashmiri Muslim regionalism represented by the PDP and Hindu nationalism represented by the BJP. I repeatedly argued in commentaries in the Indian print media, starting from the day the election result became known, for such a power-sharing government to be formed in J&K between the two largest parties.[81] That offered the potential of narrowing the divide between the Hindu majority of the Jammu region and the Valley and, crucially, of

---

81 Sumantra Bose, 'A Historic Opportunity in Kashmir', *Mint*, 24 December 2014; Sumantra Bose, 'Bringing J into K', *Open*, 9 January 2015; Sumantra Bose, 'The Power of Two', *Open*, 20 February 2015.

beginning to bridge the more than six-decade rift between the Valley's Muslims and the Indian Union. It offered Modi and his government a chance to revive Vajpayee's healing-touch approach.

After two months of behind-the-scenes negotiations, a PDP–BJP coalition government took office in Jammu and Kashmir in March 2015. Mufti Sayeed became the Chief Minister and two-thirds of ministers of cabinet rank were from the PDP. A BJP leader from Jammu became the Deputy Chief Minister and the BJP acquired the remainder of the portfolios.

The coalition government was based on a document titled 'Agenda of Alliance'. On Article 370, whilst 'recognizing the different positions of the parties' on the matter, the agreement committed to maintaining 'all the constitutional provisions pertaining to Kashmir including the [nominal] special status'. On the Armed Forces Special Powers Act, the agreement noted yet again that 'the parties have historically held different views' on its necessity, and observed that since 'the situation in the state has improved vastly ... the coalition government will thoroughly review the security situation ... [and] the need for de-notifying disturbed areas ... [to] enable the [Union] government to take a final view on the continuation of AFSPA in these areas'. Beyond these specific points, the agreement stated that 'the purpose of this alliance [is] to catalyse reconciliation and confidence-building within and across the LoC, [to] widen the ambit of democracy through inclusive politics, [and to] create conditions to facilitate resolution of all issues'. To that end, it said, 'the coalition government will facilitate and help initiate a sustained and meaningful dialogue with all internal stakeholders irrespective of their ideological views' and 'seek to build a broad-based consensus on the resolution of all outstanding issues'. On the international dimensions of the conflict, the agreement stated that as 'the [Union] government has recently initiated several steps to normalise the relationship with Pakistan, the coalition government will seek to support and strengthen that approach' and 'the same [goal] will be pursued by enhancing people-to-people contact across the LoC, encouraging civil society exchanges, and taking travel, trade, commerce and business across the LoC to the next level'.[82]

Prime Minister Modi personally attended the oath-taking ceremony of

---

82 Sumantra Bose, 'Kashmir: Can New Government Provide Healing Touch?', *BBC News Online*, 3 March 2015.

the new government in March 2015, which was held in Jammu, the winter capital of J&K (Srinagar in the Kashmir Valley is the summer capital) and a predominantly Hindu city. He warmly embraced Mufti Sayeed in the backdrop of a table decorated with equal-sized versions of the Indian national tricolour and the J&K state flag.

The Agenda of Alliance represented something previously unthinkable – a seemingly visionary pact and a joint statement of purpose of India's Hindu nationalist party and a mainly Valley-based J&K party which had premised its politics since its formation in 1999 on improving human rights, restoring meaningful autonomy ('self-rule') to J&K, and ensuring a minimally dignified life for the Valley's people. The agreement underpinning the coalition amounted to a roadmap of a peace process. I wrote in March 2015 that,

> it is premature to say that this strategic bargain between Kashmiri Muslim regionalists and Hindu nationalists heralds a Kashmir Spring. But it is unmistakably the most hopeful development since the descent into violence a quarter-century ago. The challenge over the next few years is to convert symbolism into substance, and the promise into reality.[83]

There was no subsequent initiative or action on any of the key points of the Agenda of Alliance – whether reviewing AFSPA, initiating dialogue with the spectrum of pro-independence and pro-Pakistan political groups, or enhancing cross-LoC linkages. In January 2016, ten months after the coalition government took office, Mufti Mohammad Sayeed died, just short of his eightieth birthday, after a brief illness. Six months after his death, in July 2016, the simmering Valley erupted in furious unrest triggered by the killing by security forces of a young insurgent who had acquired a large local following on social media. Since that time, the Valley has been in acute turmoil and there were about a hundred civilian deaths, as of mid-2017, in action by security forces against stone-pelting protesters. In addition to the deaths, the use of pellet guns by the security forces blinded or damaged the sight of over a thousand people – mostly young men but children and girls as well – and not just stone-pelters but bystanders too. During 2017, there was a noticeable increase in insurgent activity in the Valley as several hundred young men enlisted in guerrilla groups. That in turn led to the intensification

---

83 Ibid.

of counter-insurgency – the opposite of the normalization envisioned in the Agenda of Alliance. A lame-duck J&K government headed by Sayeed's politician daughter Mehbooba Mufti continues as of end-2017.

Prime Minister Modi first spoke about the renewed crisis in August 2016, a month after the unrest erupted, at an all-party meeting convened by his government in New Delhi to discuss the matter. He made no reference to the promises of the Agenda of Alliance but framed the problem as one of 'cross-border terrorism' and underlined that 'Jammu and Kashmir ... defines our nationalism' – the standard rhetoric of past, 'secular' Indian leaders. He added that 'like all Indians, I am also pained by the recent incidents'. By 2017, his stance discernibly hardened. Visiting the Jammu region in April 2017 to inaugurate a tunnel for motor traffic running through hilly terrain, he addressed a rally of 100,000 people, where he advised the youth of the Valley to abjure 'terrorism' and instead seek 'progress through tourism', citing 'every Indian's dream of visiting Kashmir [at least] once'.[84]

Just like Turkey's Kurdish problem – with which it shares considerable parallels – India's Kashmir problem is the making and the legacy of policies pursued over decades by professedly secular leaders and governments, in an era in which secular nationalism was the ideology of the state. And just as the anti-secular Turkish nationalists who now rule the Turkish state have reverted to authoritarian repression rather than seek a political resolution to the problem, so have the anti-secular Hindu nationalists who are steadily consolidating and advancing their ascendancy in Indian politics. This is but a reflection of both the basic nature and the electoral strategy of the movement of which the BJP represents the party-political face. The hardline approach to Kashmir, in the words of an Indian commentator, 'neatly dovetails' with the Hindutva movement's 'goal of polarising India on religious lines', which is a central element of the strategy to win Modi and the BJP a second five-year term in the national election of 2019 and secure Hindu nationalist dominance of the Indian state. So 'Kashmiris will continue to resist, [and] influential sections of the Indian media will continue to represent them as saboteurs inspired by Pakistan in ways that rallies support' for the Hindutva brand of Indian nationalism. This is 'about disciplining the Valley for internal

---

84 'Like All Indians, I am also Pained: PM Modi', *Indian Express*, 13 August 2016, 9; 'PM to Kashmir Youth: Progress through Tourism', *Indian Express*, 3 April 2017, 1.

audiences and setting the stage for assimilationist endeavours in the future', and 'if Kashmir endured the hypocrisy of the Congress [era], it is now having to live with the consequence of being central to the project of turning India into a [Hindutva-based] majoritarian state'.[85] Kashmiris and Kurds, victims and scapegoats of secular-nationalist elites, thus continue as victims and scapegoats under the anti-secular regimes of the twenty-first century.

---

85 Sushil Aaron, 'The Modi Government has a New Model for Managing Kashmir', *Hindustan Times* (internet edition), 14 April 2017.

# 7

# THE FUTURES OF SECULARISM

*My story is the story of this nation. Either this nation is going to win and come to power, or the arrogant and oppressive minority group, who look on Anatolia with contempt and are alien to Anatolian realities, will continue to remain in power. The nation has the authority to decide. Enough; sovereignty belongs to the nation.*

– Recep Tayyip Erdogan in October 2002,
just before the national election of November 2002 which brought his
Justice and Development Party (AKP) to power[1]

*India is a secular state with no state religion.*

– The Government of India's Attorney-General, at a session of the
United Nations Human Rights Council in Geneva,
Switzerland in May 2017[2]

---

1    Erdogan, then still banned from politics after being tried and convicted of anti-secular activity in 1999, was speaking to *Yeni Safak* (New Dawn), an Islamist daily newspaper. Quoted in Yavuz, *Islamic Political Identity in Turkey*, 261–262.

2    India's Attorney-General (AG) is the state's top official on constitutional and legal matters. The AG, Mukul Rohatgi, was responding to criticism from various countries at the UNHRC session that the Indian secular state is increasingly in peril under the government of Narendra Modi, India's Prime Minister since mid-2014. The Indian official's presentation further asserted that 'as the world's largest multi-layered democracy, we fully recognize the importance of free speech and expression. Our people are conscious of their political freedoms and exercise their choices at every opportunity'. He added that the Modi government 'believe[s] in peace, non-violence and upholding human dignity'. He also stated, 'The concept of torture is completely alien to our

*As the most elementary comparative analysis will show, all nationalism is both
healthy and morbid. Both progress and regress are inscribed in its genetic code
from the start. This is a structural fact about it.*

> – Tom Nairn, Scottish Marxist, in 'The Modern Janus',
> an article published in 1975[3]

Janus, the god of ancient Rome, had two faces – literally, not in a figurative
or metaphorical sense. Sculptures of Janus, and impressions of the deity on
Roman coins, invariably show him in profile, with two faces – one looking
to the left, the other to the right – mounted on a single neck and sharing
the same head. The two faces in profile, looking in opposite directions, were
sometimes identical, in other representations not identical but quite similar,
but in yet other representations depicted as very different – for example one
young, the other elderly; one bearded, the other clean-shaven; one with a
benevolent expression, the other with a stern stare. In all these variants, in the
ancient Roman version of *dharma*, Janus symbolized a composite concept of
duality – of past and future, beginnings and endings, entrances and exits, war
and peace. The Romans worshipped Janus more than any other deity in their
homes, palaces, and in temples dedicated to the god. January, the first month
of the Roman calendar, is usually said to be named after Janus; looking back
and forward at the same time, he was a symbol of change and transitions.
Both his faces were equally important, true and real – neither being a mask
nor a masquerade for the other – and together they made up Janus's wholeness
and the symbolism he represented of the nature of life and existence.

The political regimes headed respectively by Narendra Modi in India since
2014 and Recep Tayyip Erdogan in Turkey since 2003 have two faces in
the composite manner of Janus. One face expresses the *mantra*s and agenda
of progress, development, modernization – using quite similar rhetoric and
symbols in the process. For example, as Erdogan's Justice and Development

---

culture and as such has no place in the governance of our nation'. 'India is a Secular
State with No State Religion', *Greater Kashmir*, 5 May 2017, 1; 'Minority Rights, NGO
Crackdown Raised at UN Meet, India Says Freedoms Secure and Concept of Torture
Alien to Our Culture', *Indian Express*, 5 May 2017, 1.

3   Tom Nairn, 'The Modern Janus', *New Left Review* (I), no. 94 (Nov–Dec 1975), 1–28.
    Nairn (b. 1932) is a British academic and commentator. The essay was reprinted in his
    book, *The Break-Up of Britain*, first published in 1977.

Party (AKP) consolidated its grip over the Turkish state and gradually turned it into a near-stranglehold between roughly 2007 and 2014, it used,

> such catchphrases as '2023 targets' [the centenary of the Turkish Republic] and 'New Turkey' to capture the imagination of the people. In so doing, they emphasized economic development and infrastructure modernization. Consequently, grand construction projects such as a third bridge [opened in 2016] over the Bosphorus [the famous waterway between the 'European' and 'Asian' parts of Istanbul], motorway and railway tunnels under the Bosphorus, a third [gigantic] airport in Istanbul [to replace the two rather tired existing ones], massive 'urban transformation' constructions in Turkey's big cities, and hastily developed national automobile and plane [manufacturing] projects came to signify the 'New Turkey.'[4]

Many people were impressed and even awed by the ambition, verging on grandiosity, of the 'New Turkey' vision, and they were not necessarily idiots or even naïve. Between roughly 2003 and 2007 the first Erdogan/ AKP government, steered particularly by 'Foreign Minister [later President from 2007–14] Abdullah Gul and Economy Minister Ali Babacan [a highly qualified, US-trained technocrat] oversaw Turkey's remarkable economic recovery' from the collapse of 2001 (described in Chapter 1), and the economic shambles the AKP inherited from the discredited secularist establishment it replaced in government after coming first in the parliamentary election of late 2002. The recovery strategy took advantage of the 'period of global liquidity boom' prior to the Western financial crash of 2008, enjoyed the backing of the European Union, which saw the AKP as a liberalizing if not democratizing influence on the Turkish state's deep-rooted authoritarianism as represented by the military hierarchy and the Kemalist political elite, and was driven on the ground 'by a coalition of conservative [Sunni-religious] entrepreneurs, many of them supporters of Fethullah Gulen's *Hizmet* [service] movement' (the Turkish Islamist sect with a global presence now officially labelled in Turkey as the 'Fethullah Terror Organization' or FETO due to its alleged leading role in

---

4   Menderes Cinar, 'The Power Strategies of the AKP in Turkey', in *The AKP and Turkish Foreign Policy in the Middle East*, ed. Zeynep Kaya (London: LSE Middle East Centre, 2016), 14.

the failed anti-Erdogan military coup of July 2016).[5] The growth of this class of businessmen and entrepreneurs in the Anatolian heartlands since the 1990s and their vital role in supporting the political rise of the Sunni-Islamist variant of Turkish nationalism represented by the AKP is described in Chapter 5. The first AKP government faced 'a very real threat of secularist aggression'[6] from the yet to be defanged military brass and its allies in the Kemalist civilian elite – a threat the second AKP government (2007–11), which had a much stronger popular mandate, decisively overcame (see Chapter 5).

From 2002 to 2007, the politically reformist and economically developmentalist face of the newly risen Islamist counter-elite dominated over its ideological face. Thus, AKP ideologues even devised a new self-label – 'conservative democracy' (see Chapter 1) – in order to strategically distance their party and government from its ideological moorings in the Turkish Islamist movement organized around the concepts/slogans of *Milli Gorus* (National Outlook) in the 1970s and *Adil Duzen* (Just Order) in the 1990s (see Chapter 5), rooted in the Ottoman-Islamic heritage the Kemalists had so despised and tried to eradicate. The context was not yet ripe for the ideological agendas of vigorously asserting the Sunni-Islamist majoritarian definition of Turkish national identity, and revising the nature of the Turkish state in accordance with that definition.

*Hindutva 2.0* – which is what I call the contemporary incarnation of the Hindu nationalist movement in the Modi era – also has two, equally integral faces as Janus did, rising from the one neck and jutting out from the same head. The face that propelled Modi and the Bharatiya Janata Party's (BJP) emphatic victory in India's 2014 parliamentary election was not the ideological face inscribed with the features of Vinayak D. Savarkar and Madhav S. Golwalkar – whose political creed, premised on rejection of a secular conception of Indian nationhood ('pseudo-nationalistic', in the Hindutva founding ideologue Savarkar's term of the 1930s and 1940s) and implacable opposition to the Indian secular state ('pseudo-secular' in the lexicon of the post-independence Hindutva movement led by the RSS, and built under Golwalkar's leadership until 1973), is closely analysed in Chapter 6. It was the other face – promising

5 Karabekir Akkoyunlu, 'Erdogan's Victory and the Unravelling of Political Islam in Turkey', *The Middle East in London* 13, no. 4 (June-July 2017), 7.
6 Cinar, 'The Power Strategies of the AKP', 12.

socio-economic progress, modernization of India's infrastructural capacities, and the slogan of 'development with all, for all' (*sab ka saath, sab ka vikaas*) – which resonated with the 37 per cent of the electorate who voted for the BJP-led alliance charismatically fronted by Modi as the prime ministerial candidate. This sufficed to give the BJP, with 31.3 per cent of the polled votes, a (thin) single-party majority in the Lok Sabha, the popularly elected chamber of parliament, for the first time since the Congress last achieved that in 1984. This face appealed to a large chunk of what is sometimes referred to in journalistic commentary as 'aspirational India', the hundreds of millions of mainly young Indians of disparate communities and backgrounds across the vast country who share the aspiration to materially better lives than their parents enjoyed, through access to opportunities essential for such betterment: education, training and jobs that assure decent livelihoods.

The BJP campaign spearheaded by Modi tapped this aspiration to considerable effect. On the day Modi took over as Prime Minister, I wrote in an Indian national daily that to his supporters, he represents 'messiah and rock-star rolled into one'. It was a daunting image to live up to, because, I argued,

> Modi's emergence as the agent of change and hope is due less to his claimed
> credentials and qualities—which are disputed—than to a propitious set of
> circumstances. He has capitalised on a nationwide hunger for change at
> the Centre [New Delhi], in a context of weak to non-existent competition.

Modi benefited from being the only challenger to a rudderless, corruption-tainted Congress-led coalition government discredited across the country, from the tragi-comic incompetence of the Congress's dynastic scion, Rahul Gandhi, and from a longer-term trend: the withering away of the Congress's organization and popular base across most of India since the early 1990s. Meanwhile, 'the spectrum of regional [State-specific] parties' across India was simply 'too disparate, at loggerheads [with one another] in various key States, and divided by the clashing egos and ambitions of [their] leaders to throw up a coherent national alternative'. So the BJP, which in any case 'as the single-largest opposition party with a footprint in numerous States' – albeit unevenly, much stronger in northern and western India than the east and the south – was 'poised to gain the most' from the extreme unpopularity of the outgoing Congress-led government, prevailed and Modi was pitchforked from his twelve-year chief ministership of the western State of Gujarat to the office of

India's Prime Minister.[7] His successful personal re-invention during the latter half of that lengthy tenure in Gujarat from being the *Hindu Hriday Samrat* (Emperor of Hindu Hearts) – the honorific bestowed on him by hardline Hindu nationalists after the anti-Muslim pogrom in Gujarat in 2002 – to the best hope of aspirational India was crucial to the resounding return of the BJP to the corridors of power in New Delhi after a decade's hiatus.

As Prime Minister since mid-2014, Modi has worked hard to consolidate this face of Hindutva 2.0, and to inscribe his own features on it. The use of catchy phrases abounds, often combined with time deadlines. In his victory speech at the BJP office in New Delhi after the party decisively won a crucial State election in March 2017 in Uttar Pradesh, India's most populous State, Modi called for a 'New India' to be created by 2022. This signalled his and the party's growing confidence that the BJP government was on course to be re-elected to a second five-year term in the Lok Sabha election due in April–May 2019, but 2022 also happens to be the 75th anniversary year of India's independence. One of the Modi government's signature schemes – *Swachh Bharat* or 'Clean India', a nationwide drive to promote cleanliness and public hygiene – was launched shortly after he took office with a deadline of 2019, Mahatma Gandhi's 150th birth anniversary year. There is a tendency to describe infrastructure projects in grandiose terms and turn their inaugurations into public pulpits for Modi's long speeches, usually delivered in Hindi. Thus, the inauguration in April 2017 of 'South Asia's longest road tunnel', a 9-kilometre tunnel bored through mountains in the Jammu region of the State of Jammu and Kashmir, became an occasion for a rally of 100,000 people addressed by the Prime Minister (see note 84, Chapter 6). A month later, in May 2017, Modi travelled to the State of Assam in India's north-east, where the BJP won a State election in 2016 at the head of a pre-poll alliance formed with local parties, to inaugurate 'the country's longest bridge' (also 9 kilometres) constructed over a tributary of the Brahmaputra river to connect Assam with Arunachal Pradesh, a much smaller neighbouring State.[8] The date chosen for the inauguration was 26 May, the third anniversary of the Modi government, and this too became an occasion for a mass rally. These important

---

7    Sumantra Bose, 'Politics Has a Pivot Again', *Hindustan Times*, 26 May 2014.

8    'PM Modi Inaugurates Country's Longest Bridge in Assam', *Economic Times* (internet edition), 26 May 2017.

infrastructure projects were taken in hand long before Modi assumed the helm in New Delhi, but the nature of the inauguration ceremonies stamped them with Modi's highly personalized brand of developmental populism. Indeed, Modi has a keen appreciation for the value of spectacle in politics. On 21 June 2017, International Yoga Day, he travelled to Lucknow, the capital of Uttar Pradesh, where he performed yoga with a select group of young people and then addressed a 50,000-strong crowd assembled at the venue. He also has a personalized and presidential-style mass communication strategy. Modi does not hold press conferences, or give interviews to journalists. Instead, he communicates directly with the people through Twitter (daily), and through a monthly radio address called *Mann ki Baat* (Thoughts on my Mind) which is transmitted by the state-run All India Radio on Sunday mornings. The daily tweets reach a predominantly younger and metropolitan demographic and the monthly radio homily a predominantly rural audience.

The centrality in Hindutva 2.0 of the personality of the commanding, towering leader is at variance with and a marked departure from the norms of the Hindu nationalist movement, which in the pre-Modi era always stressed the pursuit of ideological aims and the building of organizational strength and cohesion towards that end over the role of individuals. When Atal Behari Vajpayee became India's first Hindu nationalist Prime Minister in the late 1990s, he had been a nationally known political figure for forty years. Yet as Prime Minister, he remained a 'first among equals' in the top echelon of the BJP leadership, consistent with the norms of the party and its broader movement. Modi, by contrast, was barely known in Indian politics until he became Gujarat's BJP Chief Minister aged 51 in late 2001, and even then gained national – and international – prominence only because of the religious violence there in 2002, a few months after he started in the post. He had spent nearly two decades through the 1970s and 1980s in anonymity as a fulltime activist of the RSS – an organization which emphasizes the cultivation of personal modesty, discipline and a spirit of service among its members, particularly its core cadre – before being seconded to work in the BJP's set-up in the late 1980s in relatively low-key roles which lasted through the 1990s. Vajpayee's recognition among the wider public, despite the marginality in Indian politics of his party until the early 1990s, rested above all on his reputation for excellent oratorical skills in Hindi, in and outside parliament. But his oratorical effectiveness was based on an understated and rather philosophical style of speaking very unusual in Indian politics, quite different from the equally effective but more tub-thumping, soapbox-style oratory of Modi. In parallel with the emphasis on ideological integrity and organization-building – rather than on nurturing and promoting charismatic personalities – in the Hindu nationalist movement built around the RSS core, the Jan Sangh and then the BJP institutionalized the practice of collective decision-making by its top leaders on important matters, subject to the final assent or veto of the RSS hierarchy. The RSS hierarchy still wields profound behind-the-scenes influence as the ultimate guardians of the Hindu nationalist movement and its ideological agenda, but the BJP in the Modi era has moved away from the ethos of collective decision-making to deference to Modi's authority, exercised through Modi's trusted associate from Gujarat, Amit Shah, who became the BJP's national president in mid-2014 after acting as the chief strategist and manager of Modi's successful Lok Sabha campaign.

The BJP's evolution towards a leader-based model is similar to that of the Congress in the 1970s, when Indira Gandhi came to wield nearly absolute authority in the party because she, like Modi today, had emerged as the party's trump card in mass electoral politics. There is some resemblance here to the Turkish Sunni-Islamist movement's series of evolutions from the ideological formulations of *Milli Gorus* in the 1970s to *Adil Duzen* in the 1990s to 'conservative democracy' in the 2000s and finally to a personality cult of Erdogan in the 2010s. When the BJP celebrated the third anniversary of its government in mid-2017 with a three-week outreach programme to all of India's nearly 700 administrative districts involving senior party leaders and ministers, the mass-contact campaign was titled 'Modifest'. In July 2017, BJP president Amit Shah released a coffee-table book chronicling Modi's life, titled *The Making of a Legend*, in New Delhi in the presence of the RSS chief Mohan Bhagwat. Bhagwat said at the event:

> Modi still follows the same lifestyle as India's PM which he had as an RSS worker and before becoming Gujarat's CM. It is not enough to praise him for what he is today, one must also realise how wedded he was to his ideals before he became PM.[9]

---

9  'Shah Ridicules 'Economic Pundits' for Criticising Jobless Growth', *Indian Express*, 13 July 2017, 7.

Indeed, every major scheme and slogan of the Modi government carries the personal imprimatur of the larger-than-life Prime Minister and serves to enhance his presidential-style aura in India's parliamentary democracy. These range from an initiative to extend basic banking facilities to India's poor launched in 2014 to an ongoing campaign to promote 'digitization' (e-governance) in all aspects of the Union government's dealings with citizens to the implementation of a '100 smart cities' proposal in his winning 2014 manifesto, which is actually a relatively limited plan to upgrade the infrastructure of some of India's urban centres. On 1 July 2017, after three years of negotiations between the Union government and State governments, an integrated Goods and Services Tax (GST) regime came into effect across India, replacing a maze of separate central and State taxes levied on goods and services. This new, unified VAT system with four slabs or tax rates was celebrated with a glitzy midnight ceremony held at India's parliament at the initiative of the Modi government, with the Prime Minister as the star speaker. The event was intended to evoke the 'tryst with destiny' speech Nehru delivered at the same venue at midnight on 14–15 August 1947, as India became an independent country. Most opposition parties boycotted the 'tryst with GST' ceremony; it was pointed out that such midnight sessions had been held in the parliament building only twice before, to mark the 25th and 50th anniversaries of India's independence (14–15 August in 1972 and 1997). The GST was launched to an advertising blitz with the punchline: 'Building a New India through One Nation, One Tax, One Market'. At the same time, mass emails reached citizens across India exhorting them to 'contribute to the Prime Minister's vision of a New India' and outlining 'five ways in which you can become a New India champion'.

At 8 pm one evening in November 2016, Modi announced on national television that Indian currency notes in 500 and 1000 denominations – amounting to 86 per cent of the liquidity in circulation – would cease to be legal tender from midnight. This extraordinary move, whose scale and suddenness is without any known precedent elsewhere in the world, was ostensibly to weed out 'black money' (illicitly acquired and hoarded cash) from the Indian economy, and to modernize the economy by encouraging non-cash modes of transactions. The move triggered chaos in India's banking system, and caused inconvenience and hardship to hundreds of millions of ordinary people in both urban and rural India for about three months until early 2017, when liquidity was restored through the gradual introduction of fresh currency notes in 500 and 2000 denominations. But Modi eventually survived the political furore more or less unscathed, and the BJP handily won the crucial State election in Uttar Pradesh held in early 2017. The episode reinforced Modi's reputation for bold, strong leadership and his efforts to project himself both as a crusader against corruption and as India's modernization messiah. The 'demonetization' decision, as it is known in India, ran the risk of adversely impacting some of the BJP's core supporters in the cash-dependent small-scale business and shopkeeper (*bania*) occupations (predominantly in northern India) the hardest, at least in the short term. Questioned by journalists about the risk of alienating long-time supporters, Amit Shah replied that the party was intent on acquiring a much wider base of support, an implicit but unmistakable signal of its ambition of emerging as the hegemon of Indian politics. As the Modi government entered its fourth year in mid-2017, the BJP launched a nationwide expansion drive, concentrating on the States in eastern and southern India where the party is relatively weak. *Vistaarak*s (from *vistaar*, a word meaning 'spread' in Hindi) drawn from various *sangh-parivar* organizations fanned out across India in a grassroots campaign.

Without a doubt, the developmentalist face of Hindutva 2.0 is the BJP's main attraction to the broader Indian electorate today, and Modi, as the charismatic, purposeful, even driven helmsman of its program of modernization and progress is the face of that face. This is very different from the Hindutva mobilization of the first half of the 1990s fronted by L. K. Advani, when the electoral strategy was built on the contentious and inherently polarizing *Ramjanambhoomi* agitation described in Chapter 4. The shift from agitational populism to Hindutva 2.0 was presciently anticipated by the American scholar Gary Jacobsohn, writing in 2003:

> While the occasional need to mobilize the *sangh-parivar*'s political base ensures that the more extreme, visceral appeals to Hindu solidarity and privilege will not soon disappear from the rhetorical landscape of Indian politics, the basic arithmetic of electoral ascendance and governing continuity means that these appeals will be muted in favour of arguments

more acceptable to moderate sensibilities within the broader Indian electorate.[10]

The accent on the developmentalist face, personified by Prime Minister Modi, has enabled the BJP to expand its appeal much beyond the geographical and social limits of its erstwhile core base. Under the Modi premiership, the party has developed at least a critical mass of support in almost all parts of India and amongst nearly all segments and communities of society barring one, Muslims. That does not worry BJP strategists not only because they feel nationwide political hegemony is achievable without Muslim support, but, more importantly, because the continued 'othering' of Muslims is an *essential element* of the strategy of realizing that hegemony in the Modi era, in a manner fully consistent with and faithful to the ideological framework of Hindu nationalism (described in Chapter 6).

The second face of the Hindutva 2.0 Janus is not, like the first, etched with Narendra Modi's physiognomy. It is blurry in comparison, but unlike Modi's semi-stern, semi-elderly visage, its features are youngish and overtly menacing. These are the roaming bands of violent *gau-rakshak*s (cow protectors) who have emerged across north India after the Modi government's rise to power. As their activities, and atrocities, sharply escalated in 2017 after more sporadic incidents ranging from hooliganism to homicide in 2015–16, these shadowy elements have emerged as the second face of the Hindutva Janus in the era of Modi. They are the new generation of the lumpen thugs of the Vishwa Hindu Parishad or VHP (World Hindu Council, the RSS's affiliate on religious matters) and its youth wing, the Bajrang Dal, who acted as the stormtroopers of the *Ramjanambhoomi* agitation during the early 1990s.

The salvation of the cow has been a major issue in the repertoire of Hindu nationalist politics from the late colonial period onwards. The Hindu nationalist espousal of the cause of the holy cow was, and is, completely different from Gandhi's compassion for the animal. Gandhi, a self-declared 'worshipper of the cow' (note 15, Chapter 2), was resolutely against any laws in independent India banning cow slaughter (and by implication, any prohibition on eating beef). Amid the bloodbath of the 1947 partition, he declared:

> The Hindu religion prohibits cow slaughter for the Hindus, not for the world ... India is the land not only of the Hindus but also of the

---

10 Jacobsohn, *The Wheel of Law*, 189.

Mussalmans, the Sikhs, the Parsees, the Christians, and the Jews ... In India no law can be made to ban cow slaughter ... How can my religion also be the religion of the rest of the Indians? It will mean coercion against those Indians who are not Hindus (note 16, Chapter 2).

A few months before his murder by a Hindu nationalist at the age of 78, he stated: 'If they can prohibit cow slaughter in India on religious grounds, why cannot the Pakistan government prohibit, say, idol worship in Pakistan on similar grounds? ... Just as Sharia cannot be imposed on non-Muslims, the Hindu law [sic] cannot be imposed on non-Hindus' (note 53, Chapter 2).

In contrast to the Gandhian perspective, the cow has featured as a *leitmotif* of Hindu nationalist discourse and activism down the decades as a means of stoking confrontation and enmity, targeted above all at the Muslim 'other' of the ideology and its movement (Savarkar, the pioneer ideologue, was ironically a partial dissenter on this matter and was sceptical of cow-fetishism because of his atheist and rationalist beliefs; see note 58, Chapter 6). As Donald Smith noted in his 1963 study of the Indian secular state, for Hindu nationalists and the like-minded, the cow issue has served as a prime means of asserting their notion of 'Hindu dominance' over India (note 21, Chapter 3). Chapter 3 has extensively discussed how, contrary to Gandhi's explicit views, a vaguely worded and convoluted 'Directive Principle of State Policy' on cow protection – on 'scientific' not religious grounds – found its way into the 1950 Indian Constitution due to a clamour raised in the 1947–49 Constituent Assembly by some Congress conservatives and like-minded elements for a total ban on cow slaughter. That chapter has also recounted how this concession did not pacify their vociferousness and how laws banning cow slaughter were enacted by Congress governments in the northern States of Uttar Pradesh, Bihar, Madhya Pradesh and Rajasthan during the second half of the 1950s. Chapter 3 also described the steadily rising spate of gratuitous violence (including a growing number of murderous attacks) perpetrated since 2015 in the name of the cow by marauding vigilante gangs, overwhelmingly targeting Muslims, in BJP-governed States of northern and western India – Uttar Pradesh (since March 2017), Rajasthan, Haryana, Jharkhand and Gujarat.[11]

---

11 A brutal attack on a family of nomadic herders in April 2017 in the Muslim-majority State of Jammu and Kashmir – where the slaughter of cows, bulls and bullocks is banned by law – is also noted in Chapter 3.

I noted in Chapter 3 that Prime Minister Modi belatedly and tepidly decried the first fatal attack by a lynch mob on a middle-aged Muslim man in his own home in Uttar Pradesh in 2015 (he was falsely accused of storing beef in the family's fridge), but promptly and strongly deplored the public stripping and beating of a group of young Dalit men – from a poor community who skin and sell the hides of deceased cows for a living – that occurred in 2016 in his home State, Gujarat. As the attacks multiplied and escalated since then, he mostly kept conspicuously silent on the matter. The RSS, his parent-organization, has been somewhat more forthcoming. I noted in Chapter 3 that the current RSS chief, Mohan Bhagwat, called for a national law banning cow slaughter in a speech in New Delhi in March 2017, notwithstanding the fact that cow slaughter is banned under State laws in all but eight of India's 29 States (six of the eight are small States in India's north-east). The holy cow thus continues to be milked for political purposes by the Hindu nationalists. In April 2017, as noted in Chapter 4, the BJP government of Gujarat passed a law making cow slaughter punishable with a minimum of ten years and a maximum of life in prison, superseding a law passed in 2011, under Narendra Modi's chief ministership, stipulating a jail term of three to seven years.[12] A year later, the head of the Dalit household whose youths were stripped and flogged in mid-2016 said, 'Our family has given up the cow-skinning business [because] the fear of attacks by *gau-rakshaks* [cow vigilantes] remains, [and] the family now has no livelihood'.[13]

The completion of three years of the Modi government was marked by official fanfare for good reason. With the government well into the second half of its mandated term and the next general election less than two years away, the anniversary provided an obvious opportunity to showcase its narrative of progress and achievement. In India's national political cycle, the long countdown to the next parliamentary election properly kicks off two years before the due date, as parties begin strategic manoeuvres and

---

12 Modi is one of the sizeable minority of Indians (less than 30 per cent) who practice vegetarianism. According to official statistics from the 2011 national census released in 2014, 71 per cent of all Indians over the age of fifteen are non-vegetarians. The extent of the non-vegetarian majority has declined slightly since the 2001 census, when it was 75 per cent. 'Vegetarian India a Myth', *Huffington Post India*, 15 July 2016.

13 'Why do Dalits always suffer?', *Indian Express*, 30 June 2017, 1.

organizational preparations. The Modi government's three-year point came two months after the decisive BJP victory in March 2017 in the State election of Uttar Pradesh, where the party won a four-fifths majority in the legislature with slightly over 40 per cent of the polled votes in a three-way contest with two regional parties and triumphantly regained the State, the cradle of the *Ramjanambhoomi* agitation of the early 1990s which propelled the BJP's rise in national politics, after a gap of fifteen years. The win in India's most populous State, nearly 90 per cent of whose eighty parliamentary constituencies had elected BJP candidates in 2014 amid a wave of enthusiasm for Modi's prime ministerial bid and enabled the BJP to gain its single-party majority in the Lok Sabha, boosted BJP morale enormously about its prospects in the 2019 national election. It was important to reinforce the momentum generated by the Uttar Pradesh success as the countdown to 2019 began, hence the elaborate celebrations of the third anniversary by both the party and the government.

It is likely, however, that the third anniversary of the Modi government will be chiefly remembered neither for the drumbeating nationwide 'Modifest' organized by the BJP, nor even for the opening of India's longest bridge in Assam which Modi inaugurated on the day, 26 May, that he had taken office in 2014.

On 23 May 2017, three days short of the anniversary, the Modi government's environment ministry issued an ordinance – technically a 'notification' – called the Prevention of Cruelty to Animals (Regulation of Livestock Markets) Rules, 2017. The order banned the sale of cattle for the purpose of slaughter in cattle markets throughout India, with 'cattle' defined as inclusive of cows, calves, buffaloes, bulls, bullocks, steers, heifers and camels. The Environment Minister claimed three weeks later, amid a nationwide uproar, '[T]he intention behind the rules is not to alter the food habits of people in any way or to cause any loss to any business or industry'. However, the order was viewed by its supporters and opponents alike as motivated by the ideological agenda of the RSS-led *sangh parivar*. It came two months after the new BJP government in Uttar Pradesh headed by the priest-politician Yogi Adityanath launched a crackdown on supposedly 'illegal' abattoirs in the State, where abattoirs are mostly owned by Muslims, who comprise a fifth of the State's population. The cattle markets across India, 'according to livestock industry insiders', account for 'over 90 per cent of cattle sold' in the country and the order required all sellers to provide a signed declaration that the cattle have 'not been brought to market for sale for slaughter'. This meant that the farmers and other livestock owners – who are largely Hindus, consistent with the overall demography of the country – could no longer dispose of their aged or diseased cattle in these markets. They would either have to abandon these animals useless for draught or milch purposes, or maintain them at considerable expense until their demise. So the order was 'expected to choke the primary supply channel' to India's booming trades in exports of bovine meat (mainly of buffaloes, not cows) and leather products.[14]

This was precisely what happened. A month after the ban was notified, it was reported that a crisis had gripped the leather industry of the eastern State of West Bengal, which employs about a million workers – mostly Muslims but also many 'low-caste' Hindus – in hundreds of medium-scale and thousands of 'micro' (home-based) units making leather products such as footwear, handbags, belts, wallets and purses both for the huge Indian market and for export (the State, where 27 per cent of the population of nearly a hundred million is Muslim, accounts for a quarter of Indian exports of leather items). The immediate problem in the hundreds of tanneries in and around Kolkata, the State capital, was that the supply of the essential raw material (bovine hides) from the major source, the northern State of Uttar Pradesh, had almost ceased. Large-scale layoffs of workers resulted, coupled with pay cuts for those retained. Meanwhile, representatives of the leather industry from the city of Kanpur in western Uttar Pradesh approached the West Bengal government – which is run by a secularist regional party, the Trinamool ('Grassroots') Congress – with a request to be allotted land near Kolkata so they could relocate their hide-curing and manufacturing facilities. Agra, the city in western Uttar Pradesh famous for the Taj Mahal, has a shoemaking industry which provides livelihoods to Muslim and Dalit workers in 150 medium-scale and 10,000 micro units. 'The notification is fatal for our industry', said the (Hindu) president of the city's association of leather manufacturers and exporters, himself the owner of a local footwear factory. In the large western State of Maharashtra, India's second most populous, a BJP-led government tightened cattle laws in 2015

---

14 'Open to Cattle Norms Feedback' and 'Unanimous Beef Message from Meghalaya', *The Telegraph*, 13 June 2017, 7.

after coming to power in State elections in late 2014, extending the slaughter ban to aged and infirm bulls and making possession, transport or sale of any form of bovine meat punishable with five years in prison. The 2017 'cattle market rules ... [spelled] a death-knell for the $4bn. meat export industry [mostly Muslim-owned, and centred in Mumbai, the State capital] that accounts for a fifth of the global output'. Kolhapur, a Maharashtrian city of nearly a million people, is famous for its eponymous (Kolhapuri) *chappals*, handcrafted designer shoes and slippers popular across India. Mass layoffs of the specialist artisans, mostly Hindus, began in 2015 as the in-State supply of hides plummeted and the industry could not cope with the higher costs of sourcing the raw material from the southern States of Karnataka and Tamil Nadu. The industry's turnover in 2016–17 was less than half the turnover in 2014–15. After the nationwide cattle-market rules were notified in May 2017, the (Hindu) president of the city's shoemakers' association said, 'I don't know what we will do'.[15]

The Hindu nationalist government's cattle-market directive elicited strong criticism. Pinarayi Vijayan, the Communist Party of India-Marxist (CPI-M) Chief Minister of the southern State of Kerala, wrote a strongly worded letter of protest to Prime Minister Modi, and the Kerala legislature passed a cross-party resolution condemning the move. Almost half of the population of Kerala – a mid-sized State by Indian standards – consists of Muslims and Christians (27 per cent and 18 per cent, respectively) who have no beef taboos, and the slaughter of all types of cattle, including cows, is legal in the State. Fried beef is one of the most popular offerings on the menus of restaurants across Kerala, and heartily savoured not only by Muslims and Christians but numerous Hindu citizens as well. The high demand cannot be met by in-State supplies and buffaloes – the main source of the meat – are imported not only from the southern States of Andhra Pradesh and Tamil Nadu but from as far afield as the northern State of Bihar. Mamata Banerjee, the Trinamool Congress Chief Minister of West Bengal, India's fourth most

---

15 Suchetana Ray and Dhrubo Jyoti, 'Hung Out to Dry: India's Leather and Meat Industries in Deep Shock', *Hindustan Times* (internet edition), 25 June 2017. According to the Government of India's commerce ministry, the value of Indian buffalo-meat exports in 2016–17 was 26,303 crores, a modest decline from the peak of 29,289 crores earned in 2014–15.

populous State where the slaughter of all types of cattle including cows is also legal, similarly criticized the move as an unacceptable violation of State autonomy and therefore of India's constitutional structure. The legislature of the small north-eastern State of Meghalaya, whose population is three-fourths Christian and where the slaughter of all types of cattle is also legal, met in a specially convened session and passed an unanimous resolution which noted that the order 'travels way beyond the scope and object[ives] set out in the preamble of the Prevention of Cruelty to Animals Act, 1960', passed in that year by India's parliament. The all-party resolution further stated – 'This House takes strong note of the shortcomings and infirmities in these Rules, and resolves that the same may be withdrawn by the Government of India with immediate effect so as to maintain the federal and secular character of our [India's] Constitution'. The resolution observed that the Modi government's order negatively 'impact[s] [both] the economy of the State and the food habits of its people' because beef is a staple of the diet in Meghalaya and 570,000 households in the State rear livestock. The Chief Minister of Meghalaya asserted that, even then, just over half of the State's beef consumption in 2015–16 (12,834 of 23,634 tonnes) had been met in-State and the rest through imports from other States.[16]

The contention of the State governments of West Bengal, Kerala and Meghalaya that the Modi government's cattle-market order contravenes Indian Constitution is well-founded. As one commentary jointly written by a political scientist and a legal scholar noted:

> The Government of India notified the Prevention of Cruelty to Animals (Regulation of Livestock Markets) Rules, enacted under Sections 38(1) and 38(2) of the Prevention of Cruelty to Animals Act, 1960. The [1960] Act intended to prevent the infliction of unnecessary pain or suffering on animals, whereas the notified Rules in substance do not come under the purview of the Act and hence are ultra-vires. Assuming for a moment that the Rules are intra-vires, the [required] approval of both Houses of Parliament as mandated by Section 38A of the Act is not complied with. There is no specific rule-making power regulating animal markets vested in the Central Government. The regulation of cattle markets and fairs are State subjects and lie within the State domain (Entry 28, List II) …

---

16 'Unanimous Beef Message from Meghalaya'.

The Central Government has sought to restrict the fundamental right to business and trade, which it can only do through a law.[17]

This is not merely a matter of constitutional jurisdictions narrowly construed, but a very significant political issue in the broader sense. The unilateral *diktat* promulgated from New Delhi in mid-2017 is completely incongruous with one of the main *mantra*s of the Modi government since it took office in mid-2014: 'cooperative federalism'. This dictum, repeatedly asserted by senior ministers and BJP leaders to be a cornerstone of the Modi government's approach to governing India, seemingly represented a radical departure from the unitary nation/centralized state paradigm of Hindu nationalist doctrine. But in fact, as I will explain later in this chapter, there is no real puzzle here because the cooperative-federalism slogan simply represented a clever strategic adjustment to India's diverse political landscape in the early twenty-first century, and not any revision of ideological fundamentals. In July 2017, responding to a clutch of petitions, India's Supreme Court stayed (temporarily suspended) the implementation of the cattle-market order. The Modi government's counsel told the hearing that in any case '[the] notification would not take effect immediately as it was the job of the states to identify and [then] notify the markets envisaged by the central notification'.[18]

In addition to the political opposition led by the State Chief Ministers, a section of civil society objected vigorously to the cattle-market regulations. A popular way of protesting was to organize public beef-eating parties. A week after the order was notified, one such 'beef festival' was organized by some students at the Indian Institute of Technology in Chennai (formerly Madras, and the capital of Tamil Nadu), one of a chain of premier universities located in different Indian cities established under the auspices of the Union government after India's independence. The student organizers were members of a campus group called the Ambedkar-Periyar Study Circle, named after B. R. Ambedkar, the Dalit leader and an architect of the Indian Constitution, and E. V. Ramasamy Naicker (1879–1973), the founder of the Dravidian

---

17 Afroz Alam and Yogesh Pratap Singh, 'Making India a Cow Republic', *The Statesman*, 22 June 2017, 16.

18 'SC extends Madras HC Stay on Cattle Trade Rules to Entire Country', *Indian Express*, 12 July 2017, 1.

movement whose offshoot parties have dominated Tamil Nadu politics since the late 1960s (he is known by the honorific *Periyar*, which means 'Elder'). The Ambedkar and Periyar philosophies share a strong aversion to Brahminical Hinduism and its strictures. A day or two after the beef festival, a small mob of other students led by a student from Bihar accosted one of those who had attended, a 36-year-old PhD student from Kerala, in a campus cafeteria and severely assaulted him; he required hospitalization from the beating and suffered a serious injury to his right eye. Two weeks after this incident, and by coincidence on the same day that the Meghalaya legislature passed its all-party resolution, a 200-strong mob on a national highway in the northern, BJP-ruled State of Rajasthan waylaid a group of officers of the Tamil Nadu government who were transporting fifty cows and thirty calves in a convoy of five trucks. The attackers damaged the trucks, tried to set one on fire, and assaulted the drivers, officers and an accompanying veterinarian. The officers, employees of the Tamil Nadu government's animal husbandry department, had purchased the cattle for breeding in their own State under India's National Agricultural Development Programme (NADP). They had come to India's north-western corner from the deep south to purchase the local variety of cattle (*Tharparkar*, named after Rajasthan's Thar desert) because the elite breed, reared locally in semi-arid conditions, yields especially rich milk and its physical strength and stamina make it a prized draught animal.[19]

In late June 2017, exactly a month after the cattle-rules notification touched off a furore, a 15-year-old boy called Junaid Khan was travelling in a train from Delhi to his village in the adjoining State of Haryana. He was returning home in the early evening after a day-shopping trip to Delhi's old town and was accompanied by two older brothers and a neighbour, all in their late teens or early twenties. They had gone to Delhi to shop for new clothes, foodstuffs and sweets in preparation for the approaching celebration of *Eid-ul-Fitr*, due a few days later at the end of the Ramzan fasting month. Their relatively short journey back home turned into a harrowing ordeal for all four, and fatal for Junaid. About a dozen men, who boarded the train and entered the compartment where the youths were seated, at some point(s) after the train

---

19 'Bovine Bullies Cross All Limits', *The Telegraph*, 13 June 2017, 7; 'Mob in Barmer Assaults TN Officials Transporting Cattle, Tries to Torch Truck', *Indian Express*, 13 June 2017, 1.

left Delhi, apparently first picked a quarrel with them over seating. Shaqir, one of Junaid's older brothers, recalled the chain of events the following day from his hospital bed in emergency care in Delhi, where he had been brought with five stab wounds, 'They flung our skull caps, pulled my brother's beard, slapped us and taunted us about eating cow meat. Beef is not cooked in our village'. The Muslim youths told their assailants that they were not carrying any form of beef in their shopping bags and packets. According to Shaqir, 'They noticed we are Muslims because of our clothing and began taunting us. It would go on for a bit, stop, then start again'. The four tried to get off the train and escape a few times when it stopped at stations but were prevented from doing so by their assailants. 'Once we reached Ballabhgarh [station]', the seriously injured Shaqir recalled, 'they took out knives. They were older than us, probably in their thirties, so we couldn't do anything'. The incident ended at the next station after Ballabhgarh, where Junaid bled to death on the platform while his other brother Hashim – who was also stabbed but suffered relatively light injuries – cradled him. The fourth youth, their neighbour, was the only one to escape being stabbed. The train compartment was found to be splattered with blood.[20]

Haryana has been a BJP-ruled State since late 2014, when the party won a majority (47 of 90 seats) in its legislature for the first time, benefiting from the unpopularity of the State's outgoing Congress government and the promise of development and progress personified by Modi, who had become India's Prime Minister four months earlier. Prior to that the BJP had been a marginal party in Haryana politics, winning six, two and four seats respectively in the 90-member State legislature in the elections of 2000, 2005 and 2009 (the Congress finished third in late 2014, behind a regional Haryana-based party). Haryana is a small State by Indian standards with a population of 28 million, of whom 7 per cent are Muslims (half the nationwide average). Almost half of Haryana's Muslim population is concentrated in the Nuh district located in the State's far south bordering Rajasthan; this district's population of 1.1 million is 80 per cent Muslim. This Muslim-majority district is part of a historical

---

20 'Boy Lynched on Train, Brother Says Were Called Beef-Eaters', *Indian Express*, 24 June 2017, 1; 'How Could They Hate Us So Much', *Hindustan Times* (internet edition), 27 June 2017; 'His Dying Image Will Haunt Me Forever: Brother of Muslim Boy Lynched on Train', *Hindustan Times* (internet edition), 27 June 2017.

region called Mewat which straddles the present Haryana-Rajasthan border, and is populated by a distinctive Muslim community called Meos. The Meos are survivors of the 1947 partition, when (then) eastern Punjab was almost emptied of its Muslim population, and western Punjab of its Hindus and Sikhs, by mass killings and expulsions. The Meos participated in the 1857 uprising against British rule and some 6,000 of the community died in battle or were executed after capture. Some Meos also joined the Indian National Army under Subhas Chandra Bose's leadership in south-east Asia during World War II. Despite the carnage of 1947, a large part of the community chose to stay on in their ancestral land rather than go to Pakistan; in late 1947 Gandhi visited the area to give them confidence to stay. The persistence of this Muslim enclave in an area close to Delhi has been a source of angst to Hindu nationalists ever since.[21] Pehlu Khan, the middle-aged dairy farmer who was murdered in a lynch-mob attack by cow vigilantes in Rajasthan in April 2017 (see Chapter 3), was a Meo from this part of Haryana. The train victim Junaid Khan – a fresh-faced teenager who was studying to become a theologian – was from a Muslim village just north of the core Meo zone.

Since late 2014, Haryana has been a laboratory for the kind of state the RSS would like to establish in India as a whole. The State's Chief Minister, Manohar Lal Khattar, is an RSS veteran in his sixties whose family origins are in western (Pakistani) Punjab. He joined the RSS in 1977 and served as a fulltime *pracharak* (preacher-activist) from 1980 to 1994 before being seconded to work in the BJP – a career trajectory very similar to Narendra Modi. From 2000 to 2014, he was the BJP's general secretary (organization) in Haryana, i.e., the designated RSS representative in the BJP apparatus in the State. In late 2014, he became Haryana's Chief Minister at the behest of RSS headquarters in Nagpur, which caused some disaffection among Jats, the caste group that has dominated the State's politics since Haryana was carved out in 1966 from the eastern part of Indian Punjab, whose western part became a Sikh-majority State of the Indian Union (Khattar is a Punjabi Khatri, not a Jat). Khattar's ministry and various official bodies in the State are literally packed with RSS men. A top priority of Haryana's BJP government has been a lavishly funded *Gau Seva Aayog* (Cow Care Commission). In 2015, the State

---

21 'What You Should Know about the Meo Muslims of Mewat', *Hindustan Times* (internet edition), 16 September 2016.

legislature passed a law that made cow slaughter, which is banned, punishable with a ten-year prison sentence. In 2016, the trade in *biriyani* (rice cooked with mutton) which is the livelihood of many Haryana Muslims, especially Meos, was badly disrupted by a campaign of vigilante and police harassment. In August 2016, two young Meo women were gang-raped by cow vigilantes; 'one of the rape survivors claimed that the attackers told her they were being punished for eating beef'.[22]

The attention to the cow is of course not unique to Haryana. In Jharkhand, another BJP-governed State on the eastern edge of north India which was carved out of Bihar's southern districts in 2000, the State government is vigorously pursuing a programme to tag each of the State's 4.2 million heads of cattle, especially the three million cows, with unique identification (UID) numbers under a scheme funded by the Modi government in New Delhi. Each head of cattle is to be 'tagged with a 12-digit UID' fixed on its left ear, which 'records age, breed, sex, lactation, height, body colour, horn type, tail switch, [and] special mark [if any]'. The programme, which is intended 'to prevent illegal transportation of cattle, improve their milk yield and monitor their health', had tagged 12,000 cows in a pilot project completed in April 2017. The full details of every bovine thus tagged are accessible by entering its 12-digit UID on a smartphone application.[23]

For 72 hours after Junaid's murder, which made headline news nationally, nothing whatsoever was heard from Haryana's State government about the incident. Chief Minister Khattar, who like Prime Minister Modi is an avid tweeter, was as usual prolifically active on Twitter during that time. Two days after the murder, for example, 'a Twitter user posted pictures of a road that had sunk in. Khattar responded by tweeting "the needful is being done" along with a picture of a heap of mud on the road. The man replied: 'Feeling proud @mlkhattar Sir! Best demonstration of listening to common citizen.

---

22 'Haryana, Hindutva Hotbed: Saffron Agenda Deepens Communal Fault-Lines', *Hindustan Times*, 9 November 2016, 7. See also 'Haryana, Hindutva Hotbed: RSS Imprint on Khattar Government Runs Deep', *Hindustan Times*, 7 November 2016, 9; 'Haryana, Hindutva Hotbed: State Largesse Provides for BJP Government's Holy Cows', *Hindustan Times*, 8 November 2016, 7; and 'Haryana, Hindutva Hotbed: Two Years on, Identity Politics Drives the State', *Hindustan Times*, 9 November 2016, 7.
23 '12,000 Cows in BJP's Jharkhand Get Aadhaar-like ID with Details of Horn, Tail', *Hindustan Times* (internet edition), 29 April 2017.

'Thank you.' Pat came Khattar's reply: 'Thank you for your kind words. It is our Government's endeavour to be accountable to the people & public welfare of the State'.[24] No representative of the State government nor any leader of the State's ruling party, the BJP, said anything about the incident. Two days after the above Twitter exchange, Khattar said he 'condemn[s]' the incident after being asked by journalists for his views. No representative of the State government visited Junaid's family as his parents Saira and Jalaluddin Khan grieved; the plight of his seriously injured older brother, who remained under treatment in Delhi, was similarly ignored (law and order, and public health, are both the responsibility of State governments in India). Meanwhile, a pall of fear gripped the dead boy's village. Rafeeq Ahmed, a resident, said that when his 'children go to the market or to college, I fear if they will return. What if someone kills them?' Another resident, Mohammad Azharuddin, who works in Delhi, explained, 'When I leave home, I wear shirt-pant and not kurta-pyjama, because that way no one can tell I am Muslim'. Yasin, a boy of twelve, added: 'We wanted to watch a movie [for Eid] but mummy-papa told us not to go anywhere'.[25]

Three days after Junaid Khan's murder, Prime Minister Modi broadcast his monthly radio homily in Hindi to the nation, *Mann ki Baat* (Thoughts on my Mind). He covered a wide range of subjects as usual, including his government's e-governance initiatives, and its efforts under the *Swachh Bharat* (Clean India) programme to create an open-defecation-free (ODF) country. On the latter point, he commended the decision of the residents of a Muslim village in western Uttar Pradesh to build toilets at their own expense. There was no mention, even obliquely, of the brutal death of a child-citizen of the country on a train. However he did recall, and at some length, the imposition of the 21-month 'Emergency' dictatorship on the country by Indira Gandhi's government 42 years earlier, at midnight on 25–26 June 1975. Remembering that 'dark night', he intoned that 'eternal vigilance is the price of liberty' and told listeners that 'one needs to be constantly alert about our democracy'.[26] On the day (26 June) that the folk of Junaid's village attended subdued Eid prayers

---

24 'On Khattar Timeline, No Word on Lynching', *Indian Express*, 26 June 2017, 5.

25 'On Eid, Fear Grips Junaid's Village', *Indian Express*, 27 June 2017, 1.

26 'On Emergency Anniversary, PM Calls for Eternal Vigilance', *Indian Express*, 26 June 2017, 1.

wearing black armbands, Modi was in Washington, DC on an official visit to the United States, where he spent four hours discussing Indo-American relations at the White House with President Donald J. Trump. Three days later, on 29 June, he said while visiting a famous *ashram* established by Gandhi in Gujarat on the occasion of its centennial celebration, 'Killing people in the name of *gau bhakti* [cow devotion] is not acceptable. This is not something Mahatma Gandhi would approve [of]'.

The expression of disapproval came a day after thousands of concerned citizens took to the streets in a dozen Indian cities to protest the spate of hate crime under the slogan 'Not in My Name!' Junaid's father Jalaluddin Khan welcomed the Prime Minister's statement 'a week after my son was mercilessly killed' but regretted that 'neither did Modiji name Junaid in his speech nor did he speak about ensuring punishment for the killers'. On the same day that Modi invoked Gandhi in Gujarat, Alimuddin Ansari a.k.a. Asgar Ali, a meat-trader aged 45, was ambushed by several dozen men in a market in a Jharkhand town. His van was set on fire and he was pulled out and beaten to death. It was not immediately clear what kind of meat he had been transporting in his van. It was noted that 'under the Jharkhand Bovine Animal Prohibition of Slaughter Act [2005], slaughter of cows and sale and consumption of beef are banned [in the State]. Violations can attract a maximum jail term of two years – not lynching'. Police investigations identified the suspects as members of the local unit of the Bajrang Dal and the *Gau Raksha Samiti* (Cow Protection Society), both affiliates of the Vishwa Hindu Parishad or World Hindu Council (VHP), a constituent of the RSS-led *sangh-parivar*. The suspects were apparently known to the victim and had been extorting money from him. This lynching happened two days after the house of Usman Ansari, 60, a dairy farmer and grocer in a different part of Jharkhand, was attacked by a thousand-strong mob after the carcass of one of his cows was spotted outside the house. The cow, which had been sick, had died of natural causes, but before the carcass could be disposed of some person(s) slit its throat during the night to make it look like a case of slaughter. The mob set Usman's small house and adjoining cow shed aflame and tried to throw him into the raging fire. He survived due to prompt intervention by the local police but suffered a fractured skull and a broken leg among other injuries. Usman's son, Kalim, stated that a sixth of the village's 250 households are Muslim and that 'it has always been peaceful', with the Hindu villagers the main customers of the family's milk and grocery trades.[27]

When the amiable Atal Behari Vajpayee served as India's first Hindu nationalist Prime Minister from 1998 to 2004, opponents of his government often referred to him as the *mukhota* ('mask' in Hindi) for the insidious political agenda of the *sangh-parivar* headed by the RSS. The Modi premiership is different, in that Hindutva 2.0 has no mask as such but two faces like Janus. During an official visit in April 2017 to India by Sheikh Hasina Wazed, the Prime Minister of Bangladesh, one face was on display in New Delhi, where Modi received her in statesmanlike fashion and emphasized cordial relations with the predominantly Muslim neighbouring nation. The other face was on display 900 miles south-east of Delhi in Kolkata, the capital of West Bengal, a State born through the partition of Bengal in 1947, when 63 per cent of Bengal's territory became the eastern wing of Pakistan and the remainder an unit of the Indian Union as West Bengal. As the Bangladeshi premier visited Delhi, the BJP and its affiliates in West Bengal were engaged in a week-long programme of raucous public celebrations of Ramnavami, the birthday of Lord Ram. This was in itself unusual because Ramnavami is a north Indian festival which has very little resonance in West Bengal, except to some State residents who are of north Indian origin. The celebrations took the form of hundreds of processions across the State of men and boys brandishing swords amid shrieks of *Jai Shri Ram!* (Victory to Ram), the slogan of the Ayodhya mobilization of

---

27  'Killing in Name of Cow Unacceptable, Not Something Mahatma Would Approve: Modi', *Indian Express*, 30 June 2017, 1; '15 Policemen Stave off 1,000-Strong Mob to Rescue Dairy Farmer Whose Cow Died', *Indian Express*, 29 June 2017, 1; 'They Killed Again, in Modi's India', *The Telegraph*, 30 June 2017, 1; 'A Father Asks: Can PM Stop the Killings?', *The Telegraph*, 30 June 2017, 4; 'Beef? Afraid to Eat Chicken, Says Mob Victim's Son', *The Telegraph*, 30 June 2017, 4; 'Jharkhand Lynching Probe Looks at Gau-Rakshaks, Bajrang Dal', *Indian Express*, 1 July 2017, 1. The lethal attacks by fringe groups on Muslim citizens escalated immediately after Modi's government took office in May 2014. A week after Modi became Prime Minister, a gang calling itself the Hindu Rashtra Sena beat a young man, Mohsin Shaikh, to death with hockey sticks and cement slabs in a suburb of the city of Pune in Maharashtra. He was returning home from evening prayers and was wearing a skullcap when he was attacked. Two other young Muslim men were injured the same evening as the gang prowled on motorbikes looking for targets. The lynching spree is reminiscent of the situation faced by African-Americans in the American South until fifty years ago. 'Three Years after Murder, Most Accused on Bail, Family Has No Lawyer', *Indian Express*, 30 June 2017, 12.

the early 1990s. West Bengal, which has 42 parliamentary constituencies – the third highest of India's 29 States after Uttar Pradesh (80) and Maharashtra (48) and whose population is 27 per cent Muslim – is the top-priority State for the BJP's nationwide expansion plan. In many towns, and the city of Kolkata, the sword-waving processions tried to come close to or even enter predominantly Muslim neighbourhoods, and scuffled with police when stopped from doing so by barricades. When prominent public personalities of the State criticized the nature of the celebrations in local media, the BJP's West Bengal president, formerly a fulltime RSS activist, threatened to send them with a kick (*laath* in colloquial, semi-obscene Bengali) across the border into Bangladesh.[28]

◆

The Turkish secular state, as established by Mustafa Kemal Ataturk, is dead. It has been replaced in all but name by a state based on an overtly religious, Sunni-Hanefi majoritarian conception of Turkish national identity. That state revolves around the person of Recep Tayyip Erdogan, Prime Minister from 2003 to 2014 and President since then, and Turkey's competitive politics has been increasingly reduced in the course of this decade to plebiscites on Erdogan's sultan-like authority, in which he has prevailed thus far. After his AKP won parliamentary majorities in three consecutive national elections in 2002, 2007 and 2011 – with almost half of the nationwide votes in the latter two cases – Erdogan was elected Turkey's President in the first-ever popular election to that post in 2014, gaining a simple majority of 52 per cent of the nationwide votes in the first round. The AKP stumbled in the mid-2015 parliamentary election, as recounted in Chapter 1 and elsewhere in this book, when it fell short of a parliamentary majority, but it was still by a wide margin the single largest party with 41 per cent of the nationwide votes. In the snap election of late 2015, the AKP regained its parliamentary majority with 49 per cent of the nationwide votes and was firmly back in the saddle. Then, after the failed coup attempt by a small section of the military against the AKP regime

---

28 '*Laath Marar Humki Dilip-er*', *Anandabazar Patrika* (Kolkata), 9 April 2017, 1. My mother Krishna Bose, a writer, retired professor and former three-time Member of Parliament (Lok Sabha) elected from West Bengal, was one of those who spoke out against the nature of the celebrations.

in July 2016, President Erdogan initiated a national referendum on dispensing with Turkey's weak parliamentary system in all but name and replacing it with a presidency invested with virtually unlimited powers. He narrowly prevailed in that referendum as well, with 51.4 per cent of the polled votes in an 85 per cent turnout. It is imponderable whether he will succeed yet again in winning the now constitutionally – not just informally – all-powerful presidency in an election scheduled for late 2019, and if he does, whether he will win a second possible term in 2024 and continue as Turkey's latter-day sultan until 2029. But regardless of that uncertain future, the Kemalist secular state is not going to revive. Turkey has undergone an anti-secular social and political transformation in the twenty-first century, which was in the making since the 1950s (see Chapter 5), but has been realized over the past fifteen years under AKP rule. Why the anti-secularists won so decisively is illustrated by the story of a woman called Merve Kavakci.

Merve Kavakci was born in the late 1960s in Istanbul to religiously devout and academically inclined parents, Gulhan and Yusuf Ziya Kavakci. When she was a child, the family moved across the country to Erzurum, a city in eastern Anatolia with a strong tradition of the Sunni-majoritarian brand of Turkish nationalism. At the provincial university there, her mother taught German and her father taught Islamic theology and law. That sojourn ended in the early 1980s when the Turkish military junta, which seized power through a coup in September 1980, launched a crackdown on headscarf-wearing women – students and teachers alike – in the nation's universities. Merve's pious mother lost her job and the family returned to Istanbul. In the second half of the 1980s, Merve was admitted to medical school but 'she arrived in a headscarf on the first day of class and [university] administrators turned her away'. Towards the end of that decade, her father was offered the position of *imam* of the Muslim community in a suburb of Dallas, Texas and the family moved to the United States. Merve's younger sister, Ravza, was 'the first student in a headscarf at [the] Lloyd V. Berkner High School' there. After her family's experiences in secular Turkey, Ravza

> was pleasantly surprised by American tolerance … She would try to leave school soon after classes to reach home for afternoon prayers. [One day] the school principal inquired about her haste; she explained. He [then] offered her a corner of his office [to pray]. 'I would pray [from then on]

in Mr Clark's office! [Ravza recalled almost three decades later]. We were filled with immense gratitude to America'.

The American idyll was beneficial for Merve as well; she graduated from the University of Texas, Dallas, majoring in computer science.

In 1999, aged 31, Merve Kavakci was elected to the Turkish Grand National Assembly. She had stood on the Istanbul list of the *Fazilet Partisi* (Virtue Party, FP), the renamed successor of the Islamist *Refah Partisi* (RP), which was the nation's single most popular party when it was closed down on charges of anti-secular politics by Turkey's constitutional court in early 1998, six months after a coalition government led by the RP was forced out of office by the military-led 'soft coup' of 1997 described in Chapters 1 and 5. During a period of severe repression designed to destroy the Islamist political alternative which had risen during the 1990s, the FP did reasonably well in the mid-term national election of April 1999, coming third in a fractured electorate with 15.4 per cent of the nationwide votes and securing a fifth (111 of 550) of the parliamentary seats. Kavakci was one of these 111 parliamentarians. During the fortnight between the election and the oath-taking ceremony of the members of the newly elected parliament, a media-fuelled hysteria gripped the country at the prospect of a headscarfed woman – Kavakci – sitting in the Grand National Assembly, unheard of in the 75 years of the Kemalist Republic, where the rare woman politician's conventional attire was the Western-style dress suit. 'The army had secretly warned President Suleyman Demirel that it might intervene if Kavakci took oath wearing a headscarf', and 'her own party's leaders advised her against it as they feared a coup'.

The parliamentarians were called to take their oaths in alphabetical order of their last names, so Kavakci's turn came about half-way through the process. As she entered the chamber wearing a navy-blue headscarf, almost all of the 136 parliamentarians (overwhelmingly men) belonging to the single largest party – the Democratic Left Party or DSP led by the veteran politician Bulent Ecevit, which had won 22.1 per cent of the nationwide votes – rose from their seats and began thumping their desks in unison. A spectacle unfolded over the next 45 minutes as they bayed: *De Sheera! De Sheera!* (Get Out!). Ecevit, the Prime Minister of the newly constituted post-poll coalition government, was apoplectic with rage and shouted: 'Put this woman in her place!' Amid

323

the chaos, Kavakci was hustled out of the parliament building. 'Go to Iran!', newspaper headlines screamed, and President Demirel publicly labelled her an 'agent provocateur'. The chief public prosecutor started a case against her under Article 312 of the Turkish Penal Code, which deals with incitement to religious or racial hatred. At the time of these events in 1999, Tayyip Erdogan was spending a few months in prison after being found guilty of such incitement (for publicly reciting a poem by the Turkish nationalist ideologue Ziya Gokalp, as recounted elsewhere in this book), and was banned from politics for five years after being forced to step down as mayor of Istanbul. A fortnight after she was ejected from parliament by the howling secularist mob, Kavakci was stripped of her Turkish citizenship, on the grounds that she had failed to duly inform the authorities that she had acquired a second, American citizenship. A few months later, she left Turkey for the United States. There, she earned a master's degree at Harvard University and then a PhD at Howard University, a predominantly African-American institution located in Washington, DC, after which she held teaching jobs at several east-coast universities. The FP was closed down in mid-2001 by a constitutional court decision on charges of anti-secular politics.

Nearly sixteen years later, in 2015, Kavakci returned to a transformed Turkey. The transformation had begun in November 2002, when it was the turn of Ecevit's DSP to be ejected from parliament – not by mob action but through the democratic process. In yet another mid-term election held in the tumultuous aftermath of the 2001 economic collapse, described in Chapter 1, and amid a growing popular backlash against the state-secularist establishment comprising the military hierarchy, the upper bureaucracy, the high judiciary and the political elite, the DSP's vote share slumped from 22.1 per cent in 1999 to 1.2 per cent in late 2002 and it faded into extinction thereafter. Meanwhile the AKP, the main successor party to the RP forcibly dissolved in 1998, won a decisive parliamentary majority with a 34.3 per cent plurality of the nationwide votes in circumstances detailed in Chapter 1 and elsewhere in this book, Erdogan was rehabilitated, and the AKP/Erdogan era began.

When Merve returned to her country in 2015, the AKP was entrenched as the country's hegemonic political force and President Erdogan was ensconced in a vast, newly built presidential mansion in Ankara. Merve was hired as a faculty member in post-colonial studies at a small private university in

Istanbul. One day, she and her younger sister Ravza – who had also earned a doctorate from Howard University, in political science – informally met the President. Erdogan suggested that Ravza run for parliament in the imminent June 2015 election. She was duly put on the AKP's list for Istanbul and was elected. A fortnight after the election, 'on 23 June 2015, Ravza Kavakci entered parliament in a long blue coat'. Matching the coat, she wore the navy-blue headscarf Merve had worn sixteen years earlier, on 2 May 1999, and took her oath along with twenty other headscarf-wearing parliamentarians. Eighteen of these twenty one women – of a total of 96 women elected to parliament in June 2015 – were AKP deputies and the other three from the mainly Kurdish People's Democratic Party (HDP). Ravza was re-elected to parliament in the snap election of November 2015. She notes with pride that in parliament and outside, people constantly refer to her as 'Merve's sister'.[29]

The perennial problem with Turkish secularism has been its symbiosis with authoritarianism. Steeped in the statist authoritarianism that is the defining trait of Kemalism, Turkish secularism was bereft of a democratic language in which to contest the rise of the anti-secular alternative. The recourse to crude tactics of repression in what was in retrospect the last years of Kemalist Turkey in the late 1990s and early 2000s was simply counter-productive. It allowed the anti-secularists to appropriate the righteous mantle of a just struggle against tyranny. That is still the unresolved problem of the beleaguered Turkish secularist opposition to the Erdogan regime. In mid-2016, the Turkish journalist and author Mustafa Akyol was interviewed in the *Times of India*, a daily newspaper, and asked sympathetically about the 'liberal backlash' to Turkey's ruling 'Islamic conservative party'. He patiently explained, 'There is not a liberal but a secular backlash in Turkey – and it's not liberal at all. [We have] Erdogan's conservative authoritarian politics aimed at social engineering of Turkey towards a more Islamized society, [and] we have fundamentalist secularists ... I oppose both. Let there be freedom for

---

29 The quotes in this and the preceding paragraphs are from Basharat Peer, 'Battle for the Headscarf: One Woman's Defiance of Turkey's Secularist Dress Code', *Open*, 10 April 2017, 16–20. See also 'Turkish Female Deputies Take Oaths for the First Time Wearing Headscarves', *Middle East Eye*, 24 June 2015. In August 2015, Aysen Gurcan, Minister of Family and Social Policy, became the first headscarfed cabinet minister in the Turkish Republic's political history, serving briefly in an interim government before the November 2015 snap election. Her two successors since then in that post are also headscarfed women.

everyone: both for those who want to wear the headscarf and those who don't'.[30] Of the competing alternatives, the anti-secular one has consistently demonstrated much greater popular support in the twenty-first century – the AKP got twice as many votes as the Kemalist-secularist opposition party, the CHP, in the most recent parliamentary election of November 2015.

During the last two decades of Kemalist Turkey, the military-led secularist establishment alternated between appeasement of the Islamist forces and tendencies, for example, through the 'Turkish-Islamic Synthesis' promoted as the *de facto* state ideology in the 1980s, and crude repression. This was a combination fatal for the cause of secularism in Turkey. The ultimately decisive victory post-2013 of the anti-secularists in the long, bitter war of attrition over the headscarf, described in Chapters 1 and 5 – the most powerful symbolic terrain of the secularist/anti-secularist conflict – confirmed the end of the Kemalist secular state. It was a self-inflicted but inevitable debacle, because Turkish secularism could not free itself from its authoritarian framework and re-invent itself as a democratic project. In India, the secularist ethic – not the same as the really existing secular state, which has anomalies, contradictions and paradoxes – seeks to express a spirit of tolerance and diversity that is both a political imperative in a multi-religious society and in keeping with an important aspect of India's historically-evolved societal traditions. In Turkey, secularism has both been coterminous with a deeply authoritarian state and a byword for intolerance and imposed homogeneity. The latter characteristic makes Turkish secularism a mirror-image and kindred spirit of India's Hindu nationalist movement, as Chapter 6 argued.

The authoritarian disease of Turkish secularism was fatally compounded over the longer run by its culturally deracinated character, and a foolish disdain for the positive aspects of historical inheritance. Thus, the Kemalist Republic 'was based on a conscious attempt to forget the Islamic-Ottoman past'.[31] The complete contextual void that resulted in the making of the Republic was sought to be filled, as this book has shown, by a misguided and futile quest to be recognized and accepted as a 'European' country, always a pathetic fantasy, and more than ever a mirage today, nearly a century after Mustafa Kemal founded his secular state. Moreover, Kemalism's Europhilia

---

30 'Turkey's Got Secular Fundamentalists', *Times of India*, 11 July 2016, 12.

31 Yavuz, *Islamic Political Identity in Turkey*, 274.

failed to convert more than a sizeable minority of Turkey's population over eight decades. That this absurd, tunnel-vision path to modernity was attempted at all was of course made possible by the fact that 'there was no colonial legacy or long period of occupation',[32] in total contrast to the Indian case. The Indian national liberation movement from almost two centuries of colonial occupation and enslavement, which assumed the form of a mass struggle under the leadership of Gandhi and the Indian National Congress from the early 1920s, invoked the indigenous traditions of tolerance and co-existence, in addition to the pragmatic considerations of political necessity in a multi-religious society, in its argument for what became the Indian secular state after independence in 1947. By contrast, due to the blanket disowning of the Ottoman past, the tradition of pragmatic tolerance of cultural, religious and other forms of diversity that was the hallmark of the Ottoman Empire was completely forfeited by the Turkish national state founded by Kemal. As a result, 'the deeply rooted legacy of the Ottoman-Islamic past'[33] was available to be monopolized and selectively exploited by Turkey's Islamist counter-elite in the early twenty-first century.

In the late 1990s, the Turkish scholar Resat Kasaba observed,

> The Kemalist, Islamist, and Kurdish nationalist ideologies share a strong intolerance for one another. Just as Kemalists are deeply antagonistic towards both Islamists and Kurdish nationalists, those two are keen on preventing each other from infringing on their respective terrains as they separately confront their common enemy, the Turkish state ... In the eyes of their adherents, each holds the key to absolute truth. It is the *sine qua non* of such fundamentalisms that their partisans reject all ambiguity, whether in their own minds or in the minds of their rivals ... As a monolithic force that tried to mould Turkish society and mentality, Kemalism is losing its

---

32  Ibid., 273.

33  Ibid., 274. The AKP regime's revivalist attachment to Turkey's Ottoman-Islamic heritage bred ambitions of renewed geopolitical influence in the region. This ambition led it into an activist and eventually failed foreign policy stance in the Middle East. The 'Arab Spring' uprisings coincided with the consolidation of AKP power in Turkey and the regime adopted a policy of extending moral and material support to what it saw as like-minded forces in the Arab world, especially the Sunni-Islamist Muslim Brotherhood movements in Egypt and Syria. The main architect of the policy was Ahmet Davutoglu, who was Foreign Minister from 2009 to 2014, and then Prime Minister from August 2014 until he was forced out of office by Erdogan in May 2016.

grip. But once released from one doctrine, the people of Turkey should not be inevitably pushed towards new absolutes, whether of the Islamist variety or the [Kurdish] ethno-nationalist sort. Some of the ideas put forth by Islamists and Kurdish nationalists are no better than the Kemalist absolutisms in their plausibility, or their capacity to provide a frame of reference for a fast-modernizing society ... one should be careful to not let the pendulum swing too far in the other direction and celebrate each and every break with the Kemalist framework as another step in liberation.

It was a prescient warning, and Kasaba underlined 'the fundamental requirement that people communicate across the divides by which they find themselves separated'.[34] Recognizing the same problem around the same time about twenty years ago, Nilufer Gole hoped for a new 'synthesis between traditional Muslim values and [the] aspiration for Western modernity', through 'a possible alliance between reformist [secular] elites and moderate Islamists'.[35] A few years later after the emergence of the AKP in the early 2000s, Hakan Yavuz noted, 'The old republican Turkey we have known has become *passe*, and a new Turkey is unfolding in a troubled and uncertain fashion. The exact trajectory of state and society may be unclear, but it is certain that the country has come to a crucial crossroads'. He wrote that 'Turkey has been evolving from a state-centric society, in which homogeneity and obedience were imperative, to an associational society in which diversity is becoming a fact of everyday life, along with the anxious emergence of a civic culture'. So, Yavuz argued, 'Turkey needs a new social contract', based on '[t]he realization that coexistence depends on [both] shared rules and recognition of differences'. He advocated: 'The founding principles of this new contract should include secularism, the rule of law, and recognition of the multicultural nature of Turkey', and 'both Kurds and Turks, and both secularists and Islamic groups, need to be involved in this search for a new social contract'.[36]

Alas, the authoritarian-state legacy of the long Kemalist era proved too strong and entrenched, and Turkey's pluralist traditions and political culture too incipient and weak in comparison, to enable such a felicitous democratic transformation. What transpired instead, as this book has shown, was the

---

34 Kasaba, 'Kemalist Certainties and Modern Ambiguities', 18, 32.

35 Gole, 'Authoritarian Secularism and Islamist Politics', 42–43.

36 Yavuz, *Islamic Political Identity in Turkey*, 263–264, 274.

replacement of secularist authoritarianism by a new form of authoritarian hegemony – ideologically anti-secular in being based on an Islamist brand of Turkish nationalism of a majoritarian and plebiscitary character, but also bearing remarkable continuities with its Kemalist predecessor's state-centrism, zero-sum and winner-take-all view of politics and power, and the cult of the strongman leader, with Erdogan replacing Ataturk. In the process, 'the AKP strategically made the sense of victimhood shared by pious Muslims [at the hands of the secular state] central to its mission and gained their unwavering loyalty' by rectifying their status as 'the pariahs of the Republic' through 'representation at all echelons of state and society'. The Erdogan regime achieved what most would have thought impossible until just a decade ago: it 'tamed the power of the military', which represented 'an existential threat to political pluralism with its history of repeated interventions', and in the 'struggle with the military, the AKP had the support of the Gulen network[s], the liberal intelligentsia, and Kurdish opinion, as well as of the EU'. But once near-total control of the state was achieved, 'Sunni-Muslim victimhood' yielded to a 'triumphalism'[37] as intolerant of difference and dissent as the Kemalists were. And the new hegemonic elite is just as hostile to any democratic accommodation of Kurdish aspirations to rights and recognition as their secularist precursors were (see Chapter 6). So Ravza Kavakci's main role, since she was elected to parliament in mid-2015, has been to appear on international television channels to defend and justify the Erdogan regime's police and military repression in the restive Kurdish areas of the east and south-east, and, since the Erdogan regime resorted to draconian authoritarianism against a much wider range of critics and opponents including its former allies in the Gulen movement after the failed anti-regime coup of July 2016, those policies as well. Kemalism including its principle of *laiklik* (laicism/secularism) is dead but its authoritarian legacy lives on, in a new garb and wrapping.[38] That is Turkey's present and its foreseeable future.

---

37 Gunes Murat Tezcur, 'Historical and Contemporary Trends in the Turkish Party System', in *The AKP and Turkish Foreign Policy in the Middle East*, ed. Kaya, 9.

38 The grip of state-centric nationalism in Turkey is visually manifested in the omnipresence of the national flag, which has a white crescent and star on a red background. Its mind-numbing omnipresence dates to the early Kemalist era, though the practice may have grown further under Erdogan's Islamist regime. In India, the public display of the national tricolour is comparatively much less as well as more low-key.

◆

The future of the Indian secular state is indeterminate by comparison, due to three major differences with the Turkish case.

First, India is not just a country of far bigger scale, with fifteen times Turkey's population, but crucially, the extent of its social diversity is unparalleled in the world. The vastness of scale and more important, the sheer complexity and degree of diversity of Indian society make the implementation of a majoritarian formula of homogeneity inherently difficult. This is the fundamental reason why Hindu nationalism languished on the margins of Indian politics until the 1990s, its ideology much too incongruous with the social reality.

Second, Turkey has had a rigidly unitary and highly centralized state structure since the birth of its Republic in the 1920s. The concentration of power at the apex of the state has facilitated authoritarian rule ever since, because the elite in control of the central institutions could impose its agenda virtually unchecked. That was how the Kemalist 'cultural revolution' (see especially Chapters 2 and 5) took place. The ruling elites of Turkey have substantially lacked both vertical accountability, due to the centralization of power at the top, and horizontal accountability because of the lack of effective institutional checks and balances – for example the constitutional court, the state's apex judicial body established by a military junta in 1961, functioned as a pillar and guarantor of the authoritarianism of the military brass and its various allies in the civilian political elite over the next five decades, rather than as an independent voice. With the military hierarchy's power neutralized over the past decade, the centralized state has been captured by the anti-secularist challengers to Kemalism, and the Erdogan/AKP regime is largely free of both vertical and horizontal restraints. India, by contrast, adopted a flexibly unitary and moderately devolved state structure in the 1950s. After four decades of single-party (Congress) dominance, this constitutional structure has *de facto* evolved in a federalistic direction post the end-1980s, an era in which coalitions have governed at the national level for most of the time, and powerful regional parties have controlled the autonomous governments of numerous States of the quasi-federalized Indian Union. That is why the BJP's hegemonic ambitions, and the fulfilment of the anti-secular agenda that fundamentally drives its politics, cannot be realized simply by controlling the national government but necessitates winning (and retaining) power in the large majority of the 29 States, especially the more populous ones – a commanding position that the Congress enjoyed for four decades after independence.

Third, India's democratic traditions and political culture are far stronger than Turkey's. This is not merely or even principally a matter of institutional factors such as judicial independence (for instance, India's Supreme Court), or the existence of a relatively empowered upper chamber of parliament – the *Rajya Sabha* or 'House of States', indirectly elected by State legislatures, in which the BJP does not (yet) have a majority. It is more fundamentally a matter of attitudes, of popular mentality. In 1975, a quarter-century after the 1950 Constitution came into effect, India's democracy faced its gravest direct challenge to date in the form of Indira Gandhi's 'Emergency' regime, under which civil liberties were suspended, leaders and activists of almost the entire spectrum of opposition parties were arrested and incarcerated, and the freedom of the press was drastically curtailed. The Indian electorate responded by inflicting a severe defeat on the Congress party when Mrs Gandhi, fortunately, misjudged the nation's mood and went for an election in early 1977. India has been a functioning democracy for almost seventy years, whereas Turkey, since the end of its first quarter-century of single-party dictatorship in 1950, has been what political scientists politely call a 'hybrid regime' – one which has superficial democratic features, but is run through with deeply embedded authoritarianism in both formal and informal ways. The weakness of Turkey's democratic development has enabled an almost seamless transition from secularist authoritarianism to anti-secularist authoritarianism in the twenty-first century. India's democratic character is much more robust in comparison, and secularism in India has always been part of a functioning democracy and not of an authoritarian or semi-authoritarian polity as in Turkey.

The crucial question, then, is whether the aims of Hindu nationalism are compatible with India's well-established democracy.

◆

Indian secularists often accuse the Hindu nationalists of intent to turn the Republic of India into a Hindu version of Pakistan. The analogy is understandable. Just as Muhammad Ali Jinnah's politics fused religion, nation and state, so does the ideology of Hindutva. However, the analogy also has limits. Pakistan has been a military-bureaucratic state since the late 1950s – the first of the nation's recurrent military coups was in 1958 – and its democratic processes and institutions are weakly institutionalized. Pakistan's regime type is a 'hybrid' – similar to Kemalist Turkey's – in which the democratic elements are fragile and weakly rooted while the military command looms over the country as an autonomous and powerful actor that calls the shots. In contrast to Pakistan, democracy has put down deep roots in India since the 1950s, both in the institutional sense and in the popular mentality. Moreover, the robustly democratic Indian state has evolved in a quasi-federal direction since the 1990s, as the trajectory of politics in the era after the end of four decades of Congress hegemony has deepened the devolved structure of state power.

There is one type of democracy which *is* compatible with the ideology and aims of the Hindu nationalist movement. This type has been labelled as 'ethnic democracy' by Sammy Smooha, an Israeli political scientist who developed the concept with primary reference to the case of Israel. The State of Israel, proclaimed in May 1948, lacks a formal written constitution to this day, but over the decades it has enacted a series of 'Basic Laws' which define the character of the state, explicitly since the 1980s, as a 'Jewish and democratic state'. Israel, in Smooha's words, represents 'an alternative non-civic form of a democratic state that is identified with and subservient to a single ethnic nation'. Smooha writes,

> [An] ethnic democracy is propelled by an ideology and movement of ethnic nationalism that declares a certain population as an ethnic nation sharing a common descent, a common language, and a common culture. This ethnic nation claims ownership of a territory that it considers its exclusive homeland ... The ethnic nation, not the citizenry [at large], shapes the symbols, laws and policies of the state for the benefit of the majority. The ideology makes a crucial distinction between members and non-members of the ethnic nation. Members of the ethnic nation may be divided into persons living in the homeland and persons living in the diaspora. Both are preferred to non-members who are 'others', outsiders, less desirable persons who cannot be full members of the society and state

> ... [Such] non-members are not only regarded as less desirable but are also perceived as a serious threat to the survival and integrity of the ethnic nation. The perceived threat can be [some] combination of biological dilution, demographic swamping, cultural downgrading, security danger, subversion and political instability. In some cases the [perception of] threat is reinforced by the [perceived] affiliation of the non-core group to an external entity ... [which is] either an enemy or an unfriendly agent.[39]

This could be a description of the doctrine of Hindutva in relation to its perennial and essential 'other', the Muslims of India (and prior to the partition of 1947, the Muslims of the undivided subcontinent). As Chapter 6 has shown, Savarkar viewed all the Muslims of the undivided subcontinent in precisely these terms, unacceptable as members of the nation and as a threatening, disloyal element whose identity and allegiance lay with a global fraternity of followers of Islam. After India's independence, as Chapter 6 has also shown, Golwalkar regarded all of India's Muslims as a fifth-column for Pakistan and as a dire, diabolical danger to India's society and state.

However, Smooha is mainly talking about the state of Israel vis-à-vis its Arab Palestinian minority. After Israel's birth in 1948, on 77 per cent of the territory of Palestine, in the early 1950s c. 15 per cent of the population of the new state consisted of Arab Palestinians, a proportion that has grown to c. 20 per cent today, mostly concentrated in Israel's northern Galilee region. Of the 900,000 or so Arab Palestinians who lived in 1948 on the territory of what became the State of Israel, about 185,000 remained in 1949 – the rest had fled, been forcibly expelled, or been killed. These 715,000-odd missing Palestinians were replaced by the early 1950s by an almost equal number of Jews who arrived in Israel from the Middle East and North Africa and supplemented the 600,000-plus largely European Jews already present there, almost all of whom had settled in Palestine in the 1920s and 1930s as part of the Zionist state-building project in the ancient Jewish homeland. As noted in Chapter 6, both Savarkar and Golwalkar were ardent admirers of the Zionist movement before the birth of Israel and supporters of the State of Israel after its formation. Savarkar was extremely upset that the representative of newly independent India at the United Nations voted against the partition of

---

39 Sammy Smooha, 'The Model of Ethnic Democracy: Israel as a Jewish and Democratic State', *Nations and Nationalism* 8, no. 4 (2002): 475, 477–478.

Palestine into Jewish and Arab states in November 1947, and had advocated instead for a federal, binational state of Palestine. As Smooha writes,

> [The] political regime [of 'ethnic democracy'] is best exemplified by Israel
> ... Israel is an ethnic democracy, based on Jewish and Zionist hegemony
> and the structural subordination of the Arab minority. At the same time, it
> keeps the procedures, flexibilities, opportunities and incremental changes
> of a viable and stable democracy.[40]

This is the kind of state, based on the majoritarian concept of Hindutva, that the Hindu nationalist movement built around the RSS's creed of 'cultural nationalism' has longed to make in India from before and ever since India's independence. It is today closer than it has ever been to realizing that goal.

Israel's polity has all the standard paraphernalia of democracy – multiparty politics, free elections, independent media, etc. Moreover, the Jewish state does not practise outright disenfranchisement of its non-Jewish citizens. The Arab population of Israel is officially recognized as a distinct minority and is accorded cultural and religious freedoms, Arabic is a co-official language of Israel alongside Hebrew, and Israeli Arabs are represented in the apex institution of Israel's parliamentary democracy, the Knesset. In 2002, for example, twelve of the Knesset's 120 members (10 per cent) were Arabs, of whom nine had been elected as candidates of Israeli Arab parties. The Arab representation in the Knesset has generally fluctuated around the 10 per cent level, and has in the twenty-first century sometimes been slightly higher if Arab candidates elected to parliament on the lists of Zionist parties (including right-wing ones such as Likud) are counted. Arab-majority areas of Israel were subject to military regulations until 1966 – the vast majority of Israel's Arabs live in exclusively Arab townships and villages, and the rest in separate Arab neighbourhoods of Jewish cities and towns – but since the mid-1970s Israeli Arabs have campaigned assertively to improve their rights and status. But despite that assertiveness and the relative improvements which have resulted, they are still a structurally subordinated minority in the Jewish state, permanently consigned to *de facto* second-class citizenship status as a suspect, undesirable element through a range of mostly informal but entrenched state policies and practices. Many and perhaps most Jewish Israelis, especially those

---

40 Ibid., 497.

of a right-wing Zionist persuasion, view them as a greater threat to Israel than the Palestinians of the Occupied Territories (the West Bank, the Gaza Strip, and East Jerusalem) or Israel's enemies in the wider Arab and Muslim international contexts. Even as Israeli Arabs are accorded some rights both as citizens of the state and as members of a recognized minority, they are essentially ghettoized in deprived enclaves since most Arab-owned land has been expropriated over the decades, '93 per cent of the lands in Israel are either owned or controlled by the state or Jewish public bodies, [and] state allotment of land to Arabs for the development of local authorities, public facilities, industrial parks and housing projects is very limited. [Meanwhile], the state's symbolic system is strictly Jewish. Israel's titular name, calendar, days and sites of commemoration, heroes, flag, emblem, national anthem, names of places, [official] ceremonies and the like are all Jewish'.[41]

In July 2017, Narendra Modi became the first Indian Prime Minister to visit the State of Israel, 69 years after its formation and 25 years after India established full diplomatic relations with the Jewish state in 1992. He was accorded an effusive welcome which went beyond the standard red-carpet protocol. Prime Minister Binyamin Netanyahu, a right-wing Zionist, welcomed him thus, 'Prime Minister Modi, we have been waiting for you for a long time, almost 70 years ... We view you as a kindred spirit'.[42]

Israel is by no means the only example of an 'ethnic democracy' in the contemporary world. There is an example in India's immediate neighbourhood, in the form of the island country of Sri Lanka located just off India's south-eastern coastline. This state, which gained independence from Great Britain in 1948, very shortly after India (and Pakistan) did, became a Sinhalese–Buddhist majoritarian state from the mid-1950s onward, even whilst retaining

41  Ibid., 485–486. On the Israeli Arabs, see also Elia Zureik, *The Palestinians in Israel: A Study in Internal Colonialism* (London: Routledge and Kegan Paul, 1979); David Grossman, *Sleeping on a Wire: Conversations with Palestinians in Israel* (New York: Farrar, Straus and Giroux, 2003); Yoav Peled, 'Ethnic Democracy and the Legal Construction of Citizenship: Arab Citizens of the Jewish State', *American Political Science Review* 86, no. 2 (1992), 432–443; Sammy Smooha, 'Minority Status in an Ethnic Democracy: The Status of the Arab Minority in Israel', *Ethnic and Racial Studies* 13, no. 3 (1990), 389–413.

42  'Defence to Development, Focus on Strategic Partnership', *Indian Express*, 5 July 2017, 1.

a democratic polity. Sinhalese are three-fourths of Sri Lanka's population, and over 90 per cent of Sinhalese are Buddhists. The process began in 1956, when Sinhala was declared the sole official and national language and an electoral slogan called 'Sinhala Only!' became state policy. In 1972, the state enacted a new constitution, which replaced a 1947 Constitution written by the British jurist Ivor Jennings. The new Constitution was proclaimed on 'the tenth day of the waxing moon in the month of Vesak in the year two thousand five hundred and fifteen of the Buddhist era that is Monday the twenty-second day of May one thousand nine hundred and seventy-two'. The Constitution renamed the country from Ceylon to Sri Lanka (Sinhalese; the island's name in Tamil, the language of the principal minority community, is *Ilankai* or alternatively *Eelam*) and declared a Republic, replacing the 'Dominion' status of the British Empire (latterly Commonwealth) in operation since 1948. It further declared: 'The Republic of Sri Lanka is a Unitary State' (Chapter I), 'The Republic of Sri Lanka shall give to Buddhism the foremost place and accordingly it shall be the duty of the State to protect and foster Buddhism while assuring to all [other] religions [their] rights [Hinduism, Christianity and Islam, the faiths adhered to by 30 per cent of the population]' (Chapter II), and that 'the Official Language of Sri Lanka shall be Sinhala as provided by the Official Language Act, No. 33 of 1956' (Chapter III). The Constitution's Chapter III stipulated that 'all laws shall be enacted or made in Sinhala' and that 'there shall be a Tamil translation of every law so enacted or made' (Tamil being the language of at least one-quarter of the population). It specified that 'any provision for the use of the Tamil language under the Tamil Language (Special Provisions) Act, No. 28 of 1958 … shall not in any manner be interpreted as being a provision of the Constitution but shall be deemed to be subordinate legislation'.[43] A new Constitution enacted in 1978, which is still in effect, reiterated that 'the Official Language of Sri Lanka shall be Sinhala' but added that 'Tamil shall also be an official language' (no capitalization) and 'English shall be the link language'. The 1978 Constitution too invoked the Buddhist calendar, and repeated verbatim the 1972 Constitution's provisions on the 'Unitary State' (in capitals) and the supreme place of Buddhism therein.[44]

---

43  http://tamilnation.co/srilankalaws/72constitution.htm#2 (accessed 5 July 2017).

44  http://parliament.lk/files/pdf/constitution.pdf (accessed 6 July 2017).

Beyond Israel in the Middle East and Sri Lanka in South Asia, there are other examples of 'ethnic democracies' which enshrine the ownership and supremacy of majority nations in the state whilst functioning as democracies. In the early 1990s Croatia, which was then still a constituent unit of the unravelling Yugoslav federation in the Balkan region of Europe, adopted such a Constitution at the initiative of a right-wing nationalist party which had taken the reins of its autonomous government. After invoking 'the millennial national identity of the Croatian nation' and asserting 'the continuity of its statehood' since the ninth century – a claim incongruous with the historical reality – the Constitution proclaimed,

> The Republic of Croatia is hereby established as the national state of the Croatian people, and a state of other nations and minorities who are its citizens: Serbs, Muslims, Slovenes, Czechs, Slovaks, Italians, Hungarians, Jews and others, who are guaranteed equality with citizens of Croatian nationality and ... ethnic rights in accordance with the norms of the United Nations and countries of the free world.[45]

At the time, Croatia's population was 78 per cent Croat and c. 14 per cent Serb, with the other communities making up the rest.

The 'ethnic democracy' state prototype is, in principle, compatible with the political ideology and aspirations of the Hindu nationalist movement. That however would entail a fundamental change in the identity and character of the Indian state – either *de facto* or *de jure* or a combination of both. India has aspired since its independence to be what is known in academic terminology as a 'civic' state, a polity in which all citizens and communities are equal (i.e., not an Israel, a Sri Lanka, or a Croatia). The 'secular' nature of the Indian state is an integral and essential part of that civic identity, and it commits the state to not accord either preferential or discriminatory treatment to any faith(s) – the impartiality principle whose troubled record in independent India has been critically examined earlier in this book, especially in Chapter 3 – and to treat adherents of all of India's multiplicity of faiths in the letter and spirit of equality. The rejection of secularism – not just the really existing secular state, which is flawed as this book has argued, but of the secular *ethic* of tolerance and co-existence that is a deeply embedded aspect of India's

---

45 http://constitution.org/cons/croatia.htm (accessed 6 July 2017).

historically evolved societal traditions – is the heart and soul of the Hindu nationalist movement and the core of its political agenda.

But it is far from clear whether such an anti-secular transformation built on an ideological construct of an essentially homogeneous Hindu majority is achievable in India, notwithstanding the current political ascendancy of Hindu nationalism. India is a vast country of almost infinite diversity and social complexity, a land where almost all citizens have multiple identities, and various forms of what social scientists call 'cross-cutting cleavages' dominate the political landscape. It is no Israel, a settler-colonialist state anomalous in the twentieth century which came into being primarily because the European Zionists who were the pioneers of the Jewish state-building project in Palestine benefited from the tolerance and support of imperial Britain, which held the 'Mandate' (a hybrid of colony and protectorate) over Palestine under the League of Nations system from 1920 until 1948. For the past five decades, since Israel overran and occupied the rest of Palestine in the six-day war of June 1967, the Jewish state's appetite for territorial aggrandizement has been sustained by the support of the United States. India is no Sri Lanka, an island of twenty million people where majoritarian Sinhalese-Buddhist nationalism came to dominate politics and captured the post-colonial state within a decade of independence by stigmatizing and victimizing Tamils, the largest minority. And it is no Croatia, a state which violently 'cleansed' its territory of the bulk of its Serb minority – most of whom refused to accept subordinate, second-class status and rose in rebellion – during the 1990s. Depopulated of most of its erstwhile Serb inhabitants, this neo-nationalist Balkan country today has barely four million people, of whom just 4 per cent are Serbs, a quarter of the number who lived there in the early 1990s.[46]

◆

In a 2015 paper, Anirudh Mathur argues that the BJP in the Modi era remains absolutely steadfast in its allegiance to Hindutva ideology and consequently, to the pursuit of the agenda of anti-secularism that is the *raison*

---

46 On the Sri Lanka and Israel-Palestine cases, see Bose, *Contested Lands*, Chapters 1 and 5. On the Yugoslav and post-Yugoslav contexts see Bose, *Contested Lands*, Chapter 3 and Sumantra Bose, *Bosnia after Dayton: Nationalist Partition and International Intervention* (New York: Oxford University Press, 2002).

*d'etre* of the RSS-led movement's existence. He debunks any notion that the Modi-era BJP has diluted the Hindutva creed in order to widen its appeal to the broader electorate, or that there is any lack of equivalence between the politics of the party (BJP) and the movement of which it is the electoral face, the *sangh-parivar* centred on the RSS. He argues that Hindu nationalism has two core principles which are 'immutable', but its politics is defined by 'core-oriented flexibility'. The first principle is the revival of the innate but largely unarticulated consciousness of the Hindu nation as conceived by Savarkar and Golwalkar, and later discussed by Upadhyaya, and the assertion of its collective strength and pride. The second is the 'Friend-Enemy distinction', a concept developed in the early work of the German political theorist Carl Schmitt (1888–1985), who emerged as a leading ideologue of Nazism during the Third Reich (1933–45). Schmitt claimed that all politics is founded on some form of the friend-enemy distinction. Mathur correctly notes that in the ideological framework of Hindutva, the friend-enemy distinction is principally manifested as a quest to unite all Hindus against the Muslim enemy, and that 'Hindutva cannot move beyond it' because it is 'an unchallengeable and axiomatic part of the theory [of Hindutva]'. My detailed discussion of Hindutva thought, in Chapter 6, focused on Savarkar and Golwalkar, supports this contention. In other words, the 'othering' of Muslims – of the subcontinent until 1947, and of India since then – as an irreconcilable and despicable foe of the Hindu nation is not simply a politically expedient tactic nor even a strategic choice (though it may well serve those purposes), but a core ideological belief.

Yet, the Hindu nationalist movement's version of the friend-enemy distinction, I think, travels much beyond the Hindu-Muslim focus to include *anyone* who does not accept the Hindutva creed as the *only* authentic and legitimate ideology of Indian nationalism. Hence, Savarkar in the 1930s and 1940s scorned the entire (and internally diverse) Congress-led movement for freedom from colonial rule as 'pseudo-nationalistic' – the term replaced in the Hindu nationalist lexicon from the 1950s by the epithet 'pseudo-secular' to describe the Indian state – and as '[a] nuisance to the Hindu cause as well as the Indian National one'. Golwalkar was even more forthright. He asserted in the late 1930s that

> Those only are nationalist patriots who ... glorify the Hindu race [sic]

and Nation ... All others, wilfully posing to be patriots and indulging in a course of action detrimental to the Hindu Nation are traitors and enemies to the National Cause or, to take a more charitable view ... mere simpletons, misguided ignorant fools (notes 60 and 62, Chapter 6).

The cardinal and unforgivable sin of the movement to liberate India from colonial enslavement – a movement the Hindu nationalists shunned – was that it sought to unite all Indians in a common cause, especially the adherents of the two biggest religious traditions of the subcontinent, Hinduism and Islam.

In what I have termed its *Hindutva 2.0* incarnation in the twenty-first century, the BJP has adopted stances on three key matters – globalization, the empowerment of lower castes, and federalism – all of which diverge from the traditional positions associated with the party and the broader movement. Yet as Mathur argues, this evolution does not imply any dilution of, let alone deviation from, Hindutva's two 'immutable' core principles but rather a capacity for 'significant flexibility' in the pursuit of the core objectives.

The Modi government has made harnessing the forces of global capitalism central to its blueprint for India's economic progress. The government's flagship programme 'Make in India' – whose logo is a striding lion – is an open invitation to foreign capital to invest, build plants and factories and manufacture their products in India. Modi highlights 'Make in India' on his very frequent globetrotting travels. The attempted embrace of global capitalism is a conspicuous departure from the traditional RSS/BJP advocacy of *Swadeshi* – indigenous enterprise and the cultivation of national self-reliance – as the model for economic policy. The BJP's manifestos for the 1991 and 1996 general elections both emphasized this long-established stance. Yet the change in approach is, as Mathur points out, completely compatible and indeed consistent with the pursuit of the first core principle of Hindutva. To make India great again in the conditions of the early twenty-first century requires abandonment of the autarkic perspective. For 'India – or Bharat, the country and nation-state of the Hindus – to be reinvigorated and revitalised' a globally attuned strategy is needed. There are still dogged advocates of the old perspective in the Hindu nationalist camp. Their main platform is an RSS-affiliated group called the *Swadeshi Jagaran Manch* (Forum for Self-Reliance Consciousness/Awakening), which persists in pushing its view of the interests of the 'little man', the small-scale businessmen, traders and shopkeepers predominantly of urban north India who constituted the backbone of Jan Sangh/BJP support until the 1990s. The SJM was a vocal lobbying group during Vajpayee's 1998–2004 premiership but its once considerable influence has faded in the Modi era, as the BJP has decisively reoriented its paradigm of economic policy in keeping with the ambition of building 'New India'.

Just as the BJP has adapted its politics to globalization in the sphere of economic policy, it has adapted to another compelling twenty-first century reality – the political assertion of middle and lower castes which has been the defining feature of politics in northern India, and especially the States of Uttar Pradesh and Bihar, since the 1990s. Chapter 4 recounted how the initial response of the Hindutva movement in autumn 1990 to the prospect of reservations in government employment for the vast and amorphous layer of middle and lower-middle castes classified as Other Backward Classes (OBC), was to sharply escalate the agitation for Ram *mandir* (temple) on the site of the Babri Mosque in Ayodhya, in order to promote an overarching Hindu unity against caste-based politics. The *mandir* was pitched as an unifying symbol vis-à-vis *mandal* – the term which denotes the politics of OBC empowerment in the lexicon of Indian politics after the surname of the chairman of a commission appointed by a non-Congress and *de facto* coalition government in New Delhi in the late 1970s that recommended the reservations policy, and which another non-Congress coalition government undertook to implement in 1990. This book has noted that the RSS, an organization of upper-caste (especially Brahmin) roots that has shaped its outlook, has historically been opposed in principle to caste-based reservations in education and employment – even for the lowest castes, the Dalits or Scheduled Castes (SCs) and the tribal or Adivasi communities (Scheduled Tribes, STs) who have had such provision since shortly after India's independence – because such policies recognize heterogeneity and inequality in 'Hindu' society.

But the Hindu nationalist movement would have had to be tone-deaf and blind to not recognize the powerful appeal of subaltern caste identities and attendant claims to opportunity and equality emanating from the middle and lower rungs of a caste-ordered society. It was an obvious conclusion that 'reservations and [subaltern] caste consciousness [were] here to stay' and that the route to building pan-Hindu unity, the ultimate goal of the movement, lay not in denying the legitimacy of those aspirations but rather in 'co-opt[ing] the Mandal framework'. There were early signs of this strategic shift. When the BJP won a majority in the Uttar Pradesh legislature in 1991 riding on the momentum of the Ayodhya agitation, a party leader belonging to a lower-OBC (Lodh) caste was made the State's Chief Minister, superseding several more senior upper-caste claimants to the position. Since Modi became Prime Minister, he has made a habit of paying obeisance to the Dalit icon, B. R. Ambedkar, at much publicized events and ceremonies. In June 2017, the BJP nominated an obscure Dalit politician of Uttar Pradesh origin to the largely ceremonial but very prestigious post of India's President. In July 2017, the candidate, Ram Nath Kovind, was resoundingly elected by the electoral college comprising members of both chambers of parliament and the legislatures of the 29 States, and became the first Hindu nationalist to occupy the presidential post since the Republic came into being in 1950.

The co-optation of subaltern castes through recognition and validation which is now a key priority of Hindutva 2.0 is completely consistent with the first core principle of Hindutva as enunciated by Mathur – the forging of a united, resurgent Hindu nation. The purpose is to transform caste from a force which fractures the Hindu nation into a force which supports pan-Hindu consolidation. Savarkar had urged precisely such an approach in his presidential address to the Hindu Mahasabha's annual convention in Calcutta in 1939, '[This] will enable you to consolidate ... your own brethren who are religiously, culturally, nationally and in every other way as much a part and parcel of Hindudom as any of us [present here] can claim to be' (note 62, Chapter 6). The co-optation of middle and low castes also dovetails neatly with the second, equally essential and abiding core principle of Hindutva since the inception of the ideology – the 'friend-enemy distinction' in which India's Muslims are the 'other'. Since the early 1990s, the emergence of durable electoral alliances between certain OBC groups (mainly Yadavs) and the large Muslim minorities of Uttar Pradesh and Bihar (19 per cent and 17 per cent, respectively) had stymied the BJP's ambitions of dominating the two populous northern States, which today elect nearly one-quarter (22.5 per cent) of the 543 members of the Lok Sabha, the directly elected chamber of India's parliament.

The most intriguing aspect of Hindutva 2.0 which is at variance with traditional Hindutva ideology is its discourse of 'cooperative federalism'. Modi,

Finance Minister Arun Jaitley and other senior ministers and BJP leaders constantly use this term since 2014, and describe it as a cornerstone of their approach to governing India. The rhetoric of cooperative federalism could not be more removed from the views of Golwalkar, whom Modi reveres. In the late 1960s, the RSS supremo called for 'the [1950] Constitution [to] be re-drafted' to 'sweep away all autonomous and semi-autonomous states within Bharat', 'bury for good all talk of a federal structure' and instead 'establish [an] Unitary form of Government' and 'proclaim 'One Country, One State, One Legislature, One Executive!'" Golwalkar believed that India's moderately decentralized state structure was an abomination which was enabling 'fragmentational [sic], regional, sectarian, linguistic [and] other types of pride' to 'play havoc with our integrated harmony' (note 7, Chapter 6).

The *mantra* of cooperative federalism of Hindutva 2.0 and the Modi-era BJP is an adaptation to the political reality of India in the early twenty-first century. Since the demise of the era of the Congress party's hegemony in Indian politics at the end of the 1980s, India's polity has *de facto* federalized as powerful regional (State-specific) parties have proliferated across the Indian Union including, most crucially, in almost all of the most populous and therefore electorally important States. Regional identities based principally on ethno-linguistic communities but also on caste as well as tribe affiliations are entrenched across most of India and many, perhaps most citizens feel a strong sense of identification with their States. It would be absolutely foolhardy of the contemporary Hindutva movement to challenge this established *status quo*.

In a book on India's democracy published in 2013, I argued that:

> Even as India's rise is contingent on the strength of its constituent parts – confident States that can deliver decent governance in the form of effective anti-poverty programmes, socioeconomic development and opportunity, and good-quality education and jobs – the prospects of the parts are linked to each other and the ultimate political community is the nation as a whole.

So, unleashing India's economic potential is critically dependent on co-operation between the Union government and State governments, through 'shared decision-making on matters of national scope and importance'.[47]

---

47  Bose, *Transforming India*, 294–295.

Hindutva 2.0 understands and accepts this. In mid-2017, Modi hailed the new nationwide GST law as a triumph of cooperative federalism in action. One of his most appealing slogans in 2014 was 'poverty elimination not poverty alleviation'. That cannot happen *sans* a coordinated Centre-State effort. And seen from a political angle, regional identities are so entrenched across Indian society and in its polity that any attempt to impose Golwalkar's prescription would not only be ineffective but would horribly backfire. If the BJP is seen as an anti-federal party, that would gift a weapon to regional parties opposed to the BJP, disturb regional parties which are BJP allies, undermine the BJP's ambitions of making strong inroads in opposition-held States such as West Bengal, Tamil Nadu, Bihar (until 2017), Odisha and Kerala where regional political identity is deeply entrenched and regional parties predominate, and possibly even damage the BJP in States where it is in government, either on its own or in coalition with regional parties. Hence Modi's repeated assertion that 'our diversity is our strength'. In 2015, the Modi government abolished the Planning Commission, established in 1950 to direct India's paradigm of state-led development which endured until the early 1990s, and replaced it with a weaker, mostly advisory body called *Niti Aayog* (Policy Unit). The new body's stated rationale is to replace 'the centre-to-state one-way flow of policy that was the hallmark of the Planning Commission era' with 'a genuine and continuing partnership with states'. Jaitley, the Finance Minister, stated in 2015 at the 'Bengal Global Business Summit', the West Bengal government's annual event for prospective investors, that a key goal of the Modi government is to ensure that 'states become more financially empowered'. Indeed, the Modi government has been more forthcoming than the Congress governments of the past ever were in sharing fiscal revenues more equitably with State governments.

Thus, especially as long as numerous States including some of the most populous ones are ruled by regional parties, 'cooperative federalism' is vital to giving substance to the first of the two faces of the Hindutva 2.0 Janus – that of progress, modernization, development. Moreover, in current conditions, the approach is completely compatible with and indeed supportive of the first core principle of Hindutva – reinvigorating Bharat through the revival of the innate unity and strength of its Hindu majority. In the context of the early twenty-first century, the path to realizing that is *not* by attacking all communitarian identities as divisive in the name of a homogeneous Hinduness asserted to be the only true form of identity, as Golwalkar did fifty years ago, but by respectfully acknowledging those identities of ethnicity, language, tribe *et al.* and *then* seeking to subsume them, as with caste, under an overarching Hindutva national identity. This is where the second core principle of Hindutva, the essential friend-enemy distinction vis-à-vis Muslims, is crucial and comes into play. The friend-enemy distinction is, according to Carl Schmitt, present in some form in *all* politics. If regional parties and their State governments cannot plausibly attack the BJP-ruled Centre as an enemy of federalism and regional identities, it becomes easier for the Hindu nationalist movement to 'change the location of conflict to *within* states' and 'shape it as a communal cleavage' between Hindus and Muslims. This is precisely what the second face of the Hindutva 2.0 Janus has been and is doing in States across India. In addition to Modi's charismatically delivered modernization-and-development message, and outreach to the most disadvantaged segments of OBCs and Dalits, a crucial element of the BJP's victorious campaign in the 2017 State election in Uttar Pradesh was its ostracization of Muslims (not one of the BJP's 380 candidates was Muslim, in a State where one of five citizens is Muslim), coupled with accusations by Modi and other BJP campaigners that the regional party which had governed the State since 2012 had favoured Muslims in a variety of ways – the familiar allegation of 'pseudo-secularist appeasement' of a minority 'vote-bank'. Mission accomplished in India's most populous State, the RSS, BJP and VHP are now deploying the same strategy in the new top target State of West Bengal, India's third most populous (and 27 per cent Muslim), with a relentless and often vitriolic campaign that charges the State's ruling regional party and its government of being 'anti-Hindu' and 'pro-Muslim'.

It will be evident from this discussion how formidable India's Hindu nationalist movement is in its current incarnation. Hindutva 2.0 has an elasticity and adaptability, whilst retaining and pursuing the ideological core principles of Hindutva as elaborated by its prophets, which makes it highly effective in the contemporary Indian context. The BJP governs almost half of India's States on its own, and a few more in coalition governments with allied regional parties. Uniquely among all of India's political parties, the BJP has a nationwide organizational apparatus built on RSS networks to draw upon, although of uneven strength – relatively weak in most of eastern and southern India compared to northern and western India. And the BJP has India's only politician with (uneven) nationwide appeal, in the person of Narendra Modi. Modi's constant globetrotting[48] reflects his personal desire for recognition on the global stage as the leader of a major country, a craving amplified by the fact that he was shunned for nearly a decade by some governments, including those of the United States and the United Kingdom, after the pogrom of Muslims in Gujarat that occurred under his chief ministership of that State in 2002. But this is also about impressing a domestic audience. He has substantially appropriated 'the narrative of India as a rising power and a force to be reckoned with'[49] in global geopolitics, in a way that resonates with a considerable part of urban, middle-class India.

◆

For all his loquaciousness, Prime Minister Modi avoids speaking directly on the issue of the Indian secular state. However, he has senior colleagues in the Hindu nationalist movement who are not reticent on the matter. One such figure is Dattatreya Hosabale, a top RSS leader who currently serves as a *sah-sarkaryavah* (joint general secretary) of the RSS. The RSS normally has four joint general secretaries, who rank just below the *sarsanghchalak* (supreme chief) and the *sarkaryavah* (general secretary) in the organizational hierarchy. All are men, of course, as the RSS is an all-male organization. Hosabale, who is in his early sixties, is originally from the southern State of Karnataka. He is known to be close to Modi and it was widely speculated in Indian media in 2015 that he was about to be elevated to the post of general secretary, the number two position in the organization. The *sarkaryavah* or general secretary functions as the chief executive of the RSS, while the *sarsanghchalak* is the final authority. Hosabale's rumoured elevation did not eventually happen in 2015 – the incumbent in the post kept his job – but it may in spring 2018, when the

---

48 As Prime Minister, Modi visited 49 countries, i.e., over a quarter of the UN's 192 member-states other than India during his first three years in office, between June 2014 and July 2017. His total number of official trips abroad during this period was 67, as he visited some countries including the United States, Germany and Japan multiple times.

49 Anirudh Mathur, 'Has the Contemporary BJP Sacrificed Fidelity to Hindutva Ideology?' (2015), unpublished paper written for 'Contemporary India: The World's Largest Democracy in the Early 21st Century', an MSc course taught by Professor Sumantra Bose at the London School of Economics and Political Science (LSE).

RSS's next three-yearly cycle of shuffling and promotions of its top staff is due. Hosabale is also spoken of in RSS circles as a future *sarsanghchalak* who may succeed the current chief (since 2009), Mohan Bhagwat, once Bhagwat turns 75 in 2025. That year will also be the centenary of the RSS's birth in 1925.

In mid-2017, Hosabale spoke frankly and expansively about India's secular state and the Indian experiment in secularism to an interviewer, an Indian woman. The interview took place in the living room, dominated by a large portrait of Guru Golwalkar, of his modest apartment on the sixth floor of the Deendayal Research Institute in New Delhi, the RSS think-tank founded in the early 1970s and named in memory of Deendayal Upadhyaya, the RSS activist-ideologue and Jan Sangh leader who died in 1968 at the age of 52. The apartment had earlier been occupied by Nanaji Deshmukh (1916–2010), an RSS stalwart of the previous generation.

Hosabale noted, correctly, that the Indian secular state is based on a concept of secularism very different from the 'wall-of-separation' (between church and state) doctrine of Western provenance. This book has shown – see especially Chapter 3 – that the Indian secular state that came into being after independence was based *not* on such a principle of separation of religion and state, as in the United States in the late eighteenth century, but on – (a) a principle of neutrality or impartiality between faiths; and (b) extensive, constitutionally-mandated powers of supervision and regulation of the religious domain and matters to do with religion, a characteristic it shares with the Turkish 'control model' of the secular state. The RSS leader then argued that the Indian secular state has failed to adhere to the neutrality/impartiality principle in the exercise of its supervisory and regulatory powers, and has instead practised 'pseudo-secularism. In India, secularism has been about minority appeasement and it has been anti-Hindu'. As an example, Hosabale cited the appointment of IAS (Indian Administrative Service) officers – state bureaucrats – to 'Hindu Religious Temple Boards or Trusts' in a supervisory/ regulatory capacity whereas this was not the usual practice with the bodies of other Indian religions. This too is substantially correct; the Indian secular state adopted such a policy from the 1950s as part of its drive against untouchability and the exclusion of Dalits, one-sixths of all Indians, from access to numerous Hindu temples and shrines across India. This rationale Hosabale omitted to mention. However, he is clearly aware of the rationale because he then went on to say, 'People despise social untouchability, but what about political and intellectual untouchability? ... Nehruvians are never ready to engage in a debate. I have seen people say that if RSS people are coming here, I am not going to share the dais with him'.

According to Hosabale,

> After Independence, we have been told that the four pillars that hold up the Idea of India are socialism, secularism, parliamentary democracy, and non-alignment [between the erstwhile USA–USSR superpower blocs]. The intellectual class of this country which became part and parcel of the ruling class or the political class, so to say, has been patronised by the Nehruvian establishment to spread these ideas as the core ideas or the fundamental ideas of India ... in the field of academics, media and intellectual activities, even spreading to art, culture and other performing arts, etc., they have said that secularism and socialism are the only ideas to be propagated. That is why, more than the British period, there was in the Nehruvian period a deliberate attempt to cut away from our cultural roots.

Hosabale contended: 'Among the renaissance masters of this country, no one has ever said that it is secularism that is the foundation of India. It is, in fact, India's cultural unity and spiritual oneness that is its foundation ... They have laid an emphasis on our cultural ties that bind'.

This too is correct. Thus Nehru, in *The Discovery of India*, which he wrote in prison during World War II, waxed nearly lyrical on this very theme: 'Ancient India ... was a world in itself, a culture and a civilization which gave shape to all things ... some kind of a dream of unity has occupied the mind of India since the dawn of civilization'.[50] A typical Congress declaration of the 1930s asserted that 'from the beginning [of history] her [India's] one mission has been to weld her myriad children into a harmonious people by giving them a political, economic and cultural unity'.[51] All nationalists invoke oneness and emphasize unity. So Subhas Chandra Bose declared in 1943: 'We are *one* [nation] whatever our individual religion' (note 10, Chapter 3). Bose's conception of secularism was very different from Gandhi's, and

---

50  Nehru, *The Discovery of India*, 62.

51  Gyanendra Pandey, *The Construction of Communalism in Colonial North India* (Delhi: Oxford University Press, 1990), 252.

more robust than the 'Nehruvian' version. Bose strongly believed that Indian national identity must transcend and not indulge (any) religious identities and sentiments, and also that it should *not* be grounded in a creed of inter-faith solidarity or a narrative of religious syncretism (note 11, Chapter 2). Notwithstanding their differences, what these Indian nationalists who – unlike the followers of Hindutva – dedicated their lives to freeing India from colonialism shared in common was a belief in the *ethic*, deeply rooted in Indian tradition, of mutual respect, equality and co-existence of all of India's faiths. They *all* considered this a *sine qua non* of the independent Indian state of the future. That is the ideological origin of the Indian secular state. Due to the deeply bruising experience of the 1947 partition, secularism became an explicit component of the discourse and identity of the independent Indian state, in contrast to the rare use of the term, noted in Chapter 2, in the discourse of the independence movement.

Hindutva is an alternative conception of Indian nationalism based on rejection of that ethic and that ideological legacy. That doesn't stop its proponents from selectively invoking Gandhi, who was murdered at the age of 78 by a Hindu nationalist for advocating tolerance and peace during and immediately after the bloodbath caused by the partition. So, according to the RSS's Hosabale:

> People, because of their cultural heritage, want to protect the cow. Gandhiji had arranged exhibitions in the AICC [All-India Congress Committee] conferences on the cow and had on repeated occasions emphasized the need for cow protection. So was Gandhiji a Hindu fundamentalist? It wasn't interpreted as parochialism and narrow-mindedness then.

This is a spurious parallel because, as noted in Chapter 2 and earlier in this chapter, Gandhi was, in contrast to the Hindu nationalists, viscerally opposed to the 'imposition' through law or otherwise of *any* prohibition on cow slaughter, and said that any such 'compulsion' or 'coercion' was 'repugnant'. In Hosabale's view,

> Gandhi Jayanti [his birthday, 2 October] is a dry [alcohol-free] day out of respect for a great man's message, so why can't you respect a community's sentiments towards cows? ... Reasonable restrictions are imposed in every society. For example, [in the name of] my freedom, I will go for a 'Slut Walk' ... semi-naked ... When it comes to a question of public decency

349

> and morality, those things have to be restricted. In a club, somebody goes
> and wears the bare minimum dress ... [but the] same thing cannot happen
> on the road.

The uninformed might gather from this that cow slaughter is rampant in India, whereas the reality is that it is strictly banned and punishable by law in more than two-thirds of India's States. When some Muslim plaintiffs went to court to challenge the laws banning cow slaughter enacted by the Congress governments of at least four States in north India in the second half of the 1950s, on the grounds that the laws violated the constitutional guarantees to both religious freedom (Article 25) and the right to livelihood (Article 19) through the beef trade, India's Supreme Court rejected their appeal and upheld the laws as 'reasonable restrictions' due to 'the Hindu sentiment' on the issue (note 19, Chapter 3).

Likewise, the Nehru government's reform of *only* Hindu personal and family law in 1955–56 – cited ever since by Hindu nationalists as 'anti-Hindu' and a prime example of 'pseudo-secularist appeasement' of Muslims because the latter's *sharia*-based laws were not subjected to a similar process of reform – is indeed another genuine and continuing anomaly of the secular state, this book has argued (see especially Chapter 3). However, even as the Hindu nationalists of the time opposed the reforms as repugnant to Hindu *shastras* (scripture) and traditions, socialists and other secularist critics based their opposition on a starkly different point of principle. In the words of Acharya J. B. Kripalani,

> I submit that we must not make laws for one community alone ... If they
> [the government] single out the Hindu community for their reforming
> zeal, they cannot escape the charge ... that they favour the Hindu
> community and are indifferent to the good of the Muslim community or
> the Catholic community ... Do we want one community to be in advance
> of other communities in India, simply because it happens to be in the
> majority? (note 5, Chapter 3).

Hosabale believes that 'a nation's soul must get expressed. It is necessary for building and achieving development of the nation. A nation without understanding its own soul, its cultural moorings, cannot express itself. A nation should get expressed in every aspect of life'. The concept of the national soul (*chiti*) is a central theme in the writings of Deendayal Upadhyaya, and the emphasis on the 'cultural' derives from the RSS's very longstanding habit of not being explicit about the organization's distinctly political purpose and aims. 'When it comes to the Idea of India', Hosabale says,

> There can be a variety of ideas and each must be permitted its space. India being a country of so many diversities can have a number of ideas ... But the problem was the approach that one idea should rule, this was enforced, and it influenced the thinking of this country through formal and informal methods and government and non-government channels.[52]

It is true that Hindutva existed on the fringes of Indian discourse for four decades after independence. That was because the movement's political party was a marginal force in India's democracy until the beginning of the 1990s. The marginality was not due to state repression as was routine in Kemalist Turkey, but derived from the failure of the Hindu nationalists to secure significant popular support. The Jan Sangh and then the BJP failed to gain a double-digit vote percentage in any national election until the end of the 1980s. The RSS and its various wings and fronts were free to pursue their activities[53] for almost that entire period with only two, brief exceptions. The first was February 1948–July 1949 when, after Gandhi's assassination, the government headed by Nehru and his deputy Vallabhbhai Patel banned the RSS for 17 months while it conducted investigations into the organization. The RSS was again banned during Indira Gandhi's Emergency regime of mid-1975 to early 1977,

---

52 'Dattatreya Hosabale: Secularism in India has been Anti-Hindu', *Open*, 2 June 2017 (internet edition). The RSS leader was interviewed by Advaita Kala, a writer.

53 The contemporary RSS's multi-faceted activities extend to eugenics. Its medical wing *Aarogya Bharati* (Healing India) runs a *garbh vigyaan* (reproductive science) programme which promises to deliver *uttam santati* or excellent children to build *samarth Bharat* (strong India). The programme, said to be based on principles of Ayurveda, claims that parents with low IQ can produce clever progeny and those of dark skin and short stature can have offspring who are fair and tall if its prescribed procedure is followed. The many requirements include intercourse at auspicious times determined by planetary configurations, strict abstinence from sex after conception of the baby, complex dietary regulations throughout pregnancy, and recitation of *shloka*s and *mantra*s – scriptural verses and prayer hymns from Hindu *shastra*s – by the expectant mother. The programme claims to have produced 450 such designer babies, mostly in the BJP-controlled States of Gujarat and Madhya Pradesh, and has ambitious plans of nationwide expansion. 'For *Samarth Bharat*, RSS Wing Prescribes Way to have Fair, Tall "Customised" Babies', *Indian Express*, 7 May 2017, 1.

but on that occasion almost the entire, diverse spectrum of Indian opposition parties were subjected to repression, and political leaders and activists across the board were arrested and imprisoned.[54]

Now, with the BJP by far India's largest political party, writes Rakesh Sinha, a Delhi University academic and prominent RSS spokesman who frequently represents the organization's positions in Indian print and broadcast media, 'forces in the Opposition, which include political parties and the predominantly "left-liberal" intelligentsia', are in a bind and denial mode. 'In the present context', he avers, 'the rise of an alternative ideology and leadership have yet to be reconciled to by the elites which enjoyed status and privileges and considered themselves authors of the destiny of modern India'. There is a hint of lip-smacking triumphalism here, although that is as yet still premature. Sinha himself recognizes that the task is not yet complete, and the remaking of the identity and character of the Indian state is still a work in progress. So in mid-2017, he called on the BJP and the Modi government, in an op-ed titled 'New President for New India' published in an Indian daily with a 'left-liberal' slant, to nominate a person to the imminent vacancy of President of the Republic who can 'act as an agent of redefining the idea of India, which is essential to restore the post-colonial identity of the Indian people'. 'The office [of president] should be filled', he stressed, 'with a philosopher-king. He must represent the soul of India, not a secularist soul. She should address not merely the present, but posterity too … his words and actions should be indicative of civilizational imperatives … It is essential that the presidential candidate … is a positive mind who embraces the arduous task of the decolonisation of the Indian mind', to complement 'Prime Minister Modi's … assertion of a genuine idea of India in the midst of ceaseless opposition from secularist forces'.[55]

The Indian presidency is a largely ceremonial post and its holder is supposed to stay strictly above the political fray (and affray) as a neutral

---

54 The RSS, the VHP and its youth wing Bajrang Dal were banned by the Congress's Union government, headed by Prime Minister P. V. Narasimha Rao, after the razing of Ayodhya's Babri Masjid in December 1992. The ban was token and ineffective and the proscription of the RSS and the Bajrang Dal was lifted after six months. The ban on the VHP ended in 1995.

55 Rakesh Sinha, 'New President for New India', *Indian Express*, 16 June 2017, 9.

figure. That aside, there does not seem to be much, if any, space in this clarion-call for transformation for 'a variety of ideas', in the words of Sinha's RSS comrade Hosabale, to shape India's society and state. A few days after Sinha's op-ed was published, the BJP president Amit Shah announced the hitherto unknown Ram Nath Kovind as the BJP-led ruling alliance's candidate for President of the Republic, and he was duly elected to the office four weeks later, in July 2017, with a decisive majority of the votes of the members of the two chambers of Parliament and the 29 State legislatures. Kovind, a former two-term (1994–2006) BJP member of the Rajya Sabha, the indirectly elected upper house of parliament, was serving as the Modi government-appointed Governor (titular head) of the northern State of Bihar when his name was announced. He thrice contested elections to the legislature of his home State, Uttar Pradesh, as a BJP candidate (in 1991, 1993 and 2007) and was defeated on all three occasions. Kovind, a Dalit, is not India's first Dalit president. K. R. Narayanan (1920–2005), who was president from 1997 to 2002, was a Dalit from the southern State of Kerala who had a long career as a diplomat in the Indian Foreign Service (IFS) after graduating from the London School of Economics and Political Science (LSE) in the late 1940s. But Kovind, 72, India's fourteenth president, *is* the first to come from the ranks of the Hindu nationalist movement. In 2002, A. P. J. Abdul Kalam (1931–2015), a professional scientist of southern (Tamil Nadu) origin who helped build India's nuclear programme, was nominated by the Vajpayee government to succeed Narayanan as President, and was elected with the support of more than 90 per cent of the electoral college of parliamentarians and State legislators. Kovind's candidature was hailed by 'Rakesh Sinha, an RSS ideologue who is a close friend of Kovind's'. 'Narayanan', Sinha asserted, 'was part of the Indian bureaucracy, while Kovind is a product of social and political movements'.[56] Indeed, Kovind joined the BJP in 1991 after becoming inspired by the *Ramjanambhoomi* agitation described in Chapter 4.

The joker in the current Hindutva pack is Yogi Adityanath, the priest-politician who became the BJP Chief Minister of Uttar Pradesh in March 2017. Known mainly as a cow crusader, he too has very definite notions of

---

56 'Ram Nath Kovind: A Profile', *Open*, 3 July 2017, 30.

what is Indian and what is not. On a visit to the neighbouring State of Bihar in June 2017, he addressed a 20,000-strong BJP rally which had gathered to hear him in the afternoon despite a torrential downpour of monsoon rain in the morning. 'Even the nature God is with us', Adityanath declared, 'the rain washed off all the impure things this spot might have had before this meeting'. He commenced his address by leading mass chants of *Jai Shri Ram* (the rallying cry of the *Ramjanambhoomi* agitation in which he cut his political teeth in the early 1990s), and the more contemporary slogan of *Gau Mata ki Jai* (Long Live Mother Cow). He then stated that 'several Muslim women come to meet me daily, narrating their woes that stem from triple *talaq* [the instant divorce of a wife permitted to Muslim men in India until August 2017]'. He went on to announce that Nitin Gadkari, the minister for road transport and highways in Modi's government and a former BJP national president, 'had approved a special road project connecting Ayodhya [the mythical birthplace of Lord Ram, in the eastern part of present-day Uttar Pradesh] with Sitamarhi' in Bihar, said to be the place of origin of Sita, Ram's consort. He then came to the punchline of his speech:

> Foreign dignitaries visiting India used to be gifted [miniature] replicas of the Taj Mahal and other minarets [probably a reference to the Mughal-era Red Fort in Delhi, which Subhas Chandra Bose rhetorically cited in 1943-1944 as the final destination of the Indian National Army's march to India from southeast Asia, where the national tricolour would be raised on its ramparts by the INA's Hindu, Muslim and Sikh soldiers to signify India's liberation from colonialism], which do not reflect Indian culture.

Under Narendra Modi's post-2014 government, he noted, the mementos gifted to visiting dignitaries are copies of the *Bhagavad Gita* (a philosophical text which is a part of the ancient Indian epic *Mahabharata*) and the *Ramayana*, the ancient epic which describes the struggles of Ram. The *Bhagavad Gita* and the *Ramayana* are without any doubt representative of Indian heritage. But the Taj Mahal, the mid-seventeenth-century monument erected in the city of Agra in what is today western Uttar Pradesh on the orders of the Mughal emperor Shah Jahan in memory of his deceased queen, Mumtaz Mahal – and where the monarch is interred in a tomb next to his consort – has been declared as antithetical to 'Indian culture' nearly four centuries later by Uttar Pradesh's BJP chief minister.[57]

♦

The future of Indian secularism depends on how far the BJP is able to expand its political base and consolidate its grip on the Indian state, because state power is essential for the pursuit and realization of the Hindutva movement's anti-secular project. As India stands at a political crossroads, it is 'advantage Hindutva'. The Congress party is an emaciated and rudderless shadow of its once-hegemonic self. Its popular base and organizational apparatus have withered away across most of India, its dynastic leadership has scant if any credibility, and the party faces an existential crisis and prospect of near-extinction. The decline is terminal and irreversible, barring a miracle. The regional parties which dot India's political landscape, and most of whom are ideologically opposed to Hindu nationalism, have their own constraints and problems. Each, unlike the BJP, is limited to (usually) one State. Moreover, the regional parties are a very variegated and disparate lot, and the prospects of a grand anti-Hindutva alliance are hindered by this factor, aggravated by an established pattern of rivalry and competition between regional parties in a number of States as well as conflicts of ego and ambition between their leaders. The BJP is well aware of these facts and seeks to manipulate and exploit them to its advantage. The regional parties

---

57 'Minarets Don't Reflect Indian Culture: Yogi Pits Taj against Gita', *The Telegraph*, 16 June 2017, 4. In 1529, Babur, the founder of India's Mughal dynasty, wrote in his Persian-language *Wasiyyat-namd-i-majchfi*: 'The realm of Hindustan is full of diverse creeds ... It is but proper that thou, heart cleansed of all religious bigotry, should dispense justice according to the tenets of each community ... And in particular refrain from sacrifice of cow, for that way lies the conquest of the hearts of the people of Hindustan'. His successors Akbar (r. 1556–1605), who tried to create an official religion combining Hinduism and Islam as described in Chapter 3, and Jahangir (r. 1605–1627), whose mother was a Hindu Rajput princess, also issued edicts disapproving of cow slaughter. However, these were in the nature of advisories. The Indian ruler who made cow slaughter an offence punishable under law was Hyder Ali, who ruled the kingdom of Mysore in southern India from 1761 to 1782 and waged an extremely tenacious resistance to British colonization of southern India, a struggle which was continued by his son and successor Tipu Sultan until he died in combat against British forces in 1799.

are also hamstrung by other damaging deficits. Most are undemocratically controlled by either a single individual or else by a proprietary family (as the Congress is). Many, especially those that recently have or currently run State governments, are steeped in corruption, a flaw the Modi government is adeptly exploiting to pin them down through criminal investigations and judicial processes.

Nevertheless, the pan-Indian BJP hegemony the Hindutva movement is striving towards is not assured. The regional parties are in most cases strongly rooted in their States and have loyal support bases. Had the two major regional parties of Uttar Pradesh – bitter rivals since the mid-1990s – formed an alliance to take on the BJP in the 2017 State election, instead of contesting against each other as well as against the BJP, they would have posed a stiff challenge to the BJP juggernaut and possibly even stalled it. Beyond the electoral arithmetic, which can prove decisive depending on the presence or absence of alliances to consolidate anti-BJP votes, the contemporary BJP has its own potential limitations. Ever since he launched his bid for the prime ministership in mid-2013, Narendra Modi has proved to be an extremely skilled dream merchant who has tapped the aspirations to progress and development in Indian society, which at the individual level means opportunity, especially decent livelihoods through gainful employment. During his premiership he has successfully turned this appeal, the first of the two faces of the Hindutva 2.0 Janus, into a powerful personal brand. In the process, however, he has aroused high expectations among those who have believed him. If he fails to meet those expectations, as he well might in due course, no amount of public-relations blitzes calling for 'New India' will compensate for the inevitable sense of disappointment. Additionally, India is still a largely agrarian country, and there are signs of peasant distress and unrest in parts of the Indian countryside which could play to the advantage of opposition parties. Moreover, the second face of the Hindutva 2.0 Janus, which is now openly visible – in the form of the violent cow vigilantes and the RSS's ideologues of revolution – could alienate some who had been attracted to the first face. There are yet other factors which could come into play, such as the Modi government's controlled but unmistakable emphasis on the primacy of Hindi. The Prime Minister, who speaks English well, increasingly uses only Hindi in his public speeches and interactions, and addressed the international media only in Hindi even during his mid-2017 visit to the Trump White House. The Hindi promotion, while consistent with the traditional Hindu nationalist approach to the issue of language, could in time alienate parts of the decisive majority of India's population who have mother tongues other than Hindi, especially in the country's south.

The battle-lines between the Hindutva movement and the anti-Hindutva forces are drawn on the issue of secularism and its future. The politics of secularism in India has several shortcomings, and the Indian secular state has genuine conundrums which need to be addressed.

Many of India's professional 'secularist' politicians manifestly lack a substantive *praxis* of secularism that goes beyond merely opposing the BJP and the RSS's *sangh-parivar* in the electoral stakes. This reduces secularism to a reactive and rather vacuous stance. Some of these politicians are also prone to opportunistically relying on the justified fear of the Hindutva movement among Muslims to secure assured votes. The phenomenon of 'minority vote-bank politics', as the Hindu nationalists call it, is much exaggerated by their propaganda but it does exist, as any serious student of Indian politics knows. Its existence is certainly more perception than reality. But perceptions crucially matter in politics, and the growth of a perception of excessive indulgence of elements of the Muslim community for opportunistic electoral purposes can be dangerous, as powerful regional parties from Uttar Pradesh's Samajwadi Party to West Bengal's Trinamool Congress have found out or are in the process of finding out. The BJP's narrative, and its strategy of 'polarization', is crucially dependent on such a perception gaining traction.

The Indian secular state has been most compromised and damaged not by any widespread rejection among ordinary Indians of the deeply rooted as well as pragmatic everyday ethic of tolerance, mutual respect and co-existence of faiths, but by elites and leaders who have sworn by the principle of secularism. Indira Gandhi's use of a *de facto* Hindu-majoritarian strategy for electoral purposes in 1983–84 is a glaring case in point, as is her son and political heir Rajiv Gandhi's even more blatant attempt to exploit the same strategy at the end of the 1980s (see Chapter 4). During the period between the two episodes, Rajiv Gandhi's Congress government reduced Indian secularism, as also detailed in Chapter 4, to parallel appeasement of the demands of militant Hindu nationalists and conservative Muslims. All of this debased Indian secularism and paved the way for the Hindu nationalist attack on not just the secular state, but on the very ethic of secularism which has been ongoing since the beginning of the 1990s, and has assumed the form of a final offensive since Narendra Modi's government came to power in New Delhi in 2014.

But, as this book has shown, the dilemmas of the Indian secular state are deeper and go back to the formative Nehru period. The BJP and the Modi government's highlighting of the triple-*talaq* issue is the most recent example of what was described by Jacobsohn in 2003 as 'the very clever appropriation of the discourse of constitutional liberalism to advance the agenda of Hindu nationalism'.[58] The triple-*talaq* debate serves the Hindu nationalist movement's purpose of barbarizing its perennial Muslim 'other'. But beyond the cynical opportunism involved in the Hindu nationalist movement taking up cudgels on behalf of Muslim women's rights, there is a genuine issue here – the fact that Muslim women in India *can* be subjected, even if its actual incidence is the exception rather than the norm, to a form of divorce to which Hindu women and women of other religious communities cannot be subjected. As the feminist scholars Brenda Cossman and Ratna Kapur pointed out in 1996,

> There has been surprisingly little attention to the meaning of equality within the dominant vision of [Indian] secularism. The continuing silence ... has become a dangerous silence that the Hindu Right has been only too willing to exploit to claim the terrain of secularism as its own ... [by] bringing a very particular [and entirely self-motivated] understanding of equality [to the debate] (note 8, Chapter 3).

In August 2017, India's Supreme Court ruled the 'instant' version of triple *talaq* – which in recent years has increasingly been conveyed not in person, as earlier, but through email, text (SMS) messages, Facebook, and even common smartphone applications such as Whatsapp – as illegal in a complex judgment. The judgment came in response to a clutch of petitions from Muslim women who had been subjected to the practice, as well as a representation made by a Muslim women's advocacy group; the Modi

---

58 Jacobsohn, *The Wheel of Law*, 189.

government's legal representatives strongly supported the petitioners' case in the hearings. The Supreme Court's judgment was widely applauded in India, the conspicuous exception being conservative Muslim organizations and their leaders.

The issue of triple *talaq* is of course merely a sub-issue of a broader anomaly of the Indian secular state which has persisted since the 1950s – the existence of different sets of personal and familial laws for different groups of citizens. As Donald Smith wrote in his otherwise laudatory 1963 study of the Indian secular state:

> That a Hindu, a Muslim, and a Christian, all citizens of the same country, should be governed by different ... laws is an anachronism indeed ... and diametrically opposed to the fundamental principles of secularism. The Constitution [moreover] declares that the state must strive for a uniform civil code [Directive Principle, Art. 44].[59]

This anomaly has been a prime weapon for over six decades of the Hindu nationalist attack on the Indian secular state as 'pseudo-secular' and a form of minority (read Muslim) 'appeasement', and today that attack is more potent than ever before. But there can as well be a principled *secularist* critique of the anomaly, which in fact was articulated, as discussed in Chapter 3 and mentioned a little earlier in this chapter, in India's parliament when the Nehru government chose to focus on reforming and codifying only Hindu laws. Members of the secularist opposition pointed out that this selective approach violated the secular imperative of equal, impartial treatment by the state of all citizens and communities irrespective of religious identity, and could be reasonably interpreted as privileging Hindus over other faiths.

There is another longstanding feature of Indian state-secularist discourse which has fed into the politics of Hindu nationalism. This is the tendency of prominent (and generally Congress-affiliated) state-secularists since at least the 1960s, as discussed in Chapter 3, to identify the Indian secular state with a romanticized notion of 'Hindu tolerance'. The habit of invoking this purported catholic spirit of Hinduism as the foundation of the Indian secular state resurfaced in 1999 when the Congress party – then fast losing ground to the BJP on the one hand and to regional parties on the other – adopted a

---

59 Smith, *India as a Secular State*, 497.

resolution that asserted the 'basic truth' that 'Hinduism is the most effective guarantor of secularism in India'. The BJP promptly welcomed the statement and then lambasted the Congress for 'its so-called secularism, essentially targeted against the majority community [and] always mortgaged to vote-bank politics' (note 17, Chapter 3). The state-secularist rhetoric locating the Indian secular state in the unique spirit of Hindu tolerance of other faiths and equating the secular state with this ethos, said to be intrinsic to the nation's majority religion, has a Hindu nationalist counterpart which has always asserted the innate virtuousness of Hinduism and its inherent superiority to other 'intolerant' religions, notably Islam. The RSS's builder M. S. Golwalkar wrote in the late 1930s that 'the average Hindu mind' is defined by 'the spirit of broad Catholicism, generosity, toleration, truth, sacrifice, and love for all life', while 'the spread of Islam' everywhere was 'the same old tale of invasion, with its attendant massacres, devastation, destruction, loot and arson, violating all sacred places, and forced conversion to the faith of the ready executioner, [everywhere] repeated in all its hideousness' (note 69, Chapter 6). Without demeaning the great faith of Hinduism in any way, it can be plausibly argued that there is no such thing as an essentially tolerant *or* an essentially intolerant religion, that all religions have both tolerant and intolerant characteristics, and that all religions can assume either a tolerant or an intolerant form depending on context and circumstance. The state-secularist fallacy of equating the Indian secular state with Hinduism's uniquely tolerant virtue leads logically to the conclusion that there is no need for a secular state as such – India can simply be a Hindu State in which the religion's innate nature will ensure a paradise for all. Indian state-secularists also need to re-examine their common assumption that the Indian secular state has invariably been democratic – the case of Kashmir, discussed towards the end of Chapter 6, shows this to not be the case.

The future of Indian secularism will rest, in part, on the capacity of Indian secularists to acknowledge and address all of these real contradictions and frailties in India's odyssey as a secular state. Simply reciting the old shibboleths of secular nationalism and uncritically defending the really existing secular state will not suffice in the age of Hindu nationalist ascendancy. Nor will cobbling together anti-BJP electoral alliances of opposition parties necessarily halt the Hindutva juggernaut.

The best guarantee of secularism's survival in India lies in a characteristic which *is* intrinsic to the Indian nation – its manifold heterogeneity. The RSS has long been given to claiming that its creed represents the collective identity and interests of '85 per cent' of India's population (i.e., all except the Muslims and possibly, Christians).[60] But in fact the Hindu nationalists remain, even in the age of their ascendancy, a vocal, ideologically motivated and highly organized political minority. They are, certainly, no longer the marginal movement they were until three decades ago; quite the contrary, they have unequivocally emerged as by far the single largest force in Indian politics. In the authoritarian framework of Kemalist Turkey, a determined minority was able to impose its ideology of secularism on the country. That sort of imposition was never possible in India's democracy, and this is more than ever the case today. So for the Hindu nationalists' anti-secular vision of the Indian state to be realized, they will have to demonstrate through the test of democracy that their vision does command the support of the overwhelming majority they claim to represent.

---

60 Julio Ribeiro, 'The Majority Complex', *Indian Express*, 17 May 2017, 9.

# SELECT BIBLIOGRAPHY

Andersen, Walter and Shridhar Damle. 1987. *The Brotherhood in Saffron: The Rashtriya Swayamsevak Sangh and Hindu Revivalism*. New Delhi: Sage Publications.

Andrews, Peter. ed. 1989. *Ethnic Groups in the Republic of Turkey*. Wiesbaden: L. Reichert.

Aslan, Senem. 2014. *Nation-Building in Turkey and Morocco: Governing Kurdish and Berber Dissent*. Cambridge: Cambridge University Press.

Aydin, Aysegul and Cem Emrence. 2015. *Zones of Rebellion: Kurdish Insurgents and the Turkish State*. Ithaca: Cornell University Press.

Barkey, Henri and Graham Fuller. 1998. *Turkey's Kurdish Question*. Lanham: Rowman and Littlefield.

Basu, Manisha. 2017. *The Rhetoric of Hindu India: Language and Urban Nationalism*. Cambridge: Cambridge University Press.

Baxter, Craig. 1969. *The Jana Sangh: A Biography of an Indian Political Party*. Philadelphia: University of Pennsylvania Press.

Beinin, Joel and Joe Stork. eds. 1997. *Political Islam: Essays from Middle East Report*. Chapters 1, 7, 12 and 13. Berkeley: University of California Press.

Berkes, Niyazi. 1957. 'Historical Background of Turkish Secularism.' In *Islam and the West*, edited by Richard Frye, 41–68. The Hague: Mouton and Co.

———. 1998. *The Development of Secularism in Turkey*. London: Hurst and Company. Reprint, originally published by McGill University Press in 1964.

Bhargava, Rajeev. ed. 1998. *Secularism and its Critics*. Delhi: Oxford University Press.

Birand, Mehmet Ali. 1991. *Shirts of Steel: An Anatomy of the Turkish Armed Forces*. London: IB Tauris.

Bose, Subhas Chandra. 1995. *Netaji Collected Works, Volume Nine: Congress President – Speeches, Articles and Letters, January 1938–May 1939*, edited by Sisir K. Bose and Sugata Bose. Calcutta: Netaji Research Bureau and Delhi: Oxford University Press.

Bose, Sumantra. 1997. 'Hindu Nationalism and the Crisis of the Indian State'. In *Nationalism, Democracy and Development: State and Politics in India*, edited by Sugata Bose and Ayesha Jalal, 104–64. New Delhi: Oxford University Press.

———. 2003. *Kashmir: Roots of Conflict, Paths to Peace*. Cambridge, Mass. and London: Harvard University Press.

———. 2013. *Transforming India: Challenges to the World's Largest Democracy*. Cambridge, Mass. and London: Harvard University Press.

Bozdogan, Sibel and Resat Kasaba. eds. 1997. *Rethinking Modernity and National Identity in Turkey*. Seattle: University of Washington Press.

Bruinessen, Martin van. 1992. *Agha, Shaikh and State: The Social and Political Structures of Kurdistan*. London: Zed Books.

Chandhoke, Neera. 1999. *Beyond Secularism: The Rights of Religious Minorities*. New Delhi: Oxford University Press.

Chatterjee, Partha. 1997. 'Secularism and Toleration.' In *A Possible India: Essays in Political Criticism*, 228–62. Delhi: Oxford University Press.

Cizre, Umit. ed. 2008. *Secular and Islamic Politics in Turkey: The Making of the Justice and Development Party*. London and New York: Routledge.

Cossman, Brenda and Ratna Kapur. 1999. *Secularism's Last Sigh? Hindutva and the (Mis)Rule of Law*. Delhi: Oxford University Press.

Davison, Andrew. 1998. *Secularism and Revivalism in Turkey: A Hermeneutic Reconsideration*. New Haven: Yale University Press.

Godbole, Madhav. 2016. *Secularism: India at a Crossroads*. Delhi: Rupa Publications.

Gokalp, Ziya. 1968. *The Principles of Turkism*. Leiden: EJ Brill.

Gole, Nilufer. 1996. 'Authoritarian Secularism and Islamist Politics: The Case of Turkey'. In *Civil Society in the Middle East*, edited by Augustus Richard Norton, 17–43. Leiden: EJ Brill.

Golwalkar, Madhav Sadashiv. 1947. *We, or Our Nationhood Defined*. Nagpur: Bharat Prakashan.

———. 1968. *Bunch of Thoughts*. Bangalore: Vikram Prakashan.

Gopal, S. ed. 1991. *Anatomy of a Confrontation: The Ramjanambhoomi–Babri Masjid Dispute*. Delhi: Penguin Books.

Graham, Bruce. 1990. *Hindu Nationalism and Indian Politics: The Origins and Development of the Bharatiya Jan Sangh*. Cambridge: Cambridge University Press.

Guha, Ramachandra. 2007. *India after Gandhi: The History of the World's Largest Democracy*. New Delhi: Pan Macmillan.

Gunes, Cengiz and Welat Zeydanlioglu. eds. 2014. *The Kurdish Question in Turkey: New Perspectives on Violence, Representation, and Reconciliation*. London and New York: Routledge.

Hale, William. 1994. *Turkish Politics and the Military*. London: Routledge.

Hanioglu, M. Sukru. 1995. *The Young Turks in Opposition*. New York: Oxford University Press.

———. 2011. *Ataturk: An Intellectual Biography*. Princeton: Princeton University Press.

Hansen, Thomas Blom. 1999. *The Saffron Wave: Democracy and Hindu Nationalism in Modern India*. Princeton: Princeton University Press.

Hansen, Thomas Blom and Christophe Jaffrelot. eds. 1998. *The BJP and the Compulsions of Politics in India*. Delhi: Oxford University Press.

Hasan, Mushirul ed. 1994. *India's Partition: Process, Strategy and Mobilization*. Delhi: Oxford University Press.

Heper, Metin. 1985. *The State Tradition in Turkey*. Beverley: Eothen Press.

Heper, Metin and Nur Bilge Criss. 2009. *Historical Dictionary of Turkey*. Lanham, MD: The Scarecrow Press.

Houston, Christopher. 2001. *Islam, Kurds and the Turkish Nation-State*. Oxford and New York: Berg.

Jacobsohn, Gary J. 2003. *The Wheel of Law: India's Secularism in Comparative Constitutional Context*. Princeton and Oxford: Princeton University Press.

Jaffrelot, Christophe. 1996. *The Hindu Nationalist Movement and Indian Politics, 1925–1990s*. London: Hurst and Company.

———. 2003. *India's Silent Revolution: The Rise of the Lower Castes in North India*. London: Hurst and Company.

———. ed. 2007. *Hindu Nationalism: A Reader*. Princeton: Princeton University Press.

Jois, M. Rama. 2015. *Supreme Court Judgment on Hindutva: A Way of Life*. Delhi: Suruchi Prakashan.

*Journal of International Affairs*. 2000 (September). Issue on 'Turkey: A Struggle Between Nation and State'. 54 (1).

Karpat, Kemal. 1959. *Turkey's Politics: The Transition to a Multi-Party System.* Princeton: Princeton University Press.

_____. 2001. *The Politicization of Islam: Reconstructing Identity, State, Faith and Community in the Late Ottoman State.* New York: Oxford University Press.

Kazancigil, Ali and Ergun Ozbudun. eds. 1997. *Ataturk: Founder of a Modern State.* London: Hurst and Company.

Kirisci, Kemal and Gareth Winrow. 1997. *The Kurdish Question and Turkey.* London: Frank Cass.

Kirisci, Kemal. 2000. 'Disaggregating Turkish Citizenship and Immigration Practices'. *Middle Eastern Studies* 36 (3): 1–22.

Kuru, T. Ahmet. 2009. *Secularism and State Policies Toward Religion: The United States, France, and Turkey.* Cambridge: Cambridge University Press.

Kuru, T. Ahmet and Alfred Stepan. eds. 2012. *Democracy, Islam and Secularism in Turkey.* New York: Columbia University Press.

Lewis, Bernard. 1961. *The Emergence of Modern Turkey.* London: Oxford University Press.

Luthera, Ved Prakash. 1964. *The Concept of the Secular State and India.* Calcutta: Oxford University Press.

Malkani, K. R. 1951. *Principles for a New Political Party.* Delhi: Vijay Pustak Bhandar.

_____. 1980. *The RSS Story.* New Delhi: Impex India.

Marcus, Aliza. 2007. *Blood and Belief: The PKK and the Kurdish Fight for Independence.* New York: New York University Press.

Mardin, Serif. 1973. 'Centre-Periphery Relations: A Key to Turkish Politics'. *Daedalus* 102 (1): 169–90.

_____. 1983. 'Religion and Politics in Modern Turkey.' In *Islam in the Political Process*, edited by James Piscatori, 138–59. Cambridge: Cambridge University Press.

_____. 1989. *Religion and Social Change in Modern Turkey: The Case of Bediuzzaman Said Nursi.* Albany: SUNY Press.

McDowall, David. 2000. *A Modern History of the Kurds.* London: IB Tauris.

Minault, Gail. 1982. *The Khilafat Movement: Religious Symbolism and Political Mobilization in India.* New York: Columbia University Press.

Morris, Chris. 2005. *The New Turkey: The Quiet Revolution on the Edge of Europe.* London: Granta Books.

366

# SELECT BIBLIOGRAPHY

Nag, Kingshuk. 2013. *The NaMo Story: A Political Life*. Delhi: Roli Books.

Nandy, Ashis. 1998. 'The Politics of Secularism and the Recovery of Religious Tolerance.' In *Secularism and its Critics*, edited by Rajeev Bhargava, 321–44. Delhi: Oxford University Press.

*New Perspectives on Turkey (NPT)*. 1987–present. Istanbul: Economic and Social History Foundation (now a Cambridge University Press journal).

Newbigin, Eleanor. 2013. *The Hindu Family and the Emergence of Modern India: Law, Citizenship and Community*. Cambridge: Cambridge University Press.

Ocalan, Abdullah. 1992. *Interviews and Speeches*. London: Kurdistan Solidarity Committee and Kurdistan Information Centre.

Olsson, Tord, Elisabeth Ozdalga and Catharina Raudvere. eds. 1998. *Alevi Identity: Cultural, Religious and Social Perspectives*. Istanbul: Swedish Research Institute.

PKK. 1983. *Programme of the Kurdistan Workers' Party*. Cologne: Wesanen Serxwebun.

Pathak, Zakia and Rajeswari Sunder Rajan. 1989. 'Shahbano'. *Signs: Journal of Women in Culture and Society*. 14 (3): 558–82.

Pettifer, James. 1998. *The Turkish Labyrinth: Ataturk and the New Islam*. London: Penguin Books.

Poulton, Hugh. 1997. *Top Hat, Grey Wolf and Crescent: Turkish Nationalism and the Turkish Republic*. London: Hurst and Company.

Rai, Vibhuti Narain. 2016. *Hashimpura, 22 May 1987: The Forgotten Story of India's Biggest Custodial Killing*. Delhi: Penguin.

Ram-Prasad, C. 1993. 'Hindutva Ideology: Extracting the Fundamentals', *Contemporary South Asia* 2 (3): 285–309.

Reed, Howard. 1957. 'The Religious Life of Modern Turkish Muslims'. In *Islam and the West*, edited by Richard Frye, 108–47. The Hague: Mouton and Co.

Reed, Howard. 1980. 'Ataturk's Secularizing Legacy and the Continuing Vitality of Islam in Republican Turkey'. In *Islam in the Contemporary World*, edited by Cyriac K. Pullapilly, 316–40. Notre Dame: Cross Roads Books.

Rustow, Dankwart A. 1957. 'Politics and Islam in Turkey, 1920–1955'. In *Islam and the West*, edited by Richard Frye, 69–107. The Hague: Mouton and Co.

Saktanber, Ayse. 2000. *Living Islam: Women, Politics and Religion in Turkey*. London: IB Tauris.

Savarkar, Vinayak Damodar. 1984. *Hindu Rashtra Darshan* [The Vision of the Hindu State]. Bombay: Veer Savarkar Prakashan.

Schick, Irvin and E. Ahmet Tonak. eds. 1987. *Turkey in Transition: New Perspectives*. New York: Oxford University Press.

Schmitt, Carl. 1988. *The Crisis of Parliamentary Democracy*. Cambridge: MIT Press.

Sen, Amartya. 1996. 'Secularism and its Discontents'. In *Unravelling the Nation: Sectarian Conflict and India's Secular Identity*, edited by Kaushik Basu and Sanjay Subrahmanyam, 11–43. Delhi: Penguin Books.

Seshadri, H. V. (ed.). 1988. *RSS: A Vision in Action*. Bangalore: Jagaran Prakashan.

Setalvad, M. C. 1967. *Secularism*. Delhi: Publications Division, Ministry of Information and Broadcasting, Government of India.

Shankland, David. 1999. *Islam and Society in Turkey*. London: Eothen Press.

———. 2003. *The Alevis in Turkey: The Emergence of a Secular Islamic Tradition*. Abingdon: Routledge.

Sherman, Taylor C. 2015. *Muslim Belonging in Secular India: Negotiating Citizenship in Postcolonial Hyderabad*. Cambridge: Cambridge University Press.

Smith, Donald E. 1963. *India as a Secular State*. Princeton: Princeton University Press.

Tapper, Richard. ed. 1994. *Islam in Modern Turkey: Religion, Politics and Literature in a Secular State*. London: IB Tauris.

Thapar, Romila. 1991. 'Communalism and the Historical Legacy: Some Facets'. In *Communalism in India: History, Politics and Culture*, edited by K. N. Panikkar, 17–33. Delhi: Manohar Books.

Tilly, Charles. 1994. 'States and Nationalism in Europe, 1492–1992'. *Theory and Society* 23 (1): 131–46.

Ullekh, N. P. 2016. *The Untold Vajpayee: Politician and Paradox*. Delhi: Penguin Random House.

Watts, Nicole. 2010. *Activists in Office: Kurdish Politics and Protest in Turkey*. Seattle: University of Washington Press.

White, Jenny. 2012. *Muslim Nationalism and the New Turks*. Princeton: Princeton University Press.

Yalman, Ahmet Emin. 1957. *Turkey in My Time*. Norman: University of Oklahoma Press.

Yalman, Nur. 1969. 'Islamic Reform and the Mystic Tradition in Eastern Turkey'. *Archives Europeennes de Sociologie* 10 (1): 41–60.

———. 1973. 'Some Observations on Secularism in Islam: The Cultural Revolution in Turkey'. *Daedalus* 102 (1): 139–68.

————. 1991. 'On Secularism and its Critics: Notes on Turkey, India and Iran'. *Contributions to Indian Sociology* 25 (2): 233–66.

Yavuz, M. Hakan. 2003. *Islamic Political Identity in Turkey*. New York: Oxford University Press.

————. ed. 2006. *The Emergence of a New Turkey: Democracy and the AK Parti*. Salt Lake City: University of Utah Press.

————. 2009. *Secularism and Muslim Democracy in Turkey*. Cambridge: Cambridge University Press.

Zurcher, Erik. 2000. *Turkey: A Modern History*. London: IB Tauris.

# INDEX

INDEX

Firat, Fuat, 247

France, 23, 37, 68–69, 71, 75, 107, 110, 208, 215, 229, 253

Free Republican Party, 229

French Revolution (1789), 7, 37, 44, 69, 76, 79

French Third Republic, 68–69

Gadkari, Nitin, 354

Gajendragadkar, P. B., 90

Gandhi, Indira, 16, 27, 40, 72, 94, 100, 123–32, 134, 142, 145, 147, 151, 156, 169, 285, 303, 318, 331, 357

Gandhi, Mohandas Karamchand (Mahatma), 38, 43, 46–52, 54, 56–58, 76–77, 88, 90, 97, 120, 122, 252, 255–58, 267–68, 281, 284, 301, 306–07, 316, 319, 327, 348–49, 351

Gandhi, Rahul, 157, 300

Gandhi, Rajiv, 94, 100, 127, 132–33, 135–36, 139–43, 145–46, 151, 154, 285, 357

Gandhi, Sanjay, 125, 127, 142

Gandhi, Sonia, 94, 96, 157

*gau-rakshak*s, 98–99, 306, 308, 320

*gecekondu*s, 112, 189, 207

Germany, 10, 19, 37, 49, 62, 69, 75, 103, 208, 264, 275–76, 346

Gezi Park, 109

Godhra, 155

Godse, Nathuram, 255

Gokalp, Ziya, 12, 60–65, 67, 163, 220, 324

Gokcen, Sabiha, 240

Golwalkar, Madhav Sadashiv (M.

S.) *see also* Rashtriya Swayamsevak Sangh (RSS), 149, 216–19, 221–22, 224–27, 238, 259–60, 265, 269–73, 274–78, 279, 280, 299, 333, 339–40, 343, 344, 345, 347, 360

Goods and Services Tax (GST), 304, 344

Grand National Assembly *see also* Turkish Grand National Assembly (TGNA), 11, 19–20, 41, 75, 102, 110, 161–63, 170, 173–74, 177, 212–14, 228–29, 238–39, 246, 249, 323

Greece, 36, 59, 167–68, 236

Greeks, 7, 43, 64, 110, 167–68

Grey Wolves, 114–15, 182, 185, 189

Gul, Abdullah, 12, 18, 206, 208–09, 212–14, 298

Gulen, Fethullah, 23, 298, 329

Gumuspala, Ragip, 178

Guney, Yilmaz, 190

Gursel, Cemal, 172, 177

Haji Bektash Veli, 113

Haq, Zia-ul (Gen.), 138, 200

Hasan, Abid *see also* Bose, Subhas Chandra, 48–49, 89

headscarf, 24, 30, 106, 198–99, 202–03, 212–14, 231, 322–23, 325–26

Hedgewar, Keshav Baliram, 217, 269–70

Hikmet, Nazim, 179

Hindu Mahasabha, 77, 83, 119–20, 256, 261–63, 265, 267, 270, 342

Hindu Rashtra, 13, 29, 77, 122, 158, 222, 225, 227, 268, 320

374

North Atlantic Treaty Organization
(NATO), 73, 106, 181

Nuri, Celal, 110

Nursi, Said, 23, 103, 187, 245

Ocalan, Abdullah *see also* Workers'
Party of Kurdistan (PKK), 241–44,
249

Okyar, Ali Fethi, 228–29

Ottoman Empire, 4, 23, 36, 42, 48,
59, 61–62, 64–66, 96, 111, 220, 327

Ozal, Korkut, 191–92, 196

Ozal, Turgut, 11, 18, 191–97, 199–
207, 211, 213, 231, 244

Pakistan, 2–3, 7, 45–47, 74–78, 120,
124, 128, 130, 138, 149, 152, 200,
218, 276–78, 282–83, 285–88, 290–
94, 307, 316, 320, 331–33, 335

Pal, Bipin Chandra, 257

Palestine, 168, 263, 275–76, 290,
333–34, 338

Palestinians, 333, 335

Pant, Govind Ballabh (G. B.), 119

Pataskar, H. V., 83, 86

Patel, Vallabhbhai, 2, 71, 76, 90, 149,
351

Peker, Mehmet Recep, 230–31

People's Democratic Party (HDP),
21–22, 116, 249, 250–51, 325

People's Houses, 65, 230, 232

People's Rooms, 65, 230, 232

Pir Sultan Abdal, 113, 115

Praja Socialist Party (PSP), 85

Progressive Republican Party, 228

Provisional Government of Free

India, *see also* Bose, Subhas
Chandra, 253

Quit India movement (1942), 58, 268,
284

Rajya Sabha, 157, 331, 353

Rama Rao, N. T. (NTR), 131–32

Ramasamy Naicker, E. V., 313

*Ramjanambhoomi*, 118–19, 122–23,
132, 135, 142–43, 149–51, 153–55,
158, 277, 279, 305–06, 309, 353–54

Rao, P. V. Narasimha, 151, 352

Rashtra Sevika Samiti, 269

Rashtriya Swayamsevak Sangh (RSS),
13–14, 77, 83, 93, 99–100, 119–22,
126, 130, 133, 148–50, 152–53,
155, 216–18, 221–22, 224–27, 238,
259–60, 265, 269–80, 289–90, 299,
302–03, 306, 308–09, 316–17,
319–21, 333–34, 339–41, 343–49,
351–53, 356–57, 360–61

Republican Peasants' Nation Party,
176–78, 181

Republican People's Party (CHP),
19, 21–22, 24, 39, 45, 63, 101–02,
116, 160–65, 168–70, 173, 175–80,
183–88, 190, 194–95, 202, 212–14,
217, 220, 223–24, 229–32, 326

Riza, Seyyit, 239

Robert College, 199

Rumi (Mevlana), 10, 67–68, 102, 162,
164

Russia, 36, 59

Sabanci University, 206

Samajwadi Party (SP), 101, 157–58,
357